Obeah and Other Powers

Obeah and

Other Powers

The Politics of Caribbean Religion and Healing

DIANA PATON & MAARIT FORDE, editors

DUKE UNIVERSITY PRESS   DURHAM & LONDON   2012

© 2012 Duke University Press
All rights reserved

Designed by Katy Clove
Typeset in Arno Pro by Keystone Typesetting, Inc.
Library of Congress Cataloging-in-Publication Data
appear on the last printed page of this book.

Duke University Press gratefully acknowledges the support
of Newcastle University, which provided funds toward
the production of this book.

For KAREN MCCARTHY BROWN

Contents

Foreword ERNA BRODBER ix
Acknowledgments xiii
Introduction MAARIT FORDE & DIANA PATON 1

PART I Powers of Representation

1 An (Un)natural Mystic in the Air:
   Images of Obeah in Caribbean Song KENNETH BILBY 45

2 "Eh! eh! Bomba, hen! hen!":
   Making Sense of a Vodou Chant ALASDAIR PETTINGER 80

3 On Swelling: Slavery, Social Science, and Medicine
   in the Nineteenth Century ALEJANDRA BRONFMAN 103

4 Atis Rezistans: Gede and the Art of Vagabondaj KATHERINE SMITH 121

PART II Modernity and Tradition in the Making

5 Slave Poison/Slave Medicine: The Persistence of Obeah in Early
   Nineteenth-Century Martinique JOHN SAVAGE 149

6 The Trials of Inspector Thomas:
   Policing and Ethnography in Jamaica DIANA PATON 172

7 The Moral Economy of Spiritual Work:
   Money and Rituals in Trinidad and Tobago MAARIT FORDE 198

8 The Open Secrets of Solares ELIZABETH COOPER 220

PART III Powers on the Move

9 Rites of Power and Rumors of Race: The Circulation of
   Supernatural Knowledge in the Greater Caribbean, 1890–1940
   LARA PUTNAM 243

10 The Vodou State and the Protestant Nation:
    Haiti in the Long Twentieth Century KAREN RICHMAN 268

11 The Moral Economy of Brujería under the Modern Colony:
    A Pirated Modernity? RAQUEL ROMBERG 288

    Afterword. Other Powers: Tylor's Principle, Father Williams's
    Temptations, and the Power of Banality STEPHAN PALMIÉ 316

    Contributors 341
    Index 345

Foreword

ERNA BRODBER

One afternoon when I was six and in standard 2, sitting quietly while the teacher, Mr. Grant, wrote our assignment on the blackboard, I heard a girl scream as if she were frightened. Mr. Grant must have heard it, too, for he turned as if to see whether that frightened scream had come from one of us, his charges. My classmates looked at me. Which wasn't strange: I had a reputation for knowing the answer. They must have thought I would know about the scream. As it happened, all I could think about was how strange, just at the time when I needed it, the girl had screamed.

I had been swimming through the clouds, unwillingly connected to a small party of adults who were purposefully going somewhere, a destination I suddenly sensed meant danger for me. Naturally I didn't want to go any further with them, but I didn't know how to communicate this to adults and ones intent on doing me harm. At the girl's scream, they swam away, quickly leaving me to tread the clouds alone but feeling that I had been abandoned and could justifiably do as I wished—and I wished to return to my place on the bench in standard 2, ready to solve the problems that Mr. Grant had written on the board. The feeling of being carried away and then abandoned to tread the clouds by myself is one I can never forget.

Twenty-four years later, suffering from a thyroid problem that brought me strange sensations, I tried to describe for my endocrinologist, a West Indian of East Indian extraction, some of these sensations, recalling for him the feeling of being carried away and treading air, which had returned. I thought this disclosure would help toward a diagnosis, which had been evading my medical team. He looked away from me, muttering that "we would now try psychiatry." *Is not everything good fi eat, good fi talk.* No matter how much contact we have had with a world not governed by the five senses, Caribbean university professors like my endocrinologist and I, Indo or Afro, are not supposed to admit to having them. A higgler or a cultivator in rural Jamaica—Indo or Afro—upon hearing my experience would have either responded with a similar one or offered a translation. I had read my culture wrongly. How stupid of me.

Understand my surprise, then, when Patricia Murray—professor at London Metropolitan University, a native of Great Britain, nonblack, and therefore, I assumed, with little personal experience of being molested by spirits—invited me to participate in a conference on "Religion and Spirituality in a Postcolonial Context: Working the Parallel World." She must have read my face, for she modified, "It is time that this aspect of African and African Caribbean life be taken seriously." This conference was aborted, but soon thereafter I was invited to an even more explicit one: "Obeah and Other Powers."

Funny. The British in 1760, as a result of the African Jamaican Tacky's rebellion, had outlawed the practice of obeah, and anti-obeah legislation has been on the statute books ever since. In order to read the de Laurence books, some of which are said to be used by obeah workers, I, with an academic interest in this parallel world of mine, had to go to Trinidad, for these books are banned in Jamaica. Yet these academics in British Newcastle were inciting people to meet for nearly a week to meditate on such things!

Perhaps the time has indeed come for these things to be taken seriously, as Patricia said. At the annual pre-Emancipation reasoning in my village, Dr. Adolph Edwards, author of the unpublished Ph.D. thesis "The Development of Criminal Law in Jamaica," asked to share with us his knowledge of legislation, and particularly obeah laws, designed expressly for handling "our" people in the days of slavery. Some young visiting academics heckled, attacking the messenger. Their behavior was an expression of frustration and anger: anger at the treatment of their ancestors—"ancestral anger," I call it—but more, frustration at knowing so little about the system of thought that their ancestors had celebrated, frustration at being robbed of the connection with their ancestors that could allow them to make a good defense of them, frustration that now initiates into Akan, Dagara, and Yoruba traditions; they still did not know the points at which their grandparents had connected with these traditions. They were now living with burning candles, wearing full white, keeping their heads covered, and leaving plates of food in their yards for the ancestors, but they still didn't know if they were connected with the feared obeah man down the road, formerly the butt of jokes in their friendship networks. Their anger was at the knowledge vacuum that made positioning themselves in the stream of spiritual history impossible, and that forced them to wonder if their newfound spiritual rituals would really lessen the sense of wearing the wrong robes that had driven them out of the Euro-American churches and in search of the African spiritual forms.

In our very active post-lecture discussion, the village passed a resolution that we should petition for the removal of the obeah laws from the statute books. Could this be enough? Whatever the answer, it is clear that enough of us in the Caribbean care about obeah and other powers. And didn't Professor Barry Chevannes of the University of the West Indies, at an international conference in his honor, sprinkle water at the four corners of the platform to acknowledge the presence of and to thank his ancestors for past kindness? We are beginning to see and to respect the alternative world that our grandparents knew to exist. But deleting an entry from a list of laws is not knowledge of a system—especially one so smothered under a bushel by British colonial policy, so bereft of the natural light that growth and development needs, that what is left might be a poor representation of what was. What my young academic friends stepping into the observance of African traditional rites need is knowledge of what exists and knowledge of what had been. Unfortunately, the meaning behind esoteric knowledge such as obeah and other powers is normally handed down from ear to ear. Can the breach fostered by colonial education systems be mended so that conduits can appear? Perhaps not. My young friends will have to design their own techniques for spiritual connection. What they need more than anything else is an environment sympathetic to this kind of creation.

Many of us in the Caribbean feel torn by the experience of living with two systems of thought that are difficult to reconcile. I for one was happier at the Newcastle conference than at any other that I have attended in my many years in academia. I think this is because I sensed not so much an attempt to use field data toward general sociological theory, but more an effort to understand a fact of my Caribbean life. I had company in this exercise of trying to understand; I was comforted. The papers presented and the post-paper discussions made me feel that data were now available to help our college-trained medical practitioners and our spirit-based practitioners make common cause, and to help our seminary-trained ministers of religion and our spirit-based ones find the path toward each other that I know the former have been trying to chart since the 1970s.

There of course have been other gatherings and sets of papers, but the one arranged by Maarit Forde and Diana Paton at Newcastle University has been much more than the usual panels at a conference. It has been for me the first to focus totally on obeah and other powers, bringing as it did the parallel world into full public view—and thus not only providing information about what was and perhaps is, but also helping to create this sympathetic environment that my young friends need for further and more private exploration. This work, valorizing the thoughts and actions of our ancestors, treating them in a matter-of-fact and therefore humanistic way, will eventuate in their shaking from their bones the epithets "stupid" and "backward," and we of this generation soon being able to share about our out-of-body experiences without thinking ourselves mentally ill, to leave plates of food outside in our yards for our ancestors without wondering how close we are to breaching the laws governing the practice of obeah.

Finally, reparations: the colonial powers have been "spirit thieves." Their obeah legislation has stymied the spiritual growth and development of transported Africans. Repairing the breach is about valorizing what they wrongly demonized. It is some kind of justice and a lighting of the way forward that descendants of those who put the bushel over Caribbean expressions of African spirituality, and those whose ancestors were thus bound, are working together—whether in conferences as college-trained intellectuals or in the field as informants—to lift the bushel and retrieve knowledge. One happy, though perhaps unintended, outcome could be the lessening of the quantum of ancestral anger felt by the descendants of Africans enslaved in the New World, as I have discussed in my book *The Second Generation of Freemen in Jamaica, 1907–1955* (University Press of Florida, 2004). May it be so indeed for the several young Afro-Caribbean academics who are waiting for this collection—not to teach about African spirituality but rather to strengthen them on their personal journey of finding their ancestors' hands, and so to link their hearts and souls to the past, allowing them to walk upright into the future, now plugged into the right ancestral source and now free from the burden of frustration and anger.

Acknowledgments

This book is the result of collaboration between the two editors, as part of a larger project, funded by the Leverhulme Trust, titled "Colonial Rule and Spiritual Power: Obeah, the State, and Caribbean Culture." It took shape at a conference, "Obeah and Other Powers," held at Newcastle University in July 2008. We would like to thank all the participants at that conference, and particularly the contributors to this book, whose initial papers made the conference so stimulating and who subsequently worked efficiently to turn their papers into book chapters. We have both learned a great deal from collaborating with them. We owe a special debt to those who generously gave their time and intellectual energy to act as chairs and panel discussants at the conference: Juanita de Barros, Jean Besson, Erna Brodber, Richard Drayton, Michael Jagessar, Projit Mukharji, Patricia Murray, Karen Fog Olwig, Stephan Palmié, James Procter, Kate Ramsey, Terence Ranger, Patrick Taylor, and David Trotman. Robert Hill delivered the keynote address at the conference; it provided a typically rich stimulus to the discussions. Unfortunately, Hill was unable to revise his paper for the book, an absence that we regret. The conference and book have depended on the financial support of the Leverhulme Trust, Newcastle University, and the Northern Centre for the History of Medicine, and the practical support of Colette Barker, Janice Cummin, Geof Ellingham, Pat Harrison, Michelle Houston, Melanie Kidd, Tom Kirk, Helen McKee, Bob Stoate, Sam Turner, and Craig White. Thanks to all of them.

At Duke University Press, we are grateful to Valerie Millholland and Miriam Angress, who supported the project from the beginning. We also thank the initially anonymous readers of our manuscript, Aisha Khan and Paul Johnson, who greatly helped us to improve it.

The onset of health problems forced Karen McCarthy Brown to withdraw from the Newcastle conference. Brown's work has been an inspiration for many of the contributors to this book; we dedicate it to her.

Obeah and Other Powers

Introduction

MAARIT FORDE & DIANA PATON

In 1905 the prison authorities at the Antigua jail, which served as the central prison for the Leeward Islands, employed a photographer to take individual and group photographs of at least eleven people who had been convicted of practicing obeah. The group shot (figure I.1) depicts nine men and two women in two rows, all staring with their faces toward the camera. All wear white prison uniforms, identical except for the differences between men and women. Each holds a small board on which is chalked his or her name and the island where she or he was convicted. The individual photographs were pasted onto preprinted documents recording that the photographed individual had been "convicted for practising Obeah under the Leeward Islands Obeah Act No 6 of 1904," and documenting his or her sentence, place of birth, age, marital status, trade or occupation ("obeahman" in some cases), religion, and a series of physical descriptors, such as skin color, hair color, and height. The images belong to the genre of the police photograph or mug shot, the chalked names providing a means for state authorities to identify these people. These photographs and identifying information were circulated "to all the neighbouring Islands, both British and Foreign," in the hope that the individuals pictured would be kept under surveillance upon their release, wherever they should travel.[1]

Someone working in the prison or the colonial civil service must have decided to group together this particular set of prisoners—obeah convicts—to photograph them collectively and individually, suggesting the significance that the colonial authorities gave to this category of crime at this time. In one sense, the photographs allowed for the fixing, classification, and control of the group. They record the fact that these prisoners had been temporarily brought to a point of stasis by confinement in prison, and thus suggest one of the themes of this book: the significance of state power, and more specifically, state hostility,

I.1 Photograph of eleven men and women convicted of practicing obeah, taken in the Antigua jail in 1905. Enclosed in Knollys to Lyttelton, no. 222, May 22, 1905, CO 152/287, National Archives, London. Reproduced by permission of the National Archives.

in shaping the environment within which Caribbean religions were sustained and practiced.

But the photographs do not merely record the disciplining of their subjects. The individuals photographed are not simply controlled by the photographer, but rather, in minor ways, take hold of the presentation of their clothing: in the group shot some wear their prison hats, for instance, while others hold them in their hands. More significant, the posing of the subjects in two rows, one seated, the other standing, resembles a photograph of a school or college graduating class, or a record of a professional convention, even more than it does a photograph of prisoners. And this resemblance is not entirely misleading, for a great deal of communication and exchange of information must have taken place inside the prison among these people from across the Eastern Caribbean. Only half jokingly, we could suggest that this photograph depicts a convention of Eastern Caribbean obeah practitioners, courtesy of the Antiguan jail authorities. Like participants in a professional convention, the men and women in this photograph were likely to have been competitors for clients but also sharers of information and knowledge. The hidden communication that lies behind the picture evokes a second theme raised in *Obeah and Other Powers*: the active role of practitioners in reshaping the religious traditions in which they participated.

As recorded by the chalkboards that the prisoners hold, all these convicts except for Cornelius Jarvis (back row, third from left) had been convicted outside Antigua. Other sources reveal that many people convicted of practicing obeah in the Eastern Caribbean in this period, including some of those photographed, were embedded in regional networks of their own making in addition to those produced by their conviction. For instance, Thomas Howe, pictured second from left in the front row, was tried in Dominica but had been born elsewhere: St. Kitts according to a newspaper report, Montserrat according to the information recorded on his prison docket (figure I.2).[2] Other convicts had connections to the Francophone and Hispanic Caribbean, as well as to other British colonies.[3] These connections suggest a third theme with which the chapters of this book engage: the importance of mobility in constructing obeah and the other powers in which we are interested, and the permeability of the borders between colonial empires that frequently confine Caribbeanist scholarship.

This book deals with religious practice in the Caribbean, primarily within contexts that have come to be known as obeah, Vodou, and Santería, and their relationship to power. It includes chapters by historians and anthropologists that discuss Jamaica, Cuba, Haiti, Trinidad, Tobago, Martinique, Suriname, Puerto Rico, and the Caribbean coast of Central America, as well as connections between several of these places.[4] The contributors are concerned with periods ranging from the late eighteenth century to the present, although most focus on the period after 1890. While they range widely in theme, the chapters share an interest in thinking through how, and by whom, the fields of religious beliefs and practices they discuss have been produced and reproduced, rather than a concern with pinning down what these formations were and are. They are concerned with the contexts in which the reproduction of Caribbean religion has taken place, and with what such religions and discourses about them *do*. By that, we mean both that the chapters in this book are concerned with the actions of those who identify with particular religious movements, and that they seek to understand the cultural and political work done by hostility to, representation of, and attempts to suppress those movements' beliefs and practices. In these concerns, this work is connected also to wider developments in history and anthropology—in particular, to the growing emphasis on analyses that approach societies and cultures not as bounded entities, but as

1.2 Tabular information about and photograph of Thomas Howe, convicted in Dominica in August 1904 of practicing obeah. Reproduced by permission of the Syndics of Cambridge University Library.

processual formations that are always being made and remade, and to lines of questioning that unveil the historical construction of many institutions, including religion, that have previously been taken for granted.

The title *Obeah and Other Powers* refers on one hand to the cross-Caribbean nature of the book's subject matter. Alongside discussions of obeah, we present studies of "other powers": formations that have occupied similar, although not identical, places to obeah in Caribbean societies. These include the power that animates Cuban *regla ocha* and *palo*; the power of the *lwa* in Haiti; and the power of the spirits accessed by *brujos* and *brujas* in Puerto Rico. At the same time, the other powers to which we refer are those that, to speak at the most general level, have dominated the lives of Caribbean people for the past five centuries. Obeah and the other powers analyzed in this book were formed, from the start, in the context of the relationships that produced the Caribbean in its modern, post-1492 form. They were produced by the power of capital and colonialism to transport millions of Africans across oceans against their will, and then set them down as enslaved people who had to rework their existing knowledge to provide some protection in a new, terror-filled setting. In the aftermath of slavery, these powers transformed as hundreds of thousands of people from India, and to a lesser extent China, migrated to the Caribbean under indenture. Asian migrants' religious experience influenced and was influenced by those who were already there. But the religious practices and knowledge of Caribbean people were also formed by a more mundane and yet highly significant set of everyday powers: the power of states to criminalize some practices and legitimize others; the power of occupying armies to rewrite constitutions and reorient economies; and the power of writers, filmmakers, lawyers, and scholars to represent Caribbean practices, both to those with little knowledge of the region and to those who live there. Such representations of Caribbean religious formations, whether by "insiders" or "outsiders"—however we might define those terms—have been carefully watched and analyzed by those they purport to represent.

Finally, the other powers of the book's title refer to a third mode of power: the power of millions of people in the Caribbean, whose relationships with one another, and with the forces of capital and the state, have been mediated through and experienced within religious formations and discourses. This power has on many occasions had a critical, combative edge, mobilizing people against colonial and authoritarian rule. It has often been unrecognizable from the point of view of conventional politics, especially the social democratic tradition that has largely dominated Anglophone Caribbean politics. It is not sufficient to conceptualize it in terms of resistance, however, for religiously mobilized powers in the Caribbean have also worked to divide, to maintain boundaries, and to generate hierarchy among non-elite Caribbean people. While many of the chapters in this book elucidate the creativity and power of Caribbean religious practitioners, they situate agency in the context of structural frameworks set up by political economy and cultural politics in the colonial and postcolonial Caribbean.

THE POLITICS OF NAMING

Examining Caribbean religion raises questions about definitions and categorization that ultimately concern methodology and epistemology. As Talal Asad has argued, the dominant scholarship and discourse in post-medieval Europe defined religion as an entity with a traceable essence, separate from other sectors of social life, such as politics, law, or science. In an enlightened, reformed Europe, religion became a system that could be studied and experienced on its own. Enlightenment thinkers saw "religion" as a private affiliation, actively separated from politics and the public sphere. The claim that religion and politics are separate realms became a mark of modernity.[5]

The chapters in this book reject this separation between religion and the rest of social life. To borrow a set of terms from economic anthropology, we adopt a substantivist rather than formalist perspective. Formalist positions have maintained that the principles of neoclassical economics can apply to all societies, as the pursuit of maximization by rational actors is universal. Substantivist economic approaches, on the other hand, have argued for plural models of economy that differentiate between capitalist and pre- or non-capitalist societies. Instead of an autonomous sector or sphere, substantivists have understood economy as embedded in a variety of religious, kinship, political, and other institutions. Similarly, we argue that religion is better understood as embedded in politics, economy, kinship, and other relevant aspects of social life, and that attempts to define religion based on universally applicable criteria tend to be ethnocentrically biased.[6]

But the problem is not only the intellectual tradition that separates religion from everything else. In addition, that same tradition has produced religion as the dominant term in a series of hierarchically paired oppositions, in which lesser terms include "magic," "superstition," "witchcraft," "the occult," "the supernatural," and "barbaric practices."[7] These categories, like the triad of magic, science, and religion that has structured much anthropological theorizing, have been insurmountably hierarchical, and have produced ethnocentric and conceptually misleading models of religion.[8]

In his important history of the concepts of "religion" and "magic" in Western thought, Stanley Jeyaraja Tambiah emphasizes the English Protestant legacy of defining religion as separate from, and morally superior to, magic. While post-Reformation theologians understood religion as a system of beliefs, cosmologically characterized by a sovereign God, they understood magic to connote "coercive rituals ambitiously attempting to manipulate the divine."[9] This division produced the foundation on which Victorian anthropologists such as Edward B. Tylor and James G. Frazer built their work. Much of the ritual practice of regla ocha, Vodou, Spiritual Baptists, Orisha, and other Caribbean religions aims precisely at "manipulating the divine," and would therefore fall into the Tylorian category of magic rather than religion; moreover, "working" the human-spirit relationship has attracted the most attention in textual representations of these religions. Further juxtapositions between Christianity (or monotheism) and paganism—and later, world religions and local religions, or book religions and oral religions—have continued to devalue religions that have developed in the Caribbean, as well as the African religions with which they are often associated. As a result, the practices and belief systems discussed in this book have operated on the borders of what has been conceptualized as religion in the Judeo-Christian tradition and in social scientific studies of religion.

A further reason for the marginality of Caribbean religions is that mainstream Christian thinking since the seventeenth century has generally understood religions to be discrete entities, adherence to or conversion into which implies rejection of all others.[10] This claim is empirically false in the Caribbean, as in many other places. As Karen Richman notes, servants of the lwa are also good Catholics.[11] It is far from unusual for family members to claim membership in two or more different denominations, and many attend different churches or shrines at different points of their lives. Across the English-speaking Caribbean, people who consult practitioners whose work is conventionally described as obeah, not to mention the spiritual workers themselves, may belong to any one (or more) of a variety of churches. Thus the "Caribbean religion" with which this book is concerned is a plural, fluid formation, intimately linked with other areas of social life, and always relational. Our goal is to examine the place of religious practice and belief in a wider context of power relations: relations of class, race, gender, and empire, but also the power of colonial and invading states, scholarship, and print and broadcast media, which have contributed to the very establishment and maintenance of these objects of study themselves.

The fact that even the appropriate names for the objects of study in Caribbean religion are contested suggests the importance of analyzing the making and remaking of these formations. For instance, adherents of what observers and outsiders refer to as "Vodou" (or voodoo, vodun, and vaudoux, among many variant spellings) rarely use that term, instead referring to themselves in relation to action, as servants of the lwa.[12] Yet the issue at stake is not simply that "native" terms for religions such as Vodou frequently differ from those used by outsiders to describe them (although that is the case), but also that even the terms used by practitioners and devotees are enmeshed with debates and definitions taking place outside the community of worshippers. Self-identifications are neither stable over time nor unanimously embraced by clear-cut communities of worshippers. Moreover, they are not distinct from the language of scholarship. The terms used both by scholars and adherents (and, of course, these are sometimes—and increasingly—the same people) contribute to the creation and especially the formalization of the objects they seek to describe.

An example of this can be seen in the response to the Afro-Cuban scholar Rómulo Lachatañeré's advocacy in the 1930s of the use of what he saw as the neutral term "Santería," in place of the derogatory "brujería." With this proposal, Lachatañeré produced a new noun for the religion as a whole, building on the practitioners' terms "santero/a" and "santo/a," which focused on specific roles and the objects of devotion. This new term came to be widely adopted, at least for the consumption of outsiders, although the terms "la regla (de) ocha" and "lucumí/lukumi" probably remained more common. By the 1990s, however, many religious leaders who sought to emphasize the African connections of the religion rejected the term "Santería" because of its implication that the religion was primarily about the worship of Catholic saints (*santos*).[13]

As this example suggests, there is no consensus within Caribbean societies and Caribbean diasporic communities about the boundaries between religions, about "orthodox" practice, or about the place of religion in social life more generally. To take further examples, Spiritual Baptists and Orisha practitioners in Trinidad and Tobago have varying opinions about which practices and beliefs constitute their religions and what differentiates one from the other.[14] Similarly, mainstream Hinduism in contemporary Trinidad and Guyana distances itself from the rituals of sacrifice and spiritual manifestation characteristic of Kali worship, but members of Kali temples do not perceive of their *puja* as separate from orthodox Hinduism.[15] In the Anglophone Caribbean, the term "obeah" was and is widely used to refer to dangerous power, but it has rarely been adopted as an identity by practitioners of its arts, who have referred to themselves as scientists, doctors, spiritual mothers, do-good men, lookmen, professors, and a range of other terms.[16]

In all these cases, terminologies have changed over time, marking the development of struggles over language that are also struggles over power. We see this particularly clearly in the shift from "Shouters" to "Spiritual Baptist religion" in Trinidad and Tobago. The name Shouters was first circulated in local newspapers and generally disapproving discourses about street preachers or religious meetings in late nineteenth- and early twentieth-century Trinidad. Although reified in legislation by the Shouters Prohibition Ordinance of 1917, Shouters referred to groups of worshippers who were never recorded as identifying themselves by that term. Instead, when allowed to do so in court, they spoke of "their religion" without a specific name, or called themselves Baptists, Independent Baptists, Mount Ararat Baptists, Spiritual Converted Baptists, and Spiritual Baptists.[17] After the Shouters Prohibition Ordinance was repealed in 1952, most of the newly legalized churches called themselves Spiritual Baptists. The originally derogatory term Shouters has remained in local parlance, however, and some churches have chosen names that retain the moniker. Such current usages have lost the negative connotations, and they may rather be understood as representing resistance and perseverance in the face of state persecutions.[18]

Names also work within different spatial frames. What we might refer to as "globalized" terms for Afro-Atlantic or Caribbean religions, such as Santería, Vodou, or Yoruba religion, tend to operate at a distance from actual devotees' lives, especially within the Caribbean itself.[19] Yet their global reach gives them the power to draw people together and for practitioners to recognize one another internationally, a process that has been deliberately fostered in some cases—as, for example, by the leadership of the World Congresses of Orisha Tradition and Culture that have met regularly since 1981.[20] At the same time, these dominant terms can exclude other forms of African-Caribbean religion, such as Cuban *palo monte*, or occlude their differentiation from more widely discussed formations. Moreover, more local terms can be markers of insider knowledge of specific religious communities, both within the Caribbean and within Caribbean communities overseas. Because terms such as "obeah," "Vodou," and "Santería" designate a shifting array of practices, attempts to pin down and define the referents they index are fruitless. But as Lara Putnam pointed out at the conference at which much of the work collected in this book was discussed, this problem does not mean that we should abandon all attempts to investigate the meaning of these terms. Rather, such explorations focus our attention on contingencies and specificities. What practices are given which name, in which circumstances, by whom, and with what effects?

Many of the chapters in this book suggest that distinctions between religion and other categories, or boundaries constructed between differently named religions, stem largely from on-the-ground practices and negotiations of those practices. In this way, the chapters complicate the work of scholars who have focused on the significance of colonial states and Western scholarly practices in shaping such boundaries.[21] For example, low-level state agents like police officers played a central role in elaborating these distinctions. Elizabeth Cooper's chapter on early twentieth-century Cuba documents discussions within the police force about whether the people they arrested were indeed "true practitioners of authentic ñáñiguismo." Diana Paton's chapter suggests that similar discussions took place in Jamaica in relation to obeah, and shows that ordinary people's choices about who to report to the police for practicing obeah were also significant in constructing official definitions of the crime. Looking at exchange relationships between ritual specialists and their clients in Trinidad and Tobago, Maarit Forde's chapter points out a correlation between more established, successful practitioners who were arrested mainly by police entrapment, and less convincing entrepreneurs whose clients reported them to the police. On the other hand, Karen Richman's chapter on Haiti shows that similar processes can be located in higher-level state practices, like the appropriation of Vodou imagery in the self-representations of the Duvalierist state and of President François Duvalier himself (along with a simultaneous embrace of anti-Vodou Protestantism as a bulwark against the power of the Catholic Church). Focus on such actors gives us a nuanced view of how various agents and institutions of colonial and postcolonial states suppressed, engaged with, and categorized religious practice, and how ordinary subjects could affect and manipulate these processes.

The risk involved in noting the inescapably hierarchical nature of distinctions like that between religion and magic is that we leave ourselves unable to make necessary analytic distinctions. There is a difference, after all, between Vodou's ritual cycle, ritual specialists, and deities, and obeah's designation of a looser constellation of practices and powers that can be accessed autonomously but are also often consulted in the context of, or as supplements to, differently named religions with their own rituals, specialists, and spirits. No less important, whereas *serviteurs des lwa*, members of Orisha shrines, Spiritual Baptists, santeros, Hindus, and Roman Catholics speak of "their religions," there is little evidence of people who practice or talk about obeah in the Anglophone Caribbean or brujería in Puerto Rico conceptualizing it within a similar category. Bearing these reservations in mind, it may not always prove useful to stretch the analytic category of religion to cover all spiritual practice. But at the same time, if we think of religion not as a bounded category of institutionalized dogma and rituals, but rather as a constantly negotiated, internally heterogeneous field of knowledge and practice whose composition varies according to the perspectives of differently positioned adherents, then analytic boundaries between religious practice, sorcery, and magic seem untenable. While we recognize the usefulness of categories like magic, sorcery, and witchcraft in analyses and cross-cultural comparisons of practices that aim at controlling or coercing "persons, powers, beings, or even events,"[22] we do not want to divorce the rationales and practices of such categories from those of a larger category of religion.

WRITING CARIBBEAN RELIGION THROUGH AND AGAINST EMPIRE

As the above discussion suggests, when examining Caribbean religion it is neither possible nor desirable to avoid the long history of prior representations. In this section, we present a brief historical account of writing about these traditions, focusing on the key themes of analysis in history and anthropology and their relationship to politics and historical developments. We group this writing into three major paradigms. The first, inaugurated with colonialism, and becoming fully formed by the late eighteenth century, was dominated by hostility to African-Caribbean religions, understanding them as signs of backwardness and barbarism. From around the late nineteenth century, and gaining force from the 1920s on, a new set of voices, including those of Caribbean intellectuals and anthropologists from outside the region, sought to reclaim Caribbean religions as the region's "tradition," often presenting them as an inheritance from Africa. Most recently there has been an effort—of which we see this book as a part—to situate Caribbean religions within historicized understandings of Caribbean societies, and to rethink the terms within which we understand religion, in order to present analyses less focused on questions of origins and more concerned with issues of power. Defining these paradigms inevitably simplifies a more complex story, as elements of each have frequently coexisted. Nor can all literature on Caribbean religion be included in one or another of these paradigms. In addition, each paradigm is complex and contradictory in its own right, and has also developed differently in and for different parts of the Caribbean. Nevertheless, dividing the literature in this way can help to orient thinking about the history of writing Caribbean religion.

The earliest European writers about the Caribbean were interested in the religion of the Taíno people of the region primarily in order to determine whether they could be converted to Catholicism. Columbus concluded that conversion would be easy because, he repeatedly declared, the people he encountered "do not know any religion" or had "no religion or idolatry."[23] Later, when this proved overly optimistic, the refusal of indigenous people to adopt Christianity, along with the alleged cannibalism of the Caribs (or Eastern Taíno), was used to justify their enslavement. A few Spanish missionaries, notably Ramón Pané and Bartolomé de Las Casas, wrote detailed and knowledgeable accounts of Taíno culture and beliefs that were in some ways sympathetic, despite their overall framework that assumed the desirability of conversion. Nevertheless, the dominant mode of early Spanish reports was to stress the demonic nature of indigenous religion, to the extent that it was recognized as religion at all.[24]

As enslaved Africans began to outnumber indigenes, the focus of proto-ethnographic writing shifted to describing their cultures and lifeways in texts that sought to make sense of the new world that slavery was creating.[25] While many writers discussed these issues, a few in English and French became reference points for future debates. These texts became foundational for later discussions of Caribbean religions (as well as other topics), both describing in general terms the religious practices of enslaved people, and incorporating narratives of specific instances of African "sorcery" or "obeah" that proved highly memorable and repeatable. Spanish writers did not produce equivalent texts in this period. This was partly because of their greater attention to indigenous belief, but also because Spanish concern with African (and, indeed, mestizo, Spanish, and indigenous) sorcery was instead channeled largely through the Inquisition, which engendered enormous quantities of archival material documenting popular belief, but not the same kind of widely circulated printed texts.[26]

One of the oldest such foundational texts is the Dominican missionary Jean-Baptiste Labat's *Nouveau Voyage aux Isles de l'Amerique*, published in Paris in 1722 and then in an expanded edition in 1742. Based on Labat's time in the Eastern Caribbean (primarily Martinique and Guadeloupe) from 1694 to 1705, this multivolume work includes extensive discussion of poisoning and sorcery. Labat's account of an African woman who used what he calls witchcraft (*sorcellerie*) to prevent the progress of the slave ship on which she was imprisoned is one example; another is his description of his attack on an African healer-diviner who had told an enslaved woman that she would die within four days.[27] Doris Garraway's recent study of eighteenth-century Francophone writing about the Caribbean emphasizes Labat's continuing resonance: not only is his work mined as a source of evidence by many historians (about all kinds of issues aside from religion), it is also widely read in contemporary Martinique, where "Pere Labat" has become a kind of bogeyman (or *macoute*) figure, used to frighten children.[28]

In the late eighteenth century, a group of English and French texts were published that proved equally influential: Edward Long's *History of Jamaica* (1774), Bryan Edwards's *History, Civil and Commercial, of the British Colonies in the West Indies* (1793), and Mederic Louis-Elie Moreau de Saint-Méry's *Description topographique, physique, civile, politique et historique de la partie française de l'isle Saint-Domingue* (1797).[29] These books were written in a more secular vein than Labat's work, and worked within the developing genres of history and geography rather than memoir. Importantly, all of them were published in a context in which slavery had come under attack by abolitionists and revolutionaries, and were part of the wider defense of slavery. But like Labat's work, they each included significant sections regarding African understandings of the spirit world, which they conceived of as indicators of African lack of civilization. Long and Edwards both framed their discussions with the term "obeah," while Long also discussed "myal." Moreau published the first extended discussion of religious practice by enslaved people in colonial Saint-Domingue, and used the term "vaudoux" to describe aspects of it.[30]

Like Labat, these planter historians also included memorable individual stories that were much repeated over time. Bryan Edwards's *History*, for instance, included a long quotation from a parliamentary inquiry into obeah, which incorporated an episode in which an enslaved woman in Jamaica "from the Popo country" was discovered to be the cause of multiple deaths on her plantation.[31] Edwards's quoted description of the "Popo woman," or the original parliamentary report, became a classic in colonial literature and then made its way into the scholarship on obeah, appearing, sometimes without attribution, in later works on Africa and the Caribbean by Thomas Winterbottom, Bessie Pullen-Burry, Martha Beckwith, Joseph Williams, and Orlando Patterson, among others.[32] Moreau's description of "vaudoux," while more abstract than Edwards's account of obeah, gave a detailed description of ritual and dance, focused around the worship of the snake and the initiation of people into the "sect."[33] His description included a chant beginning "Eh! eh! Bomba hen! hen!"—words that, as Alasdair Pettinger's chapter in this book shows, were reproduced and discussed in multiple locations, and for multiple purposes. Pettinger traces scholarly trajectories and interpretive efforts concerning the chant, showing how a late eighteenth-century text continues to generate debates and questions relevant to contemporary intellectual climates. He argues that even the most scholarly of these repetitions have paid too much attention to issues of translation, and too little to the kinesthetic and corporeal meaning and effect that the words, when chanted in a specific ritual context, produced. As Pettinger's chapter suggests, the repeated citation and reproduction of texts like Moreau's and Edwards's has produced a powerful discursive universe within which obeah, Vodou, and their analogues have been understood.

Despite differences between them, Long's, Moreau's, and Edwards's texts all adopted a hierarchical and racist standpoint, in which European Christianity was presented as superior while Africa was marked as savage, backward, and sometimes horrifying. They were written during a period of intense production of knowledge about other parts of the non-European world besides the Caribbean, including Africa, which influenced the development of European understandings and definitions of religion.[34] Writers such as Long, Edwards, and Moreau not only drew on but also reinforced European "knowledge" that Africans (or "Negroes") had no religion but instead worshipped "fetishes."[35]

Between them, these texts created a resonant picture of Caribbean religion that focused on manipulation of the spirit world, and stressed the hostile purposes for which such manipulation took place. They characterized enslaved people's religious practice as magic or witchcraft rather than religion. Nevertheless, they are also ambivalent texts, displaying fascination with the spiritual power that the authors perceived in the enslaved Africans who surrounded them. This fascination has added to their attraction as sources for later historians and anthropologists, who have found in them suggestive information for reconstructing societies from which those in whom we are often most interested left practically no written records. The temptation has been strong to use them as transparent descriptions of practice, rather than to interrogate them as texts.

With few exceptions, this discourse—in which the religious practice of people in the Caribbean was understood as primitive and barbaric—dominated representations of the topic until the late nineteenth century. It fed into later representations of Caribbean religions in travel writing and memoir, such as the work of Froude, St. John, and Kingsley.[36] As part of the larger body of literature engendered by European colonists' encounters with faraway peoples, early Caribbean historiography and ethnography contributed—at least indirectly—to the body of knowledge on which Galton, Tylor, Frazer, Lévy-Brühl, and other anthropologists built evolutionary models of race, mentality, and religion.[37]

Depictions of Indian religions in the first decades of indentureship in the

Caribbean were more ambiguous about these religions' location on the ladder from barbarism to civilization.[38] Observers like John Morton and Louis de Verteuil exoticized indentured Indians' religious practices in the Orientalist vein, but in contrast to most depictions of African-Caribbean religion, a certain level of sympathy and even respect toward Hindu and Muslim religious knowledge and literature emanates from these writings. Although Morton, a Presbyterian missionary, disapproved of Hindu "idolatry," he characterized Indians in Trinidad as being "of a philosophical turn of mind" and as "wonderfully acute and metaphysical," going on to describe a Brahman's insightful queries about the Christian concept of sin. He also recognized "Mohammedans'" intelligence and reverence for their sacred text, and noted how challenging it was to argue with them about the authority of the New Testament or, even more so, the Qur'an.[39] The local press was not always as cordial when reporting on Indo-Trinidadian rituals, and occasionally the vocabulary and tone of these articles was identical to those denouncing Afro-Trinidadian practices.[40] But the press never launched campaigns against Hindu or Muslim ritual practice, like it did against Shouters or the funerary rituals of working-class Trinidadians, or against alleged brujos in Cuba. Even the reportage of the notorious Hosay massacre in 1884 highlighted the "coolies'" disobedience in the face of law, rather than questioning the legitimacy of their religious practices as such. Indeed, the government defended its position by claiming that the 1882 ordinance prohibiting Hosay or Muharram processions did not apply to the religious aspects of the festival, but merely purged it of non-Hindu and non-Indo-Trinidadian elements.[41] Instead of religious persecution, scholars have read the Hosay riot against the background of deteriorating conditions for the Indo-Trinidadian labor force on the estates.[42] Before and after the Hosay massacre, Hindu and Muslim rituals attracted few state interventions in the form of repressive legislation and policing; freedom of religious worship was indeed part of the indentureship contract, and state persecutions of religious practice in the Caribbean could have jeopardized the recruitment process in India.[43]

Eventually, racist and hostile depictions of Caribbean religions began to face written challenges from within the Caribbean. Across the region (and the African diaspora more generally), intellectuals began defending (or "vindicating," as they often put it) people of African descent, producing texts like the Haitian scholar Anténor Firmin's *De l'égalité des races humaines* or the Trinidadian John Jacob Thomas's *Froudacity*.[44] These works, along with the journalism of writers like Robert Love in Jamaica, argued for the unity of the human race in the face of polygenist positions that had become powerful in the nineteenth century. Unlike the earlier historiography, travel writing, and memoirs they were writing against, these authors paid little explicit attention to religion. In a sense, their perspective shared in European contempt for African religious traditions, seeking to differentiate the Caribbean from Africa, and their "own" parts of the Caribbean from areas that seemed more closely connected to Africa. Thus John Jacob Thomas, like many non-Haitian Caribbean intellectuals, worked in his response to Froude to emphasize the difference between Haiti and the rest of the Caribbean, leaving unchallenged Froude's assertion that Vodou was barbaric.[45] Despite this, their work paved the way for the next generation of scholar-activists who did take up questions of religion in a serious, if often contradictory, way, including Jean Price-Mars and Fernando Ortiz.[46] Price-Mars's work on Haiti, and particularly his 1928 book *Ainsi parla l'oncle*, brought the search for African "survivals" in the New World to the Caribbean. Importantly, Price-Mars argued that Haitian Vodou should be regarded as a religion in its own right, although a "primitive" one.[47]

But such early defenders of Caribbean religion were swimming against the political tide. This period saw increased attention from states in the Caribbean and beyond to religious practice deemed dangerous and uncivilized, and a series of moral panics that crossed imperial and linguistic boundaries. In the Anglophone Caribbean, obeah law was reconstructed, and there appears to have been a significant increase in prosecutions (see Forde's and Paton's chapters on obeah arrests in this period). The Shakers and Shouters Prohibition Ordinances of St. Vincent and Trinidad and Tobago in 1912 and 1917, respectively, brought hundreds of people to court in the subsequent decades. Street preaching as well as funerary rituals were also targeted in media and police campaigns in Trinidad and Tobago in this period. The Brazilian Penal Code of 1890 made both Candomblé and Umbanda illegal.[48] In Cuba, there were a series of arrests of alleged *ñañigos*, and from 1904 onward a panic about *brujería*.[49] Meanwhile in Haiti, the Catholic Church sponsored a campaign against sorcery in the late nineteenth century.[50] After 1915, the United States occupation of the country both produced a large number of spectacular representations of "voodoo" that strongly influenced international understandings of Haiti and the Caribbean as a whole, and led to major efforts to suppress Vodou practice.[51] As Richman's chapter in this book shows, the Catholic Church continued these efforts after the occupation by the United States ended, in particular through the "anti-superstition campaign" of the early 1940s.[52] Recent scholarship, including Alejandra Bronfman's and Lara Putnam's chapters in this book, has elucidated the interrelationships between this increased legal, police, and media attention to religious practice and the coinciding, voluminous labor migration in the Greater Caribbean, the formation of the Cuban republic, the institutionalization of anthropology, and the augmenting knowledge of African religions gathered in newly acquired frontiers of European empire.[53]

Yet while Caribbean states treated it as a problem, social scientific study of Caribbean religion began to take a different, relativist view. In Cuba, Fernando Ortiz's scholarship, although starting from the assumption that Afro-Cuban religion was "atavistic" and criminal, developed into work that valued Cuba's African "past" as part of a celebration of its "transcultural" present.[54] Stephan Palmié has persuasively argued that the shift in Ortiz's vision was stimulated by his encounter with Fernando Guerra, a santero who corresponded with Ortiz, wrote to many other Cuban intellectuals and politicians, and published broadsides in defense of his religion at the time of the brujería persecutions.[55] This process of influence from marginalized to powerful took place on an international scale as well as within nations. The work of both Ortiz and especially Jean Price-Mars substantially influenced Melville Herskovits. Through his position as professor of anthropology at Northwestern University, Herskovits went on to popularize and extend the Haitian scholar's paradigm, which focused primarily on African cultural continuities.

As well as undertaking important research himself on Suriname, Trinidad, and Haiti, Herskovits also influenced a generation of American anthropologists who studied the Caribbean, including Katherine Dunham, Zora Neale Hurston, and George Eaton Simpson.[56] Adopting a Boasian, cultural relativist view, these scholars sought not to measure Caribbean culture on a hierarchical scale, but instead to analyze its content and meaning, and in particular, its origins. Their work was central in asserting the importance of continuities between Africa and the Caribbean. For the first time, African-Caribbean people were seen as bearers of a culture that was equivalent in status to that of European Americans. Although Herskovits and his colleagues (both Caribbean and American) were interested in a wide range of cultural "traits," including folklore, land tenure, kinship and so on, religion was frequently at the heart of their studies. Along with kinship, religion already occupied a privileged site within evolutionary anthropology. In the Caribbean, which many early anthropologists saw as uninteresting because it appeared insufficiently exotic and because its heterogeneous, mobile societies fit poorly into the structural-functionalist concept of society and culture, ritual practice that involved spirit possession and divining, and beliefs about duppies, jumbies, loup-garous, and other extraordinary beings, produced scope for what was understood as genuinely interesting research.[57]

While important in valuing African-Caribbean culture and seeing it as a serious object of study, Herskovits's research method—reflecting the anthropological ideas of society and culture of his time—was divorced from history. When he and Frances Herskovits went to Trinidad to conduct field research in 1939, they looked for a field site as far as possible from areas populated by Trinidadians of Indian descent, from the commercial capital, Port of Spain, and from the oil fields where labor rebellions had taken place only two years before. Writing in his diary about their choice to base themselves in Toco, in northeastern Trinidad, Herskovits noted, "The south should be difficult, if only because of the labor troubles that they have been having there the past two or three years and because of its intense industrialization."[58] It turned out that this search for a place where "African ways of life . . . would be met in greatest purity" led them away from the "Shango cult" for which they had been searching, whose affiliates generally lived close to the capital.[59] Similarly, anthropological studies of Haiti typically failed to mention the occupation of the country by the United States from 1915 to 1934, despite the fact that many anthropologists conducted research during or very soon after the occupation, and despite the substantial impact of the occupation on the regulation and thus the development of Vodou.[60] In this paradigm, Caribbean religion was most interesting when it took place in rural, isolated, and remote parts of the region—those areas, like Toco, that could be imagined as coming as close as possible to the ideal of a "pure," precolonial anthropological field site. Scholars chose Haiti over Jamaica, and Jamaica over Barbados. They focused on maroons rather than non-maroons, and rural rather than urban populations.

Concern about the lack of historical specificity in the Herskovitsian project of tracing African cultural retentions and continuities underlay Sidney Mintz and Richard Price's influential 1976 book *An Anthropological Approach to the Afro-American Past*, which called for a move toward historicized, context-specific research on African American culture.[61] Their work, which, as we discuss below, has become controversial, initiated what we see as a third paradigm in representations of Caribbean religion, characterized by a renewed attention to historical processes. Mintz and Price argued that the transportation, placement, and disciplining of slaves made it impossible for entire cultures or cultural practices to be transferred intact to the Caribbean; rather, what crossed the Atlantic were cognitive orientations or underlying logics that enabled enslaved people to create new institutions. Slavery, and enslaved people's limited autonomous activities, then, rather than the African past as such, underpin Mintz and Price's model for cultural creation. Instead of neglecting the significance of African influences in the New World, as some readings have suggested,

Mintz and Price posited that "Africanisms"—continuums or retentions of African cultures in the Americas—should be studied as products of New World history.[62] In the following sections of this introduction, we examine two central themes in the study of Caribbean religion in recent decades, influenced by the creolization debate initiated by Mintz and Price: the reproduction of culture, and the question of the nature of modernity in the Caribbean.

THE REPRODUCTION OF CULTURE IN THE CARIBBEAN

For scholars of Caribbean religions—and Caribbean sociocultural systems more generally—notions of plurality, syncretism, and creolization seem inescapable, yet little has been agreed on in theories about cultural production in the region. Although some contributions to the ongoing debate on the origins and development of Caribbean cultures prefer to divide the literature into "schools," distinguishing followers of Sidney Mintz and Richard Price's "creolization" model from African-centered history and anthropology, there is hardly a unitary theory for these "creolists" to draw on.[63] A potentially powerful tool for interpreting culture and cultural change in the contemporary world, the term "creolization" has attracted authors from way beyond the Caribbean.[64] The concept is useful in theorizing interaction and continuums rather than bounded, isolated cultures and societies, and as a result, many writers—not least those informed by the "postmodern shift" in anthropology—have found it appealing. Creole, however, has a long history in scientific as well as everyday parlance in and of the Caribbean. Printed sources dating back to the sixteenth century mention creole people, plants, or animals—those born in the New rather than the Old World.[65] The signification has, quite predictably, varied in different contexts, so that the connotations of hybridity or mixing, central to most contemporary social scientific usage of "creolization," have by no means always accompanied the term. In Caribbean media and everyday discussions, creole often highlights division—particularly between sections of populations identifying as African-Caribbean (or "Creole") and Indo-Caribbean, respectively—rather than inclusion or synthesis.[66]

Cultural change and synthesis as a result of mobility is, of course, not a uniquely Caribbean phenomenon. We recognize, in agreement with Marilyn Strathern and others, that cultural and social reproduction everywhere requires the crafting of novel forms out of old materials.[67] The *circumstances* in which the cultural reproduction often described as creolization has taken place in the colonial as well as postcolonial Caribbean, however, are particular and deserve to be studied as such. The unprecedented migrations of both enslaved people from Africa and other, more or less coerced laborers from Asia and Europe; the hierarchical and violent colonial regimes of plantation societies during and after slavery; and the prolonged engagement of the region with the development of global capitalism and Atlantic modernity have produced cultural contact zones marked by specific forms of social stratification and power relations. Universalizing applications of the concept of creolization risk diluting the term's analytical potency.

Much theorizing on creolization in Caribbean religions focuses on the integration or merging of African- and European-derived models, practices, and beliefs into new forms within strictly hierarchical and oppressive plantation societies. Such analyses have been indebted to Kamau Brathwaite's creole society model as well as to the Herskovitsian project of locating a "Negro Past" in the New World.[68] Brathwaite, focusing on the plantation regime during slavery, identifies two discrete groups, black and white, as producers of not only a mediating colored population but also acculturation and "interculturation," which he describes as imitation and mimicry.[69] Analyses of Caribbean religions have largely depended on a similarly selective matrix, and have portrayed syncretism[70] or creolization as a somewhat mechanical process between European powers and African subalterns.[71] Thus what could be called a "camouflage" theory of syncretism—developed, for example, in Roger Bastide's and George Eaton Simpson's work—maintains that practitioners of illegal or marginalized African-Caribbean and Brazilian religions covered their actual ritual practice under legitimate Roman Catholic symbolism, like statues and pictures of saints.[72] Syncretism, in this view, was purely pragmatic and the resulting religion a mosaic of separate African and European parts.

We seek to complicate such models by illuminating the internal heterogeneity and hierarchies within what sometimes appear as undifferentiated notions of African or European influences, and by emphasizing Asian contributions to the formation of Caribbean religions. For instance, scholarship has divided the Caribbean into Protestant and Catholic worlds, and attributed the development of formations such as regla ocha to the specific syncretism that could develop in the context of Catholic saints and African deities. While this distinction has important analytic power, it is too binary. It fails to allow for the complex pasts of places like Trinidad, Grenada, and Dominica, where Catholicism flourished among elites although it was no longer the officially dominant religion after the British took over, nor does it describe the effects of the mobility of subaltern people and knowledge within the region, including movement across the boundaries drawn by imperial powers. As a result of these movements, which were especially significant in the Southern and Eastern Caribbean, religions like Spiritual Baptist and Orisha include Protestant-derived forms of worship alongside Catholic saints and African and Indian deities. Moreover, as Richman's chapter demonstrates, even in places like Haiti where Protestant Christianity has never had official status, Protestant missionaries have successfully converted large numbers of people. Richman argues that in Haiti this has led to interesting rapprochement between official Catholicism and Vodou leaders, despite the Catholic Church's historical hostility to Vodou.

Other aspects of Caribbean societies also limit the applicability of a model of creolization based primarily on contrasts between Europe and Africa. Rhoda Reddock and Verene Shepherd, among others, have noted that Brathwaite's creole society model fits uneasily in analyses of the demographically diverse societies of the Caribbean.[73] An important line of critique in the ongoing debate on Caribbean cultural reproduction addresses the exclusive politics of nationalist or elite applications of creolization, creoleness, and *creolité*. Aisha Khan, Viranjini Munasinghe, and Deborah Thomas, among others, have shown how nationalism in the postcolonial states of Trinidad and Tobago and Jamaica has promoted certain features of African-Caribbean culture at the expense of the multiple others—but most notably the Indo-Caribbean populations—that these nations comprise.[74] As Thomas Hylland Eriksen puts it, anti- and postcolonial ideologies have been *models for* society rather than reflecting actual social reality.[75] The Asian presence in the Caribbean has had a profound influence on local cosmologies, ritual symbolism, and practice, the plurality of which the shorthand "African-Caribbean" effectively hides.

Colonies like Guyana, Suriname, and Trinidad were important nodes in cross-oceanic networks connecting this Atlantic world to the East, and particularly India. The more than half a million indentured Indians who crossed the Kala Pani between 1838 and 1917 made Asian cosmologies and ritual knowledge a part of Caribbean religious landscapes. These indentured laborers were placed on estates mainly in Guyana and Trinidad, but also in smaller numbers in Jamaica, Suriname, and on the French islands of Guadeloupe and Martinique.[76] In Indo-Caribbean identity politics, religion has emerged as a primary marker of ethnic difference.[77] Notions of authenticity and orthodoxy have marked Hindu discourses in Trinidad particularly since the 1950s, as Sanatanist pundits have sought to disassociate orthodox Hinduism from what Arthur and Juanita Niehoff identified as "the folk religion."[78] Rituals of healing and counseling, called *jharaying*, as well as rituals of sacrifice to Kali, Dee (or Di) Baba and other marginalized gods and goddesses, were part of Guyanese and Trinidadian Hinduism during indentureship. From the 1950s onward, Shakti practice has been purged from mainstream Hinduism, and Kali's puja is spatially confined to particular *mandirs* or temples.[79] India remains a source of religious authority to Sanatanist as well as more inclusively oriented Hindus, however, and both Shakti and orthodox ritual specialists travel to the subcontinent in search of "authentic" models for their temples and pujas.[80]

Such marginalized—and yet vibrant—modes of worship are often brought to the fore in discussions of creolization in Indo-Caribbean religions; other examples include the annual Ramleela performances in Trinidad, fusing carnival aesthetics and poignant social and political criticism with more conventional representations of "Indianness," or Hosay processions in which Hindus and Christians celebrate along with Muslims. In early twentieth-century Trinidad, ritual practitioners' self-definitions often reflected the heterogeneous milieu in which they worked: charged with practicing obeah, some defendants declared themselves a "Hindoo doctor," an "Indian doctor," or a "Hindu." While it is remarkable that numerous Indo-Caribbean religious practitioners were charged under obeah legislation in Guyana, Trinidad, and Jamaica, even more indicative of the permeability of ethnic and religious boundaries was the fact that one "Hindoo doctor" was reported to be "a man of the bold negro type, answering to the name of Baboo Khandas Sadoo."[81] Finally, elements of Hinduism have become an integral part of most Orisha practice and shrines in Trinidad, and India is present as part of the spiritual landscape in Winti, Comfa, Spiritual Baptist, brujería, and Revival Zion cosmologies.[82]

The issues at stake here do not relate only to relationships within the Caribbean. Indeed, the variety of participants in cultural reproduction and the nuanced, albeit hierarchical, power relations this reproduction entails become even more complex when we look at the Atlantic as a space of multidirectional movement and influences. Recent important contributions have situated New World history within a larger field of commerce, migrations, and discourse.[83] The sociocultural systems in the Caribbean have not merely been fed by unilinear streams from cultural "sources" flowing from the Old World to the New, but should also be seen as part of a cross-oceanic dialogue, a system of mutual appropriations, re-evaluations, borrowings, and syntheses. J. Lorand Matory traces the development of the transatlantic Jeje and Nagô (Yoruba) nations across different empires, nation-states, and regions, and sheds light on the agency of a mobile class of merchants and travelers sailing between Brazil and the West African coast in the making of these imagined communities. Constructed as part of a cross-oceanic field, the African societies Matory describes differ sharply from the ahistorical, unchanging, or unspecified cultures of origin implied by much of the literature on African cultural continuums in the New World.[84] Bronfman argues in her chapter that while early twentieth-century American, Cuban, and Brazilian anthropology conceived of the African past as disconnected from the social order of the New World, and therefore produced an atavistic image of Africa, Henri Dumont's 1876 study of Cuban medicine and healing portrayed Africa as a changing and heterogeneous region with a continuous presence in the lives of Cuban slaves. The twentieth-century project of imagining a distant and static African past correlates both with the aforementioned resurgence of moral anxiety about and new legislations implemented to suppress African-Caribbean religious practice in various parts of the English-speaking Caribbean, Cuba, and Haiti, and with the actual expansion of European colonial rule in Africa.

European contributions to the making of the New World cannot be studied as unaffected by these multidimensional and multidirectional processes of cultural production. While some historians have criticized the presumption of dominance of European influences over subsumed African cultures in the creolization model of cultural change in the Caribbean and in the Americas, we deem it necessary to place European, African, Asian, and American influences under similar scrutiny.[85] Without overemphasizing their importance in Caribbean cosmologies and rituals, we need to look into the multiple, differently valued European-originated belief systems and ritual practices that have been embraced and appropriated by religious specialists and healers in the Caribbean (see Lara Putnam's and Raquel Romberg's chapters in this book). Although outside the scope of this book, it is also necessary to investigate the ways in which knowledge produced in and about colonial societies has influenced European definitions and practice of religion. Indeed, it may be the case that further investigation of "European-originated" belief systems would reveal the ways in which they drew on and were crafted in response to evolving religious beliefs and practices elsewhere in the Atlantic world and beyond.[86]

The differently valued range of European influences in Caribbean ritual practice is well exemplified by people convicted of practicing obeah in Trinidad, especially since the late nineteenth century. Ritual specialists were *bricoleurs*, drawing from belief systems and cultural traditions indigenized in the Caribbean over the course of centuries of coexistence and synthesis between Judeo-Christian and West African religiosity. More recent imports, like the variants of Hinduism and Islam practiced by indentured Indians, Freemasonry, spiritualism, hypnotism, and the occult publications of the Chicago-based De Laurence Company all fed into the field of symbols and knowledge evoked in obeah trials. Putnam in her chapter writes, "Like their contemporaries in Paris, Liverpool, and Long Island, Caribbean folks sought supernatural power by means of an eclectic array of elements drawn from Victorian and Edwardian imaginings of otherness."

Although state prosecutors were keen to use the legal category of obeah as a gloss for various types of non-institutionalized ritual practice, many defendants in Jamaican and Trinidadian courtrooms preferred titles such as "palmist," "hypnotist," "scientist," "medical electronic specialist," "phrenologist," and "mesmerist," reflecting the circulation of overlapping religious and scientific knowledge between Europe and the Americas. Local newspapers covered séances in London, Paris, and St. Petersburg, published learned debates on the virtues and dangers of hypnotism or mesmerism, and described witchcraft, fortune-telling, and spiritual encounters in European centers. In Putnam's analysis, this plurality reflected shared notions of and interests in manipulating spiritual powers and material relations: "The association of the exotic and alien with dangerous and useful power meant that boundaries of perceived race, culture, and origin could encourage bridge building rather than impede it."

In addition to cross-oceanic connections, regional mobility between Caribbean colonies and between the Caribbean and the United States has been integral to the development of Caribbean religions. The period between 1890 and 1940 was marked by voluminous migrations within the insular and mainland Caribbean driven by United States investment in the plantation industry, especially in Cuba and the Dominican Republic, the nascent oil industry in Trinidad and Venezuela, and the massive construction projects of the Panamanian and Costa Rican railways and the Panama Canal.[87] Putnam's chapter in this book examines the practice of obeah and the circulation of rumors concerning illegitimate ritual practices in the Greater Caribbean migratory sphere. Putnam describes obeah as "magic of and for a mobile modern world," and argues that "engagement with the contemporaneous North Atlantic and the disparate and contentious technologies of healing and knowledge for sale within it" were a commonality shared by so-called obeah practitioners around the Greater Caribbean. As the stories of the prisoners in the Antigua jail discussed at the beginning of this introduction suggest, many defendants in late nineteenth- and early twentieth-century obeah prosecutions had moved at least once between different Caribbean colonies, and some were quite widely travelled. Regional mobility and the resulting networks of social relations, particularly networks of kinship and exchange, have also led to the spreading of religions like the Spiritual Baptist faith to St. Vincent, Trinidad, Tobago, Barbados, Grenada, and Guyana. In recent decades, northbound migration to the metropoles of the United States, Canada, France, the Netherlands, and Britain have expanded Caribbean religions to hemispheric proportions, producing intense social fields of spiritual families, ritual practice, and exchange that span the borders of nation-states.[88]

Closely linked to this discussion about ethnically and geographically situated agents of creolization are questions of power and agency. Cultural resistance, creativity, and agency in relation to dominating structures have been at the heart of much scholarship on Caribbean religions. But studies of creolization can become ahistorical and decontextualized if, in their desire to empower the marginal and oppressed, they highlight agency and cultural creativity at the expense of analyzing the manifestations of power and inequality shaping such agency.[89] Aisha Khan warns us that models of creolization devoid of concrete events leave us unable to account for political and economic processes and unequal power relations, which are essential to cultural construction.[90] Drawing on Marxist social theory, O. Nigel Bolland's view of creolization as a dialectical process brings agency to the forefront without reducing it to merely individual practice. Along with race, status differences can be based on ethnicity, gender, class, and age. Resistance emanating from creolization can be subtle to the verge of "infinitesimal," but nevertheless meaningful.[91] Raquel Romberg's work on Puerto Rican brujería dwells on the concept of ritual piracy, portraying a dialectic not unlike that described by Bolland.[92] Ritual pirates such as brujos illicitly appropriate and reposition central symbols of oppressors, like Catholic prayers or the cross. Rather than mixing, creolization here is an empowering tactic that challenges the exclusivity of hegemonic symbols, but also one that recognizes their power. Brujos' ritual practice is highly individual and non-institutional, but, according to Romberg, it works to reproduce rather than subvert the social order of the "modern colony" of Puerto Rico.

In contrast, practices labeled as "ñáñiguismo" in Cuba were an example of politically potent, dissident action: arrests of *ñáñigos* at the end of the nineteenth century, as analyzed in Cooper's chapter, reflected the intensifying anticolonial struggle in Cuba and were brought about by the political, not only religious, nature of the rituals. Katherine Smith's chapter provides another perspective on the relationship between the state and religious practice. Smith focuses on artistic representations of the lwa Gede in Haiti in order to investigate the relationship between the Haitian state and this multifaceted guardian of regeneration and death. She shows that representations of Vodou spirits reflect changes in social, political, and economic circumstances. Although the Haitian artists discussed by Smith view Vodou from a perspective that is in many ways completely opposite to the viewpoints of colonial, exoticizing onlookers, they nevertheless sculpt their work to be viewed (and possibly purchased) not only by Haitians, but also by foreign tourists and consumers.

While accounts highlighting individual choice and agency in religious practice elucidate important aspects of Caribbean religiosity and power, we need to be wary of representing Caribbean cosmologies as infinitely open and inclusive, or ritual practitioners as purely pragmatic.[93] Although inspirational and lacking centralized organization, there are powerful discursive and ritual mechanisms in Caribbean religions that give structure to individual interpretations and limit practitioners' agency.[94]

It should also be borne in mind that while analyses of Caribbean religious practices often see them as an arena of positively valued agency and subversion for the practitioners themselves, many people in Caribbean societies perceive these practices as potentially dangerous. Robert Hill, in his address to the conference from which most of this book's chapters are drawn, emphasized the ambivalence of Jamaican appropriations of religious imageries, particularly around the persona of Marcus Garvey. Rastafarians' and others' negative attitudes toward obeah, as depicted in Kenneth Bilby's chapter, range from ridicule to genuine fear. And it is a sense of danger or awe before lwa's might and demands that stimulates Haitian conversions to Protestantism, as explored in Richman's chapter. This ambiguous, even threatening power of religious practice is real to many members of Caribbean societies but not always appreciated in scholarship more inclined to stress the emancipatory potential of religion. As Bilby's analysis shows, negative perceptions of religious practice do not necessarily align with racial or cultural binaries.

CARIBBEAN RELIGIONS IN THE "SAVAGE SLOT": THE QUESTION OF MODERNITY

Considerations of how Caribbean religions have been defined, named, and represented, as well as the debates on cultural reproduction delineated above, are closely connected to another significant discussion in which many Caribbeanists have recently engaged: that surrounding Caribbean modernity. The most influential accounts of Caribbean modernity have focused largely on both the sugar plantation as a highly rationalized form of production and the central position of the Caribbean in intercontinental chains of commerce.[95]

Caribbean religions have scarcely been drawn on in depictions of the Caribbean in the creation of modernity. On the contrary, as the above discussion of Caribbean ethnography and historiography since Labat and Long shows, religion and ritual practice have largely been understood as antithetical to the modern, at best picturesquely traditional, but often at the very core of what Michel-Rolph Trouillot has called the "savage slot."[96] According to Trouillot, Western modernity is inherently dual or Janus-faced; it has taken shape against a spatially and temporally differentiated counterpoint, its other. The Caribbean as imagined by the West (along with other spaces, utopian or real) has occupied this savage slot in the heterology of modernity. We would go beyond this, however, to argue that the imagined topographies of modern and non-modern (or differently modern) spaces and times are heterologous in an additional sense. For hierarchies, boundaries, and comparisons along binaries like modern/primitive or civilized/barbarous inhere even within and between places and times positioned outside Western modernity. The presence of other, distanced, and exoticized places and people has been visible in Caribbean media since the nineteenth century, and particularly during the period of high colonialism. Reports of "the hostile savages of the Amazonia," cannibalism in the Solomon Islands, headshrinking Pygmies in "the Darkest Africa," or headhunting in Borneo were common in local newspapers like the Trinidadian *Port of Spain Gazette*, illuminating the planetary scale of European imperialism but also presenting the newly "discovered," yet-to-be-civilized cultures in contrast to colonies like Trinidad (which were depicted as "modern" and "civilized").[97] A wide array of differently valued peripheries, then—not unlike that in the global hierarchy of value between the nation-states of the contemporary world order[98]—was presented in public discourse in the colonial Caribbean.

And yet, although Caribbean journalists and writers presented the region as being superior to the savagery of those distant others, ritual practice posed an underlying threat to the modernity and potential sovereignty of Caribbean societies. Mostly religious but also profane rituals like carnival would be deemed as "barbarous relapse into Savagedom," "Voodooism" or obeah in Demerara was a "relic of African savagery," wakes a "nuisance" and a "savage practice," Shouters' meetings in Trinidad a "combination of African fetish dance and devilish possession," and Jamaican "obeah and myalism [meant] degradation and a relapse into savagery."[99] The colonial imagination had long held "Voodoo" in Haiti as the very antithesis of modern and civilized social order. Portrayals of Caribbean religions have been most flagrant in both local and foreign media and popular culture, like the song lyrics explored in Bilby's chapter in this book. Anthropological and historical studies have frequently contributed to understandings of the beliefs and ritual practices of mainly Afro-Caribbean people as the other to what is modern, civilized, and desirable.

Trouillot's heterologous model adds to recent discussions of modernity as comprising geographical and historical variants.[100] Critics of such plural approaches to modernity have questioned the validity of relativizing the concept, arguing that to do so may conceal relations of power and dominance integral to the making of world capitalism. To such critics, European agency appears to define modernity.[101] But, as Stephan Palmié argues, given that capitalism, as well as other tenets of modernity (such as nation-state, democracy, and Enlightenment philosophy), were formulated in the context of imperialism, massive migrations, and cultural encounters of unprecedented variety, "modernity may well be, not a metropolitan export, but a colonial reimport."[102] Richard Drayton suggests that we look at European imperialism as "the colonization of Europe by extra-European interests"; as his work on the profound, and continuing, impact of empire on centers as well as peripheries shows, the modern world was produced through the "collaboration of the labour, wit, and learning of all the world."[103] The cross-oceanic networks of mobility, discourse, and capitalist commerce engendered by sugar production in Caribbean plantations require less unilinear and Eurocentric models for comprehending modernity than mainstream social scientific theory has generally provided.

As noted above, the Caribbean has been a bountiful source of exoticized representations of "primitive" religiosity in European and North American literature and media. Indeed, the influence of such colonial knowledge on the development of apparently autochthonous European fin de siècle belief systems deserves further research. Novel modes of accessing the spiritual world, such as mesmerism or Spiritism, took shape in imperial centers engaged in Atlantic fields of discourse and mobility, and came ashore in the Caribbean as products of the empire, if not part of Atlantic culture itself. Thus the modernity visible in early twentieth-century obeah in Putnam's chapter may entail various layers of cultural encounters within the empire, rather than autochthonously European religious imports to the Caribbean.

Forde's and Romberg's chapters bring new perspectives to the debate on capitalism in Caribbean modernity. Forde argues that although capitalism has shaped Caribbean societies from the dawn of the plantation economy, and although money has been a medium of exchange in Caribbean ritual practice for hundreds of years, the norms and values associated with a ritual sphere of exchange in Trinidad and Tobago do not align with those of capitalism. Whereas related, non-capitalist modes of exchange in most other parts of the colonized world had existed prior to colonialism, and were reshaped by it, transactions between ritual specialists and their clients in the Caribbean follow codes developed *within* imperial structures. Romberg, on the other hand, looks to Puerto Rico as a modern colony characterized by welfare capitalism.

Puerto Rican brujos adhere to the pursuits and norms of consumer capitalism, but they rationalize it through Spiritist tenets and morality. For these practitioners, accumulation is a sign of blessing.

CONCLUSION

As we write, the importance of understanding the historical longevity, complexity, and political work done by representations of Caribbean religions has become especially pressing. In the aftermath of the earthquake that devastated Haiti in January 2010, representations of Vodou became intertwined with debates about the historical and political reasons for Haiti's poverty, the difficulty of reconstruction, and the question of who controls aid. While Pat Robertson's claim that Haitians have been "cursed" since the revolution due to their having made a "pact with the devil" quickly became notorious and was widely condemned, some liberal commentators attacked Vodou (or rather, voodoo) as the cause of Haiti's ills in not entirely dissimilar terms.[104] Writing in the online edition of the British newspaper the *Guardian*, Caroline Saunders blamed Haiti's poverty on two things: corruption, and "Haiti's cultural traditions," by which she meant "the prevailing belief in voodoo," which leads to "the village witch doctor" being "for many Haitian parents the first port of call when their child falls ill."[105] Her comments suggest the continuing power of negative interpretations of Caribbean religion as backward and superstitious across much of the political spectrum in the Global North.

Such interpretations, widely published in Caribbean media, add to the long history of using culture (and especially religion) to explain social problems and suffering. Effectively silent on political and economic contexts, this discourse has concrete repercussions in our contemporary world. At worst, sedimented ideas of religions like Vodou as backward or demonic can serve to justify continued marginalization and even violence; for example, consider an attack on "Voodooists" by a group of evangelical Christians, who destroyed Vodou altars and offerings and urinated on ritual symbols in Cité Soleil a few weeks after the earthquake.[106] In addition to influencing public opinion on religious groups and practices, scholarly and media interventions, including more nuanced and less condemnatory understandings of Caribbean religion, reflect but also shape discussions within religious groups. This mutually influential relationship between practitioners and scribes has been visible, for example, in the emergence of ideologies of anti-syncretism in Orisha, Candomblé, and regla ocha, especially since the 1990s. If the recent discourse on Voodoo relies on old, racialized notions of superstition and sovereignty, these developments reference authenticity and anti-colonialism. By denying substantial or semantic syntheses of African and other, mainly Asian and Christian, elements in creole religions, many educated, middle-class religious leaders with transnational connections to Orisha elders in the United States, Nigeria, and elsewhere in the Caribbean seek to purify their religions of non-African symbols and practices and add elements considered more authentic and African, such as Ifa divination.[107] Such anti-syncretic views sometimes adopt, but also invert, the image of an unchanging and undifferentiated Africa that marks much of the twentieth-century anthropology of African American and Caribbean religion.[108] As this book suggests, moves such as these are part of an ongoing dialogue in which a multitude of actors in and around the Caribbean have debated and redefined the authenticity, validity, and origins of spiritual power. We advocate paying greater attention to that dialogue not because it proves that Caribbean religions are in any way inauthentic, but rather because it demonstrates just how integral Caribbean faiths and practices have been to the political, economic, and social processes that have shaped the world we inhabit today—and the multiple places of Caribbean peoples within it.[109]

This book may offer little to those practitioners, students, or advocates of Caribbean religions who, for motives personal or political, yearn for clear-cut depictions of obeah or other local forms of religious practice that accentuate uniqueness and authenticity by playing down change and interaction in cultural reproduction. But it may prove helpful for those who seek to understand Caribbean religions, or identify with them, in the societies in which they are practiced. Addressing the centuries-long processes of cultural encounters, appropriations, and reproduction that have gone into the making of religion and spiritual work in the Caribbean, the chapters in this book tell us about agency and identity politics, about the need to find common ground, and the need to draw boundaries. No less important, they describe the practices of governing, policing, and representing religion as projects that both affect and are affected by the cultural politics of religious practitioners. Throughout, the chapters emphasize the powerful presence of the spiritual in the lives of Caribbean people past and present, in milieus sacred and mundane. At the most fundamental level, it is the acknowledgment of this power that unifies these chapters and inspires the analyses and debates this book evokes.

NOTES

1. Knollys to Lyttelton, no. 222, May 22, 1905, The National Archives of the UK (hereafter TNA): CO 152/287. On police photography, see Mary Warner Marien, *Pho-*

tography: A Cultural History (New York: Harry N. Abrams, 2002); and, in a colonial context, Clare Anderson, *Legible Bodies: Race, Criminality and Colonialism in South Asia* (Oxford: Berg, 2004), 141–62.

2. "An Obeah Case," an undated clipping from unnamed newspaper reporting on a court case of August 30, 1904, puts Howe's birthplace as St. Kitts. Howe's record of conviction for practicing obeah lists his birthplace as Montserrat. Both in Cambridge University Library: Royal Commonwealth Society Library, Sir Henry Hesketh Bell Papers, RCMS 36, notebook C (newspaper clipping); file A12, subfolder on "West Indian Superstition: Obeah" (record of conviction).

3. Colonial officials described Lucy Emile Bernard, convicted of practicing obeah in Dominica, as a "French woman from Guadeloupe." Young to Sweet-Escott, June 20, 1906, enclosed in Sweet-Escott to Bruce, no. 275, July 23, 1906, TNA: CO 152/290. Their Virgin Islands colleagues noted of Isaac Williams that he had been caught and prosecuted after "returning home" to the Virgin Islands "after spending several months in Santo Domingo." Earl to Lyttelton, May 9, 1905, enclosed in Knollys to Lyttelton, no. 218, May 19, 1905, TNA: CO 152/287.

4. A book such as this might have included chapters on other societies in the Americas, particularly Brazil and the United States. In order to include as much material as possible on the Caribbean, however, we have limited our focus to the Greater Caribbean (including mainland Central America and the Guyanas). Even so, it has not been possible to discuss all parts of the region.

5. Talal Asad, "Anthropological Conceptions of Religion: Reflections on Geertz," *Man*, n.s., 18, no. 2 (June 1983): 237–59. See also Talal Asad, *Genealogies of Religion: Discipline and Reasons of Power in Christianity and Islam* (Baltimore: Johns Hopkins University Press, 1993).

6. On the substantivist/formalist debate, see, for example, George Dalton, "Theoretical Issues in Economic Anthropology," *Current Anthropology* 10, no. 1 (February 1969): 63–102; Karl Polanyi, Conrad M. Arensberg, and Harry W. Pearson, eds., *Trade and Market in the Early Empires: Economies in History and Theory* (1957; Chicago: Regnery, 1971).

7. James G. Frazer, *The Golden Bough: A Study in Comparative Religion* (London: Routledge, 2003); E. E. Evans-Pritchard, *Witchcraft, Oracles, and Magic among the Azande*, with a foreword by C. G. Seligman (Oxford, Clarendon, 1937); Lucien Lévy-Brühl, *How Natives Think*, trans. Lilian A. Clare (1926; Princeton: Princeton University Press, 1985); Bronislaw Malinowski, *Magic, Science, and Religion, and Other Essays* (New York: Doubleday, 1954).

8. A large body of anthropological literature has historicized these categories and challenged their applicability as markers of autonomous entities. See, for example, Asad, *Genealogies of Religion*; Robin Horton and Ruth H. Finnegan, eds., *Modes of Thought: Essays on Thinking in Western and Non-Western Societies* (Cambridge: Cambridge University Press, 1997); Morton Klass, *Ordered Universes: Approaches to the Anthropology of Religion* (Boulder: Westview Press, 1995); Stanley Jeyaraja Tambiah,

Magic, Science, Religion, and the Scope of Rationality (Cambridge: Cambridge University Press, 1990).

9. Tambiah, *Magic, Science, Religion, and the Scope of Rationality*, 19.

10. Peter Harrison, *"Religion" and the Religions in the English Enlightenment* (Cambridge: Cambridge University Press, 1990).

11. Karen Richman, "A More Powerful Sorcerer: Conversion, Capital, and Haitian Transnational Migration," *New West Indian Guide* 82, nos. 1/2 (2008): 3–45.

12. On the history of these spellings, see Alasdair Pettinger, "From Vaudoux to Voodoo," *Forum for Modern Language Studies* 40, no. 4 (October 2004): 415–25. Arguing that Vodou practitioners understand their relation to the spirits as analogous to the relation of disciplined and obedient children to parents, Karen McCarthy Brown argues that "existence and essence are the theological preoccupations of Great Atlantic [i.e., white Euro-American] culture." Alourdes, her main informant and collaborator, stressed action, not belief, and always spoke of serving the spirits instead of worshipping or believing in them. Karen McCarthy Brown, *Mama Lola: A Vodou Priestess in Brooklyn* (Berkeley: University of California Press, 2001), 49.

13. David H. Brown, *Santería Enthroned: Art, Ritual, and Innovation in an Afro-Cuban Religion* (Chicago: University of Chicago Press, 2003), 129, 285; Stephan Palmié, *Wizards and Scientists: Explorations in Afro-Cuban Modernity and Tradition* (Durham: Duke University Press, 2002); Jorge Castellanos, *Pioneros de la etnografía afrocubana: Fernando Ortiz, Rómulo Lachatañeré, Lydia Cabrera* (Miami: Universal, 2003), 166–67.

14. On negotiations of who and what practices make up the Spiritual Baptist religion, see, for example, Hazel Ann Gibbs de Peza, *My Faith: Spiritual Baptist Christian* (Mona: University of the West Indies Press, 1999); James Houk, *Spirit, Blood, and Drums: The Orisha Religion in Trinidad* (Philadelphia: Temple University Press, 1995); Maarit Laitinen, *Marching to Zion: Creolization in Spiritual Baptist Rituals and Cosmology* (Helsinki: Research Series in Anthropology, 2002). On similar contestations in Santería, see George Brandon, *Santería from Africa to the New World: The Dead Sell Memories* (Bloomington: Indiana University Press, 1997); Kristina Wirtz, *Ritual, Discourse, and Community in Cuban Santería* (Gainesville: University Press of Florida, 2007).

15. William Guinee, "Ritual and Devotion in a Trinidadian Kali Temple" (master's thesis, Indiana University, 1990), 9, 15; Keith McNeal, "Ecstasy in Exile: Divinity, Power, and Performance in Two Trinidadian Possession Religions" (PhD diss., Emory University, 2004), 248, 307; Teruyuki Tsuji, "'They don't do culture': Kali-Mai as a Matrix of National Culture in Trinidad," *Wadabagei* 12, no. 3 (2009): 59–86.

16. Diana Paton, "Obeah Acts: Producing and Policing the Boundaries of Religion in the Caribbean," *Small Axe* 13, no. 1 (2009): 1–18. Richard Allsopp, in *Dictionary of Caribbean English Usage* (Oxford: Oxford University Press, 2006), lists "mama-do-good," "papa-do-good," and "scientist" as alternatives for "obeah-man" or "obeah-woman," attributing the first two to Grenadian usage alone and the last to Guyana, Grenada, Jamaica, and Nevis.

17. See, for example, "A Shouter's Meeting," October 1, 1904; "Riotous 'Shouters' Heavily Fined," January 17, 1909; "Shouters Raided," March 10, 1909; "Shouters' Meeting Interrupted by Police," January 23, 1918; "In A Shouters' Camp," November 1, 1924; "Shouters at Baden Powell Street," January 15, 1930; "'Shouters' Raided," July 29, 1930; all in *Port of Spain Gazette*; and "Shouter's Meeting Down South," *The Mirror* (Trinidad), April 29, 1906. See also Bridget Brereton, *Race Relations in Colonial Trinidad, 1870–1900* (Cambridge: Cambridge University Press, 2002), 159.

18. Similarly, what used to be referred to as the "Shango cult" in Trinidadian media and scholarship is today called Orisha work or Orisha religion by most practitioners and researchers.

19. On the globalization of what is today identified as Yoruba religion, see Jacob K. Olupona and Terry Rey, eds., *Òrìṣà Devotion as World Religion: The Globalization of Yorùbá Religious Culture* (Madison: University of Wisconsin Press, 2008); J. Lorand Matory, *Black Atlantic Religion: Tradition, Transnationalism, and Matriarchy in Afro-Brazilian Candomblé* (Princeton: Princeton University Press, 2005); Stephan Palmié, "The Cultural Work of Yoruba Globalization," in *Christianity and Social Change in Africa*, ed. Toyin Falola (Durham, N.C.: Carolina Academic Press, 2005), 43–81.

20. For a discussion of the Sixth World Congress, held in Trinidad in 1999, see Frances Henry, *Reclaiming African Religions in Trinidad: The Socio-political Legitimation of the Orisha and Spiritual Baptist Faiths* (Mona: University of the West Indies Press, 2003), 146–56.

21. Asad, *Genealogies of Religion*; Tambiah, *Magic, Science, Religion, and the Scope of Rationality*.

22. Klass, *Ordered Universes*, 89.

23. Christopher Columbus, *The Journal of Christopher Columbus (during His First Voyage, 1492–93), and Documents Relating to the Voyages of John Cabot and Gaspar Corte Real* (1893; edited and translated by Clements R. Markham, New York: Burt Franklin, 1971), 47, 90; see also pp. 38, 65, 73.

24. Fray Ramón Pané, *An Account of the Antiquities of the Indians*, ed. José Juan Arrom, trans. Susan C. Griswold (Durham: Duke University Press, 1999); Luis N. Rivera-Pagán, "Freedom and Servitude: Indigenous Slavery and the Spanish Conquest of the Caribbean," in *Autochthonous Societies*, vol. 1 of *General History of the Caribbean*, ed. Jalil Sued Badillo (Paris: UNESCO Publishing, 2003), 316–62; Antonio M. Stevens-Arroyo, *Cave of the Jagua: The Mythological World of the Taínos* (1988; Scranton: University of Scranton Press, 2006), 71–83.

25. Gordon K. Lewis, *Main Currents in Caribbean Thought: The Historical Evolution of Caribbean Society in Its Ideological Aspects, 1492–1900* (Kingston: Heinemann Educational Books, 1983), chap. 3.

26. For studies of the Inquisition that emphasize cases involving Africans and people of African descent, usually in close interaction with mestizos/as, Spaniards, or Indians, see Joan Cameron Bristol, *Christians, Blasphemers, and Witches: Afro-Mexican Ritual Practice in the Seventeenth Century* (Albuquerque: University of New Mexico

Press, 2007); Laura A. Lewis, *Hall of Mirrors: Power, Witchcraft, and Caste in Colonial Mexico* (Durham: Duke University Press, 2003); Luz Adriana Maya Restrepo, "Paula de Eguiluz y el arte del bien querer: Apuntes para el estudio de la sensualidad y el cimarronaje femenino en el Caribe, siglo XVII," *Historia Crítica* 24 (June 2002): 101–24; and Ruth Behar, "Sex and Sin, Witchcraft and the Devil in Late-Colonial Mexico," *American Ethnologist* 14, no. 1 (February 1987): 34–54. For an important work on the Inquisition's concern with indigenous "sorcery" and "heresy," see Serge Gruzinski, *Man-Gods in the Mexican Highlands: Indian Power and Colonial Society, 1520–1800*, trans. Eileen Corrigan (Stanford: Stanford University Press, 1989).

27. Cited in Doris Garraway, *The Libertine Colony: Creolization in the Early French Caribbean* (Durham: Duke University Press, 2005), 167–69; Garraway cites the 1728 edition of *Nouveau Voyage*, 2:396.

28. Garraway, *The Libertine Colony*, 192–93.

29. For important discussions of all these texts, and many others, see Lewis, *Main Currents in Caribbean Thought*.

30. Pettinger, "From Vaudoux to Voodoo," 415.

31. Bryan Edwards, *The History, Civil and Commercial, of the British Colonies in the West Indies* (London: John Stockdale, 1793), 1:171–74.

32. Thomas M. Winterbottom, "An Account of the Native Africans in the Neighbourhood of Sierra Leone; to Which Is Added, an Account of the Present State of Medicine among Them" (1803), in *Slavery, Abolition and Emancipation: Writings in the British Romantic Period*, ed. Peter Kitson and Debbie Lee (London: Pickering and Chatto, 1999), 7:212–14; B[essie] Pullen-Burry, *Jamaica as It Is, 1903* (London: T. F. Unwin, 1903), 136–37; Martha Beckwith, *Black Roadways: A Study of Jamaican Folk Life* (Chapel Hill: University of North Carolina Press, 1929). Joseph J. Williams, in *Voodoos and Obeahs: Phases of West India Witchcraft* (New York: AMS Press, 1970), 114–16, quotes the Popo woman story directly from the original parliamentary inquiry, as well as quoting extensively from Edwards and many other sources. Orlando Patterson, in *The Sociology of Slavery: An Analysis of the Origins, Development and Structure of Negro Slave Society in Jamaica* (London: Macgibbon and Kee, 1967), 192–93, likewise quotes from the original source.

33. Moreau's description of vaudoux was, for instance, extensively quoted in the notorious Spencer St. John, *Hayti; or, The Black Republic* (London: Smith, Elder, 1884), which popularized the claim that Vodou involved cannibalism.

34. See, for instance, Emmanuel Chukwudi Eze, ed., *Race and the Enlightenment: A Reader* (Cambridge, Mass.: Blackwell, 1997).

35. On the idea of fetishism, see William Pietz, "The Problem of the Fetish, I," *Res* 9 (Spring 1985): 5–17; William Pietz, "The Problem of the Fetish II: The Origin of the Fetish," *Res* 13 (Spring 1987): 23–45; and especially William Pietz, "The Problem of the Fetish, IIIa: Bosman's Guinea and the Enlightenment Theory of Fetishism," *Res* 16 (Autumn 1988): 105–23.

36. James Anthony Froude, *The English in the West Indies; or, The Bow of Ulysses*

(London: Longmans, 1888); Sir Spencer B. St. John, *Hayti; or, The Black Republic* (London: Smith, Elder, 1884); Charles Kingsley, *At Last! A Christmas in the West Indies* (London: Macmillan, 1871).

37. In contrast to these early armchair anthropologists, Henri Dumont's work on Cuban slaves in the latter half of the nineteenth century, as examined in Alejandra Bronfman's chapter in this book, is a rare example of nascent anthropology produced in the periphery rather than in the center.

38. On proto-ethnographic descriptions of Indian-Caribbean people in the early decades of the indentureship period, see Aisha Khan, *Callaloo Nation: Metaphors of Race and Religious Identity among South Asians in Trinidad* (Durham: Duke University Press, 2004), chap. 2.

39. Sarah E. Morton, ed., *John Morton of Trinidad: Pioneer Missionary of the Presbyterian Church in Canada to the East Indians in the British West Indies* (Toronto: Westminster Company, 1916), 52, 121.

40. For example, the *Port of Spain Gazette* of April 24, 1906, 6, report of an "East Indian" funeral procession in Port of Spain, depicts the bereaved as "indulg[ing] in a sort of glorified crapeau dance, and hootchi kootchi combined, and tom tomming away to their hearts' content."

41. The bloodiest repression of religious proceedings in Trinidad was targeted at Indo-Trinidadians, when the colonial police opened fire against the annual Hosay or Muharram procession on its way to San Fernando on October 30, 1884, killing at least fifteen and wounding well over a hundred Muslim and Hindu participants. Indo-Trinidadian estate labourers had been prohibited from entering the main towns during the Hosay festival as a precaution against possible riots. Kelvin Singh, *Bloodstained Tombs: The Muharram Massacre, 1884* (London: Macmillan Caribbean, 1988), 1, 16–17.

42. Ibid., 9; Frank J. Korom, *Hosay Trinidad: Muharram Performances in an Indo-Caribbean Diaspora* (Philadelphia: University of Pennsylvania Press, 2003), 116.

43. In the following decades, a relatively small number of Indo-Trinidadians were prosecuted for allowing drumming after 10 p.m. See, for example, "Coolie Drum Beating," *Port of Spain Gazette*, May 14, 1915, 8.

44. Anténor Firmin, *De l'égalité des races humaines* (Paris: Librairie Cotillon, 1885); John Jacob Thomas, *Froudacity: West Indian Fables by James Anthony Froude* (1889; London: New Beacon, 1969). For recent discussions of these intellectuals, see Laënnec Hurbon, *Le Barbare imaginaire* (Paris: Editions du Cerf, 1988), 55–58; Carolyn Fluehr-Lobban, "Anténor Firmin: Haitian Pioneer of Anthropology," *American Anthropologist* 102, no. 3 (September 2000): 449–66; Faith Smith, *Creole Recitations: John Jacob Thomas and Colonial Formation in the Late Nineteenth-Century Caribbean* (Charlottesville: University of Virginia Press, 2002). On vindicationism, see David Scott, *Conscripts of Modernity: The Tragedy of Colonial Enlightenment* (Durham: Duke University Press, 2004), 79–83.

45. Thomas, *Froudacity*, 53. See also Smith, *Creole Recitations*, 21–22.

46. For an analysis of Price-Mars's work in relation to Firmin, see Gérarde Magloire-

Danton, "Anténor Firmin and Jean Price-Mars: Revolution, Memory, Humanism," *Small Axe* 9, no. 2 (September 2005): 150–70.

47. Jean Price-Mars, *Ainsi parla l'oncle* (1928; Ottawa: Leméac, 1973), 194–95, 230–32.

48. Yvonne Maggie, *Medo do feitiço: Relaçoes entre magia e poder no Brasil* (Rio de Janeiro: Arquivo Nacional, 1992). See also Denise Ferreira da Silva, "Out of Africa? Umbanda and the 'Ordering' of the Modern Brazilian Space," in Patrick Bellegarde-Smith, ed., *Fragments of Bone: Neo-African Religions in a New World* (Urbana: University of Illinois Press, 2005), 32–51.

49. As well as Cooper's chapter in this book, see Alejandra Bronfman, *Measures of Equality: Social Science, Race, and Citizenship in Cuba, 1902–1940* (Chapel Hill: University of North Carolina Press, 2004); Aline Helg, *Our Rightful Share: The Afro-Cuban Struggle for Equality, 1886–1912* (Chapel Hill: University of North Carolina Press, 1995); Palmié, *Wizards and Scientists*; Reinaldo Román, *Governing Spirits: Religion, Miracles, and Spectacles in Cuba and Puerto Rico, 1898–1956* (Chapel Hill: University of North Carolina Press, 2007); Rafael Ocasio, "Dancing to the Beat of Babalu Aye: Santería and Cuban Popular Culture," in Bellegarde-Smith, *Fragments of Bone*, 90–107.

50. Laënnec Hurbon, *Voodoo: Search for the Spirit*, trans. Lory Frankel (New York: Harry N. Abrams, 1995); Kate Ramsey, "Legislating 'Civilization' in Postrevolutionary Haiti," in *Race, Nation, and Religion in the Americas*, ed. Henry Goldschmidt and Elizabeth McAlister (Oxford: Oxford University Press, 2004), 231–58.

51. Kate Ramsey, *The Spirits and the Law: Vodou and Power in Haiti* (Chicago: University of Chicago Press, 2011), 118–76; Mary A. Renda, *Taking Haiti: Military Occupation and the Culture of U.S. Imperialism, 1915–1940* (Chapel Hill: University of North Carolina Press, 2001).

52. For more on the anti-superstition campaign, see Kate Ramsey, "Without One Ritual Note: Folklore Performance and the Haitian State," *Radical History Review* 84 (Fall 2002): 7–42; David Nicholls, *From Dessalines to Duvalier: Race, Colour and National Independence in Haiti*, 2nd ed. (New Brunswick: Rutgers University Press, 1996), 181–83.

53. See, for example, Bronfman, *Measures of Equality*; Palmié, *Wizards and Scientists*; Palmié, "The Cultural Work of Yoruba Globalization"; Román, *Governing Spirits*.

54. Brown, *Santería Enthroned*, 3–4.

55. Palmié, *Wizards and Scientists*, 250–56.

56. On Herskovits's influence, see Kevin Yelvington, "The Invention of Africa in Latin America and the Caribbean: Political Discourse and Anthropological Praxis, 1920–1940," in *Afro-Atlantic Dialogues: Anthropology in the Diaspora*, ed. Kevin Yelvington (Santa Fe: School of American Research Press, 2006), 35–86; and Jerry Gershenhorn, *Melville J. Herskovits and the Racial Politics of Knowledge* (Lincoln: University of Nebraska Press, 2004).

57. See Michel-Rolph Trouillot, "The Caribbean Region: An Open Frontier in

Anthropological Theory," *Annual Review of Anthropology* 21, no. 1 (October 1992): 19–42. The increasing number of ethnographic inquiries into Caribbean societies and cultures can be contrasted with the discipline of history's almost complete lack of concern with the worldviews and culture of Caribbean people at this time. Historians, to the extent that they attended to the Caribbean at all, focused instead on the development of colonial policy and the plantation economy.

58. Melville and Frances Herskovits Papers, MG 261, box 15, folder 82, Schomburg Center for Research in Black Culture, New York; Melville J. Herskovits and Frances S. Herskovits, *Trinidad Village* (New York: Octagon Books, 1964), vi, 3. On the labor rebellions in Trinidad, see O. Nigel Bolland, *The Politics of Labour in the British Caribbean: The Social Origins of Authoritarianism and Democracy in the Labour Movement* (Kingston: Ian Randle, 2001), 250–79; Kelvin Singh, *Race and Class Struggles in a Colonial State: Trinidad, 1917–1945* (Mona: University of the West Indies Press, 1994), 158–85.

59. Herskovits and Herskovits, *Trinidad Village*, 173. For similar comments regarding Cuba and Brazil, see Stephan Palmié, "Ethnogenetic Processes and Cultural Transfer in Afro-American Slave Populations," in *Slavery in the Americas*, ed. Wolfgang Binder (Würzburg: Königshausen and Neuman, 1993), 340–41.

60. Ramsey, "Penalizing and Promoting 'Voodoo' "; Gérarde Magloire and Kevin Yelvington, "Haiti and the Anthropological Imagination," *Gradhiva* 1 (2005): 127–52.

61. Republished as Sidney Mintz and Richard Price, *The Birth of African-American Culture: An Anthropological Perspective* (1976; Boston: Beacon, 1992); Richard Price, "The Miracle of Creolization: A Retrospective," *New West Indian Guide* 75, nos. 1/2 (2001): 35–64.

62. Stephan Palmié, "Is There a Model in the Muddle? 'Creolization' in African American History and Anthropology," in *Creolization: History, Ethnography, Theory*, ed. Charles Stewart (London: UCL Press, 2007), 185.

63. Price, "The Miracle of Creolization." See Stephan Palmié, "Creolization and Its Discontents," *Annual Review of Anthropology* 35 (October 2006): 433–56; and Palmié, "Is There a Model in the Muddle?" for thorough reviews of creolization studies and the apparent opposition between paradigms.

64. See, for example, L. Caplan, "Creole World, Purist Rhetoric: Anglo-Indian Cultural Debates in Colonial and Contemporary Madras," *Journal of the Royal Anthropological Institute* 1, no. 4 (1995): 743–62; James Clifford, *The Predicament of Culture* (Cambridge: Harvard University Press, 1988); James Clifford, *Routes: Travel and Translation in the Late Twentieth Century* (Cambridge: Harvard University Press, 1997); Ulf Hannerz, "The World in Creolization," *Africa* 57, no. 4 (1987): 546–59; Ulf Hannerz, *Transnational Connections* (New York: Routledge, 1996).

65. Palmié, "Creolization and Its Discontents."

66. See Viranjini Munasinghe, *Callaloo or Tossed Salad? East Indians and the Cultural Politics of Identity in Trinidad* (Ithaca: Cornell University Press, 2001) on creoles as an ethnic category in Trinidad and Tobago.

67. Marilyn Strathern, *Reproducing the Future* (New York: Routledge, 1992).

68. Kamau Brathwaite, *The Development of Creole Society in Jamaica, 1770–1820* (Oxford: Clarendon, 1971).

69. Brathwaite, *The Development of Creole Society in Jamaica*, 299–303.

70. The term "syncretism" has been applied cross-culturally in studies of religious synthesis and change. See Sidney M. Greenfield and André Droogers, eds., *Reinventing Religions: Syncretism and Transformation in Africa and the Americas* (Lanham, Md.: Rowman and Littlefield, 2001); Rosalind Shaw and Charles Stewart, eds., *Syncretism/Anti-syncretism: The Politics of Religious Synthesis* (London: Routledge, 1994).

71. Roger Bastide, *African Civilisations in the New World*, trans. Peter Green (London: C. Hurst, 1971); Brandon, *Santería from Africa to the New World*; Leslie G. Desmangles, *The Faces of Gods: Vodou and Roman Catholicism in Haiti* (Chapel Hill: University of North Carolina Press, 1992); Herskovits and Herskovits, *Trinidad Village*; Joseph M. Murphy, *Santería: An African Religion in America* (Boston: Beacon, 1988). For a useful appreciation and critique of Brathwaite's approach to creolization, see Garraway, *The Libertine Island*, 18–21.

72. Bastide, *African Civilisations in the New World*; George Eaton Simpson, *Black Religions in the New World* (New York: Columbia University Press, 1978).

73. Rhoda Reddock, "Contestations over Culture, Class, Gender and Identity in Trinidad and Tobago: 'The Little Tradition,'" in *Questioning Creole: Creolisation Discourses in Caribbean Culture*, ed. Verene A. Shepherd and Glen L. Richards (Oxford: James Currey, 2002); Verene A. Shepherd, "Indians and Blacks in Jamaica in the 19th and Early 20th Centuries: A Micro-study of the Foundations of Race Antagonisms," in *After the Crossing*, ed. Howard Johnson (London: Frank Cass, 1988).

74. Khan, *Callaloo Nation*; Deborah Thomas, *Modern Blackness: Nationalism, Globalization, and the Politics of Culture in Jamaica* (Durham: Duke University Press, 2004); Munasinghe, *Callaloo or Tossed Salad?*; Sally Price and Richard Price, "Shadowboxing in the Mangroves," *Cultural Anthropology* 12, no. 1 (February 1997): 3–36.

75. Thomas Hylland Eriksen, "Creolization in Anthropological Theory and in Mauritius," in Stewart, *Creolization*, 153–77.

76. Steven Vertovec, *Hindu Trinidad: Religion, Ethnicity, and Socio-economic Change* (London: Macmillan Caribbean, 1992), 4.

77. Khan, *Callaloo Nation*.

78. Arthur and Juanita Niehoff, *East Indians in the West Indies* (Milwaukee: Milwaukee Public Museum Publications in Anthropology, 1960), 158. On the development of orthodox Hinduism in Trinidad, see Vertovec, *Hindu Trinidad*.

79. Guinee, "Ritual and Devotion in a Trinidadian Kali Temple," 8–9; McNeal, "Ecstasy in Exile," 227.

80. McNeal, "Ecstasy in Exile," chap. 5; Tsuji, "'They don't do culture.'"

81. "Alleged Assumption of Supernatural Powers," *Port of Spain Gazette*, February 7, 1919, 9–10. See also "An East Indian Trickster," *Port of Spain Gazette*, May 29, 1924, 12,

on Biroo alias Sadoo, "an East Indian man describing himself as a worshipper of the Sun," charged with practicing obeah; or "Obeah Charge," (Jamaica) *Gleaner*, December 10, 1909, 3, on Pearial Maragh, an East Indian who claimed to be a professor and saw his clients at Queen's Hotel. Like at least fifty other practitioners identified as East Indian in Jamaica and Trinidad between 1890 and 1940, Maragh was charged with practicing obeah.

82. See, for example, Kean Gibson, *Comfa Religion and Creole Language in a Caribbean Community* (Albany: State University of New York Press, 2001); Maarit Forde, "Rituals, Journeys, and Modernity: Caribbean Spiritual Baptists in New York," in *Constructing Vernacular Culture in the Trans-Caribbean*, ed. Holger Henke and Karl-Heinz Magister (New York: Lexington Books), 101–22; Kenneth Lum, *Praising His Name in the Dance: Spirit Possession in the Spiritual Baptist Faith and Orisha Work in Trinidad, West Indies* (Amsterdam: Harwood Academic Press, 2000); Raquel Romberg, *Witchcraft and Welfare: Spiritual Capital and the Business of Magic in Modern Puerto Rico* (Austin: University of Texas Press, 2003); Wallace Zane, *Journeys to Spiritual Lands: The Natural History of a West Indian Religion* (New York: Oxford University Press, 1999).

83. J. Lorand Matory, "The English Professors of Brazil: On the Diasporic Roots of the Yorùbá Nation," *Comparative Studies in Society and History* 41, no. 1 (January 1999): 72–103; Matory, *Black Atlantic Religion*; Palmié, *Wizards and Scientists*; Palmié, "The Cultural Work of Yoruba Globalization"; Kristin Mann, "Shifting Paradigms in the Study of the African Diaspora and of Atlantic History and Culture," *Slavery and Abolition* 22, no. 1 (April 2001): 3–21.

84. Matory, *Black Atlantic Religion*.

85. For such critiques, see, for instance, James H. Sweet, *Recreating Africa: Culture, Kinship, and Religion in the African-Portuguese World, 1441–1770* (Chapel Hill: University of North Carolina Press, 2003); Michael Gomez, *Exchanging Our Country Marks* (Chapel Hill: University of North Carolina Press, 1998); Paul Lovejoy, "The African Diaspora: Revisionist Interpretations of Ethnicity, Culture and Religion during Slavery," *Studies in the World History of Slavery, Abolition and Emancipation* 2, no. 1 (1997): 1–24; John Thornton, *Africa and Africans in the Making of the Atlantic World, 1400–1680* (Cambridge: Cambridge University Press, 1998).

86. Thanks to Lara Putnam for helping us to formulate this point.

87. César Ayala, *American Sugar Kingdom: The Plantation Economy of the Spanish Caribbean, 1898–1934* (Chapel Hill: University of North Carolina Press, 1999); Jorge L. Giovannetti, "The Elusive Organization of 'Identity': Race, Religion, and Empire among Caribbean Migrants in Cuba," *Small Axe* 10, no. 1 (March 2006): 1–27; Marc C. McLeod, "Undesirable Aliens: Race, Ethnicity, and Nationalism in the Comparison of Haitian and British West Indian Immigrant Workers in Cuba, 1912–1939," *Journal of Social History* 31, no. 3 (Spring 1998): 599–623; Velma Newton, *The Silver Men: West Indian Labour Migration to Panama* (Mona: Institute of Social and Economic Re-

search, University of the West Indies, 1984); Lara Putnam, *The Company They Kept: Migrants and the Politics of Gender in Caribbean Costa Rica, 1870–1960* (Chapel Hill: University of North Carolina Press, 2002).

88. Such religious, transnational networks have been particularly well depicted in recent studies of Vodou. See, for example, Brown, *Mama Lola*; Elizabeth McAlister, *Rara! Vodou, Power, and Performance in Haiti and Its Diaspora* (Berkeley: University of California Press, 2002); Karen Richman, *Migration and Vodou* (Gainesville: University Press of Florida, 2005). On Spiritual Baptists' transnational connections, see Forde, "Rituals, Journeys, and Modernity"; Maarit Forde, "Modes of Transnational Relatedness: Caribbean Migrants' Networks of Child Care and Ritual Kinship," in *Everyday Ruptures: Children, Youth, and Migration in Global Perspective*, ed. Cati Coe, Rachel R. Reynolds, Deborah A. Boehm, Julia Meredith Hess, and Heather Rae-Espinoza (Nashville: Vanderbilt University Press, 2011), 79–96.

89. Andrew Apter, "Herskovits's Heritage: Rethinking Syncretism in the African Diaspora," *Diaspora: A Journal of Transnational Studies* 1, no. 3 (Winter 1991): 235–60; Margarite Fernandez-Olmos and Lizabeth Paravisini-Gebert, *Creole Religions of the Caribbean: An Introduction from Vodou and Santeria to Obeah and Espiritismo* (New York: New York University Press, 2003). On this problem, see Walter Johnson, "On Agency," *Journal of Social History* 37, no. 1 (Fall 2003): 113–24.

90. Aisha Khan, "Journey to the Center of the Earth: The Caribbean as Master Symbol," *Cultural Anthropology* 16, no. 3 (August 2001): 273; Aisha Khan, "Creolization Moments," in Stewart, *Creolization*, 238.

91. Nigel O. Bolland, "Creolization and Creole Societies: A Cultural Nationalist View of Caribbean Social History," in Shepherd and Richards, *Questioning Creole*, 15–46. Bolland draws largely on Michel de Certeau's *The Practice of Everyday Life*, trans. Steven Rendall (Berkeley: University of California Press, 1984).

92. See also Raquel Romberg, "Symbolic Piracy: Creolization with an Attitude?," *New West Indian Guide* 79, nos. 3/4 (2005): 175–218.

93. For example, Huon Wardle has argued for heightened individualism in Jamaican religious practice in "Ambiguation, Disjuncture, Commitment: A Social Analysis of Caribbean Cultural Creativity," *Journal of the Royal Anthropological Institute* 8, no. 3 (September 2002): 493–508; and "A Groundwork for West Indian Cultural Openness," *Journal of the Royal Anthropological Institute* 13, no. 3 (September 2007): 567–83.

94. Kristina Wirtz has argued in *Ritual, Discourse, and Community in Cuban Santería* (Gainesville: University Press of Florida, 2007) that discursive, reflective practices around Santería produce and integrate a moral community. Discourse, then, is at least as significant as ritual practice in integrating a religious group and religion.

95. Sidney Mintz's work is vitally important here; see also Hilary McD. Beckles, "Capitalism, Slavery, and Caribbean Modernity," *Callaloo* 20, no. 4 (1998): 777–89; Richard Drayton, "The Collaboration of Labour: Slaves, Empires, and Globalizations in the Atlantic World, c. 1600–1850," in *Globalization in World History*, ed. A. G. Hopkins (London: Pimlico, 2002), 98–114; Eric Williams, *Capitalism and Slavery* (Chapel

Hill: University of North Carolina Press, 1944); C. L. R. James, *The Black Jacobins: Toussaint L'Ouverture and the San Domingo Revolution*, 2nd ed. (1938; New York: Vintage Books, 1963).

96. Michel-Rolph Trouillot, *Global Transformations: Anthropology and the Modern World* (New York: Palgrave Macmillan, 2003), 7–28.

97. For examples of such reports recurring in the *Port of Spain Gazette*, see "Cannibal Monarch," February 16, 1913, 2; "Lost in Wilds," February 1, 1908, 7; "New Guinea," January 6, 1924, 14.

98. Michael Herzfeld, *The Body Impolitic: Artisans and Artifice in the Global Hierarchy of Value* (Chicago: University of Chicago Press, 2004).

99. West India Committee Circular of March 1910, quoted in "The Crying Shame of Trinidad," *Port of Spain Gazette*, February 2, 1913, 11; "Ghastly Tragedy in Demerara," *Port of Spain Gazette*, January 23, 1917, 9–10, reprinted article from *Demerara Argosy*, January 20, 1917; "The Wake Nuisance," *Port of Spain Gazette*, March 25, 1917, 9; "A Shouter's Meeting Down South," Trinidad *Mirror*, April 29, 1906, enclosed in Cameron to Harcourt, no. 127, 24 October 1912, TNA: CO 321/269; "The Need of Caution," Jamaica *Gleaner*, August 20, 1906, 8–9.

100. Bruce M. Knauft, "Critically Modern: An Introduction," 1–56; and Donald L. Donham, "On Being Modern in a Capitalist World: Some Conceptual and Comparative Issues," 241–57; both in *Critically Modern: Alternatives, Alterities, Anthropologies*, ed. Bruce M. Knauft (Bloomington: Indiana University Press, 2002).

101. Partly in response to Trouillot's insistence on the modernity of the colonial Caribbean, Jonathan Friedman defines modernity as "the cultural field of commercial capitalism, its emergent identity space," but lists its systematically interrelated attributes as follows: "individualism, public/private division, democracy, nation-state, Enlightenment philosophy/critical rationality, capitalism, global economy/imperialism, modernism/developmentalism/evolutionism." Any alternative modernity must include these invariables. See Friedman, "Modernity and Other Traditions," in Knauft, *Critically Modern*, 294, 298.

102. Palmié, *Wizards and Scientists*, 42.

103. Richard Drayton, *Nature's Government: Science, Imperial Britain, and the "Improvement" of the World* (New Haven: Yale University Press, 2000), xviii; Drayton, "The Collaboration of Labour."

104. Ryan Smith, "Pat Robertson: Haiti 'Cursed' after 'Pact to the Devil,'" CBS News, January 13, 2010, http://www.cbsnews.com/.

105. Caroline Saunders, "Haiti Needs Our Help," *Comment Is Free*, January 13, 2010, http://www.guardian.co.uk/commentisfree/.

106. Paisley Dodds, "Voodooists Attacked at Ceremony for Haiti Victims," *Seattle Times*, February 23, 2010.

107. Nicole Castor, "Trinidad Ifa: Performing African Identity in Trinidad Orisha" (paper presented at the annual conference of the American Anthropological Association, Philadelphia, December 3, 2009); Sidney M. Greenfield, "The Reinterpretation

of Africa: Convergence and Syncretism in Brazilian Candomblé," in Greenfield and Droogers, *Reinventing Religions*, 113–30; Henry, *Reclaiming African Religions in Trinidad*; Houk, *Spirits, Blood, and Drums*; James Houk, "Chaos, Compromise, and Transformation in the Orisha Religion in Trinidad," in *Religion, Diaspora, and Cultural Identity: A Reader in the Anglophone Caribbean*, ed. John W. Pulis (New York: Gordon and Breach, 1999), 295–310; Roberto Motta, "The Churchifying of Candomblé: Priests, Anthropologists, and the Canonization of the African Religious Memory in Brazil," in *New Trends and Developments in African Religions*, ed. Peter B. Clarke (Westport, Conn.: Greenwood Press, 1998), 45–58.

108. With the opposite effect, but operating on a similar logic, some members of the Spiritual Baptist religion wish to purify their faith from "African forms of worship." See de Peza, *My Faith*.

109. Thanks to Lara Putnam for helping us to formulate this point.

PART I

Powers of Representation

1.

An (Un)natural Mystic in the Air:
Images of Obeah in Caribbean Song

KENNETH BILBY

As one who has worked as an anthropologist and ethnomusicologist in a range of different Caribbean locations, I have long been aware that there is considerable disagreement about what the term "obeah" might mean. Such disagreements about meaning, in my view, tell us something fundamental about the nature of cultural experience in the colonized and still decolonizing societies of the Caribbean. Obeah, whatever else it might be, remains a primary site of cultural contestation in many of these societies. Because the semantic domain of this term almost always overlaps with spiritual concepts that have profound existential significance—and because, in the minds of those who speak it, the term almost invariably remains associated with an ancestral African past—it occupies a particularly prominent and highly charged place in this zone of cultural contestation. One way to get at the complex tangle of meanings surrounding an ideologically charged term such as "obeah" is to carry out in-depth ethnographic interviews with individuals for whom the term is, in fact, richly endowed with meanings, including spiritual practitioners themselves, as I have done on many occasions over the years.[1] Another way is to listen in on conversations that take place in vernacular or popular culture, which I have also done. The two sources of data, in fact, are complementary; each can be used to shed light on the other. Unlike most of my previous work on the topic, the present chapter focuses on the latter—the imagery of obeah purveyed through vernacular cultural expressions in various parts of the Caribbean.

Some idea of just how profound the existential implications of the term may be can be gleaned from the words of a prominent Ndyuka Maroon living in the Netherlands, himself a practitioner of spiritual arts, who characterizes obeah (which he spells "obiya") as "an all-encompassing, all-pervasive and all-inspiring force." "This spiritual force," he adds, "is present in all modes of being."[2] Viewed through this Surinamese Maroon lens, obeah would seem to be quite similar to concepts such as *ache* (or *ashe*) in Cuban Santería and *ase* in the Yoruba religion—a kind of life force or energy that permeates the universe, which can be tapped and used in concentrated form by knowledgeable human beings. And indeed, this force sounds not altogether different from Bob Marley's "natural mystic blowing through the air," to cite one of the reggae icon's most revered songs.[3]

Marley himself was no stranger to obeah.[4] According to his biographers, he came from a spiritually gifted line.[5] Many today regard him not only as a prophet, but also as one of the most spiritually powerful people who ever lived—what in the language of Surinamese Maroon spiritual practitioners might be called "a great obeah man." But to characterize Robert Nesta Marley, the world's most famous exponent of the Rastafarian faith, as an obeah man would not sit well with most of those who now share the faith he helped to spread around the world. A typical attitude to obeah is revealed in the response of one Jamaican Rasta woman when asked by a naive North American visitor her thoughts on obeah. Bursting into peals of laughter, the woman replied, "You're asking a Rastafarian about obeah? Well, the most I can tell you is by giving you a simile. Bob Marley said in one of his songs, 'I am a duppy conqueror.'[6] We don't really pay the duppy [spirit] world any mind. The practice of obeah is to use the spirits of iniquity to perform works. And, of course, you know that there can be no good in that as far as we can see." "We just scoff at it," the Rasta woman continued. "We refuse to be afraid of it, so people realize that our power must be much greater. We know we shall win because we are confident that good wins over evil."[7] Here, the same term used by a well-respected Surinamese Maroon spiritual healer to index "an all-encompassing, all-pervasive and all-inspiring force" serves as a label for working with "the spirits of iniquity," a practice that is portrayed as the very embodiment of wickedness in a cosmic struggle of good against evil.

In a recent song by a young Jamaican reggae artist who calls himself I Maroon, obeah is represented as a source of confusion.[8] But unlike I Maroon and many of his Rastafarian colleagues, who tend to view this confusion as something inherent to the practice and nature of obeah itself, I see this as a type of historically derived cultural confusion caused by the production over time of several layers of contradictory and competing meanings that continue to inhabit the same cultural space. This particular example of cultural confusion revolving around the term "obeah," I would argue, is one of the more enduring and tenacious legacies of colonialism in the Anglophone Caribbean.

The only societies in the region that seem to have escaped this confusion are those constructed beyond the European colonial orbit, such as the Maroon peoples of Suriname and French Guiana. And this may change soon, depending on the outcome of the ideological battles now being waged by Christian missionaries and evangelists in the various Maroon territories. For the moment, most Maroons in this part of the world continue to use the term "obia" in overwhelmingly positive ways. For them, in addition to its several other positive senses, the term still refers to the all-pervasive spiritual power referenced by the Surinamese Maroon practitioner quoted above, which in practice is tapped primarily for healing, spiritual protection, and addressing the problems of daily life. Guianese Maroons see the knowledge of how to work with this healing and protecting obia as a precious gift handed down from their ancestors.

Elsewhere in the Caribbean, as I have argued in a number of other writings, obeah is most often publicly represented in largely or entirely negative terms, as a form of sorcery or malevolent witchcraft, even though there is widespread acknowledgment in more private contexts that the spiritual powers to which it refers are—perhaps in the majority of cases—sought out and employed for positive ends, such as healing and inducing good fortune.[9] The cultural ambivalence that goes hand in hand with these contradictory ideas and images lends itself to the scapegoating of anyone thought to be an obeah practitioner, including those healers, herbalists, and other benevolent ritual specialists who identify themselves, or are identified by their patients or clients, as obeah men or women. (The blame for all the harm and suffering supposedly caused by the negative use of spiritual power tends to be placed on obeah men or women rather than those among their clients who, motivated by jealousy, envy, and greed—according to popular belief—pay them to abuse their powers to harm others.) This current cultural confusion is clearly the product of a historical process of colonization and cultural domination that has led, in most parts of the Caribbean, to the reduction of all forms of African religiosity and spirituality in public discourse to inherently antisocial sorcery or witchcraft meant to harm fellow human beings.

Many spiritual practitioners in Jamaica—to take one particularly important theater in what I would characterize as an ongoing ideological war over representations of African spirituality in the Caribbean—reveal through their words some awareness of the process of cultural domination that has fundamentally shaped the often-contradictory world of meanings within which they must operate. As one man, a longtime practitioner of the Afro-Jamaican religion known as Convince or Bongo, recently told me, "The name 'obeah,' it no sound good in the English. But the work from it, it a pretty fine work.... We no rate it fe go out deh [in public], go seh [the word] 'obeah.' We just say it local [i.e., among ourselves]."[10] Implicit in this statement is a recognition that in the Jamaican context, part of what makes the word "unspeakable" is its perceived Africanness, which renders it problematic when inserted into the dominant colonial language; in private, however, where the "goodness" of the English that one speaks is not an issue, the word can still be used to refer to something that is "pretty fine."

As this chapter (and others in this book) will show, the term "obeah" has been constructed in a variety of ways in different contexts, and therefore should not be seen as having any single, essential meaning. This of course makes it problematic to argue that any of these meanings is more correct than any other; all of them may be properly understood as historical products of particular social and cultural processes. But from the perspective of Guianese Maroons or the Jamaican Convince practitioner quoted above—or, indeed, many other people in the Caribbean—the notion that obeah or obia is a kind of spiritual power that is both African and "pretty fine" is correct; and the widespread coexisting idea that it is a kind of inherently antisocial, malicious witchcraft or sorcery is a misrepresentation. These dissenters from the dominant view may have a good point. The fact that there are still many voices making such assertions suggests that the ideological war over representations of African spirituality in the Caribbean, which began during the period of colonization and slavery, has yet to end. Indeed, its dissonances, I would contend, can still be heard—though often in muted, subtextual forms—in the popular music of the region.

OBEAH, ARTISTS, AND ANCESTRAL POWER

One of the richest forms of popular cultural expression throughout the Caribbean is music. In much of the region, topical songs offer one of the best and most effective means of gauging public sentiment and teasing broadly shared cultural understandings out of the cacophony of contentious public discourse. The topic of obeah is no exception. We can gain insight into the complex polysemy of this term not only from song lyrics, but also from certain other forms of expression associated with popular music, such as naming practices. Several artists and groups are known by stage names that include the word "obeah."[11] Why would popular musicians—some of them Rastafarians—name themselves with a term that is generally thought to denote an inherently evil form of spiritual power used to cause suffering and destroy innocent human beings?

In an interview published in the 1990s, the revered Trinidadian session guitarist Lynn Taitt told of how he had once played in a band called Obeah—adding, without further explanation, that this "is a bad word in Trinidad."[12] A few years ago, I asked Taitt why he had told the earlier interviewer that "obeah" was considered a bad word in his homeland. He suggested that it was because it is something that deals with "witches and spirits" and was used to "put hex" on people. When I pressed him on why anyone would name a band after such a destructive thing, he said, "You could use it both ways, you could use it for good or evil."[13]

If one reads between the lines, it is easy to see that the choice of Obeah (or Obeah Man) as a moniker in popular culture most often represents a kind of indirect or unspoken cultural revindication—a gesture toward reclaiming ancestral power through music or other African-related forms of cultural expression, and in some cases an attempt to reassert control over the language used to characterize such ancestral power. Similar rhetorical gestures, acknowledging a positive connection between ancestral obeah and the power of music, are found at times in the writings of academics as well. Manuel Monestel, for instance, tells us that "the calypsonian, both in the Caribbean in general and in Limón [Costa Rica], is more than a conventional composer of songs. He is a magical character, with certain power in the style of the obeah man."[14] Similar claims have been made for the Jamaican dancehall, where, according to Agostinho Pinnock, "the Dancehall male artiste becomes the modernized (African) obeah man. Hence, he and his vast array of psychic and verbal powers, brought through the Middle Passage as part of the retention of a distinctly African identity in the 'New World' are recuperated into the present in an effort to resist the modern-day enslavement of 'ghetto people' under the guise of Jamaican Independence."[15]

Does the more nuanced (and even positive) view of obeah suggested by images and passing comments such as these represent the concrete ways in which spiritual power is actually used in the Caribbean today more fully than the monolithically negative one that Rastafarian hard-liners (not to mention Christians) tend to project? In fact, the themes of ancestral power and cultural reclamation do sometimes crop up in the lyrical content of popular songs touching on the theme of obeah. But they are far from the norm, and they exist alongside—and sometimes explicitly in opposition to—a great many other, less positive images. In the following section, I look at the range of themes with which representations of obeah are associated in Caribbean song, before arriving at some general conclusions about the ways that popular music in this part of the world both reflects and helps to shape social consciousness.

INIQUITOUS BY DEFINITION

In Jamaica, the word "iniquity" has a special sense. According to the eminent lexicographers Frederic Cassidy and Robert Le Page, in Jamaican usage this term is actually a synonym for obeah.[16] Thus, in Jamaica, when one hears the phrase "iniquity worker," it is usually taken to mean "obeah worker." Here we have a particularly striking illustration of how thought may be colonized (and cultural hegemony at least partly achieved) through a lexico-semantic process of cultural domination. The Jamaican-specific sense of the term in question clearly betrays the enormous influence of nineteenth-century Protestant missionaries and the role they and their successors played in the ongoing colonization of Jamaica and other parts of the region. In their preaching, drawing selectively on the Bible, "iniquity" captured in a single word one of the fundamental concepts of the Manichean theology they sought to impose on African Jamaicans, both during and after slavery. It was a word and a concept that formed an important part of their armament in the long struggle they waged against the understandings of the cosmos that Africans brought with them to the Caribbean. There can be little doubt that, over time, as they insistently identified obeah as a primary example of what they called "iniquity," a great many of their converts came to agree with them.

It is not surprising, then, that the majority of songs referencing obeah in the Anglophone Caribbean are populated with workers of iniquity of one kind or another. One of the more common images of obeah in popular music is as a kind of antisocial witchcraft or sorcery, used—whether at the request of an obeah man's client, or out of pure evil-mindedness on the part of the practitioner him- or herself—to cause illness, misfortune, and general suffering. One of the best-known Jamaican popular songs about obeah, Admiral Bailey's "Science Again" (1989), is a good example:

> Dem is me enemy and a gwan [go on; i.e., behave] like me friend
> Me a tell dem, dem deh sinting [things] cyaan work again
> It's a serious ting, nuh badda tek it fe no laughter ...
> Just wet up you *Star* [newspaper] when dem throw dem obeah
> Wet up you gate when dem plant dem obeah
> Spray out you car 'fore you drive it go no further
> Tell it to me sister, tell it to me brother
> It's a serious ting, nuh badda tek it fe no laughter.[17]

Admiral Bailey is counseling listeners to be on guard, so that they will know when to wash and cleanse ("wet up" or "spray") the objects and places that evil spirit workers typically invest with harmful obeah—the ground in front of one's "gate" (residence), for example, in which an obeah worker might bury something to make the proprietor sick, or one's car, on which the sorcerer might sprinkle some spiritually empowered powder to cause an accident. A number of other songs make similar general allegations about obeah practitioners.[18]

When a specific motive for such evil uses of spiritual power *is* spelled out, it is often—and this will come as no surprise to those who have studied the logic of witchcraft accusations cross-culturally—jealousy or envy (frequently glossed in the Anglophone Caribbean as "badmind"). A typical example suggesting this motive is Leo Graham's reggae song "Black Candle" (1973), in which the singer rebukes an iniquity worker who, unlike himself, allows envy to govern his actions:

> You could burn black candle little more, iniquity worker
> I'm gonna out it, I'm gonna out it
> Who God bless, no man curse
> I'm gonna prove it, I'm gonna prove it
> I envy no one
> I always try to do the good I can.[19]

This theme of envy is found in songs about obeah in other parts of the Caribbean as well. A particularly clear example is Sheik Ally's popular chutney soca song from Guyana, "Neighbour Working Obeah" (2004), which suggests that Indo-Caribbean people are no less prone to such representations of obeah than others in the region.[20] Like many other popular songs touching on obeah, this one relies on humor (and, as is often the case, ridicule) for its effect:[21]

> Me neighbor, me neighbor
> Me badminded neighbor, they want to see me suffer
> When I buy some cement to fix up me house
> Me neighbor dem get mad, dem only peeping like a mouse
> When I try to rise up, they want to see me drop
> They must be the only one to reach to the top
> They working hard on me, they working vigorously
> They trying to run this Indian real crazy
> They working hard on me, they working furiously
> They trying to send this Indian to the cemetery
> Me neighbor working obeah [repeat seven times]
> In the night I dreaming, I see a lot of things
> Me neighbor and the jumbie [spirit] in the backyard bubbling

They jumping like a crapaud, they jumping like a toad
And when dem shake dem bambam, they blow out a load
Dem killing de chicken, de pig, and de goat
They doing all kind of things to cut this Indian throat
They running 'round and 'round, they jumping up and down
And the name of the jumbie is James Bond
Me neighbor working obeah [repeat multiple times].[22]

One of the most common themes in Caribbean songs about obeah is that of "tying" a lover with spiritual power—rendering him or her incapable of rejecting or leaving the person who does the tying. In the vast majority of these songs, the one who does the tying is a woman. (One of the favored methods is to spike someone's food with magical substances, including a woman's menstrual fluids; this is what is meant when a man accuses a woman of "steaming his rice.") The process can also be used to win a lover away from a competitor. In some cases, as in "G.O. Go" (1973), a spouge song from Barbados by Draytons Two, the representation of tying appears to be neutral:

G.O. go
Gal, a weh you go?
Me ben down Speightstown
Me ben a wuk obeah
Me wuk obeah
Me wuk obeah
With two white fowls
And two candles
A black candle
With some bush rum
Me wuk obeah
"Don't marry Janie
Ah go join Johnny."[23]

Often, the theme provides a pretext for humorous commentary about gender relations, usually from a male perspective. The Mighty Sparrow's "Obeah Wedding" (1966)—undoubtedly the best-known song about tying, and probably the most famous of all songs with the word "obeah" in the title—is a good example.[24] Trinidad calypsos recorded during the 1930s and 1940s often treated this same theme, and it remains a popular topic in song lyrics to this day.[25]

While tying a lover might seem like a positive use of spiritual power from the perspective of the person doing the tying, it is generally seen—because of its denial of free will to the person targeted—as an unnatural and immoral practice. (It is also widely believed that it can cause physical illness in the person on whom it is used, even as it creates irresistible feelings of attraction toward the perpetrator.) In most representations, therefore, tying serves as but another example of the evil nature of obeah. Most of the songs treating this topic, in fact, amount to complaints by the (usually male) singer about what is seen as a reprehensible abuse of spiritual power. A particularly popular example was the Jamaican deejay Yellowman's hit "Nuh Tie Me" (1987):

> Why she waan tie me ina rice and peas?
> Why she waan tie me now ina stew peas?
> Why she waan tie me ina rundung [Jamaican dish]?
> A tie you waan tie me and then give me bun? (i.e., cheat on me)
> Gal, a so me know your life woulda done . . .
> Nuh badda tie me
> Gal, nuh badda tie me
> Nuh badda tie me
> *You* nuh badda tie me![26]

Yet other negative representations of obeah are encountered in popular music. One of the more common stereotypes of obeah practitioners portrays them as charlatans who knowingly deceive clients and charge exorbitant fees for fraudulent services. In Jamaica, there is a word for this, "samfai" (sometimes spelled "samfie"), which means con man or trickster. But another of the term's senses—indeed, according to Cassidy and Le Page, its primary sense—is obeah man.[27] The clearest example of the tendency in popular music to reduce obeah practitioners to swindlers is the Pioneers' early reggae song "Samfie Man" (1969):

> Woi, samfie man, woi, woi
> You no fe tek de man money under false pretense
> Now you're acting so funny just to build a defense
> You go up a Mass Rob fe go get de job
> You dig de hole, sinner man, you plant de pole.[28]

Songs such as these, accusing obeah workers of charlatanism, at least leave open the possibility (even if they discourage entertaining it) that *some* honest obeah practitioners may exist. More important, these songs betray the fact that obeah workers are often involved in transactions that actually have positive ends—acquiring a job, for instance, or combating an illness.[29] Thus the common refrain that the obeah man is not a person to depend on (a sentiment often repeated in the lyrics of Jamaican dancehall deejays during the early 1980s) reveals a fundamental contradiction. The obeah practitioner is represented as being undependable only when it comes to positive goals. If the aim is to damage or kill someone by sending spirits, however, the obeah worker is often portrayed as being quite capable. As Admiral Bailey warns, "It's a serious ting, nuh badda tek it fe no laughter." In short, obeah, insofar as any real efficacy is attributed to it, is reduced to malevolent witchcraft.

The Rastafarian repudiation of obeah represents a variation on this type of reductionist thinking. Accepting the hegemonic recasting of obeah as a symbol of spiritual corruption and evil in general, Rastas now often explicitly identify obeah with Babylon. A well-known expression of this tendency in popular music is the Ethiopians' classic reggae song "Obeah Book" (1977):

> I'm not an obeah man
> I am a Rasta man
> I am the righteous one
> Do not study iniquity, Jah Jah know, yaw
> Do not act wickedly, I say, Jah Jah know, yaw
> Back 'way wid your obeah book
> No, no, no, I-man nuh dwell deh
> Back 'way wid your obeah book
> No, no, no, Rasta nuh dwell deh.[30]

When I interviewed the composer of this song, Leonard Dillon, a few years ago, I asked him what he had intended to convey with it. He explained that because he often comes across as a "spiritual man" who is "very mystic," a man with "a certain amount of wisdom," people would sometimes suggest that he might be a "scientist" who knew how to "work obeah." Because they would associate him with the word "obeah"—a word, he reminded me, that is used to describe "evildoers"—he wrote this song to emphasize that he would never "do anything that is wicked." When I asked him whether obeah was necessarily evil, he replied, "Me no know what obeah mean, you know." When I tried to pursue the question further by saying that I had heard that obeah could also refer to spiritual power used to heal, he ended that part of our conversation by saying with finality, "These are the things now weh me no dwell ina, I don't dwell in those"—closing off further examination of the meaning of the term by repeating the lyrics of his song.[31] Clearly, the proposition I was suggesting was not one with which he was comfortable.

In some songs, reductive representations of obeah as "all negativity" amount to a kind of synecdoche, in which the term stands for all things evil. In such cases, the possibility of discussing whether the word might actually have more than one meaning is foreclosed; obeah is simply emblematic of evil (and often explicitly represented as satanic). A good example of this is Kiprich's song "Obeah Man" (2005), in which the basic premise that an obeah man cannot enter a church prefaces a list of examples of evil and "unchristian" behavior and thought that do not belong in the house of God:

> No obeah man can't go ina no church
> Tell me weh it work fe you come and sprinkle dirt
> And a rejoice over when somebody a get hurt.[32]

Of course, Christian dancehall music—a dancehall subgenre associated specifically with preaching the gospel—tends to be even more explicit in its reduction of obeah to Satanic wrongdoing. Minister Goddy Goddy's "Obeah Man Poppy Show" (2004) uses ridicule to score points in the evangelical battle against obeah:

> Dis ya one dedicated to everybody weh obeah man a turn ina
>   poppyshow [foolish spectacle]
> Some a dem a call scientist a run up dem phone bill, Satan turn
>   dem ina poppyshow
> Some a dem a cut green lime and wash down dem stall, but a Jesus
>   keep me secure[33]
> Some a dem gone a nine night [wakes], gone sprinkle white rice,
>   talk bout seh dem feeding de dead
> Jesus a de resurrection, put it ina you head—at de name of Jesus
>   demon a fled
> Some a dem gone a obeah man gone read up pon palm, but a Bible
>   me read instead
> Some a dem a bathe ina Mother [i.e., a Revival Mother's] wash pan,
>   seh dem a quote scripture, but dem a Satan
> Some a dem tek country bus gone a "St. Weh-It-Name-Deh-Again?"
>   gone pon oil fe catch man[34]
> Some a dem a purchase oil-of-comeback, oil fe turn people pickney
>   ina idiot
> But Father God Him is watching from above and Him will send
>   down Him wrath, so a full time you stop
> Some a tie red cloth round de pickney hand, pass him over top fe
>   get protection

An (Un)natural Mystic in the Air

> But a one protection I and I recommend, mek me tell you bout the blood of the lamb
> You see de ring pon you finger weh dem give you seh a guard? Mek me tell you something: a no guard, that a fraud!
> If you want de real guard, invite in Jesus, and run Satan out of you yard!³⁵

Obeah intended for positive purposes, such as healing, protection, bringing good fortune, or attending to the needs of ancestor spirits—which is what is described in almost all the examples condemned in the lyrics above—comes under the same fire as obeah meant to cause harm to others.

Such representations of obeah as fundamentally and inherently immoral are not limited to straitlaced Christian productions. Some of the most lyrically hard-core Jamaican dancehall music—often thought of as contemporary "rebel music"—is filled with the same kinds of damning judgments. Munga Honourable's (aka Honourebel; i.e., "honor rebel") hit "Na Hear" (2007), for instance, puts obeah near the top of a virtual checklist of sinful and aberrant acts and ways, delivered in language that few Christians would welcome in church—a list that also condemns, rather predictably, the behavior of another archetypal scapegoat in the current Jamaican dancehall lexicon of opprobrium, the "batty man" (male homosexual):

> After me say batty [buttocks] no fe fuck, and dem naa hear
> After me say pussy no fe suck, and dem naa hear
> After me say obeah no fe wuk, and dem naa hear
> A de same ting weh me a tell dem from last year
> Tell dem tight pants is not fe us, and dem naa hear
> Tell dem tight blouse is not fe us, and dem naa hear
> Tell dem lipstick is not fe us, and dem naa hear
> A de same ting weh me a tell dem from last year
> If me no know nothing else, a one ting I know
> Badman [gangsters] no bleach [their skin] and shave dem eyebrow
> Burn dem from Timbuktu to Cairo . . .
> Tell dem bleach face is not fe us, and dem naa hear
> Tell dem bore tongue [pierced tongues] is not fe us, and dem naa hear
> Bore navel [pierced navels] is not fe us, and dem naa hear.[36]

Obeah is, in fact, a frequent topic of gossip in the world of the Jamaican dancehall, and lyrics also sometimes include accusations (sometimes explicit, sometimes veiled) that one deejay is working obeah against another to try to hold him back. It is also understood that entertainers competing for attention in the dancehall may sometimes go to an obeah man or woman simply for help in achieving a hit song or for other kinds of help, rather than to wield spiritual power negatively against competitors. As an article in Jamaica's main entertainment tabloid put it, "Anecdotal stories about the use of 'science' abound in the dancehall. DJs have been known to wear guard rings, Lodge rings and walk with the names of rival DJs written on parchment paper in their shoes. Several artistes also believe that other artistes are sprinkling obeah in the dancehall-reggae game to maintain their dominance or rise to the top."[37]

A stir was caused recently by the deejay Determine, whose controversial song "Science" (2008) became an instant hit. Among the other deejays and singers named in the song are Capleton, Beenie Man, Alliance, Guidance, Elephant Man, Gyptian, Turbulence, Ninja Man, Merciless, Lexxus, Captain Barkey, Fantan Mojah, Junior Gong (Damian Marley), Sizzla, Natural Black, Munga, and Roundhead. With cleverly crafted lyrics, Determine decries the ubiquity of obeah ("science") in the dancehall:

> Me seh dem have science everywhere a dash, but only time will tell
> We soon know a who a go wind wid de monkey pon de hilltop [a pejorative reference to the obeah man][38]
> Dem bring you weh de zugu [obeah] man a mek, you see how zugu tan[39]
> Now dem a walk and a talk—a weh you duppy a nyam?
> Tell me what's the plan that a mek you a better man?
> You have dub plate science, forty-five [i.e., 45 rpm] science
> Stage show science, and dancehall science
> Cyaan-bus' science, and must-bus' science [obeah to prevent another deejay from becoming big, and obeah to make oneself get big]
> Nobody cyaan tell me seh dem no science Alliance . . .
> A who a talk bout dem science Guidance?—
> turn him ina one-hitter like a wear-out pants
> Dem seh science mash up Gyptian and de camp . . .
> Dem have science fe mek police tear up go run
> Science mek judge piss up dem skirt and pant
> Dem seh science rise and fall Elephant Man . . .
> Tell me weh you think about Father Capleton?
> Dem seh dem naa seh nothing, dem just a gwan sing de song

You shoulda know a St. Mary him a come from
And you know dat a straight science land.⁴⁰

The majority of songs that go so far as to provide concrete descriptions of obeah—including most of those that represent it as inherently evil—depict situations in which the spiritual powers denoted by this term are actually called on to address and seek solutions to personal problems. We can see this particularly clearly in a song like Lloyd Lovindeer's Jamaican dancehall hit "The Oil" (1987), which has the comical deejay taking on the persona of an obeah man who possesses an astonishing panoply of magical oils to offer those in need. These range from "oil-of-mek-you-get-promotion" and "oil-of-get-rid-of-all-diseases" to "oil-of-mek-ugly-man-look-handsome" and "oil-of-record-reach-number-one." Particularly remarkable are "oil-of-get-U.S.-visa," "oil-of-mek-politician-stop-lie," "oil-of-prevent-Christian-from-turn-back," and "oil-of-get-loan-from-America-while-keeping-ties-with-Russia-and-Cuba"—not to mention "oil-of-write-lyrics-like-Lovindeer."⁴¹ One thing that is striking about Lovindeer's fanciful list of obeah oils is that not a single one has as its purpose harming another person or causing suffering. While the song does make fun of the grandiosity of some obeah practitioners' claims, using this as a pretext for broader social and political satire, it nonetheless tells us something about the positive motivations widely understood to be behind the actual practice of obeah in a great many cases.

CONSCIOUS OBEAH: KNOWING ONESELF AND RECLAIMING THE ANCESTORS

Among Maroons living in the interior of Suriname and French Guiana, many songs mention the term "obia"—not surprising, since the spiritual powers denoted by the term are an ever-present part of daily life. For them (and certain non-Maroons living in coastal areas who share their spiritual concepts), the term is entirely uncontroversial. There is general agreement about the range of meanings attached to it (except perhaps where Christian missionaries have won converts). When the word does appear in a song, it is, in a sense, morally unmarked—that is, it does not form part of an explicit statement about the morality of the spiritual power to which it refers. This was the case, for instance, when an Aluku Maroon *obiaman*, a specialist in the Kumanti (Kromanti) spiritual tradition, sang the following song in my presence in 1987:

Obeah—instead of firing, may it [a gun] split open.⁴²

The song references the protective power of obeah when used in warfare, which is said to be able to cause an enemy's gun to shatter rather than fire in battle. Of course, the song has an implicit moral dimension, in that it also points to a history in which this spiritual power played an important positive role in helping the ancestors of the Aluku fight their Dutch enslavers. The moral dimension of this power came to the fore again when Maroons became embroiled in a civil war in Suriname in the late 1980s, during which they once again resorted to some of these spiritual powers. But my point is that in performances of the song, obeah or obia is normally mentioned in a matter-of-fact way, simply to describe (and in some cases, invoke) the spiritual power to which the term refers, rather than in connection with some explicit moral commentary. The fact that obia in all its senses generally lacks any negative moral charge or any hint of moral ambivalence among Surinamese Maroons helps to explain the total lack of irony, humorous banter, or ridicule in their songs mentioning obia—one way in which such Surinamese songs clearly contrast with many of the popular songs commenting on obeah in various parts of the Anglophone Caribbean.

The same is true of songs performed by young Surinamese Maroons and Creoles, Afro-Surinamese people from the coastal region who have migrated to Dutch cities and joined there to form cultural associations devoted to the performance of their ancestral cultural heritage. In this case as well, songs are occasionally performed that mention obia in an unmarked way. One such young Afro-Surinamese group based in the Netherlands is Sangrafu.[13] A passage from their song "Madjo So We Madja"—also tied specifically to the Kumanti tradition—represents a matter-of-fact statement about the types of knowledge any obia man deserving of the name is expected to have (though it also criticizes a particular individual for pretending to have more knowledge of a certain kind of obeah than he actually does):

> When you're an obeah man, you're able to speak the language of the spirits [or gods]
> When you're an obeah man, you're able to sing the obeah songs
> When you're an obeah man, you're able to dance with the spirits [or gods]
> When you're an obeah man, you're able to speak the language of the spirits [or gods]
> When you're an obeah man, you're able to do obeah work
> You're pretending to do *ankama* [a particular type of obeah], but you don't know *ankama* obeah.[44]

In such songs, the term "obia"—which refers to all kinds of socially sanctioned African-derived spiritual power—is morally unproblematic, for it is rarely, if ever, used to refer to sorcery or harmful witchcraft.[45] In Suriname, such antisocial use of power is typically denoted by an entirely different word, *wisi*, derived from the English word "witch" (or, in the case of Saramaka Maroons, *sibá*). This difference between Suriname and other parts of the Caribbean where the term "obeah" is common can be explained, at least in part, by its different colonial history. Not only were Maroons in that colony able to develop their cultures with a minimum of interference from the ruling colonial power, but the entire colony changed hands early in its history, becoming Dutch after only a few short decades of English rule. Because of this, the English-lexicon creole language of coastal Suriname—which continued to function as the lingua franca for the enslaved population even after the departure of the English colonists—was essentially cut off from the language that had originally provided the majority of its vocabulary. Under Dutch rule, English no longer served as the colonial language of prestige, and because of this, Afro-Surinamese people, whose languages included the word "obia," were spared the brunt of the campaign against obeah that was waged across the Anglophone Caribbean. In the Surinamese case, the Dutch colonial campaign against African forms of spirituality was focused on other local labels for specific religious practices, such as Winti. The power to construct public meanings and resignify widely used terminology played an important role in the process of colonial domination. The reductive construction of obeah (which came to stand for all forms of African religiosity) as malevolent, antisocial witchcraft, I would argue, is best understood as an outcome of such processes.

But even in the Anglophone Caribbean, one can find songs that clearly demonstrate that obeah was never completely redefined, and that stigmatization of obeah as the work of evildoers was never absolute—at least among certain segments of the population. We can see this, for example, in the following Jamaican folk song. This is one of a number of related mento songs centering on the theme of controlling troublesome duppies.[46] (Such spirits, as the song suggests, are not always sent by obeah workers; sometimes duppies interfere with the living on their own.) Such situations call for an obeah man who knows how to manage unruly spirits. Songs of this kind are often humorous, and sometimes the duppy gets the better of the presiding obeah man, who ends up looking foolish—but not in this case. The obeah man mentioned in the following song is in fact a real person—a famous and respected spirit worker who died many years ago but is still remembered by obeah practitioners in St. Mary parish. The song relates his exploits rather matter-of-factly, without any hint of disapproval:

> Miss Matty was cooking and selling
> She were getting on very well
> All on a sudden she took a sick
> She says the duppy gave her a lick
> Then she go and made a report
> To the Nine-Day William
> That's the reason why them said
> Nine-Day William, the good obeah man
> For when him cut him "ri-bamba-ree"
> The duppy say, "You not speaking to me"
> And then him dodge him around the bedpost
> And then him bawl like a wind a ghost
> That's the reason why them said
> Nine-Day William, the good obeah man.[47]

This song helps us to interpret a pattern we have already seen in popular music, since it expresses the positive side of obeah more clearly than most. Even some of the more negative depictions of obeah in popular songs betray an underlying recognition that the spiritual power in question—regardless of whether the singer gives it any credence—is sought out most often with positive intentions, because of the widespread belief that it can be put to beneficial uses. This contradiction, contained in many songs, reveals serious cracks in the reductive image of obeah as pure antisocial witchcraft. Songs such as this one about Nine-Day William ("the good obeah man"), which stress only the positive side of obeah, lack this contradiction, and therefore stand in clear opposition to prevailing images of obeah as inherently evil.

Because the understandings reflected in songs such as this survive among a significant portion of the population, there remains, despite all the damning images in circulation, a residue of positive sentiment toward obeah—or at least toward those spiritual practitioners who use their knowledge and powers in benevolent ways. Perhaps because of the growth of new spaces for cultural contestation and reclamation in the postcolonial era, this positive undercurrent surfaces from time to time in popular culture, in one guise or another.[48] The obeah man—or the implied obeah man, called by another name—emerges as a figure of awe, a "mystic man," or man of "mystery," who draws his power from a vaguely understood reservoir of ancestral "science" or spiritual wisdom. This kind of imagery is not incompatible with Rastafarian mysticism, so long as it steers clear of duppies (or other spiritual beings) and avoids the actual word "obeah." All three founding members of the Wailers—Bob Marley, Peter Tosh, and Bunny Wailer—have at one time or another been portrayed in these terms. Tosh, in particular, embraced such imagery, explicitly identifying himself as a "bush doctor," a term widely used in Jamaica and other parts of the Anglophone Caribbean to refer to an obeah man who specializes in herbal medicine.[49]

Another important figure in Jamaican popular music who often plays around with the imagery of obeah, without embracing it overtly, is the brilliant producer Lee "Scratch" Perry, responsible for some of the most important creative contributions to the emergence of reggae as a distinct style of music in the late 1960s. Perry has long behaved as a kind of trickster figure whose image vacillates between that of a madman and mystic scientist. Several of his albums feature iconography suggestive of obeah, or at least a kind of African mysticism, and some of his songs reference "spells."[50] In interviews, in which he tends to ramble in highly opaque language, he most often rejects outright any suggestion that he might be involved with obeah, yet he has been known to refer to himself on occasion as an "obeah man" (along with many other things).[51]

The Bahamian singer Tony McKay, otherwise known as Exuma, the Obeah Man, was a pioneer in the use of this kind of imagery. Beginning with his 1970 song "Exuma, the Obeah Man," he cultivated the image of the obeah man as an awe-inspiring figure naturally gifted with mystic power:

I came down on a lightning bolt
Nine months in my mama's belly
When I was born, the midwife scream and shout
I had fire and brimstone coming out of my mouth
I'm Exuma, I'm the obeah man.[52]

Since portions of the song, and other parts of the album on which it first appeared (*Exuma*, 1970), summoned up certain staple images associated with the disfigured version of Afro-Caribbean religion served up by Hollywood—for example, "voodoo" and "zombies"—McKay had to clarify this disturbing imagery for the international rock audience to which his music was originally marketed. In one interview for a North American newspaper, he tried to set things straight: "[Obeah] was with my grandfather, with my grandmother, with my father, with my mother, with my uncles who taught me. It has been my religion in the vein that everyone has grown up with some sort of religion, a cult that was taught. Christianity is like good and evil. God is both. . . . It's the same thing, the whole completeness—the Obeah Man, the spirits of the air." Here the interviewer interjects, "It isn't voodoo or witchcraft, he says. It is based on earthly things, 'people to people.' It is the idea of the healer." "We have vibrations," McKay continues, "a relationship, but not in the way that the man goes home at night and makes a secret potion. He doesn't do that. He goes home and writes songs, paints, makes some scenarios—ideas always on a practical sense, on a visual sense. . . . I'm trying to put out good vibrations through my music, or bad vibrations through my music. It depends on my mood, angry or loving vibes."[53]

As we can see in this statement, McKay's representations were consistent with the duality of conceptions of obeah in the Bahamas (and most of the rest of the Caribbean). If the powers referenced by the term "obeah" could be used to heal, they could also be used to injure. There is, then, an element of potential threat in McKay's imagery. In fact, there is ample reason to believe that obeah—in addition to its continuing use for problem solving—never lost its associations in popular consciousness with cultural resistance and the struggle against slavery. Even construed primarily as malevolent witchcraft, obeah could be turned into a useful tool when brought into the service of struggles against oppression. After all, it would not be difficult to justify the aggressive use of negative spiritual power against the enemies responsible for one's enslavement and suffering—or those responsible for one's continuing subjugation and persecution in the post-slavery era. So the element of threat that accompanies the possibility of abusing power in most indigenous African religions certainly forms part of the imaginary of Caribbean obeah.

Closely tied to this aspect of obeah is its association with social control in various Caribbean societies, a capacity that shades into its frequent use as an extralegal means of seeking redress—a side of obeah that deserves more careful ethnographic investigation in future. McKay clearly revealed this aspect of obeah in his later song "Obeah, Obeah" (1972), the first section of which consists of the following repeated lyrics:

Obeah, obeah-oh
Obeah, obeah-oh . . .
We don't molest nobody
Unless they mess with somebody
Don't molest nobody
Unless they mess with somebody.[54]

A similar element of threat (and the possibility of using obeah for social control) is suggested in a piece by Guyanese dubmaster the Mad Professor,

"The Coming of the Obeah Man" (1990).[55] Weaving in and out of his heavy dub mix are two repeating spoken phrases: "The obeah man is coming . . . coming to get you raas [ass]."[56] I once ran into the Mad Professor at a performance and took the opportunity to ask him to sum up the meaning of this piece. His succinct response was, "Well, you see, the obeah man is a kind of mystic man."[57] Clearly, the "mystic" quality of the obeah man that is conveyed to the listener in this case is his ability, should you do him (or someone else) wrong, to come and "get you raas."

Viewed overall, Tony McKay's adoption of the obeah man persona must be understood as part of a larger project of cultural reclamation. As reported in a commemorative article several years after his death, when summing up why he had chosen to call himself the Obeah Man, "he said it was important to keep your identity and your roots."[58] Even though they are in the minority, there do exist other examples of popular songs that portray obeah primarily as a positive force that deserves to be reclaimed as an important part of the ancestral cultural heritage. One of the most interesting is the calypsonian Mighty Chalkdust's song "Try Obeah" (1989), which uses the notion of reclaiming obeah—although not literally, or in an entirely serious way—to frame a political critique of the government then in power in Trinidad and Tobago:

> A old lady, she accosted me
> Talking like if Trinidad gone through
> And the government don't know what to do
> Tell Robbie [Prime Minister A. N. R. Robinson] that longtime old
>   people
> When their problems were unbearable
> They would never sigh, they would never cry
> They knew what to do, so tell this guy:
> The answer to all your problems, Mr. Robinson
> We must all return to our people's great tradition
> Stop stretching out your hand and begging Washington
> It's only obeah could save the nation . . .
> Big speech in Washington can't solve the recession
> Is only obeah to save the nation . . .
> The old lady say to tell Robbie
> Get some rachette [type of cactus] and detapeyi [another plant]
> Cousin mahoe and some purpleheart
> And with a lime take a good bush bath

> Tell him wear a jersey back to front
> Wrap with red lavender for a month
> Tell Robbie take heed, wear some jumbie bead
> In his pocket put a obi seed . . .
> Is only obeah to save the nation.[59]

In portions of the lyrics not included here, various other politicians and policies are named and other obeah prescriptions recommended, such as bathing with specially prepared "water from down in Moruga" to achieve prosperity. There is no shortage of witty humor, and one might wonder whether the calypsonian actually intends to mock the practice of obeah along with the politicians he is critiquing, since it seems highly unlikely that he really believes that the obeah recipes suggested by the old lady in the song are the only thing that can "save the nation" from its predicament.

Some years ago, I had the chance to ask Hollis Liverpool (Chalkdust) about his intentions in composing this song. He assured me that he in no way meant to poke fun at obeah or its practitioners, despite the tongue-in-cheek treatment. On the contrary, the premise with which the song begins—that "we must all return to our people's great tradition"—was to be taken seriously. Instead of looking outside for the solutions to the nation's problems, politicians should draw more on the people's own resources, and obeah was employed in the song, even if with a calypsonian's teasing wink, as a genuine symbol of the need for a return to ancestral sources.[60]

Particularly interesting is "Sang Versé" (Spilled blood), a recent recording by a group of young rappers from French Guiana who call themselves Obia—a name that in itself represents a gesture of cultural reclamation. Interviewed about their motives for composing this piece, one of the members had this to say: "Many people in the Diaspora are alienated. . . . They don't know their history. They live in stereotypes, they have a real inferiority complex. There are blacks who don't want one to speak about their history, who say, 'No, that's in the past.'"[61] The lyrics of the song, in French, recount the story of the Maroons whose ancestral territories are in the interior of French Guiana and Suriname, stressing the crucial part that obeah—as the Maroons themselves define it—played in their survival in the forest and their successful struggle to liberate themselves:

> Alukus, Ndyukas, Saramakas escaped
> Regained the forest, to find once again their freedom
> Not even thinking of meeting [the Amerindians] on their journey
> Already settled, guardians of the secrets of the forest

The exchange of knowledge allowed them to adapt
To live together far from the colonized world . . .
Today I've opened my eyes, and I've seen beyond
Where many no longer stop
The truth is there, the truth is there
It was necessary to protect oneself to live in the Amazonian wilderness
Obeah against evil reinforced your spirit
This vital force necessary once in the *busi* [forest]
Especially and in no case used to cause harm
Neither for meddling, vengeance, or jealousy
This hurdle overcome, you committed *wisi* [sorcery]
For support in battle, invoking the warrior spirit
That performed during the *faya dansi* [fire dance].[62]

Although this song is performed by young French Guianese Creoles (people of African descent from the coastal region who do not share the Maroons' languages and cultures), it unapologetically expresses a Maroon perspective on obeah. In the context of neocolonial French Guiana—where Maroon peoples such as the Aluku and Ndyuka remain marginalized and stigmatized minorities, and the African cultural heritage remains in many ways problematic—this is in itself an act of cultural resistance. There is clear recognition in the group's lyrics that for Maroons in the past, as in the present, "obeah against evil" was the norm. As they point out, in the culturally autonomous zones that Maroons were able to establish, "far from the colonized world," obeah was a form of "protection," a "vital force" necessary for survival. It was never to be used to cause harm to one's own people, and never to be employed in the vendettas that inevitably arise in human society because of interpersonal tensions and jealousies. Obeah was purely good; and negative power, or "wisi," was to be used, if at all, only in battle against the enemy. The young members of this group, Obia, have been able, as they say, to "open their eyes" and "see beyond" the colonial fallacies about the African spirituality of their ancestors no doubt because they hail from a solidly Francophone area in which Anglophone Caribbean constructions of obeah, shaped by centuries of interference from Protestant missionaries, legislators, educators, and other colonial agents, have yet to make a significant impact—this, and the fact that in recent years, growing numbers of young Maroons have migrated to coastal French Guiana and Suriname, where they are increasingly able to exchange ideas with young Creole artists.

CONCLUSION: THE HEATHEN BACK DEH PON THE WALL

It is not the purpose of this chapter to make an argument about the greater "authenticity" of indigenous or African-derived forms of spirituality (whether in Africa or the Americas) that show fewer traces of hegemonic colonial ideologies, the cosmological systems of the Guianese Maroons being but one of many possible examples of such forms. Nor am I arguing that African or African-derived spiritual systems that are relatively free of such remnants of colonial thinking are necessarily any more benevolent—that they are not open to politically motivated abuses or hegemonic tendencies of their own. Anyone familiar with the Maroon societies of the Guianas is well aware that harmful use of spiritual power (wisi) is very much a cause for concern. At times, Guianese Maroons show considerable anxiety about the spiritual implications of envy and jealousy; and the figure of the *wisiman* is as loathed among these peoples as the obeah man is in the Anglophone Caribbean. And so, much as in Jamaica and other parts of the Caribbean, evil-minded abusers of spiritual power sometimes appear in the lyrics of the young Maroon popular musicians who frequent the recording studios of the Surinamese capital of Paramaribo and a number of Dutch cities.[63]

The crucial difference, however, is that among the Ndyuka and other Guianese Maroons (except possibly some Christian converts among them), these manifestations of evil in the cosmos are never represented as anything like the sum total of "traditional" ancestral African (or more specifically, Maroon or Ndyuka) spiritual practice or experience. The evil use or abuse of power is never understood to be an inherent or primary characteristic of one's "ethnic" group or identity, defined in part by religiosity, and wisi never serves as a totalizing symbol of ancestral spirituality. By the same token, no matter how real and inescapable wisi is felt to be, one's "original [i.e., precolonial] religion"—the combination of spiritual concepts and practices understood to have been handed down from the ancestors—is never reductively defined in terms of this negative form of power. Quite to the contrary, as we have seen, the means of dealing with this destructive power (and many other evils and problems in life)—known not coincidentally as obia—is a fundamental part of the cosmos; and the knowledge of how to harness this obia and turn it toward positive ends *is* understood as something handed down from previous generations and *does* function as a source of ethnic pride and a symbol of ancestrality.

Conversely, an imposed stigma, based on the ostensible deficiencies of an ancestral past, is entirely absent from Guianese Maroon understandings of the very important part of the universe that they know as obia. In short, the kinds of contradictions that bedevil discourses surrounding obeah in most parts of the Anglophone Caribbean play no role here. Nor does one encounter among these Maroons the psychic "confusion" that causes people in many parts of the region to disparage forms of spiritual practice perceived as "black" or "African," even as they consult practitioners understood to be operating within such traditions when all else fails.

To the extent that Rastafari represents an attempt to decolonize consciousness and resolve the historically accrued ideological contradictions with which African descendants in the Caribbean, along with other colonized peoples, must contend, one might argue that it has already succeeded. From one perspective, what is important is that the basic terms of the imposed logic that supported the colonial project (white/European is good, black/African is evil) have successfully been reversed, and the actual cultural "contents" of the inverted equation are, or should be, of little consequence. Human beings everywhere, after all, are as much active producers and inventors as passive recipients of culture or tradition. And who is to say, to take a different example, whether obeah centering on de Laurence magic manuals or European grimoires, or making use of the Bible for that matter, qualifies as African? What matters, then, is that in the case of Rastafari, the personally felt psychic contradictions represented by expressions such as "mental slavery" have been resolved, and cultural ambivalence in certain conceptual domains that have fundamental existential significance has been reduced or eliminated. Whether this has been achieved with fidelity to an actual ancestral past might be seen as immaterial. The reduction of culturally based psychic dissonance, one might argue, need not be beholden to history.

However philosophically defensible such a position might be, I would suggest that it vastly underestimates both the complexity of the "live dialogue" between African and African American cultures in which Rastafari will of necessity continue to participate, as well as the continuing power—within this dialogue, and also at a global level—of hegemonic ideologies related to the forces that historically produced the contradictions we see in the "confusion" over obeah.[64] Guianese Maroons are increasingly a part of this Afro-Atlantic dialogue, and those I have spoken with about this question show no indication that they are about to relinquish their fundamental understandings of the cosmos.[65] And what of practitioners of African and African-related religions in Haiti, Cuba, Brazil, and a great many other diasporic locations—not to mention others on the African continent—who bring their own understandings to the dialogue? Inevitably, history (including many local forms of historical consciousness) and its interpretation will continue to play a major role in this dialogue, ensuring that questions of historical authenticity continue to animate debates.

One thing that an examination of the treatment of obeah in Caribbean song clearly shows is that even within a single society in the Anglophone Caribbean, such as Jamaica, there is much variation in views and attitudes; and we can detect in this internal variation at least some local consciousness of the existence of historically based contradictions of the kind I have tried to lay bare in this chapter. Despite prevailing representations of obeah as pure evil, alternative perspectives on the subject do find their way into popular music, some of them explicitly anti-hegemonic; and these alternative views certainly reflect currents of thought already circulating within the societies out of which these songs emerge. As it turns out, one need not leave Jamaica and go to the rainforests in Suriname where Maroons rule, or anywhere else for that matter, to begin to realize that whatever obeah might really be, it is not (at least not entirely) what it is most often said to be.

That obeah has been constructed in different ways over time, and has taken on different meanings and connotations in different locations and contexts, is hardly surprising. All language, after all, is socially constructed and changes over time. Clearly, the word "obeah" today does not stand for a single thing or concept, and one could argue that it never did. Whether, as I believe, the term once had meanings in various parts of the Anglophone Caribbean much closer to those held by Guianese Maroons today—primarily positive or neutral meanings that became partly displaced over time through a hegemonic process of lexico-semantic domination and negative resignification—is a question for further study. But the other possible explanation—that the Guianese Maroons originally used the term "obia" to denote an African-derived concept of malicious witchcraft or sorcery, and then over time redefined it among themselves to mean benevolent power used mostly for healing and protection—seems to me a very difficult argument to make. In any case, the question is not whether we should view older meanings as correct, and newer ones as incorrect because they have strayed from original meanings. Rather, to my mind, the question is this: to what extent are the power relations and hegemonic processes that led to these linguistic shifts in the first place still operative in the Caribbean, and to what extent do the current meanings attached to this highly charged Afro-Caribbean term continue to reflect, and be implicated in, such processes?

Although the word "obeah" may have complex, multiple meanings, it also serves in the present at a more general level, like the English-language term "voodoo" (derived from Haitian *vodou*), as a monolithic signifier for African or neo-African forms of religiosity or spirituality still existing in the Caribbean—all of which risk continued stigmatization, discrimination, and demonization so long as pejorative, more recently imposed meanings and understandings (themselves, as colonial and postcolonial constructions, certainly no more correct than the older ones) go unchallenged. It is my contention that popular music is one arena in which challenges to hegemonic views, or what many Guianese Maroons would characterize as colonized understandings, of obeah continue to occur, providing one more confirmation that the struggles over cultural valuation and meaning that were fundamental to the construction of slave societies in the colonized Caribbean have yet to be fully resolved. Indeed, the outward flow of Caribbean popular music has helped to ensure that these unresolved cultural contradictions remain connected to similarly contradictory cultural phenomena elsewhere in the diaspora and in postcolonial Africa itself.

No doubt, Caribbean popular music, including Rasta music, will continue to play an important part in Afro-Atlantic dialogues.[66] Whether the already proven capacity of such music to contribute to new forms of consciousness might eventually play a role in resolving the deeper cultural contradictions embedded within the polysemic mysteries of obeah and other such colonized signifiers of African spirituality remains to be seen.

NOTES

1. I have undertaken long-term fieldwork among both the Aluku Maroons of French Guiana and Suriname and the Maroons of Jamaica (as well as less extensive work in a variety of non-Maroon Jamaican communities). In each of these places, I have carried out interviews with self-identified obeah/obia practitioners. Works that draw on these materials include Kenneth Bilby, "The Remaking of the Aluku: Culture, Politics, and Maroon Ethnicity in French South America" (Ph.D. diss., Johns Hopkins University, 1990); and Kenneth Bilby, *True-Born Maroons* (Gainesville: University Press of Florida, 2005).

2. André Pakosie, *I Greet the New Day: Classical Songs and Music of the Ndyuka Maroons of Suriname*, booklet accompanying album of the same title (Utrecht: Stichting Sabanapeti, 2002), 11. Another definition from a recent publication on the Guianese Maroons also reveals the existential and philosophical depth of the concept: "*Obia* is a magico-mystical concept with multiple resonances which, according to the Maroon elders, encompasses 'science and consciousness, experience and its object, operation and operator'—that is, the Obia Man." Apollinaire Anakesa, *Musiques et chants traditionnels Busikondé Sama de Guyane*, booklet accompanying album of the same title (Cayenne: CADEG, 2008), 7.

3. Bob Marley and the Wailers, "Natural Mystic" (produced by Lee Perry, Kingston,

1975, and released at that time as a single with a blank label; later rerecorded and released in 1977 by Island Records on the *Exodus* album).

4. Despite the widespread depiction of obeah by Rastafarians as a false "superstition," it is clear that Marley felt that the spiritual powers associated with the term were real, and that such powers had affected his life in important ways. For example, sources close to him say that he often expressed the feeling that he had been led to marry his wife Rita (and was unable to split with her definitively) only because an "obeah woman" had spiritually tied him to her. See Don Taylor and Mike Henry, *Marley and Me: The Real Story* (Kingston: Kingston Publishers, 1994), 33, 107; Cedella Booker and Anthony C. Winkler, *Bob Marley: An Intimate Portrait by His Mother* (London: Viking, 1996), 115–16; Chris Salewicz, *Bob Marley: The Untold Story* (London: HarperCollins, 2009), 313. At one point, after the initial diagnosis of the cancer that was eventually to kill him, he consulted a Jamaican "bush doctor" named "Bungo"; and on a number of occasions, he told people that he could sense the presence of duppies (spirits of deceased human beings). Booker and Winkler, *Bob Marley*, 162, 199–201.

5. Adrian Boot and Chris Salewicz, *Bob Marley: Songs of Freedom* (New York: Viking Studio, 1995), 29; Salewicz, *Bob Marley*, 29, 37.

6. The reference is to Bob Marley and the Wailers, "Duppy Conqueror" (Kingston: Upsetter, 1970), which was rerecorded and released by Island Records for the international market a few years later. "Duppy conqueror" is actually an old expression in Jamaican Creole, traditionally used to mean "a belligerent or bullying person." See Frederic Cassidy and Robert Le Page, *Dictionary of Jamaican English*, 2nd ed. (Cambridge: Cambridge University Press, 1980), 165.

7. Debbie Smoker, *Adventures of Coconut Woman* (Madison: Joy Won, 2006), 267–68.

8. I Maroon (Barrington Dixon), "Mi Salt" (Kingston: Downsound, 2007).

9. Kenneth Bilby, "The Strange Career of 'Obeah': Defining Magical Power in the West Indies" (paper presented at the Institute for Global Studies in Culture, Power, and History, Baltimore, November 1993); Jerome S. Handler and Kenneth M. Bilby, "On the Early Use and Origin of the Term 'Obeah' in Barbados and the Anglophone Caribbean," *Slavery and Abolition* 22, no. 2 (2001): 87–100; Kenneth M. Bilby and Jerome S. Handler, "Obeah: Healing and Protection in West Indian Slave Life," *Journal of Caribbean History* 38, no. 2 (2004): 153–83.

10. Interview with the author, January 18, 2004. In all cases in which an interviewee admitted to me that he or she practiced "obeah" (and at other times "science"), I do not include the interviewee's name, since the practice of obeah (however defined) remains illegal and prosecutable in Jamaica and most other parts of the Anglophone Caribbean.

11. Probably the most famous popular singer and recording artist from the Bahamas—to take a particularly intriguing example—was known to most of the world not by his birth name, Anthony Mackey (aka Tony McKay), but by his stage name, Exuma, the Obeah Man. Lloyd Denton, a well-respected Jamaican keyboardist, is known to

most people (and on album credits) simply as Obeah—his Jamaican "pet name." Lord Sassafrass, a deejay who during the 1980s had a number of hits referencing Afro-Jamaican religions, such as "Pocomania Jump" (1985) and "Kumina to Kumina" (1985), bore the title Obeahman unofficially. Several Afro-Caribbean bands (or bands with Afro-Caribbean members) working in various musical genres—including a reggae band based in France—have given themselves the name Obeah as well. A rap group from French Guiana that has recently begun to attract international attention calls itself Obia (using the most common Guianese spelling).

12. Jim Dooley, "Lynn Taitt," in *More Axe: Mud Cannot Settle without Water*, ed. Tero Kaski (Kuusankoski, Finland: Black Star, 1998), 16.

13. Nearlin (Lynn) Taitt, interview with the author, August 30, 2001.

14. Manuel Monestel, "The Calypso Limonense of Costa Rica," in *Regional Footprints: The Travels and Travails of Early Caribbean Migrants*, ed. Annette Insanally, Mark Clifford, and Sean Sheriff (Kingston: Latin American–Caribbean Centre, University of the West Indies, 2006), 292–302. Similarly, Stefano Harney reveals that "several informants have confided to me that [the calypsonian and soca star] Superblue uses some kind of Obeah to render crowds so entranced." Stefano Harney, "Soca and Social Formations: Avoiding the Romance of Culture in Trinidad," in *Caribbean Romances: The Politics of Regional Representation*, ed. Belinda J. Edmondson (Charlottesville: University of Virginia Press, 1999), 48.

15. Agostinho M. N. Pinnock, "'A Ghetto Education Is Basic': (Jamaican) Dancehall Masculinities as Counter-Culture," *Journal of Pan African Studies* 1, no. 9 (2007): 47–84.

16. Cassidy and Le Page, *Dictionary of Jamaican English*, 236.

17. Admiral Bailey (Glendon Bailey), "Science Again" (Kingston: Jammys, 1989). All transcriptions of song lyrics or interviews are by the author, unless otherwise noted. Translations of lyrics (from Jamaican Creole, Aluku, Ndyuka, or French) are also mine.

18. See, for example, Captain Barkey (Wayne Hamilton), "Obeah Worker" (Kingston: Firehouse Crew, 1993); Lone Ranger (Antony Waldron), "Obeah Man" (Kingston: Thrillseekers, 1979); Kiprich (Marlon Plunkett), "Obeah Man" (Kingston: Birchill, 2005).

19. Leo Graham, "Black Candle" (Kingston: Justice League, 1973). In his later song "Voodooism," Graham returns to this theme, once again defying the obeah man (or the client employing his services), who is driven by badmind, being envious of the singer's relatively good fortune. Leo Graham, "Voodooism" (Kingston: Black Art, 1977).

20. For a useful discussion of concepts of obeah among Indo-Trinidadians, see Aisha Khan, "On the 'Right Path': Interpolating Religion in Trinidad," in *Religion, Diaspora, and Cultural Identity: A Reader in the Anglophone Caribbean*, ed. John W. Pulis (New York: Gordon and Breach, 1999), 247–76.

21. There are many instances of such ridicule in early Trinidadian calypso recordings. A good example of this in early Jamaican popular music is the mento song "Guzoo Doctor," which tells of a "new man in town" who some people say is a "high bush

doctor," but others call "the guzu clown." Alerth Bedasse and Chin's Calypso Sextet, "Guzoo Doctor" (Kingston: Chin's, 1956).

22. Sheik Ally, "Neighbour Working Obeah"; lyrics transcribed from a recording of a live performance posted on YouTube.com, "Me Neighbour Wuking Obeah," uploaded by johnalliproductions on April 7, 2007. This song was a finalist in the Chutney Soca Monarch competition held in Guyana on September 18, 2004.

23. Draytons Two, "G.O. Go" (Kingston: WIRL, 1973). A version of this song is also well-known in Guyana. The spouge version by the Draytons Two may actually represent a Barbadian adaptation of what was originally a Guyanese folk song. (Spouge is an indigenous genre of Barbadian popular music that enjoyed a brief period of popularity during the 1970s.)

24. Mighty Sparrow (Slinger Francisco), "Obeah Wedding" (aka "Melda") (on LP: *The Calypso Genius*, Diego Martin, Trinidad: National Recording Company, 1966).

25. For a trenchant analysis of Trinidadian calypsos on the theme of using obeah for tying, see Gordon Rohlehr, *Calypso and Society in Pre-independence Trinidad* (Port of Spain: Gordon Rohlehr, 1990), 258–63. See also Donald R. Hill, "Calypso, Magic, Religion, and Folklore," in *West Indian Rhythm: Trinidad Calypsos on World and Local Events*, ed. Classic Calypso Collective and John Cowley (Hamburg: Bear Family, 2006), 73.

26. Yellowman (Winston Foster), "Nuh Tie Me" (Kingston: Black Scorpio, 1987).

27. Cassidy and Le Page define "samfai" as "A. 1. An obeahman or other person professing magic powers; 2. one who tricks others by supposed magic powers; a confidence man; 3. The trick of a samfai man; 4. Monkey or ugly person; B. To practise pretended witchcraft so as to trick people; C. dishonest, deceiving." Cassidy and Le Page, *Dictionary of Jamaican English*, 392.

28. Pioneers, "Samfie Man" (Kingston: Beverley's, 1969). There are many more such examples. In his song "Obeah Man" from the early 1980s, the Jamaican deejay Welton Irie expresses similar sentiments. See Welton Irie (Welton Dobson), "Obeah Man" (Kingston: Well Charge, ca. 1980). Songs in this vein go back a long way, as evidenced by an old Vincentian folk song known as "Obeah Man." The song, which remains popular in Saint Vincent, has been recorded by Grupo Amistad on the CD album *Come to St. Vincent* (Kingstown: SVG DOC, 2003).

29. Unlike tying a lover, the use of obeah to obtain employment is generally not seen as an abuse of power, even though it may involve bending the employer's will. Since large-scale unemployment and job discrimination are widely understood to be parts of a larger oppressive system—among other ways in which the disadvantaged masses are victimized and kept in a condition of dependence and poverty—using obeah in this way may be seen as a defensive act meant to correct a systemic injustice experienced at the individual level.

30. Ethiopians, "Obeah Book" (Kingston: Observer, 1977).

31. Leonard Dillon, interview with the author, January 20, 2005. In 2003, I asked Joseph Hill, the lead singer of Culture, how he felt about having the word "obeah" in

the title of a bootleg CD containing his work, *Peace, Love, and Obeah*. He responded, "I wouldn't have that in my camp—never. No, never." When I pointed out that there seemed to be some confusion about the term, for I had often heard it used to mean something positive, he replied, "I know what it means. I would not have that in my camp. [It means] nothing elevating—like voodoo, et cetera. I don't deal wid dem tings. I definitely don't want to have any part, nor lot, with those type of things—Devil works." I cautiously suggested that some people actually think of obeah as a type of "African science" that is often used for positive purposes, such as spiritual healing. His final answer to this was, "Well, I understand it to be something negative, and I don't deal with negativity. [Obeah is] all negativity." Joseph Hill, interview with the author, May 29, 2003.

32. Kiprich (Marlon Plunkett), "Obeah Man" (Kingston: Birchill, 2005).

33. The reference here is to a form of spiritual cleansing sometimes used by street vendors and market sellers to remove negative energy from their "stalls," thus opening the way for good fortune and improved sales and offering protection from competitors who might use spiritual power negatively to keep them from prospering.

34. "St. Weh-It-Name-Deh-Again?" is a clever verbal construction suggesting the ignorance of urban Jamaicans whose search for obeah takes them to country areas with which they are not familiar. In the minds of many Kingstonians, St. Thomas and St. Mary—two of the poorest and most rural parishes—have a special association with obeah.

35. Minister Goddy Goddy (Howard Reynolds), "Obeah Man Poppy Show" (on CD: *Warfare*, Spearhead Records, Kingston: Spearhead Records, 2004).

36. Munga Honourable (Damian Rhoden), "Na Hear" (Kingston: Don Corleon, 2007).

37. "Entertainers Practicing Obeah?," *Xtra News*, February 27–March 4, 2008, 2–3.

38. See Cassidy and Le Page, *Dictionary of Jamaican English*, 392, where one of the senses given for samfai is "monkey or ugly person."

39. "Zugu" appears to be a Rastafarian inversion of "guzu"; but see Cassidy and Le Page, *Dictionary of Jamaican English*, 489, where "zuzu-man" is defined as a "name for an obeahman."

40. Determine (Rohan Bennett), "Science" (produced by Marvin Williams, Kingston, 2008). In good dancehall style, Guidance—one of the deejays targeted in the song—came back with "Destruction Tek You," an "answer song" recorded on the same riddim (dancehall instrumental backing). Guidance (Donovan Walker), "Destruction Tek You" (produced by Marvin Williams, Kingston, 2008).

41. Lloyd Lovindeer, "The Oil" (Kingston: TSOJ, 1987). Another humorous song in which obeah is treated (facetiously) as a catchall remedy for every imaginable problem is "Take Me to the Obeah Man" (aka "Obeah Man") by Mighty Sparrow (Slinger Francisco) (on LP: *Pussy Cat Party*, Port of Spain: SH, 1978).

42. "Suku a sole bambam / Obia—pe fu a piki, a piiti nou." Transcribed from a field recording made by Kenneth Bilby in Saint-Laurent-du-Maroni, French Guiana,

August 8, 1987. Sections of this recording can be heard on the album *The Spirit Cries: Rainforest Music from South America and the Caribbean* (New York: Rykodisc, 1993). Similar examples from the Saramaka Maroons can be found in Melville J. Herskovits and Frances S. Herskovits, *Suriname Folk-Lore* (New York: Columbia University Press, 1936), 546–47, 568; and Richard Price, *Travels with Tooy: History, Memory, and the African American Imagination* (Chicago: University of Chicago Press, 2008), 283.

43. Interestingly, the name of this band refers to a particular variety of herbs of the *Costus* family that are among the most important plants used by Guianese Maroons in compounding obia (in the sense of spiritually powerful medicinal mixtures).

44. Te i de obiaman-ee, da i man taki obia tongo
Te i de obiaman-ee, da i man singi obia singi
Te i de obiaman, da i man dyompo obia dyompo
Te i de obiaman-ee, da i man taki obia tongo
Te i de obiaman, da i man du obia du
i e pele fu ankama, yu no sabi fu ankama obia-ee.

Sangrafu, "Madjo So So We Madja" (on CD: *Na Wan Ray*, Amsterdam: Walboomers, 2006).

45. The phrase *taku obia* ("bad obeah" or "evil obeah"), though rarely heard, is not inconceivable. It might be used, for instance, to describe a situation in which a variety of spiritual power normally associated with positive aims turns out to have been used by an individual improperly, for negative ends, although the much more common term used to denote this is "wisi."

46. A few songs in this vein have been released as mento-reggae singles, including Murphy Romeo, "Ghost Affair" (Kingston: World Wide, 1975); and Wisdom and the All Stars, "Lizard in Bed" (Kingston: High Note, 1978).

47. From a field recording made by the linguist David DeCamp in Bermuda Mount, St. Andrew, Jamaica in 1958; the singer was a woman whose name was recorded by DeCamp only as Trefina. Recording archived in the David DeCamp collection of field recordings at the University of Texas, Austin.

48. One might wonder whether many examples of popular songs containing positive views of obeah (or obeah practitioners) can be written off as mere faddish attempts to reclaim symbols of African culture—that is, products of current political maneuvering that have no real connection with attitudes to obeah carried down from the past. While a few examples may fit this description, the vast majority of cases that I know of suggest the opposite. Many Caribbean popular musicians and singers have understandings that remain rooted in historically deep vernacular forms of culture, even as they participate in contemporary political trends and cosmopolitan (and globalizing) forms of pop culture. Even such international stars as Bob Marley, Peter Tosh, Mighty Sparrow, and Tony McKay (Exuma) clearly reflect understandings in much of their work that owe a great deal to the rural folk heritage of their countries. Some of them (such as Tosh and McKay) also had considerable personal experience with obeah and obeah men (or women) in the rural communities where they grew up.

The same can be said of most of the dozens of lesser-known Jamaican studio musicians and singers I have interviewed over the years. There is every reason to believe that, even today, most of the understandings of obeah reflected in Caribbean popular song, while certainly of the present, are not simply products of the current moment.

49. Cassidy and Le Page define "bush-doctor" as "one who practises herb remedies; esp one who practises obeah under the guise of medicine—a euphemism for OBEAHMAN." Cassidy and Le Page, *Dictionary of Jamaican English*, 84. One of Tosh's albums was titled *Mystic Man* (New York: Rolling Stones Records, 1979), and another one *Bush Doctor* (New York: Rolling Stones Records, 1978). His longtime manager and friend, Herbie Miller, reveals that Tosh was deeply involved with spiritual beliefs and practices that many in Jamaica would consider obeah. For instance, "Especially before a major tour was undertaken, Tosh would pay a visit to his 'Bush Doctor'—who he sometimes called 'mi four-eye man' [a synonym in Jamaica for obeah man]—returning with vials of oils, charms and medicine. His four-eye man advised when he should or would travel." Yet, according to Miller, "Tosh never used the description 'obeahman' or 'obeah' in positive ways. Indeed, he referred to them as 'iniquity' ('outaquity') workers." See Herbie Miller, "Peter Tosh: The Mystic Man," booklet accompanying the DVD/CD box set *The Ultimate Peter Tosh Experience* (Newton, N.J.: Shanachie, 2009). For definition of "four-eye(d) man" as "an obeah-man or myal man, who supposedly has second sight," see Cassidy and Le Page, *Dictionary of Jamaican English*, 186–87.

50. See, for instance, "Mr. Arkwell Spell" (Washington, D.C.: Ariwa/Ras, 1996) in which he intones, "Here comes another Black Ark spell from Mr. Arkwell Perry . . . Arkwell magic."

51. In one interview, Perry said, "The whole of them things them say, like me deal with Obeah, that cannot be true, because how could I deal with good and evil? I never have no contact with Obeah man, the person who say that are a goddam liar. The only people I have contact with is righteous, spiritual people who know about God. Me want to know about things that happen in Africa, long time before we reach Jamaica—not idiot Obeah man, for me no need curse." See David Katz, *People Funny Boy: The Genius of Lee "Scratch" Perry* (Edinburgh: Payback Press, 2000), 182. In another interview, he stated, "People believe in obeah-man and I don't believe in that. . . . I believe in fire, and I'm Lee Scratch Perry who's on the wire burning with fire." Later in the same interview, he said, "I am a teacher and a doctor, I am number one scientist and number one obeah-man and number one voodoo expert and number one voodoo doctor. . . . I am good and I am evil, depends on what you want." Interview by Reto Baumann and Raphael Gretener, 1998, URL no longer available.

52. Exuma (Tony McKay), "Exuma, the Obeah Man" (on LP EXUMA, Chicago: Mercury Records, 1970).

53. Lew Harris, "Music to Call up Zombies by and Dr. John's Healing Sound," *Chicago Tribune*, May 31, 1970, G3. McKay's ideas about obeah are based partly on firsthand experience. He was originally from Cat Island, the part of the Bahamas most strongly identified with obeah.

54. Exuma (Tony McKay), "Obeah, Obeah" (on LP *Snake*, New York: Kama Sutra, 1972).

55. Another recent song that references this element of threat and its potential use for social control is "Obeah Man" (2001), by the Trinidadian soca/dancehall/rapso artist Maga Dan (now known as Maximus Dan). At one point, the lyrics (which mix Jamaican and Trinidadian) tell us:
Dem call me de Shango [practitioner of the Orisha religion] Maga Dan
Otherwise known as Obeah Man . . .
Everybody say me a nice person
Nah get me vex and diss me program
Me go chook me dolly foot and he hand
Next ting you know you end up sick man.

Later in the song, he says:
Today me a go deep down ina de bush
Sit down and read ina me obeah book
Learn how fe give some people sore foot
Specially de nasty rapist and crook.

Despite his fearsome powers, the imaginary obeah man in this song is known to his community as "a nice person"; the only people he makes sick with his powers are those who trouble or disrespect him, or those who are a threat to the community, such as "nasty rapists" and "crooks." The song was a hit. Maga Dan, "Obeah Man" (on CD: Various Artists, *Pelau*, Port of Spain: KMC, 2001).

56. Mad Professor (Neil Fraser), "The Coming of the Obeah Man" (on CD Mad Professor, *Science and the Witchdoctor*, Washington, D.C.: Ariwa/Ras, 1990).

57. Conversation with Neil Fraser, Woodstock, New York, April 20, 2001. Fraser's stage name, Mad Professor, is of interest here. In Jamaica, the word "professor" has a special sense, which Cassidy and Le Page give as "an obeah-man—euphemistic term." Cassidy and Le Page, *Dictionary of Jamaican English*, 364.

58. Monique Forbes, "Tony McKay, the Obeah Man," *Nassau Guardian*, January 19, 2004, 1.

59. Chalkdust (Hollis Liverpool), "Try Obeah" (on LP Chalkdust, *Total Kaiso*, Port of Spain: Strakers, 1989).

60. Conversation with Hollis Liverpool, Port of Spain, Trinidad and Tobago, May 27, 2001. Very much in the same vein is the song-poem "Obeah Man," by the Trinidadian poet and performance artist Roi Kwabena. In this piece, obeah is the wished-for remedy for problems that are similarly systemic, rooted in large-scale structural circumstances—as well as for various kinds of individual corruption and deception. Roi Kwabena, "Obeah Man" (on CD Y42K, Port of Spain: Blue Planet, 1999). Print version published in Roi Kwabena, *A Job for the Hangman* (Birmingham, United Kingdom: RAKA, 1997).

61. "Beaucoup du monde, de la diaspora, sont aliénés. . . . Ils ne connaissent pas leur histoire. Ils vivent dans les clichés, ils ont un réel complexe d'infériorité. Il y a des Noirs

qui ne veulent pas qu'on parle de leur passé, qui disent, 'Non, c'est du passé.'" Transcribed from interview posted on YouTube.com, "African Consciences: EPK (artists Interview) Part 3," uploaded by Tieddo on December 30, 2007.

62.   Bonis [a French name for Alukus], Ndyukas, Saramakas se sont échappés
Regagné la forêt, pour retrouver la liberté
Ne pensant même pas rencontrer sur leur trajet
[les Amérindiens] déjà installés, gardiens des secrets de la canopée
L'échange de connassiance leur a permis de s'adapter
De cohabiter loin du monde colonisé . . .
Aujourd'hui j'ai ouvert mes yeux, et j'ai vu au-delà
Où beaucoup ne s'arrêtent plus
La vérité est là-bas, la vérité est là-bas
Il faut se protéger pour vivre en Amazonie
Obia contre le mal renforce ton énergie
Cette force vitale nécessaire une fois dans le *busi*
Surtout en aucun cas utilisée pour nuire
Ni mêle, ni vengeance, ni jalousie
Cette étape franchie, tu commets le *wisi*
Pour soutenir dans le combat, invoque l'esprit-guerrier
Qui intervient lors du *faya dansi*.

Obia, "Sang Versé" (on CD *African Consciences*, Paris: Universal International, 2003). The terms "obia," "busi," "wisi," and "faya dansi" are all taken from the Ndyuka language. I would like to thank Bruno Blum for his help with my transcription of this passage from the song; the translation is mine alone.

63. Take, for instance, the contemporary kaseko song "Djaroesoe Mang" (Jealous man) (ca. 1995), by the Ndyuka Maroon band High Class.

64. See J. Lorand Matory, "The 'New World' Surrounds an Ocean: Theorizing the Live Dialogue between African and African American Cultures," in *Afro-Atlantic Dialogues: Anthropology in the Diaspora*, ed. Kevin A. Yelvington (Santa Fe: School of American Research Press, 2006), 151–92.

65. In the last few years there has been an explosion of young Maroon (mostly Ndyuka) Rastafarian reggae bands in Suriname and French Guiana, and it is interesting to consider their use of language when they sing about the negative use of spiritual power. Although they tend to employ the typical Jamaican Creole or English terms used by young Jamaican and international Rasta recording artists to "burn" symbols of evil such as Babylon, the batty man, or the chi-chi man (the latter two referring to male homosexuals), to my knowledge they never—unlike their Jamaican counterparts—burn obeah workers or the obeah man. Rather, for this purpose, they use their own non-cognate term for malicious abusers of spiritual power, "wisiman." Guianese Maroon Rastafarian reggae songs verbally burning the wisiman have become quite common recently. A few examples of such recordings are the following: Intervibration, "Faya eke Dondru" (Paramaribo, ca. 2009); Westkantoro, "Tja Tja Faya" (Paramaribo,

ca. 2009); and Positif Vibration, "Wishiman" (Paramaribo, 2008). The recently coined Aluku term "busi data," used as the title of a recent CD by the Maroon reggae band Positif Vibration, is also of interest here. It is both a calque and a cognate of the Jamaican Creole term "bush doctor" (as pointed out earlier, a synonym for obeah man, but with more positive connotations). It is interesting that the Aluku Maroon members of this band, in creating symbolic linkages with their Jamaican Rasta counterparts, chose to use obviously cognate terms from their own language ("busi," meaning bush, and "data," meaning doctor) to reference one Jamaican term for a spiritual worker, "bush doctor"; but they seem to have avoided another, even closer cognate from their own language, "obia man" (which is very similar to the Jamaican Creole "obeah man" in pronunciation), presumably because it would not have properly translated the negative meanings of the Jamaican usage, heard so often in contemporary Rastafarian-oriented Jamaican dancehall recordings.

66. There are no signs that the popularity of obeah as a topic is diminishing among Caribbean songwriters, performers, and audiences. For instance, two much-played soca songs during the Trinidad and Tobago carnival season of 2011 centered on obeah. Both of them display striking ambiguities. Pelf's "Obeah" blends sometimes macabre humor (especially in the accompanying video) with stereotypical images of obeah used in both harmful ways (e.g., to tie a man and make him leave his wife) and more positive ways (e.g., to help a performer achieve a hit song). The chorus references the common concern about being a target of negative obeah. But then the final verse comments ambiguously on a crowd of people waiting in line to get an obeah "blessing":

It could be obeah
They working on me
It could be obeah
They working it night and day . . .
I getting blessed, you getting vex
And I know your blessing is next
So tek your time to join the line
You know how long I wait for mine?

Pelf (Victor St. Louis), "Obeah" (Brooklyn, NY: Nxt Level Productions, 2011). Bunji Garlin's "Obeah" is even more ambiguous. It begins with a story about a man who escapes from jail miraculously using obeah. At one point the song tells of a fearsome vampire that sheds its skin (known in Trinidad as "sukuyan"), and at another point comments negatively on "using voodoo to try to bless me." A portion of the chorus, however, could be read in either positive or negative ways:

When you are sick, what you healing with?
When you feeling the vibe, what you feeling with?
When gunshot fly, what you shielding with?
It's obeah, it's obeah.

Bunji Garlin (Ian Alvarez), "Obeah" (Castries, St. Lucia: Slu Records, 2011).

2.

"Eh! eh! Bomba, hen! hen!":
Making Sense of a Vodou Chant

ALASDAIR PETTINGER

UNE CHANSON AFRICAINE

>   Eh! eh! Bomba, hen! hen!
>   Canga bafio té
>   Canga moune dé lé
>   Canga do ki la
>   Canga li.

These words made their first appearance in print in Moreau de Saint-Méry's classic survey of the French colony of Saint-Domingue, which he compiled from notes made during his long residence there in the years immediately preceding the revolution that ended with the creation of the independent state of Haiti in 1804.[1] They can be found in a section devoted to the religious beliefs and practices he calls *vaudoux*, named after the snake god to which its followers are devoted, and who communicates his wishes through a high priest and priestess (or "king" and "queen"). We are told how the initiates are led into a circle by the king, who taps each one lightly on the head with a piece of wood while intoning this "African song," which Moreau de Saint-Méry transcribes in a footnote. But while he is quite precise about how some of the words are to be spoken or sung ("the first two vowel sounds of the first line are wide open, the last two, mere muted inflections"), he makes no attempt to translate them.[2] And, indeed, this chant proved a mystery for several subsequent generations of writers on Haitian religious beliefs and practices, none of whom had any idea what it meant.[3]

The first part of this chapter examines some of the ways the chant has been deployed by travel writers and other foreign observers, both sympathetic and hostile toward the new republic, and tries to account for its appeal. Translations of the chant began to appear in the 1930s. In the second part, I consider the role they play in two key twentieth-century Caribbean works on the Haitian Revolution, and in the debates over the chant's interpretation that followed. Finally, I try to identify what is at stake in these attempts to make sense of the chant, and whether translators of the chant can indeed fix its meaning any more than their predecessors for whom it was unintelligible. How we understand the chant certainly has implications for our understanding of the history of Vodou, especially during the revolutionary period. But it is also important to recognize the limits of what it can tell us.

In a pamphlet written during the reign of Faustin Soulouque, who governed Haiti in the 1850s (and under whom the religion briefly enjoyed official recognition), Théophile Guérin quotes the chant and asks, "What does it mean, this euphonious, pure-blood African dialect? No one knows."[4] The chant is also described as unintelligible in a full-length book on Soulouque published the same year by the French consul writing under the name Gustave d'Alaux. He is not sure which language it is in, just that it is a "Negro" language.[5] He observes that colonists in Saint-Domingue, upon hearing the chant, immediately stepped up the defense of their plantations (counting their slaves and calling out mounted troops), even while revealing that the ceremonies, somewhat anticlimactically, always ended with scenes dominated by "the triple excitement of promiscuity, drunkenness, and darkness."[6]

Alaux's account is significant because in it we see the emergence of a pattern by which the relatively rich detail of Moreau de Saint-Méry's description of vaudoux is whittled down to two key, related elements: the dangerous power of its leaders and the bacchanalian frenzy of its followers, which, in due course, can be evoked by the words of the chant alone.[7] Thus Alaux proves a valuable source for the Baptist missionary Edward Bean Underhill, who visited Haiti in 1860 as a guest of a Mr. Webley, whose firsthand acquaintance with vaudoux is no match for the more literary pretensions of the Frenchman, who grants him the authority to link "Eh! Bomba!" with a "wild dance" and that "triple excitement."[8]

All this reinforces Underhill's claim that "the black . . . is strongly imbued with the superstitions of his African origin, which no cultivation has removed."[9] But he is equally emphatic that missionary effort is not wasted, and further, that this effort is much more likely to succeed now that slavery has been abolished: "Freedom alone is the true school in which men's faculties can be trained for the higher purposes of life, and the black is as capable of attaining them as the fairer-skinned peoples of more favoured climes."[10]

An anti-abolitionist pamphlet published in the United States the same year, however, shows that the chant could be used in support of the opposite point of view. Citing Underhill against himself (and culminating in the reference to that "triple excitement" he borrowed from Alaux), the author wonders how such "a disgusting picture of savageism and heathenism" can possibly support "the idea that negroes can remain civilized when left to themselves." On the contrary, it exemplifies "the relapse of these negroes into their original barbarism."[11]

The chant also turns up in several descriptions of New Orleans toward the end of the century. George Washington Cable's study of "Creole slave songs" includes a free, imaginative rendering of Moreau de Saint-Méry's account—in which the transcription of the chant is revised for English-speaking readers ("Eh! eh! Bomba, honc! honc!") to better capture the "horrid grunt" of those last two syllables. For Cable this chant shows how things were "in the times when the '*veritable Vaudaux*' had lost but little of the primitive African character," in contrast to the "rather trivial affair" the rituals had now become, with formal religious "worship" largely superseded by more diffuse "superstitions."[12]

Other writers were more willing to collapse the differences between late eighteenth-century Saint-Domingue and late nineteenth-century Louisiana, as the chant's verbatim reappearance in an avowedly eyewitness account of a "Voudoo Dance" in a street just off Congo Square in the late 1880s would seem to suggest.[13] The strange familiarity of the "history, mysteries and practices" of the "Voodoo" outlined in *New Orleans as It Was* (1895) is explained by its reliance on a memoir of 1883 whose anonymous "creole" author evokes her Louisiana childhood by quoting long passages from Moreau de Saint-Méry's study of colonial Saint-Domingue—including, of course, "Eh! Bomba!"[14]

From this condensed survey, we can see how a few lines in an unknown language can anchor a whole network of associated meanings. From the beginning, they connote both the dangerous power of religious leaders and the moral and intellectual confusion of those who follow them, a confusion manifested above all in intoxication and sexual license. If these associations are all made to point to the inferiority of people of African descent, and are invariably thought to indicate the extent to which they are capable of governing themselves (economically, socially, politically), they can support both abolitionist and proslavery arguments.

The whole history of this chant as it appears in print from the 1790s onward appears to consist of one writer citing another.[15] It seems perfectly possible that none of Moreau de Saint-Méry's successors had heard it firsthand. Arguably, the versions of the chant resemble one another more closely than they would had they been direct transcriptions. Indeed, it is even tempting to believe that Moreau de Saint-Méry simply made it up. At any rate, one can surely understand the weary complaint of the Haitian writer Frédéric Marcelin, who in 1913 accuses travellers of turning lazily to the same old sources for the exotic content of their narratives that present-day Haiti seems unable to supply. And he singles out the "strange guttural sounds" of Moreau de Saint-Méry's "baroque incantation," which he dismisses as "meaningless" and no more authentic than the elaborate "fetish-drums" manufactured specifically for export to museums overseas.[16]

The association of the chant with the superficial (and largely patronizing, even derogatory) attitudes of foreign visitors is one reason why the chant does not figure at all in the considerable body of Haitian literature in which Vodou is an important theme (although I later refer to one possible, if encrypted, exception). Its absence from anthropological studies of the religion would tend to confirm the suspicion that it is, indeed, a fabrication.

But the citational history of the chant intersects at various points with that of another chant, whose associations—and fortunes—are markedly different. Drouin de Bercy first recorded this chant in a short book supporting the restored Bourbon monarchy's plan to retake the colony, some ten years after independence. He refers to "the Vaudou" as "the most dangerous of all the Negroes"[17] and goes on to describe a ceremony in which the participants sing and repeat in chorus the following lines, beginning and ending with a beat on the *bamboula* drum:

A ia bombaia bombé,
lamma samana quana,
é van vanta, vana docki.

This translates to: "We swear to destroy the whites and all that they possess, let us die rather than renounce this vow [*mourrons plutôt que d'y renoncer*]."[18]

Drouin de Bercy not only translates the chant but also notates the melody to which it is sung. The words and the music reappear forty years later in Henry Rowe Schoolcraft's massive study of the Native American population of the United States in a passage whose source, however, is identified as a certain "William S. Simonise, Esq. of Port au Prince, a native of Charleston, South Carolina, but for many years a resident of Hayti, and one of her first lawyers."[19] This time a translation is not deemed necessary, for the most notable feature of the transcription—which differs considerably from that found in Drouin's text—is the proper name that is embedded in it:

Making Sense of a Vodou Chant

Aya bomba ya bombai (Bis)
Lamassam Ana-coana (Bis)
Van van tavana dogai (Bis)
Aya bomba ya bombai (Bis)
Lamassam Ana-coana (Bis).

This suggests to Simonise that the chant is in praise of "Anacoana, the Carib Queen," described by Las Casas, Oviedo, and other Spanish chroniclers of the sixteenth century.[20]

Native Caribbean warrior-leaders like Anacaona (to use the more common spelling) were anointed as heroic, romantic figures in the first half of the nineteenth century by such biographers of Columbus as Washington Irving and Alphonse de Lamartine. Her story is also told by the Haitian author Emile Nau, who claims that the chant—in the truncated form of "Aya Bombé"—was popularized by the advisers to King Henry Christophe (1811–20), apparently fascinated by his namesake, Anacaona's nephew, sometimes referred to as Cacique Enrique or Henri, who waged a guerrilla war against the Spanish until 1533. Their translation—"Rather die than be enslaved" (*Mourir plutôt que d'être asservis*)—is less specific than Drouin's, although it preserves the same general form.[21]

The Dominican poet José Joaquín Pérez opens his collection *Fantasías indígenas* (1878)—which acknowledges Irving, Lamartine, and Nau as historical sources—with a poem titled "Igi aya bongbé (Primero muerto que esclavo)."[22] But it was the reproduction of the words and music from the Schoolcraft version a few years later in *Cuba primitiva* by Antonio Bachiller y Morales that seemed to establish the *areíto de Anacaona* (as the chant was called) as an iconic reference point for proponents of *indigenismo* in Cuba, the Dominican Republic, and Puerto Rico.[23]

If, elsewhere in the Caribbean, indigenismo has a tendency to marginalize the role of black slaves and their descendants in the anti-colonial movement, and indeed to marginalize Haiti itself,[24] in Haiti emblems of indigeneity had for a long time been associated with black self-definition, most obviously in the name of the republic.[25] And—as Nau recognized—"Rather die than be enslaved" neatly mirrors the "Haitian marseillaise,"[26] namely, the "liberty or death" motif that adorns Jean-Jacques Dessalines's Declaration of Independence. This motif colors subsequent invocations of "Aya Bombé" in Haitian literature.[27]

If the first chant has acquired (generically) African connotations, thereby allowing it to serve as a convenient shorthand for a primitive level of moral and political development, always in various ways requiring the civilizing influence of Europeans, the second chant has assumed a more distinctly (and more historically specific) Caribbean form that imaginatively fuses native Indian and black resistance to slavery and colonialism around 1500 and around 1800. This perhaps explains why Haitian writers have been much more inclined to make use of the second chant rather than the first.

But it may be unwise to make too much of this contrast, especially as both chants have been quoted together on several occasions.[28] In one case, the rebellious overtones of the "Aya Bombé" seem to have spilled over into the "Eh! Bomba!," as Louis Elie offers the theory that the latter was a "war chant . . . composed by the followers of Telemaque Canga," a Maroon leader who was active in the 1780s.[29] We should also remember that the first chant has always carried a certain menace, too, not only through its first appearance in a text published in the middle of the Haitian Revolution, but also in the flurry of citations in the 1850s during the regime of Soulouque (when the mulatto elite were perhaps most on the defensive).

Nor should we place too much emphasis on the fact that the second had been translated while the first remained inscrutable. The translations offered for "Aya Bombé" (by Drouin de Bercy and by Nau) are not very convincing. Neither identify the source language, and if Drouin's openly propagandist text hardly suggests that his rendering is supported by participant observation or careful scholarship, Nau himself claims that the chant was invented by Christophe's advisers in an attempt to flatter him, thus rejecting the assumption that it is of Amerindian origin.

In any case, when the chants appear together in at least two of the many sensationalist North American travel books that appeared during the occupation of Haiti between 1915 and 1934 by the United States, neither are translated and any sense of their different histories is missing. In *The Magic Island*, William Seabrook lays before us (one immediately after the other) "two Voodoo invocations made up almost entirely of old African words. The first ["Eh! eh! Bomba, Hen! hen! . . ."] I have heard, with slight variations, in several Voodoo temples. The second ["Aia bombaia bombé! . . ."], which was given to me by Dr. Price Mars, of Pétionville, I have never heard in actual use. I do not know the meaning of either."[30] Richard Loederer's *Voodoo Fire in Haiti* reduces the differences further by quoting them together as if they formed a single song, performed before a frenzied crowd by a highly sexualized *mamaloi* (priestess).[31]

Seabrook's and Loederer's accounts are typical of the period in the way vaudoux—now thoroughly Americanized as "Voodoo"—figures largely as a

Making Sense of a Vodou Chant

form of entertainment, comfortably satisfying a taste for the macabre and the pornographic, Haiti having been made safe for prurient visitors by the United States Marine Corps. Far cry, perhaps, from the rather more pointedly allegorical reports of the nineteenth century, when more explicit hopes and fears regarding the emancipation of slaves were at stake. Nevertheless the chant continues to enjoy its special status as a particularly convincing demonstration of a primitive mentality and way of life.[32]

From this perspective, "Eh! Bomba!" might be compared to other citations of African and pseudo-African vocal and drummed rhythms in Euro-American modernism. After all, there is more than a hint of Moreau de Saint-Méry's *chanson africaine* in the *chants nègres* of early Dadaist performances.[33] There is also Vachel Lindsay's notorious poem "The Congo" (1914), in which the heavy meter of the "blood-lust song" of the "fat black bucks" frequently slips into onomatopoeia and nonsense: "Boomlay, boomlay, boomlay, BOOM."[34] The gap between the author's avowed intention to defend and celebrate "the negro race" and the uproar of protest he faced from those who condemned his negative stereotypes testifies to the ambivalence of blackface performance, popular since the mid-nineteenth century and a tradition on which the poem—and these early twentieth-century voicings of the Haitian chant—conspicuously draw.[35]

In Rachel DuPlessis's reading of Lindsay's poem—particularly its provocative "hoo" syllable (and the way it is taken up by apparently more respectable figures such as T. S. Eliot and Wallace Stevens)—she speaks of it as a form of "white conjure" that seems to substitute the cartoon menace of savages ("Boom, kill the white men") for the historical realities of colonial and racist violence.[36]

FOUND IN TRANSLATION

"Eh! Bomba!" did not resist translation for much longer. Several independent lines of research in the 1930s and 1940s allow us to see the mysterious refrain in a whole new light.

In his study of the Haitian Revolution, *The Black Jacobins* (1938), C. L. R. James seems to make the first breakthrough. He quotes the "Eh! Bomba!" chant on two occasions: first, in the opening chapter that outlines the situation of the slaves on the eve of the revolution, and then (this time with the fourth line, "Canga, do ki la," printed twice) as the epigraph to his fourth chapter, in which the narrative of the slave uprising takes off, beginning with an account of the gathering of the night of August 22, 1791, in the forests overlooking Le

Cap Français.[37] On the first occasion, James does something his predecessors had singularly failed to do. He provides a translation: "We swear to destroy the whites and all they possess, let us die rather than fail to keep this vow."[38]

Attentive readers will realize that this could easily be an English rendering of the French translation Drouin de Bercy provided for the *other* ("Aya Bombé") chant. James was clearly careless with his source, possibly Vaissière (whom he cites several times in the same chapter), who quotes both chants (as they appear in Moreau de Saint-Méry and Drouin de Bercy) on the same page.[39] But one can also suggest reasons why this translation might have appealed to James and why he might have found it plausible.

In Drouin de Bercy's text, the slaves' willingness to fight to the death is meant to serve as a warning to a future invasion force: his translation deglamorizes this determination by grounding it in premodern sentiments and values (e.g., oaths, revenge, witchcraft). Transplanted to *The Black Jacobins*, where the struggle to "destroy the whites" is ennobled by the higher cause it serves, the *mourir plutôt* acquires the characteristically modern twist in the "liberty or death" motif as it circulated in the Age of Revolution, when the preference for death became identified with the assertion of universal, human rights rather than the defense of a family's honor or good name. In Haiti, the scope of these rights was pushed further than anywhere else.

In an article on Toussaint Louverture and the slave revolt in Saint-Domingue, Paul Foot argues that "Liberty or death" was "the slogan which dominated the entire slave campaign."[40] This claim would certainly be supported by James's account, not only because it culminates in Dessalines's creation of the Haitian flag by removing the white from the French tricolor and replacing the initials "R. F." (République Française) with the motto "Liberty or Death,"[41] but also because of the way James punctuates his narrative with cited pronouncements that express similar sentiments using the same propositional form. These include Robespierre's outburst from 1790 ("Perish the colonies... if the price is to be your happiness, your glory, your liberty"); a message from Sonthonax to his officers in 1794 ("Let us perish... rather than... fall again into enslavement and servitude"); and Toussaint's letter to the Directory in November 1797 ("We have known how to face dangers to obtain our liberty, we shall know how to brave death to maintain it").[42] As James's remarks on the latter document suggest—he compares it to "Pericles on Democracy, Paine on the Rights of Man, the Declaration of Independence, the Communist Manifesto"—this rhetoric is indeed distinctly modern, pointing both back and forward in time and space to emphasize its universal application and appeal.

James's remarks on the chant itself follow a similar pattern. Its appearance in the first chapter is in a section that characterizes the "intellectual level" of the slaves, to support his point that "one does not need education or encouragement to cherish a dream of freedom." James introduces the chant with the following words: "At their midnight celebrations of Voodoo, their African cult, they danced and sang, usually this favourite song."[43] And after quoting and "translating" it, he observes, "The colonists knew this song and tried to stamp it out, and the Voodoo cult with which it was linked. In vain. For over two hundred years the slaves sang it at their meetings, as the Jews of Babylon sang of Zion, and the Bantu to-day sing in secret the national anthem of Africa."[44]

As the earliest citation of the chant dates from 1797, James's claim that it was sung by slaves as far back as the late sixteenth century would appear to be purely conjectural (although there is certainly evidence that the colonial authorities outlawed vaudoux). The "two hundred years," though, prepares us for the much vaster historical sweep of the comparison that follows—one that underscores James's reading of the chant as expressing a general principle rather than particular interests, tracing its sentiment back to biblical times and forward to "Nkosi Sikelel' iAfrika" in the present and beyond. In a footnote added to a revised edition, James writes, "Such observations, written in 1938, were intended to use the San Domingo revolution as a forecast of the future of colonial Africa."[45]

If the repositioning of the chant at the head of this revolutionary sequence emphasizes its implicit appeal to generalized liberty, the fact that James quotes the chant (in its original language) and makes no attempt to hide its associations with oaths, revenge, and a religious "cult" allows him to show "Eh! Bomba!" occupying two planes simultaneously. "Voodoo" may have been "the medium of the conspiracy," as he puts it,[46] but its message was clearly that of the Enlightenment and the Age of Revolution.

The reputation and authority of *The Black Jacobins* is such that the mistranslation of the chant has largely gone unnoticed—in fact, it has been reproduced numerous times.[47] In George Lamming's essay on the book, "Caliban Orders History," Caliban might stand for Toussaint and the revolutionary slaves as they make history, or James as he writes history, or even Lamming himself, whose account reorders James's material so as to book-end his summary of the narrative with two vocal performances: "Eh! Bomba!" in 1791 and a song overheard by one of Leclerc's officers in 1803.[48] For Cedric Robinson, the chant appears to underscore his argument in *Black Marxism* that "bourgeois culture and thought and ideology were irrelevant to the development of revolutionary consciousness among Black and other Third World peoples," while

Darcus Howe quotes it in order to show that "Caribbean musicality has always been a fundamental part of the revolutionary movement."⁴⁹

But the story does not end here. For while James was working away in the archives in Paris, elsewhere two other researchers were making some interesting discoveries about the chant that point in another direction entirely. One was Jean Cuvelier, a Catholic missionary based in the Belgian Congo, whose history of the first attempt to Christianize the region in the early sixteenth century by King Afonso I was—after a long delay caused by the Second World War—published in 1946. In one chapter he describes at length the native animistic beliefs Afonso aimed to eradicate, such as the belief in shape-shifting witches or *ndoki*. In a footnote citing some sources that testify to the worship of animals, particularly snakes, he refers, almost in passing, to a chant recorded in a book on Haiti written by a fellow missionary, Henri Op-Hey. Cuvelier presumably had not read Moreau de Saint-Méry, but Op-Hey certainly had, for his account—written in Flemish—of the "initiation of the vaudoux" draws heavily on the master. "Then he taps him gently on the head with a small wooden stick," writes Op-Hey, "while intoning an unintelligible African song: 'Eh! eh! Bomba, hen! hen! / Canga, bafio té.' "⁵⁰ Cuvelier instantly recognizes it as a Congolese chant "dedicated to the snake Mbumba (Bomba)," which he renders in the orthography then current and translates into French:

Eh, eh, Mbumba,
Kanga bafioti
Kanga mundele
Kanga ndoki (la)
Kanga (li)

Eh, serpent Mbumba
Arretez les noirs
Arretez le blanc
Arretez le ndoki
Arretez-les.⁵¹

In a separate development, the Cuban anthropologist Fernando Ortiz came to question the by-then-widespread assumption that the areíto de Anacaona was of Indian origin. Already in 1934 he was expressing his opinion that it was "an African-derived song of the Negroes of Haiti."⁵² Thirteen years later, he would support this claim with a close reading of sources, including a phonetic analysis of the chants recorded by Moreau de Saint-Méry and Drouin de Bercy. Their close resemblance to the Afro-Cuban incantations with which he had firsthand acquaintance led Ortiz to conclude they must be of Congo origin, and he arrives at the following translation into Spanish:

¡Eh!¡Eh! ¡Bomba! ¡Eh! ¡Eh!
¡Conjuro a los negros!
¡Conjuro a los blancos!
¡Conjuro a los espiritus! ¡Allá!
¡Conjúralos![53]

Ortiz did not come across Cuvelier's work until he came to revise his article, which became the first chapter of his monograph *La africanía de la música folkórica de Cuba* (1950), but he is sufficiently confident of his own translation to insert a passage that takes issue with the Belgian's confused rendition of Mbumba as "snake," insisting that the term signifies "image, fetish" and also "secret and mysterious."[54]

Aimé Césaire offers both translations in his major study *Toussaint Louverture* (1960), which, somewhat fancifully, has the chant sung at the famous Bois Caïman ceremony that launched the slave rebellion in August 1791. Césaire breaks his study into three parts. The chant marks the entrance of the slaves in his narrative near the beginning of the third part, after the extensively documented debates in the French National Assembly concerning the revolt first of the white colonists and then of the mulattoes, which make up the first two. The invocation of "African gods" could not be more different from the parliamentary speeches quoted earlier at great length, and if its appearance conveys the sudden change of pace of historical events, it also signals a shift in the style of Césaire's commentary. Previously limited to terse summaries and perfunctory link passages, it suddenly becomes more expansive and oratorical, making use of the same rhythmic repetitions found in the chant itself. The anaphoric "canga" (which appears five times, because, as in James, the fourth line is printed twice) echoes the incantatory quality of the chapter's opening paragraph: "The Negroes were ready, always ready; one could even say that in colonial society it was only they who were really ready, only they who were able to fully comprehend the revolution."[55]

But in order to prepare for the imminent appearance of Toussaint, Césaire is anxious to stress the limitations of this first phase of the rebellion, as it is Toussaint's historical role to move beyond it. For all that it is "touching and picturesque," the vaudou ceremony of August 22 was nothing more than a shot of rum to boost a fighter's courage. "It could not sustain the energy of a military campaign."[56] More specifically, the "feverish inspiration and prophetism" of the insurrection needed to give way to the "cold reflection" that would convert it into a revolution.⁵⁷

Césaire's book prompted a response from René Bourgeois, formerly a colonial administrator in the Belgian Congo. His "open letter"—printed in *Présence Africaine* in 1969—outlines the shortcomings of the translations Césaire uses. That of Ortiz he abruptly dismisses as "the product purely of his imagination," while Cuvelier's apparently demands more serious consideration.

First, he argues, Mbumba is not a snake but rather a good-luck name traditionally given to the surviving children of families who have suffered heavily from infant mortality; indeed, snake worship is unknown in the areas where the language of the chant is spoken. Second, *canga* or *kanga* has several meanings, depending on the inflection of the first vowel, and while it may mean "stop or exterminate," it may also mean to "open the mind" of someone.

This allows Bourgeois to render the chant more consistent not only with what he knows of vaudou (for him, evidently not a snake cult but rather an animistic religion), but also with its role in the revolution (inspiring the black slaves to revolt against their white masters). If "stop the European" makes sense in this context, "stop the blacks" does not, suggesting that the intended meaning here is rather to "open their minds." Thus he offers the following alternative:

> Eh, eh esprit benefique / Mbumba, hen hen.
> Ouvre l'intelligence aux Noirs.
> Arrete / extermine l'Europeen.
> Arrete / extermine ce sorcier.
> Arrete / extermine lui.⁵⁸

Césaire incorporates the full text of this letter in a footnote added to the next edition of his book (adding, incidentally, yet more iterations of the chant, making six in total), hoping that it would "put an end ... to the controversy."⁵⁹ But, of course, it does no such thing. At least three scholars have since made further attempts to make sense of the chant, and there is considerable disagreement among them.

In her study of the revolution, *The Making of Haiti*, Carolyn Fick argues that "voodoo," being "one of the first collective forms of resistance, ... was both a cultural and, in its practical applications, a politically ideological force."⁶⁰ She makes much of what she claims is an eyewitness report that suggests that the chant (described as "a sacramental voodoo hymn") did indeed form part of the ceremony at Bois Caïman in August 1791.[61] Advised by the Kongo expert John Janzen, she provides the following translation:

> Eh! eh! Mbumba [rainbow spirit = serpent]
> Tie up the BaFioti [a coastal African slave-trading people]
> Tie up the whites [i.e., Europeans]
> Tie up the witches
> Tie them.[62]

David Geggus, in an article on "Haitian Voodoo in the Eighteenth Century," casts doubt on the authenticity of the source used by Fick, which was not published until 1898. And in general he is rather skeptical of the widespread tendency to romanticize Vodou—in other words, to identify it as a major inspirational force for the revolution—when there is very little evidence either way.[63] He reviews previous attempts to make sense of the chant (e.g., Cuvelier, Bourgeois) before offering his own:

> Oh! Mbumba, oh!
> Render harmless the blacks
> Render harmless the European
> Render harmless the witch[es]
> Render them harmless.[64]

He explains that Mbùmba was an old Kongo deity in the form of "both a rainbow and a great snake that lived near the water's edge,"[65] while the "basic meaning of *kànga* is 'to bind or tie,'" but "in the context of sorcery it would seem best translated as 'to bewitch, keep at bay, or render harmless.'"[66]

Two years later, John Thornton reinstates Cuvelier's translation, which he renders in English as follows:

> Eh! Eh! Mbomba [Rainbow] hen! hen!
> Hold back the black men
> Hold back the white man
> Hold back that witch
> Hold them.[67]

A Kongo expert himself, he discusses previous interpretations of the chant, marking his distance from both those (such as Bourgeois and Fick) who urge a translation that stresses "its place as the anthem of the Haitian rebels," and those (such as Geggus) who insist that its meaning is not primarily political but rather "simply a part of initiation into a Voodoo society in which the sectarian hoped to find personal protection against the witchcraft, often worked by fellow slaves."[68]

Those in the first camp tend to register a certain unease about the apparent equivalence of "black" and "white" in the chant: why would slave rebels appeal to Mbumba to restrain or otherwise limit themselves as well as their enemies? Bourgeois resolves the contradiction by applying different senses of kanga in each case, while Fick does so by suggesting that BaFioti does not refer to blacks in general but rather to a particular group despised by the rest.

Thornton is not convinced by these maneuvers, but nor is he content (as Geggus seems to be) to limit the significance of the chant to the local realm of sorcery:

> Its general terms of address, to blacks (*bafiote*) and whites (*mundele*) alike, and the invocation of *Mbumba* suggest that it had a social as much as a personal significance. Furthermore, the invocation of *Mbumba* also suggests that it expressed the spirit of harmony and peace as an alternative to personal greed and witchcraft that was rampant in prerevolutionary Haiti. As such it could serve as a sort of shorthand expression of a particular revolutionary creed that sought to restore justice and harmony to all, as expressed in Kongo politico-religious ideology. The fact that the verb *kanga* can mean to save and deliver, combined with the Christian context of the verb in Kikongo, might mean that it had a more universalistic message than simply one of murder or revenge.[69]

LOWERING THE TONE

Let me try and step back a little and consider these new interpretations in a broader context. There seems to be general agreement that the chant is in the Kongo (or Kikongo) language and is readily understood by current speakers of this language. So Moreau de Saint-Méry did not make it up; indeed, the accuracy of his transcription testifies to the reliability of his account, and reminds us that not all colonial sources are to be dismissed as self-serving fictions. It also suggests that by the late eighteenth century, different African cultures—and languages—were already fusing together in various ways. At this stage the vaudoux sect, as described by Moreau de Saint-Méry, was probably not dominant in the colony, since its followers were primarily *nègres aradas*, slaves, and descendants of slaves, from the Fon-speaking region of West Africa (who at the time made up less than 20 percent of the slave population); but it is significant that its rituals were beginning to incorporate elements from other parts of the continent.[70]

There is also fairly general (but not unanimous) agreement that the chant invokes Mbumba, a deity or spirit that takes the form of a snake (or rainbow-snake). This fits in well with Moreau de Saint-Méry's understanding of vaudoux as a snake-cult. If he was right, it suggests how much vaudoux has changed, and that it was only during the course of the nineteenth century that vaudoux became the dominant Afro-Haitian religion—embracing other forms under its ecumenical umbrella—a process that seems to have been accompanied by a diminution of the role of the snake. Certainly by the twentieth century—when reliable ethnographic studies began to appear—the snake enjoyed only a relatively minor role, associated with just one of the *lwa* in the Haitian pantheon, Damballah, who is regularly represented by Catholic lithographs of Moses and St. Patrick. The possibility that the religion has changed over time does not seem to occur to René Bourgeois, who does not recognize that if vaudoux was not a snake cult when he was making his remarks in the 1960s, it may yet have been one in the eighteenth century.[71]

But perhaps we should question such an exclusive focus on the *meaning* of the chant. Certainly the revelations of Cuvelier and Ortiz and their successors have done little to dispel the existing associations that make it—and Vodou more generally—answer questions about the level of political development of the slaves and their descendants. This is not just because this debate over the finer points of translation remains the province of specialized scholars, but also because these historically accumulated connotations structure the debates themselves, predisposing them to one version rather than another.

James's mistranslation and Césaire's multiple translations (and their later refinements) share a good deal of common ground with their perplexed predecessors—not least in the way the chant is conceived as a privileged signifier that captures a whole culture in miniature or condenses fundamental social forces. Either way, it is assumed that large generalizations may be derived from it—and further, generalizations that tend to figure the chant (and the culture it has been made to symbolize) as emphatically not (or not yet) of the modern world, standing outside it, whether submissively or defiantly.

We might also consider that if those singing the chant were nègres aradas, then they would probably not have known what the words meant. And indeed this may have been one reason favoring their adoption, since the power of ritual invocations such as prayers or curses are often enhanced by their unintelligibility. A semantic analysis of a chant, then, cannot tell us much about what it does for those who actually give voice to it: we are not any closer to appreciating it as part of an absorbing physical activity that emotionally binds the participants together but does not necessarily "communicate" anything at all.

To help us think about Moreau de Saint-Méry's chant in this way, we could do worse than to turn, after James and Césaire, to that third great Caribbean reconstruction of the Haitian Revolution, Edouard Glissant's play *Monsieur Toussaint* (1961). Although "Eh! Bomba!" does not appear in the script, it may yet in performance, as the closing stage direction calls for "a Haitian chant in the distance."[72] In the context of a work whose inclusion of chants and incantations (according to the preface to the second edition) "signal above all the unbridled pleasure of finally writing a language *as it is heard*,"[73] this might help restore to "Eh! Bomba!" a certain irreducible materiality or (to use Glissant's key term) opacity. Having grown used to imagining that the familiar syllables were entirely transparent, opening onto an entire culture or mentality that observers had convinced themselves they fully comprehended, could its listeners be persuaded to attend to them as pure sound?

We have seen how white modernists (Lindsay, Seabrook, Loederer) habitually slipped into the language of "the primitive," mimicking the voice and intonation of African religious and musical forms, in order to challenge prevailing orthodoxies. To the extent that this is a somewhat cynical, mercenary gesture (projecting onto *other* cultures impulses one dare not fully acknowledge as one's own), it is not surprising that their black counterparts developed alternative strategies. As Michael North has argued, primitivism may have been liberating for whites, but for black modernists it was a trap they worked hard to avoid.[74]

Rachel DuPlessis briefly mentions the response of Sterling Brown and Langston Hughes to "'The Congo,' the one parodying its simplicity, the other inverting its valuation of blackness.[75] W. E. B. Du Bois—who was among those who publicly denounced the racism of Lindsay's poem—had himself earlier in *The Souls of Black Folk* (1903) transcribed a "heathen melody," passed down in his family from his grandfather's grandmother, "seized by an evil Dutch slave trader two centuries ago":

Do bana coba gene me, gene me!
Do bana coba gene me, gene me!
Ben d'nuli, nuli, nuli, nuli, ben d'le.

"And we sing it to our children," he writes, "knowing as little as our fathers what its words may mean, but knowing well the meaning of its music."[76] The domestic setting here makes all the difference: the chant is not a curious sound heard in the distance in a foreign land (as it is in Lindsay's work), but one the writer is accustomed to singing at home. It forms a link in a genealogical chain, pointing back four generations to slavery and forward to the Harvard-educated scholar who honors it in print. The emphasis is not on its semantics, but on the more obscure emotional effect of its "music," alluding to a history of change and transformation rather than a fixed culture or mentality.

If this may suggest an unexpected affinity between Du Bois and Glissant, it may also invite us to reconsider the deployment of "Eh! Bomba!" in the works of James and Césaire, who, for all the various translations (spurious or otherwise) they provide for the chant, do not place the same importance on its meaning as did the academic debates over its translation in the 1990s.

We have seen how James uses the chant as a poetic device to suggest a certain symbiotic relationship between "Voodoo" and Enlightenment, a hypothesis that does not stand or fall on the authenticity of the chant. And for Césaire, what matters is the spontaneous recourse to the theological or prophetic language of the chant (rather than the detail of what it says), and especially the way this contrasts with the considered, secular, political discourse of Toussaint that emerges in its wake. That they choose to reproduce—and repeat—the original chant (rather than simply describe or paraphrase it) implies that what attracts them is the pleasure of the sounds themselves. Uttered less as an illustrative quotation than as a way of introducing a marked change in the narrative voice, the strange syllables and insistent rhythms of the chant herald an unexpected change of pace of both historical events and the manner in which they are presented.

Understood in this way, James and Césaire are more than a match for Lindsay's sonic booming. For they, too, share a modernist delight in provocation and bad taste, forcing the chant's unreadability to loudly interrupt the more formal, measured tone of their accounts. But rather than serving a primitivism that locates "Eh! Bomba!" elsewhere, in a disappearing world of undisciplined satisfactions that industrial capitalism has all but displaced, their performances insist on the distinctly modern project it makes possible: citizenship for all.

In the end, however, we must still ask, do these two studies of the revolution dispel the colonial accretions of "Eh! Bomba!"? Their realignment of the chant introduces a certain dissonance that may weaken the apparent obviousness with which, for two centuries, it has disclosed the persistent condition of a race or a population. Nevertheless, this approach still runs the risk of exaggerating the importance of the chant by having it mark an irrevocable historical rupture through which a nation of citizens comes into being. The words continue to bear a colossal symbolic weight.[77]

As Du Bois's example suggests, however, there is another way of responding to the power of the chant, one that turns down its volume rather than adds to its noise. In the first section of this chapter I referred to Frédéric Marcelin's exasperation at the lazy reliance on "Eh! Bomba!" by travel writers in search of exotic mystification. In his first novel, *Thémistocle-Epaminondas Labasterre* (1901), there is a passage in which his young protagonist, enjoying a walk in the country, is mesmerized by the sight of young women washing clothes by the riverbank. In an erotically charged reverie, he hears them singing. While one of them tells the story of a scandalous pregnancy, the others respond, every two lines, with "Bombé, manzai Calistra, bombé."

Marcelin does not let Epaminondas persist in his fantasy for long, as the narrator reverses perspective. "Mostly," he writes, "it's only a jumble of words which mean little, lacking finesse and originality. What they cherish is the sound and the laughter that helps take their mind off the dreary task, their feet submerged in water the whole day."[78]

Like the chants we have been considering, and whose phonemes turn up again here, mangled but not beyond recognition, this refrain is not allowed to meet the demand for cheap exoticism. In what I like to think of as a kind of allegory of Bomba interpretation, Marcelin sends up the pretensions of the male onlooker, who only too easily fixes the women in a *tableau vivant* designed for his entertainment, by juxtaposing them with the point of view of the women he objectifies. Marcelin does not disclose the meaning of the chant (which he implies would be impossible and irrelevant in any case), but he hints—rather more prosaically—how it helps them bear the physical toil of their labors. From this rediscovery of the ordinary,[79] students of "Eh! Bomba!" still perhaps have much to learn.

NOTES

1. In this chapter, I am especially indebted to the analysis of this chant and its citational history by Fernando Ortiz, *La africanía de la música folklórica de Cuba* (Havana: Ediciones Cardenas y Cia, 1950), 61–87; David Geggus, "Haitian Voodoo in the Eighteenth Century: Language, Culture, Resistance," *Jahrbuch für Geschichte von Staat, Wirtschaft und Gesellschaft LateinAmerikas* 28 (1991): 21–51; and Stephan Palmié, "Conventionalization, Distortion, and Plagiarism in the Historiography of Afro-Caribbean Religion in New Orleans," in *Creoles and Cajuns: French Louisiana*, ed. Wolfgang Binder (Frankfurt am Main: Lang, 1998), 315–44. Unless indicated otherwise, all translations are mine.

2. M. L. E. Moreau de Saint-Méry, *Description topographique, physique, civile, politique et historique de la partie Française de l'isle Saint-Domingue*, ed. Blanche Maurel and Etienne Taillemite (1797; Paris: Société de l'histoire des Colonies Françaises, 1958), 1:67.

3. In this chapter I adopt the spelling of "vaudoux"/"vaudou"/"voodoo"/"Vodou" (etc.) used by the text under discussion. When I need to refer to the religion more generally, I use the now widely accepted "Vodou." For a discussion of the historical and orthographic issues involved here, see Alasdair Pettinger, "From Vaudoux to Voodoo," *Forum for Modern Language Studies* 40, no. 4 (2004): 415–25.

4. Théophile Guérin, *Biographie de l'empereur Soulouque: Solution de la question haïtienne* (Paris: Auguste Durand, 1856), 27.

5. Gustave d'Alaux, *L'empereur Soulouque et son empire* (Paris: Michel Lévy, 1856), 63. The book grew out of a series of articles the author wrote for *Revue des deux Mondes* in 1850/51.

6. Ibid., 64, 68. The African American abolitionist James McCune Smith expressed the opinion that the chant—which he found in Alaux—was the basis for the famous lines of Tennyson ("Cannon to the right of them, / Cannon to the left of them, / Cannon in front of them / Volley'd and thunder'd") in "The Charge of the Light Brigade" (1854). See "The Critic at Chess," *Frederick Douglass' Paper*, January 12, 1855, reprinted in *The Works of James McCune Smith*, ed. John Stauffer (New York: Oxford University Press, 2006), 109–11.

7. Moreau de Saint-Méry already associated vaudoux with "disgusting prostitution" and warned that the power of its leaders meant that there was "nothing more dangerous . . . than the cult of vaudoux." *Description topographique, physique, civile, politique et historique de la partie Française de l'isle Saint-Domingue*, 1:68.

8. Edward Bean Underhill, *The West Indies: Their Social and Religious Condition* (London: Jackson, Walford and Hodder, 1862), 159–61.

9. Ibid., 109.

10. Ibid., 176.

11. *Free Negroism; or, Results of Emancipation in the North and West India Islands* (New York: Van Evrie, Horton, 1862), 12–13.

12. George Washington Cable, "Creole Slave Songs," *Century Magazine* 21, no. 6 (1886): 818–20.

13. Charles Dudley Warner, *Studies in the South and West, with Comments on Canada* (London: T. Fisher Unwin, 1890), 71.

14. Henry C. Castellanos, *New Orleans as It Was: Episodes of Louisiana Life* (1895; Gretna, La.: Pelican, 1990), 90–95; [Hélène d'Aquin Allain], *Souvenirs d'Amérique et de France par une créole* (Paris: Bourguet-Calas, 1883), 149.

15. It is precisely this "plagiarism" that preoccupies Palmié in "Conventionalization, Distortion, and Plagiarism in the Historiography of Afro-Caribbean Religion in New Orleans."

16. Frédéric Marcelin, *Au gré du souvenir* (1913; Port-au-Prince: Editions Fardin, 1978), 15–17.

17. [Louis Marie César Auguste] Drouin de Bercy, *De Saint-Domingue* (Paris: Chez Hocquet, 1814), 176.

18. Ibid., 177–78.

19. Hamilton W. Pierson, "Anacoana," in *Information Respecting the History, Condition and Prospects of the Indian Tribes of the United States*, ed. Henry Rowe Schoolcraft (Philadelphia: Lippincott, 1853), 2:309.

20. Ibid., 2:312. For a survey of the literature on the *areíto*, see Donald Thompson, "The 'Cronistas de Indias' Revisited: Historical Reports, Archaeological Evidence, and Literary and Artistic Traces of Indigenous Music and Dance in the Greater Antilles at the Time of the 'Conquista,'" *Latin American Music Review/Revista de Música Latinoamericana* 14, no. 2 (1993): 181–201.

21. Emile Nau, *Histoire des caciques d'Haïti* (Port-au-Prince: T. Bouchereau, 1855), 334.

22. José Joaquín Pérez, *Fantasías indígenas, y otros poemas* (1878; ed. José Alcántara Almánzar, Santo Domingo: Ediciones de la Fundacion Corripo, 1989), 35.

23. Antonio Bachiller y Morales, *Cuba primitiva: Origen, lenguas, tradiciones e historia de los Indios de las Antillas y las Lucayas*, 2nd ed. (Havana, 1883), 44–45.

24. See Sibylle Fischer, *Modernity Disavowed: Haiti and the Cultures of Slavery in the Age of Revolution* (Durham: Duke University Press, 2004), 155–68.

25. See David Patrick Geggus, "The Naming of Haiti," in *Haitian Revolutionary Studies* (Bloomington: Indiana University Press, 2002), 207–20.

26. Nau, *Histoire des caciques d'Haïti*, 334.

27. See Arsène Chevry, *Areytos: Poésies indiennes* (Port-au-Prince: Maison Athanase Laforest, 1892), vii, 23–25, 61; Jean Price-Mars, *Ainsi parla l'oncle: Essais d'ethnographie* (Port-au-Prince: Imprimerie de Compiégne, 1928), 116–17; Jacques-Stéphen Alexis, "Dit de la fleur d'or," in *Romancero aux étoiles* (Paris: Gallimard, 1960), 161; Jean Metellus, *Anacaona* (Paris: Hatier, 1986), 114–15; and Berthony Dupont, *Jean-Jacques Dessalines: Itinéraire d'un revolutionnaire* (Paris: Harmattan, 2006), 22–24. *Aya Bombé* was also the name of a Haitian literary journal published between 1946 and 1948, whose title Léon-François Hoffman explained as follows: "Supposedly 'Liberty or Death' in the pre-Columbian dialect of the first inhabitants of Haiti." See "The Climate of Haitian Poetry," *Phylon* 22, no. 1 (1961): 66.

28. Pierre de Vaissière, *Saint-Domingue: La société et la vie créoles sous l'ancien régime* (Paris: Perrin, 1909), 179; Price-Mars, *Ainsi parla l'oncle*, 116–17.

29. Louis Elie, *Histoire d'Haïti* (Port-au-Prince, 1945), 2:184. I have not seen this claim made elsewhere. Jean Fouchard, in *Les marrons de la liberté* (Paris: Editions de l'Ecole, 1972), makes reference to both Telemaque (508, 522) and the "Eh! Bomba!" chant (536) but does not suggest any connection between them.

30. William B. Seabrook, *The Magic Island* (London: Harrap, 1929), 304.

31. Richard Loederer, *Voodoo Fire in Haiti*, trans. Desmond Ivo Vesey (1935; Gretna, La.: Pelican, 2005), 272–73.

32. According to at least one source, a reference to the chant was implied in Pat Robertson's notorious remarks about the Haitian "pact with the devil," made in the

immediate aftermath of the January 12, 2010, earthquake. See Jonathan Turley, "Pat Robertson: Haitians Were Punished by God for 'Pact with the Devil,'" *Jonathan Turley*, January 14, 2010, http://jonathanturley.org/.

33. On the *chants nègres*, see Michael North, *The Dialect of Modernism: Race, Language, and Twentieth-Century Literature* (New York: Oxford University Press, 1994), 28–32.

34. Vachel Lindsay, "The Congo: A Study of the Negro Race," in *Collected Poems*, rev. ed. (New York: Macmillan, 1925), 178–84.

35. On the controversy, see Ann Massa, *Vachel Lindsay: Fieldworker for the American Dream* (Bloomington: Indiana University Press, 1970), 167–70.

36. Rachel Blau DuPlessis, *Genders, Races, and Religious Cultures in Modern American Poetry* (Cambridge: Cambridge University Press, 2001), 81–105, esp. 84, 93, 105.

37. C. L. R. James, *The Black Jacobins: Toussaint L'Ouverture and the San Domingo Revolution*, rev. ed. (London: Allison and Busby, 1980), 18, 85.

38. Ibid., 18.

39. Vaissière, *Saint-Domingue*, 179.

40. Paul Foot, "Man's Unconquerable Mind," *Socialist Worker Review* 144 (1991): 18.

41. James, *The Black Jacobins*, 365.

42. Ibid., 76, 136, 197.

43. Ibid., 18.

44. Ibid.

45. Ibid., 18n.

46. Ibid., 86.

47. James's error was first identified in Geggus, "Haitian Voodoo in the Eighteenth Century," 24.

48. George Lamming, "Caliban Orders History," in *The Pleasures of Exile* (1960; London: Allison and Busby, 1984), 124, 149.

49. Cedric J. Robinson, *Black Marxism: The Making of the Black Radical Tradition* (London: Zed, 1983), 386; Darcus Howe, "Revolutionary Threads of Slavery," *New Statesman*, March 26, 2007, 22.

50. H. Op-Hey, *Haiti: De parel der Antillen*, 2nd ed. (Antwerp: De Paters Montfortanen Te Kontich-Kazernen, 1937), 260.

51. "Eh, serpent Mbumba / Stop the blacks / Stop the whites / Stop the *ndoki* / Stop them." Jean Cuvelier, *L'Ancien royaume du Congo* (Bruges: Desclée de Brouwer, 1946), 290; brackets in the original.

52. Fernando Ortiz, *De la música afrocubana: Un estímulo para su estudio* (Havana, 1934), 6.

53. "Eh! Eh! Bomba! Eh! Eh! / Cast out the blacks! / Cast out the whites! / Cast out the spirits! Go! / Cast them out." Fernando Ortiz, "Preludios étnicos de la música afrocubana," *Revista Bimestre Cubana* 59, nos. 1–3 (1947): 100.

54. Ortiz, *La africanía de la música folklórica de Cuba*, 83.

55. Aimé Césaire, *Toussaint Louverture: La révolution Française et le problème colonial*, rev. ed. (Paris: Présence Africaine, 1981), 191.

56. Ibid., 196–97.

57. Ibid., 195.

58. "Eh, eh, kind spirit / Open the minds of the Blacks / Stop (or exterminate) the European / Stop (or exterminate) this witch / Stop (or exterminate) him." R. Bourgeois, "Lettre à Aimé Césaire," *Présence Africaine* 70 (1969): 209.

59. Césaire, *Toussaint Louverture*, 192.

60. Carolyn Fick, *The Making of Haiti: The Saint-Domingue Revolution from Below* (Knoxville: University of Tennessee Press, 1990), 57.

61. Ibid., 265–66.

62. Ibid., 290n, 58; brackets in the original. Although the translation is different, one finds a similar reading of the chant by Ned Sublette, who finds in it an example of the ways that one "transmits secrets in order to accomplish a revolution." See Sasha Frere-Jones, "Roundtable: Haitian Music, Part 2: 'What Does Revolution Sound Like?,'" *New Yorker* blog, July 13, 2009, http://www.newyorker.com/.

63. Geggus, "Haitian Voodoo in the Eighteenth Century," 44–50.

64. Ibid., 26; brackets in the original.

65. Ibid., 27.

66. Ibid., 28. Incidentally, Geggus also offers a translation of the "Aya Bombé" chant: this, too, appears to be in the Kikongo language and turns out to mean something quite different from that claimed by Drouin de Bercy.

67. John K. Thornton, "'I am the subject of the king of Kongo': African Political Ideology and the Haitian Revolution," *Journal of World History* 4, no. 2 (1993): 210; brackets in the original. He refers elsewhere in his article to "Mbumba," so we may assume the spelling "Mbomba" here is a misprint.

68. Ibid., 211.

69. Ibid., 213.

70. Moreau de Saint-Méry, *Description topographique, physique, civile, politique et historique de la partie Française de l'isle Saint-Domingue*, 1:64; Geggus, "Haitian Voodoo in the Eighteenth Century," 36.

71. On the changing role of the snake in Vodou, see Hénock Trouillot, *Introduction à une histoire du vaudou*, 2nd ed. (Port-au-Prince: Editions Fardin, 1983), 44–51. The assumption that Vodou has remained fixed over time is made by Madison Smartt Bell, who transposes twentieth-century versions of Vodou in his fictionalization of the 1791 rebellion—which, incidentally, does not forget to include the chant (untranslated) in its account of the famous ceremony at Bois Caïman. See Madison Smartt Bell, *All Souls Rising* (London: Granta, 1995), esp. 118.

72. Edouard Glissant, *Monsieur Toussaint*, 2nd ed. (Paris: Gallimard, 1998), 160.

73. Ibid., 12.

74. North, *The Dialect of Modernism*, 11.

75. DuPlessis, *Genders, Races, and Religious Cultures in Modern American Poetry*, 93–95.

76. W. E. B. Du Bois, *The Souls of Black Folk*, in *Writings*, ed. Nathan Huggins (New York: Library of America, 1986), 538–39. The chant also appears in his subsequent autobiographical writings. See Du Bois's *Darkwater: Voices from within the Veil* (New York: Harcourt, Brace, 1921), 5; and *Dusk of Dawn: An Essay toward an Autobiography of a Race Concept*, in *Writings*, 638.

77. I thus share the skepticism toward supposedly revolutionary chants and anthems voiced by Michel Beaujour in "Flight out of Time: Poetic Language and the Revolution," *Yale French Studies* 39 (1967): 29–49. But Beaujour, in questioning their revolutionary value, then goes too far the other way, I think, and exaggerates their danger and threat as reactionary diversions.

78. Frédéric Marcelin, *Thémistocle-Epaminondas Labasterre* (1901; Port-au-Prince: Editions Presses Nationales d'Haiti, 2005), 45–46.

79. I borrow this expression from Njabulo S. Ndebele, "The Rediscovery of the Ordinary: Some New Writings in South Africa," in *South African Literature and Culture: Rediscovery of the Ordinary* (Manchester: Manchester University Press, 1994), 41–59.

3.

On Swelling:
Slavery, Social Science, and Medicine in the Nineteenth Century

ALEJANDRA BRONFMAN

By the time it was published in 1922, *Antropología y patología comparada de los negros esclavos* (Comparative anthropology and pathology of black slaves) had survived a long and mostly obscure, unpublished existence. Written in 1876 by a French physician named Henri Dumont, the text contained a series of observations drawn from his work on Cuban plantations. The anthropologist Luis Montané brought the manuscript to the attention of the Cuban Academia de Ciencias Médicas Físicas y Naturales, which praised it as a significant contribution.[1] Soon thereafter, however, it seems to have sunk into obscurity and remained in the academy's archives until building renovations resulted in the dispersal of most manuscripts. Years later it came into the possession of a bricklayer who then sold it to the criminologist Israel Castellanos. Castellanos translated the text from its original French and published it as a series in the *Revista Bimestre Cubana* in 1916. In 1922, the Cuban intellectual Fernando Ortiz reissued it in book form.[2]

As social scientists primarily interested in people of African descent, Montané, Castellanos, and Ortiz named Dumont one of the precursors of Cuban anthropology, a field to which they all contributed. They may or may not have known about an additional book Dumont published in Cárdenas in 1865 about his sojourn in Cuba. A more narrowly medical text, *Investigación general sobre las enfermedades de las razas que no padecen la fiebre amarilla* (General investigation of the illnesses of the races that do not suffer from yellow fever) recounted more of Dumont's experiences treating ill slaves on plantations. The few subsequent studies of Dumont's work have followed the interpretation that places him in a national framework, and that understands the significance of his writing insofar as it preceded that of better-known Cuban social scientists of the twentieth century.[3] At first glance, these texts do not seem terribly surprising. Recent studies of the production of knowledge have alerted us to the ways that social science and anthropology in particular incorporated people of African descent and multiply inflected notions of race into emerging theories and debates about human behaviors and capacities.[4] Since it was not until the late nineteenth century that the discipline of anthropology was established in Cuba, just as it was being institutionalized in Europe, it seems reasonable to name Dumont one of its foundational figures.[5]

However, a closer look at the text and the intersections of slavery, medicine, and social science renders this book quite strange and worthy of further consideration. Although the book was written in 1876, it was based on observations that Dumont had made in 1864 and 1865. This was a rare moment when the emerging discipline of anthropology coincided with the waning institution of slavery. Moreover, both texts offer a sense of how practices of slave medicine might have looked. In effect, Dumont offers unusual representations of slaves in two respects. First, they are objects of anthropological scrutiny. Second, slaves are patients, behaving in particular ways not often found in the historical record. These traces of slave behavior in Dumont's account add another dimension to the study of slavery and medicine, which has not often paused to consider the ways that patienthood might change or challenge power dynamics on a plantation.[6]

This chapter will use Dumont's texts to ground reflections on the relationships among slavery, social science, and medicine. The two texts together challenge some prevailing understandings of periodization. They suggest that "tropical medicine" did not spring only from European laboratories in the late nineteenth century, but rather that it was preceded by centuries of slave healing. On the other hand, the anthropological aspects of the texts belie simple ascription as predecessors to later Cuban social science. Instead, I argue that Dumont's work occupied a window in which the waning of slavery and the emergence of institutionalized anthropology converged to produce a rare anthropology of slavery.

Dumont's work points beyond national parameters. He was a French physician working in the Caribbean and drawing from knowledge produced in Africa, Europe, and the Caribbean. Analysis premised on the nation does not do justice to the scales and networks in which he operated, which both extend to an Atlantic space of healing and the production of knowledge, and narrow to the specificities of the local, in this case a single plantation where different modes of healing interacted and collided.

WINDOWS OF OPPORTUNITY

Anthropology obtained accepted status among social scientific circles just as slavery was ending in the New World. The process of abolition and emancipation, begun with the Haitian Revolution in the late eighteenth century, had reached much of Latin America by the early nineteenth century, the British Caribbean by 1838, and the United States by 1865. By the time Dumont published his earlier text, slavery persisted only in Cuba and Brazil. In Cuba, the decades of the 1860s and 1870s were a period of transition concerning slavery. As Dumont gathered materials, slavery was being challenged both by slaves themselves and by the Moret Law of 1870, which freed all children born to slave mothers.[7] The Ten Years' War (1868–78) eroded slavery's long-standing dominance and appeal for many Cubans. After 1886 in Cuba, and 1888 in Brazil, slaves would no longer be available to social scientists anywhere in the world as objects of study *as slaves*.

Arguably, discourses and practices that might fall under the rubric of anthropology did not originate in the mid-nineteenth century. Historians of anthropology have located its origins in a number of different moments from the seventeenth to the nineteenth centuries. They agree nevertheless that the institutionalization of the discipline, along with a greater emphasis on empirical evidence gathered ideally from participant observation, or fieldwork, arose in the mid-nineteenth century.[8] This occurred in Cuba and France at about the same time. In France, the Société d'Ethnographie Américaine et Orientale and the Société d'Anthropologie de Paris were both founded in 1859.[9] In Cuba, the Academia de Ciencias Médicas Físicas y Naturales was founded in 1861 and the Sociedad Antropológica in 1877. Regardless of whether institutionalization marks the origins of a discipline (and many have argued persuasively that it does not), it can nonetheless open possibilities for formalized channels of interaction and opportunities for far-flung exchanges among participants. In short, texts like Dumont's may have been more likely to have an audience at this moment than they would have before. Indeed, he might have written his book precisely as a way to gain entry into scientific circles, both in France and in Cuba.

In its European origins, the discipline of anthropology had taken as its primary object of study the cultures of the world. Eventually, the geographies of primitiveness designated Africa and the Pacific Islands as sites worthy of study, locations where uncivilized people might be held up as a mirror, either flattering or not, to Europeans. The Americas were largely left out of this equation. Slavery, the institution that bound Africa to the Americas, seemed to be of no interest to European anthropologists—perhaps because, as I have noted above, it was on the wane as anthropology was being instituted. But perhaps it was also an epistemological problem: did the fact of slavery strip Africans in the Americas of their status as "pristine primitives" and put them in a category not easily integrated into an intellectual project premised on the primitive/civilized binary?[10]

When Dumont traveled to the Caribbean and conceived of it not only as a place to practice medicine but also as a new "field" for anthropologists, the concerns of anthropology (race and culture) meant that the subjects (or perhaps objects) of his study were people of African descent, since indigenous cultures had largely disappeared centuries earlier. In Cuba, this included both free people of color and slaves. Thus circumstances converged to make the anthropology of slavery part of an Atlantic intellectual conversation.

That conversation had for many years included medicine. Dumont's earlier text, *Investigación general sobre las enfermedades*, places Dumont much more squarely in the medical field. This text serves as a reminder that the relationship between slavery and healing had been a necessary part of the slave trade since its inception.[11] In that sense, Dumont's more narrowly medical text ought to be situated as part of multiple exchanges and lengthy periods of experimentation and accumulation of knowledge regarding the ailments of slavery.[12] Tropical medicine was forged out of this long history and in an Atlantic space that brought together slaves and healers from Africa, physicians from Europe, and diseases from the Americas. As Dumont worked in this space, he can be imagined not as a precursor of a national discipline, but rather as the inheritor of an Atlantic network of knowledge and practices.

SELF-SUBVERSION

This chapter revisits arguments I have made elsewhere that proposed a transformation in the tone of social scientific thought in the wake of independence and the extension of citizenship. My book *Measures of Equality: Social Science, Citizenship, and Race in Cuba, 1902–1940* took as its point of departure a moment in Cuban history in which universal manhood suffrage coincided with the growth and institutionalization of anthropology.[13] I argued that social science, in particular anthropology, became very concerned with criminality precisely as large groups of men of color became citizens with rights to suffrage. Social science also developed a new interest in religion, as African-derived faiths were imagined as autonomous spaces that perpetuated "pre-modern" ways of being and secret forms of associational life perceived as threatening to an expanding public sphere. Fernando Ortiz and Israel Castellanos were among those who produced a body of work concerned with race, criminality, religion, and biology. The book traces the way their work was part of a larger conversation about race among journalists, scientists, politicians, and, eventually, black activists in the first decades of the twentieth century. Complex ideas about race emerged in this context and changed over time, in part because of a dialogue between anthropologists and activists. By 1940, a constitutional amendment criminalizing racial discrimination revealed the polarized aspect of race in Cuba: voices calling for a correction of injustice had achieved the passing of this amendment, but the very necessity to declare discrimination illegal served as a reminder that it persisted in many spheres of life.

In a thoughtful review, Steven Palmer pointed out that my periodization might be called into question by taking into account colonial anthropologies and their claims about race and criminality. How well founded, Palmer asked, was my argument that anthropology in the Cuban republic took on these new concerns?[14] It seemed appropriate to turn to Dumont, who had been designated a precursor by the very anthropologists about whom I wrote. If anybody's work could challenge my claims about the intellectual shifts ushered in by Ortiz and Castellanos, Dumont's would. At stake was the nature of the production of knowledge about people of African descent—knowledge that was so easily used against them in the early decades of the twentieth century. I argue that, in fact, Dumont's concerns were quite different from those of Castellanos and Ortiz in their neglect of criminality and distinct understanding of slaves' relationship to Africa.

But Dumont wrote in two guises, both as an anthropologist and as a physician, and in the latter we can see the inheritance of a long history of practices made necessary by the system of slavery, which required that ill slave bodies be tended and healed. That circumstance necessitated relationships among slaves and doctors that afforded roles beyond mere subservience and coercion. Taken together, the two facets of Dumont's work give rise to new reflections about the nature of modernity. My emphasis on anthropology in the context of an emerging republic allowed an overly facile equation of citizenship, sovereignty, and social science with modernity. To be sure, this echoes contemporary discourses in which many Cubans equated modernity with independence.[15] But there are different kinds of modernities, and they do not all line up so neatly with one another.

Sidney Mintz has long argued that the Caribbean is the quintessentially modern place, and that slavery and colonialism did not precede modernity but rather created it and must be central to any conception of it.[16] The point here is not to argue over when modernity started, but rather to understand the ways it might work as an analytical category. If slaves were, as David Scott (echoing Mintz) argues, conscripts of modernity, then it might be useful to examine the kinds of institutions that were shaping their lives and drafting them into modern subjectivities.[17] Social science, tropical medicine, and anthropology incorporated slaves into their purview very differently than did legal and political institutions at the same time. If politics and law could afford to exclude or ignore people of African descent, medicine and anthropology *required* them, and profited from studying, treating, and understanding slave bodies and practices.

THE LIFE

Born in Paris in 1824, Henri Dumont received his medical degree there a few years before he was sent to Veracruz in 1863, to study and contain the yellow fever that was afflicting French troops stationed there. Yellow fever was a major concern for Europeans in the Americas, as many imperial endeavors eventually foundered in the face of the deadly disease. As soldiers and workers died quickly and rather dramatically, the search for the causes and cures of yellow fever became a central concern of not just the French, but the Spanish and Americans as well.[18] The French extended their mission toward collecting additional forms of knowledge. They formed scientific commissions dedicated to mapping, archaeological explorations, and what they called natural history. French officials justified the creation of these commissions by arguing that "by studying indigenous races and métis, the new science of anthropology would 'raise questions of the most elevated order, at once physiological, moral, and social.' Medical doctors could shed light on acclimatization and tropical disease."[19]

Dumont participated in this project for one year, after which he proceeded to Cuba, where he would remain for six months working in plantations and hospitals and gathering the materials for his texts. From there he traveled to St. Thomas, Guadeloupe, Guyana, and finally Puerto Rico, where he died in 1878. Further biographical details about Dumont are scarce. One source is the 1922 edition of *Antropología y patología comparada de los negros esclavos*, in which the Puerto Rican historian Cayetano Coll y Toste offers some observations about Dumont's personality and demeanor. He seems to have been a rather austere and mysterious man who dressed mostly in black, had few possessions, slept in hammocks when he traveled in the countryside to see patients, and was never seen consuming anything other than hard-boiled eggs and black coffee. In some places he was met with suspicion because he tended to not charge patients for consultations and rarely wrote prescriptions for medication.[20]

Far from limiting his writings to Cuba, he wrote on many of the places he lived, using in one title the phrase "intertropical regions of America."[21] Even when he was writing directly on Cuba, his observations suggest that he was working within a framework that envisioned regions of tropical disease as unbounded by state borders. His interests in plantation medicine, diseases like yellow fever, and race place him in an Atlantic medical dialogue that included not just the islands in the titles of his work, but also New Orleans, Havana, Veracruz, and Philadelphia.[22]

THE TEXTS

Dumont's earlier text seems to be drawn more closely from his experiences on a single plantation called La Granja in the town of Cárdenas, which was then a relatively new settlement (founded in 1828) about seventy-five miles east of Havana. It is a port town, so it might be safe to speculate that a plantation would have access to the contraband slave market that grew after the official banning of the slave trade in the 1850s. There—working, as he put it, "on commission by the government of France to study the diseases peculiar to the Americas," and with the blessing of the town council and other local official bodies—Dumont installed himself at the plantation.[23] He was assisted by a local physician named Dr. D. Miguel Bravo y Senties (resident surgeon), about whom we know little.

Here Dumont focuses on a single disease, what he calls "hinchazón," which might be translated into English as "swelling." Although he drew a distinction between hinchazón and beriberi, later studies identified them as the same disease, and texts in tropical medicine came to list them as synonyms.[24] Whatever the name of the disease, his claim was that it affected black and Chinese people, but not whites. As the first to identify the ailment, he may have conceived of it as an important contribution to French medicine. Dumont wrote a thorough analysis of the causes, the progression of the disease, and the treatment. One of the most detailed sections describes the results from autopsies, with notes about the state of a number of internal organs in the aftermath of the illness. In a final section, he offers some thoughts on the treatment of the disease.

The more varied observations in *Antropología y patología comparada de los negros esclavos* included those related to anthropology as well as portions devoted to medicine. In particular, it lingers on case studies of slaves with various kinds of tumors. These case studies detail patients' symptoms and the kinds of treatments they received. One account of a young man with elephantiasis whose leg was amputated and who subsequently died is contrasted with another, in which surgery was withheld and the patient recovered. Dumont is also concerned in this text with something he calls "curvature of the legs" ("desviación de piernas"), a painful condition that prevented slaves from working at full capacity and may have been another version of hinchazón.

As most of his patients were slaves, the conjunction of slaves and medicine merits some consideration. Long before they were citizens, and while they were struggling over their status as legal subjects, slaves were patients. Dumont's texts disclose the way slaves acted as patients. They explained their symptoms, narrated medical histories, and requested certain kinds of treatments. In one account, Dumont notes that "those who were sick came to us saying that they had felt ill for four or five days," and that others "indicated that they felt pain in other places."[25] In some cases, they made their desires for treatment very clear: "A man of color, born here and twenty-six years old, presented himself at the hospital, asking that his leg be amputated. The subject begged the physicians to amputate his leg, which was invaded by elephantiasis."[26]

At times he notes their emotional states as well. In the case of Alejandro Lima Valdes, a nineteen-year-old freedman who had elephantiasis in the face and neck, he made the following observations: "The patient's horrible appearance makes him deeply repulsive to others. He knows this and suffers ... as a man still affected by the insatiable desires typical of his youthful age."[27]

These are small details, but the ways in which slaves in this text sought out doctors and were relied on to give accurate accounts of their symptoms speaks to a complex dynamic whereby slaves were acting within a patient-doctor script. Indeed, Dumont helped write the literal version of this script when he included a glossary of phrases for doctors and patients in Spanish and Lucumí, a language commonly spoken by Cuban slaves. This included phrases indispensable to medical exchanges, such as "Where does it hurt?" ("Voló un duan?"), "Are you tired?" ("Etin sco linó?"), and "Stick out your tongue" ("Yanguán sodé quenlí"). Never losing sight of the power dynamics at play, it also included commands that European visitors might have found useful when interacting with slaves, such as "Sweep here" ("Ma ogua ovalé"), "Carry this" ("Ve rumí"), or "Go home" ("Ma lolé").[28]

Dumont's text and the interactions that informed it seem to be not so much about slaves engaged in resistance or rebellion as it is about their participation in a set of practices from which they seemed to believe they would benefit. Although still guided by fairly rigid hierarchies, the circumstances of being a patient allowed slaves to deviate from simple servility and total obedience. Medicine not only necessitated a degree of subjectivity, but it also incorporated slaves into particular practices of modern personhood.[29]

More problematically, some of the accounts quite clearly demonstrate the extent to which Dumont and other doctors took advantage of slave bodies as experimental data, as they tested various theories and treatments and compared results. The use of slaves for testing purposes is striking as well in contrast to post-slavery narratives of the fight against yellow fever, in which doctors used soldiers' bodies, or their own, to test remedies and vaccines.

FINDING TREATMENT

Dumont's comments on remedies and medications allow for an exploration of plantation medicine. If it is difficult to distinguish where "European" theories and practices end and "African" ones begin, it may be that these categories are inadequate to the task. Following David Wade Chambers and Richard Gillespie, it may be more fruitful to imagine knowledge in this instance as distinctly local and influenced by "vectors of communications, exchanges and control."[30] While Dumont never accounts for the provenance of his methods, he does mention others with whom he interacts and who have deployed their healing practices, including the owner and overseers, local healers whom he identifies variably as "medicos," "curanderos," "curanderas," and of course the slaves themselves. While in the text he is literally the author and authority, this works to assert in a singular voice (his) knowledge that comes from many distinct sources.

According to Dumont, hinchazón occurs in hot, dry environments, but the heat does not technically cause it. Instead, he identifies the habits of slaves and plantation workers who drank large quantities of water mixed with fermented sugar or honey. The gases emanating from these liquids were, according to him, the immediate cause of swollen limbs, usually the legs. Other symptoms were fatigue and lethargy, with the occasional burst of irascibility. It afflicted only those working on sugar plantations or honey farms, distinguishing the ailment further by race.

This diagnosis seems to draw at least partly from some currents in what would come to be called "tropical medicine" once it was institutionalized. As environmental explanations for disease came to mingle with other theories, one in particular stands out as relevant. Physicians studying disease in India and other British colonies had by the 1850s and 1860s developed theories in which different illnesses, specifically fevers, began with decaying organic matter, which would then cause the blood to undergo its own version of fermentation. This idea, originated by the German chemist Justus Liebig, was popular among physicians working in the British colonies in the 1860s.[31] This connection begs the question, certainly, of Dumont's relationship to networks of knowledge not just in France, but also in Europe more broadly.

At the same time, there are also points of convergence between Afro-Caribbean beliefs, as described by Michel Laguerre, and Dumont's descriptions. The relevance of heat and cold, for instance, is shared by many healing traditions. Laguerre points out the strong causal power granted to temperature and its relation to the blood, often at the center of Afro-Caribbean healing beliefs. Similarly, Liebig's theories about fermentation extended and refined European environmentalist beliefs about excessive heat as the source of many illnesses.[32]

When it came to treatment, Dumont was critical of both European and Afro-Caribbean remedies, but in the end his own practices (as he described them) were eclectic and not easily classified. He cited as one of the most common remedies the use of *vejigatorios*, or blistering plasters, noting that he might find up to five placed in different parts of the bodies of those who suffered from hinchazón. These he dismissed as completely useless.

Another remedy about which he was skeptical was the use of "Le Roy's purgative," which he claimed did more harm than good. This is not surprising, as the medication, created in France and known to induce vomiting, had been faulted for causing too violent a reaction and in some cases leading to death. It had been officially banned in France in the 1830s, but a brisk black market trade kept it in circulation. In this instance, Dumont seemed to be echoing a well-established official French opinion. But his remarks allow for a tantalizing glimpse into who was treating slaves and workers on the plantations: they were "managers, overseers, and nurses."[33] People who fit this description may have been drawing from any number of traditions and experiences, depending on their ages, family networks, and access to published work or other healers. In any case, it hints at a complicated picture in which illness and treatment were not necessarily cordoned off for specialists, but rather were integrated into the daily life of the plantation. Those whose responsibility was to make sure the work was done included among their responsibilities the well-being (or capacity to work) of slaves. Dumont reserved his most pointed professional arrogance for this group: "It seems only natural that doctors and medicine take possession of plantation infirmaries, and that therapeutic practices acknowledge the rightful place of medicine as instituted by our colleagues and not to practitioners (however intelligent) who lack training."[34] Nonetheless, he later revealed himself to be in a tight spot, unwilling, apparently, to condemn the use of Le Roy's purgative altogether, wanting only to control its dispensation.

But other actors participated in the drama of ailment on the plantation. Dumont's most cryptic allusion refers to the "curanderas negras"—specifically gendered female—whose secret remedies he grudgingly admits do work to alleviate hinchazón. Since they were secret, he cannot describe them, so—with what might be a bit of resentment—he claimed that though they were effective, they merely treated the symptoms and not the cause. This is the most direct reference to the presence and effectiveness of an alternative method of healing on these plantations. Tellingly, he was not as quick to be rid of their services as he was of the others.' There is no suggestion in his discussion of the curanderas that professionals replace them. Rather, one can discern a desire that they share their knowledge. He demonstrates ambivalence, and perhaps even a grudging respect, but does not entertain their dismissal.

Dumont had most likely been trained in the context of French campaigns against unauthorized healers that arose in the Napoleonic era. Early nineteenth-century efforts by doctors to obtain more patients, greater status, and more revenue had spurred a crackdown on "itinerant quacks" and other healers in rural France. His ambivalence toward those who lacked training was not surprising. But his role as a physician in the Caribbean altered his position, since what was at stake was not necessarily the loss of revenue or status as much as the exigencies of a labor system (the crucial thing was to get slaves back to work), and the claim on the discovery of the disease (not necessarily its treatment). Would that have led him to be slightly more catholic in his approach, despite his stated intentions to defend the boundaries of the legitimate?[35]

When he offered his own recommendations, they seemed to be rooted in a practical need to see results rather than focusing on the legitimacy of their origins. First, he emphasized the importance of allowing the digestive functions to operate without interference (as an antidote to the use of purgatives, perhaps). That included the ingestion of red wine and fresh meat, echoing an Afro-Caribbean folk belief that red substances cured ailments of the blood.[36] In addition to recommending antispasmodics, he ultimately advised close attention to the skin and the promotion of perspiration through stimulants, massage, and aromatic therapy. Though antispasmodics were common European remedies, the treatments in which Dumont put the most store, such as bloodletting, leeching, massages, and baths, cannot be said to belong exclusively to one tradition or another.[37]

These extensive reflections on medical practices suggest that searching for their national or even ethnic origins is a futile exercise. Perhaps it is more interesting and relevant to look at the ways that healing worked in local settings, taking note, as Chambers and Gillespie suggest, of "social infrastructures that support knowledge and work in both traditional and western settings."[38] These divisions, between traditional and Western, between colonial and metropole, between African and European, are at play in the narratives of healing produced by people like Dumont, but perhaps only because his ability to defend them is at risk. Along these lines, many questions arise from this preliminary exploration: What were the most common ailments afflicting slaves and what were the local healing practices before Dumont arrived at the plantation? What precisely was the population of this plantation? How isolated was it from town and from incoming ships? These lie beyond the scope of this chapter. Instead, I suggest a reading of Dumont's work that begins, to borrow from Chakrabarty, to provincialize European medicine.[39]

AFRICA

In *Antropología y patología comparada de los negros esclavos*, Dumont writes extensively about Africa in order to locate the slaves who are his subjects. Beginning with his descriptions of the physical geographies of slaves' lands of origin, he distinguishes among African ethnicities. He seems to echo prior assessments made by slave traders over the years: Mandingas, for example, were thought to be educated, while Congos were deemed unintelligent and lazy.[40] His observations tend to be about Africans' physique and strength, as well as their capacities for work. With an emphasis on whether they are likely to rebel, to follow orders, or to fall prey to certain diseases, he writes portraits of Africans as potential workers. In contrast to the work of Ortiz and Castellanos, who were interested in black men as *brujos* or criminals, Dumont's concerns are to describe the best labor force. This leads him to also include women in his study—notably absent from most of Ortiz's and Castellanos's work—as workers and as potential reproducers of the labor force. In one example, he writes of "Genoveva, a black lucumí, twenty-two or twenty-three years old, arrived in Havana three years ago. Has a son that is six or seven months old. She has had enteritis, fevers, and colds."[41] Where Castellanos and Ortiz looked for physiognomic signs of what they called atavism, such as the nature of the gaze or the shape of facial features, Dumont concentrates instead on ethnicity as an indicator of workforce potential and health.

His work differs from later Cuban anthropologies in his rendition of African culture and history. In a recent work, Kevin Yelvington attributes the social scientific invention of Africa in large part to Melville Herskovits's work and his search for "retentions" and "survivals."[42] Those involved with American anthropology, enmeshed in a debate during the early twentieth century about the relative personhood of people of African descent, believed that one key to this question had to do with the state of African culture and the destruction wrought by slavery. Africa was imagined as an isolated, tribal place where people practiced polytheistic rituals in minimal material comfort. Moreover, Africa was placed in the past and understood as a place in which time had not moved forward. Anthropologists looked for evidence of primitive beliefs and rituals, imagined as remnants from another era in the cultural practices of people of African descent in the Americas. In much of their work, Castellanos and Ortiz drew from this paradigm, with particular emphasis on retentions and survivals as evidence of savagery or propensities to crime.[43]

Dumont's is a very different invention of Africa. In *Antropología y patología comparada de los negros esclavos*, Africa is not a distant memory as much as a continuing presence and source of slaves only recently arrived in Cuba. Dumont's concern is not with retentions or survivals, but rather with the complex social and cultural institutions that shaped their lives in Africa. Typical of his observations is the following, made most likely about wealthy African traders and merchants: "The houses of the wealthy *carabalí* are made of wood, and they are furnished in the best taste. The sons of *carabalí* from prominent families, like those of prominent European families, speak several languages; in addition to their own, they speak English, French and Spanish."[44] The text describes polygamy, gender relations in terms of work, and the value of women in religious rituals. It distinguishes among different forms of government, and offers details about urban organization, commerce, trade, and production of textiles. Dumont is interested in religious plurality, including forms of Islam and Christianity as well as what he called animism and cannibalistic practices. He also notes the participation of Africans in the slave trade. As in the above quote, he is keen to provide accounts of class distinctions among Africans and to point out the habits and practices of the elite. The emphasis on an African present rather than an African past is striking.[45] At the same time, it also coincides with an imperial moment in which France was in the process of acquiring African territories and in search of ethnographic knowledge.[46] In contrast to the American anthropological invention of Africa in the early twentieth century, premised on a distant and fading culture, French anthropology was forced to confront a present Africa. This strange hybrid text, more than much Cuban anthropology that followed, places Cuba and Africa alongside one another in parallel presents.

If Dumont was indeed the inaugurator of anthropology in Cuba, how much did his Africa resonate with subsequent ones invented by Castellanos and

Ortiz? Very little, I would argue. The conjunction of slavery, medicine, and anthropology conscripted slaves into a modernity that imagined them as patients, as unfree labor, and as Africans who came from complex and sophisticated cultures. In the fleeting liaison I have tried to elucidate, all were possible at once.

CONCLUSION

To return to the critique that animated this chapter, how different was colonial, nineteenth-century anthropology from anthropological studies written in the republican, post-emancipation context of the twentieth century? There are two answers. The first is that they were very different. And the second is that consideration of these differences calls into question the categories on which they are premised. Once the political landscape changed, the very fact of their inclusion as citizens rendered black men more threatening to the stability of the republic than they had been as slaves. Social scientists began to scrutinize them for their propensity to crime and their adherence to "primitive" cultural practices. Dumont's observations about ethnicity, work ethic, and robustness were drowned out by Ortiz's and Castellanos's cries that *brujería* was infecting the body politic. But on the other hand, Dumont's work reminds us to look beyond electoral politics in the production of knowledge about people of African descent. Institutions dealing with health and medicine were also influential, and when they coincided with slavery they inflected the production of knowledge in distinct ways. As patients, slaves were enlisted into a series of practices that superseded their status as property and would persist post-emancipation. Dumont's work suggests different modes of modernity that do not necessarily coincide with one another. The anthropology of slavery generated in a nineteenth-century window reveals just how much slaves and non-European medical practices founded the practices we might recognize as modern.

NOTES

All translations are mine. I would like to thank Neil Safier, Rebecca Scott, Steve Palmer, Danny Vickers, and Adrian López Denis for their comments on early versions of this chapter.

1. Fernando Ortiz, preface to *Antropología y patología comparada de los negros esclavos*, by Henri Dumont (1876; ed. Fernando Ortiz, trans. Israel Castellanos, Havana: Colección Cubana de Libros y Documentos Inéditos o Raros, 1922), 6 (hereafter cited as *Antropología*).

2. Ortiz, "Prólogo," 1–6, in *Antropología*.

3. Gabino La Rosa Corzo, "Henri Dumont y la imagen antropológica del esclavo africano en Cuba," in *Historia y memoria: Sociedad, cultura y vida cotidiana en Cuba, 1878–1917*, ed. José Amador (Havana: Centro de Investigación y Desarrollo de la Cultura Cubana Juan Marinello, 2003), 175–82.

4. See, for example, George Stocking, *Race, Culture, and Evolution: Essays in the History of Anthropology* (Chicago: University of Chicago Press, 1982); James Clifford, *The Predicament of Culture: Twentieth-Century Ethnography, Literature, and Art* (Cambridge: Harvard University Press, 2002); Olívia Maria Gomes da Cunha and Flávio dos Santos Gomes, eds., *Quase-cidadão: Histórias e antropologias da pós-emancipação no Brasil* (Rio de Janeiro: Editora FGV, 2007); Elazar Barkan and Ronald Bush, eds., *Prehistories of the Future: The Primitivist Project and the Culture of Modernism* (Stanford: Stanford University Press, 1995); Kevin Yelvington, ed., *Afro-Atlantic Dialogues: Anthropology in the Diaspora* (Santa Fe: School of American Research Press, 2006); Stephan Palmié, *Wizards and Scientists: Explorations in Afro-Cuban Modernity and Tradition* (Durham: Duke University Press, 2002).

5. Manuel Rivero de la Calle, *Henri Dumont: Precursor de los estudios antropológicos en Cuba* (Santo Domingo: s.n., 1982).

6. See, for example, Todd Savitt, *Medicine and Slavery: The Diseases and Health Care of Blacks in Antebellum Virginia* (Chicago: University of Illinois Press, 1978); Ronald L. Numbers and Todd Savitt, eds., *Science and Medicine in the Old South* (Baton Rouge: Louisiana State University Press, 1989); Richard Sheridan, *Doctors and Slaves: A Medical and Demographic History of Slavery in the British West Indies, 1680–1834* (Cambridge: Cambridge University Press, 1985); Sharla Fett, *Working Cures, Healing, Health, and Power on Southern Slave Plantations* (Chapel Hill: University of North Carolina Press, 2002); Karol Weaver, *Medical Revolutionaries: The Enslaved Healers of Eighteenth-Century Saint Domingue* (Chicago: University of Illinois Press, 2006); Geneviève Leti, *Santé et société esclavagiste à la Martinique (1802–1848)* (Paris: L'Harmattan, 1998).

7. Rebecca Scott, *Slave Emancipation in Cuba: The Transition to Free Labor, 1860–1899* (Princeton: Princeton University Press, 1985).

8. Han F. Vermeulen and Arturo Alvarez Roldán, "Introduction: The History of Anthropology and Europe," in *Fieldwork and Footnotes: Studies in the History of European Anthropology*, ed. Han F. Vermeulen and Arturo Alvarez Roldán (New York: Routledge, 1995), 1–18.

9. Martin Staum, "Nature and Nurture in French Anthropology, 1859–1914," *Journal of the History of Ideas* 65, no. 3 (2004): 475–95.

10. Stocking, *Race, Culture, and Evolution*; Stephen Jay Gould, *The Mismeasure of Man* (New York: Norton, 1981); Vermeulen and Alvarez Roldán, *Fieldwork and Footnotes*. Very few anthropological texts deal explicitly with slaves. Two that approximate the subject are Henry Clarke Wright, *Anthropology; or, The Science of Man: In Its Bearing on War and Slavery, and on Arguments from the Bible* (Cincinnati: E. Shepard, 1850); and John Van Evrie, *The Six Species of Men, with Cuts Representing the Types of the*

Caucasian, Mongol, Malay, Indian, Esquimaux, and Negro (New York: Van Evrie, Horton, 1866).

11. See, for example, Adrian López Denis, "Melancholia, Slavery, and Racial Pathology in Eighteenth-Century Cuba," *Science in Context* 18, no. 2 (2005): 179–99; Michel Laguerre, *Afro-Caribbean Folk-Medicine* (South Hadley, Mass.: Bergin and Garvey, 1987).

12. David Arnold, "Introduction: Disease, Medicine and Empire," in *Imperial Medicine and Indigenous Societies*, ed. David Arnold (Manchester: Manchester University Press, 1988), 1–26.

13. Alejandra Bronfman, *Measures of Equality: Social Science, Citizenship, and Race in Cuba, 1902–1940* (Chapel Hill: University of North Carolina Press, 2004).

14. Steven Palmer, review of Bronfman, *Measures of Equality, American Historical Review* 111, no. 1 (2006): 237–38.

15. Louis A. Pérez, Jr., *On Becoming Cuban: Identity, Nationality, and Culture* (Chapel Hill: University of North Carolina Press, 1999); Marial Iglesias Utset, *Las metáforas del cambio en la vida cotidiana: Cuba, 1898–1902* (Havana: Ediciones Unión, 2003).

16. Sidney Mintz, *Sweetness and Power: The Place of Sugar in Modern History* (New York: Penguin, 1985).

17. David Scott, "Modernity That Predated the Modern: Sidney Mintz's Caribbean," *History Workshop Journal* 58, no. 1 (2004): 191–210.

18. John Lawrence Tone, "How the Mosquito (Man) Liberated Cuba," *History and Technology* 18, no. 4 (2002): 277–308; Nancy Stepan, "The Interplay between Socio-Economic Factors and Medical Science: Yellow Fever Research, Cuba, and the United States," *Social Studies of Science* 8, no. 4 (1978): 397–423.

19. Victor Duruy cited in Paul Edison, "Conquest Unrequited: French Expeditionary Science in Mexico, 1864–1867," *French Historical Studies* 26, no. 3 (2003): 468.

20. Cayetano Coll y Toste, preface to Dumont, *Antropología*.

21. Henri Dumont, *Memorias sobre la historia médica y quirúrgica de las regiones intertropicales de América/Islas de Cuba, Puerto Rico, Méjico, Santomás, Guyana, etc.*, cited in La Rosa Corzo, "Henri Dumont y la imagen antropológica del esclavo africano en Cuba," fn. 5.

22. Tone, "How the Mosquito (Man) Liberated Cuba"; Stepan, "The Interplay between Socio-Economic Factors and Medical Science."

23. "En comisión por el Gobierno de Francia, nuestro país, para estudiar las enfermedades peculiares á las Américas." Henri Dumont, *Investigación general sobre las enfermedades de las razas que no padecen la fiebre amarilla: Y estudio particular sobre la enfermedad de los ingenios de azúcar l'hinchazón de los negros y chinos* (Cárdenas, 1865), 2 (hereafter cited as *Investigación*).

24. See, for example, B. Scheube, *Diseases of Warm Countries: A Guide for Medical Men* (n.p., 1903). Thanks to Adrian López Denis for this reference.

25. "Los enfermos se presentaron diciendo que padecían desde hacia cuatro o cinco días"; "localizaron los dolores en otras regiones." Dumont, *Antropología*, 71.

26. "Un hombre de color, criollo y de 26 años, se presentaba en el hospital civil de la ciudad de Cárdenas, solicitando la amputación de su extremidad inferior. El sujeto reitero a los médicos sus ruegos para que le amputasen la pierna invadida por la elefantiasis." Ibid., 83.

27. "El horrible aspecto del enfermo produce honda repugnancia, repugnancia que a el no le pasa desapercibida y que le aflige . . . inquieto por los deseos insaciables de su edad nubil." Ibid., 76.

28. Dumont, *Antropología*, 65–66.

29. Manuel Barcia, *Seeds of Insurrection: Domination and Resistance on Western Cuban Plantations, 1808–1848* (Baton Rouge: Louisiana State University Press, 2008); Matt D. Childs, *The 1812 Aponte Rebellion in Cuba and the Struggle against Atlantic Slavery* (Chapel Hill: University of North Carolina Press, 2006); Laurent Dubois, *Avengers of the New World: The Story of the Haitian Revolution* (Cambridge: Harvard University Press, 2004).

30. David Wade Chambers and Richard Gillespie, "Locality in the History of Science: Colonial Science, Technoscience, and Indigenous Knowledge," *Osiris*, 2nd ser., 15, Nature and Empire: Science and the Colonial Enterprise (2000): 227.

31. Mark Harrison, "Tropical Medicine in Nineteenth-Century India," *British Journal for the History of Science* 25, no. 3 (1992): 299–318.

32. Laguerre, *Afro-Caribbean Folk-Medicine*, chap. 5.

33. "Administradores, mayordomos y enfermeros," Dumont, *Investigación*, 69.

34. "Parece natural que los médicos y medicina sean los que tomen posesión de las enfermedades del ingenio, y que la terapéutica sumaria ceda el punto a una medicación instituida por nuestros comprofesores y no a practicantes (inteligentes quizá) que carecen de facultades." Dumont, *Investigación*, 69.

35. Matthew Ramsey, "Medical Power and Popular Medicine: Illegal Healers in Nineteenth-Century France," *Journal of Social History* 10, no. 4 (1977): 560–87.

36. Dumont, *Investigación*, 8; Laguerre, *Afro-Caribbean Folk Medicine*, 7.

37. Dumont, *Investigación*, 70; Laguerre, *Afro-Caribbean Folk Medicine*, 30.

38. Chambers and Gillespie, "Locality in the History of Science," 227.

39. Dipesh Chakrabarty, *Provincializing Europe: Postcolonial Thought and Historical Difference* (Princeton: Princeton University Press, 2000).

40. Dumont, *Antropología*, 6–30.

41. "Genoveva, negra lucumí, de 22 a 23 años de edad, llegada a la Habana hace tres años proximamente. Tiene un niño de seis a siete meses. Ha padecido enteritis, fiebres catarrales y resfriado." Dumont, *Antropología*, 27.

42. Kevin Yelvington, "The Invention of Africa in Latin America and the Caribbean: Political Discourse and Anthropological Praxis, 1920–1940," in *Afro-Atlantic Dialogues: Anthropology in the Diaspora*, ed. Kevin Yelvington (Santa Fe: School of American Research Press, 2006), 35–82.

43. See, for example, Fernando Ortiz, *Hampa afro-cubana: Los negros brujos (apun-*

tes para un estudio de etnología criminal) (Madrid: Editorial-América, 1917); Israel Castellanos, *Medicina legal y criminología afro-cubanas* (Havana: Molina y Cia, 1937).

44. "Las casas de los carabalís ricos son de madera y están amueblados con el mejor gusto. Los hijos de los carabalís pertenecientes a las familias elevadas, como los hijos de las familias europeas, hablan varias lenguas; la de su país y el inglés, el francés y el español." Dumont, *Antropología*, 36.

45. Dumont, *Antropología*, 50–66. This resonates with the work of J. Lorand Matory, who has argued that frequent crossings and interaction between Africans in Brazil and Africans in Africa throughout the nineteenth century constituted Brazilian Candomblé and kept it vital. See Matory, *Black Atlantic Religion: Tradition, Transnationalism and Matriarchy in the Afro-Brazilian Candomblé* (Princeton: Princeton University Press, 2005).

46. Staum, "Nature and Nurture in French Anthropology, 1859–1914."

4.

Atis Rezistans:

Gede and the Art of Vagabondaj

KATHERINE SMITH

This chapter begins on the Grand Rue, the main street of Port-au-Prince, Haiti. The Grand Rue stretches from the sprawling slums of Cité Soleil in the north to the city's lively necropolis in the south, a place inhabited by both spirits and transients. To the west lies the city's shoreline, a repository of history, spirit, and human waste. From the east side of the street, downtown distends toward the hills recalled in Haiti's popular proverb "Beyond the mountains, more mountains."[1] Amid the sensual dissonance of downtown, at a spot where mechanics ply their trade street-side, there is a courtyard where the artist André Eugene lives and shares a workspace with Frantz (Guyodo) Jacques and Jean-Hérard Céleur. These three artists form the core of a collective called Atis Rezistans, or Artists of Resistance. While the artists all have workshops of their own, Eugene describes this courtyard as a museum, and in practice it functions as much more.

Eugene's courtyard would be unremarkable if not for the proliferation of Vodou-inspired sculpture that inhabits it. For most of the neighbors that share the space, and for the artist himself, it is still an urban *lakou*, or compound. Meals are still cooked there, dominoes are played, children turn plastic bags into kites, and in an unoccupied corner someone has planted a small patch of beans and corn. Yet the industrial waste, the car parts and other First World debris that clog the rest of the city have been transformed into images of Vodou's cosmic recycler of life and death, the spirit Gede. There are other spirits represented as well, but it is Gede—master of all aspects of life's beginning and end, from ancestors and future progeny to sex and death—who takes center stage in Eugene's courtyard. Just beyond the shadows of the love hotels of the Grand Rue, with the cemetery over the horizon, there is a statue of Gede that looms taller than the other buildings on the block. Named after the chief of the Gede family, the statue titled *Bawon*[2] stands near the entrance of the

4.1 This sculpture of Bawon, who is closely related to Gede, stands just outside André Eugene's courtyard. Photo by the author, 2005.

4.2 The artist André Eugene with *Bawon*. Photo by the author, 2005.

lakou (figures 4.1 and 4.2). The body is made of welded pieces of recovered metal, with a head made of a large muffler. The *Bawon* smokes a pipe, as the spirit himself characteristically does upon "mounting" a bodily host. The statue features a wooden phallus attached to its steel frame by a shock coil, effectively rendering the appendage kinetic. On days when the neighboring women do the wash in the shadow of this towering monument to tumescence, the phallus is draped in clothes hung to dry. The statue has been there since 2002, and it no longer garners much attention from the neighbors unless an outsider is actively engaging the piece. But even this happens frequently enough that it attracts little attention.

Sometimes, when the artist sees fit, *Bawon* wears a Haitian flag, but rather than obscuring Gede's genitals, the flag is draped just below and behind them as if to serve as a backdrop for the impressive appendage. The *Bawon*'s salute to

Haitian nationalism is more than ironic, though humor is always relevant to a discussion of Gede. Eugene is demonstrating that Gede is the spirit closest to the Haitian people. But the question of how this spirit of *pèp la* (the people) is imagined is complex, at the very least because of Gede's overwhelming phallocentrism. In this chapter, I present my reading of Eugene's answer to this question. I assert that what emerges from his work is an idea of Gede that expresses an incarnation of masculinity that may be best described as the urban *vagabon*, or vagabond. I situate this transgressive masculinity historically, and trace two more sculptures of Gede. I begin, however, with introductions, first to the Atis Rezistans, then to Gede.

ATIS REZISTANS: AN URBAN ART COLLECTIVE

While Guyodo, Eugene, and Céleur are the core members of the Atis Rezistans collective, some neighbors have begun making sculpture as well. Eugene has encouraged this by teaching children the art of painting and assemblage in a group he calls Ti Moun Rezistans or Children's Resistance. Eugene and Céleur began their careers as artisans who worked in wood to create tourist souvenirs and kitchen goods for the domestic market. Céleur was the first in the area to begin carving pieces that parted from the conventions of the trade. Eugene joined him shortly thereafter. Guyodo, the youngest of the three, began training as an artist under the tutelage of Céleur.[3] Before Guyodo joined, the two artists had collaborated with Nasson and Mario Benjamin, two established Haitian artists who helped Atis Rezistans gain recognition. Barbara Prézeau-Stephenson, founder of the organization AfricAmerica, who arranged their first international exhibition, also promoted their work.[4]

It is important to understand the artists and their works as a collective because they live and work in close proximity to one another. This is a conscious choice on their part, and an effort that they see as part of a movement based in their community. The three artists have traveled and exhibited internationally, and in 2007 they were commissioned to create a piece for the International Slavery Museum in Liverpool. Despite this success, the artists choose to remain in their neighborhood. And I have heard repeatedly from the neighbors that their work is good because it brings in money and foreigners. The Atis Rezistans are taking garbage and making it live again, as each of them phrased it. In doing so, they are transforming their neighborhood. Guyodo envisions the place as a "garden of artists."[5]

While I stress that it is important to understand the artists as a collective, I will be focusing on the work of André Eugene in particular because his courtyard is an important hub of neighborhood activity and creative work. Also, while all the artists make images of Gede, Eugene has been dedicated to the spirit since he was born.[6] While he serves all the spirits, he clearly has a close affinity for Gede: "I like to work with Gede because no one can hide anything from him. When Gede appears, he exposes the truth."[7] It is not surprising, then, that the images he creates of Gede are poignant and prolific. Eugene's affinity for seditious tricksters extends to the human realm as well. The walls of his home feature photographs and news clippings of Karl Marx, Osama bin Laden, and Charlemagne Péralte, leader of the guerilla fighters who resisted the first United States occupation (1915–34).[8] Eugene, in fact, styles his carefully angled haircut after the latter. There is also a picture of the signing of the United States Constitution printed on velveteen. Eugene identifies all these images as influences, as portrayals of men who had a vision for the future and who broke laws to accomplish their goals.

Eugene was born in 1959 and, like the other two artists, he grew up in an area of the Grand Rue known as Ghetto Leanne. His home is modest in scale, but the ambiance and décor of the simple concrete structure can only be described as Gede baroque. He almost constantly hosts an assortment of neighbors, friends, children, artists, art collectors from uptown, foreign journalists, "adventure tourists," international art marketers, culture brokers, ethnographers, photographers, NGO workers and more. Everyone who enters must at some point bend, bow, or otherwise negotiate the protuberance of a phallus, a doll's head, a skull, or some other carefully placed aberrance. The sheer abundance of sculptures—all with faces of marble, plastic, or nails, eyes that glint from just beyond the ebb of the light—effects a dissonance of the senses. This orchestrated excess reflects the conditions of life itself in the city. But excess also describes Gede's dual appetite for death and fornication. Ultimately, Eugene presents an image of Gede that embodies the city in all its vivacity and decrepitude. As Céleur has said, "We are an artist collective, but we are artists of the city, too."[9]

Figures for the population of Haiti are usually given around 8.5 to 9 million, with an estimated one-fourth of the population residing in the capital, Port-au-Prince.[10] More than half of the city's population arrived in the last two decades, though its infrastructure was designed for a population of 200,000. But statistics are specious in a place where the nature of urban survival is peripatetic. As a friend once said of the city, "Not even God knows how many people live in Port-au-Prince."

The layout of Port-au-Prince is defined both by the grid of major boulevards and by the maze of makeshift homes and passageways between them. The city is a palimpsest of decay and development; rebar rusts at the unfinished ends of buildings whose concrete skins begin to crumble long before completion. But completion is a fallacious lens for viewing a city that is so clearly improvised—or, better put, *improvising*. Daily its denizens increase, expanding into the narrowing gangways, precariously piling cement on cement, and mounting labyrinths of corrugated tin up into the hills. Yet if there is more life here, then there is also more death. Eugene has said of his space, "This is an art museum, but it is also a cemetery in its own way."[11] Sometimes Port-au-Prince has the same feel. In a place crowded with so much life and death, it seems only fitting to speak of Gede as a spirit at home in the city.

WHO IS GEDE?

The images of Gede presented by Eugene in *Bawon* and other works may be shocking, but they are culturally intelligible. The sculpture employs a lexicon of symbols that most Haitians would recognize as referencing Gede. The artist has said, "For me, Gede symbolizes life and death."[12] Gede is commonly represented by the phallus, the skull, and the cross—the cross being a tomb, but also more generally the place where the world of the dead finds a place in the world of the living. In Vodou cosmology, these worlds are always coeval, suspended in mirrored communion above and below the ancestral waters. Maya Deren describes the immanent presence of the spiritual world in Vodou, "the metaphysical world of *les Invisibles* is not a vague, mystical notion; it is as a world within a cosmic mirror, peopled by the immortal reflections of all those who had ever confronted it."[13] Eugene made a similar point describing another sculpture: "Everything in the world below is the same as the world above."[14] That includes, of course, sex.

For Gede, the world begins and ends in the realm of the corporeal. He embodies a resolution to those seemingly intractable oppositions that power so much human creativity: sex and death, consumption and excretion. He is the nexus between the sexual reproduction of the individual body and the regeneration of the social body. By this I mean that in him lies the realization that the most base and pungent physical aspects of sexual reproduction are also the most fecund semantic generators. This is graphically performed when Gede possesses someone. As Eugene explains, "When Gede arrives he immediately pulls out his dick and shows you the symbol of life." Yet as the spirit who is best able to contravene the boundaries of the social and physical body, he is also a healer employed in the direst of circumstances. As Marilyn Houlberg has said, "Gede is the special guardian of infant children and the *lwa* (spirit) best able to help human beings avoid death."[15]

It is difficult to overstate the prominence Gede enjoys in Vodou, and more generally in Haitian popular culture. Gede is the most ubiquitous spirit of the pantheon because he is common to everyone. A temple may serve any combination of spirits, but it will always have a tomb for Gede, usually outside the peristyle. Likewise, every individual has a spirit that "rules" his or her head, but additionally, as the esteemed priestess Mama Lola said, "Some people got Ogou. Some got Papa Danbala . . . not everybody. But everybody got Gede. Everybody."[16] Or as another associate of Atis Rezistans, Claude Sentius, stated, "We are all Gede spirits. I am a Gede. It's a Gede that is speaking to you. I've already died, I just haven't been buried yet. When I die I will be a Gede and dance inside someone's head."[17]

Gede is a spirit associated with the family and ancestors, and by extension, the rural family compound, or lakou. The lakou is the locus of ritual service for Gede, with the family tomb (often more elaborate than the homes of the living) serving as an altar. But urbanization marks a radical restructuring of the lakou.[18] In the city, one may share the same space with other families, and the space may be rented rather than inherited.[19] Impermanent as it is, the urban lakou is hardly a fit repository for ancestors.

Instead, urban necropolises have become sites of devotion, prayer, magic, and partying. Fet Gede has become a holiday celebrated in public on a massive scale, rather than a private, family affair. In 2007 at Fet Gede in Port-au-Prince, I saw families quietly attending to their tombs; delegations of devotees from temples passing out coffee and bread; street children asking for alms; pilgrims on their own mystical missions; foreign and local photographers, videographers, and journalists vying for the best vantage point to observe the spectacle; market women selling libations, candles and cigarettes; showmen who eat glass, pierce their skin with needles, or hold burning embers; marauding bands of adherents possessed by Gede; and the onlookers who follow the spirit. Finally, there were bands of young men (although there are occasionally women, too) who sang lewd songs and generally *fe dezòd* (misbehaved). I saw one young man pounding on the tombs yelling, "Leve bouzen! Leve!" (Get up, whore! Get up!). Outside the cemetery, the streets filled with *bands à pieds*, and even the most dormant temples enlivened to celebrate and sacrifice goats and offer food to the poor.

Guyodo explained to me that the scene in the cemetery was "normal" for Gede: "Well, the reason why people call Gede a vagabon is because of the way he is when he arrives [when he possesses a person]. When Gede first comes he acts boldly, and some of them [Gedes] might go as far as hitting someone on the leg with a stick or even putting hot pepper in someone's eye. You can sometimes see in Carnival someone will be possessed with Gede. You will see this in the Raras [popular street bands],[20] that they become possessed with Gede. That is why they call it the 'vagabon religion.' "[21] Guyodo is describing a behavior of Gede that is direct and provocative. It is significant, however, that he labels Vodou as "the vagabon religion." On the one hand, the phrase would frame Vodou as almost carnivalesque. Yet this also acknowledges that the most public face of Vodou is Gede, and that the image presented is masculine and transgressive. In the following section, I examine another sculpture by Eugene that manifestly references the uniform of Duvalierist agents, but also reveals a historically situated and gendered concept of *vagabondaj*—a Creole term for vagrancy, but also more generally for misbehaving.

CHEF SEKSYON

In André Eugene's home and courtyard, the statues of Gede and his Vodou compatriots come and go. If a piece is not sold, or if Eugene tires of it, it is taken apart and turned into something else. One of the pieces that has remained in its place since I first met the artist in 2003 is a sculpture titled *Chef Seksyon* (Section chief; figures 4.3a and 4.3b). Upon entering Eugene's home, one is greeted by *Chef Seksyon*, who stands opposite the front door. The piece takes its name from the paramilitary force popularly known as the Tonton Makout under the two Duvalier dictatorships. Eugene is making an analogy between Bawon and the Makout: "Chef Seksyon under the Duvaliers was someone who was a chief of their community.... If you wanted to do something in that zone, you have to pass him. It's the same with Bawon Samdi in the cemetery, he's the chief." Bawon Samdi is the master of the dead, and therefore the spirit marshal of *zonbis*. Eugene is suggesting that negotiating with Bawon is a kind of clientelistic relationship with the dead. He signifies this linkage visually with a steel pan from the underside of a car, positioned on the *Chef*'s head to resemble a military officer's hat. The *Chef* also dons a scarf around his neck, which, as Eugene pointed out, resembles the uniforms of the Tonton Makout.

Gede and the state have been engaged in a mimetic pas de deux since at least the early twentieth century.[22] The intertwining of masculinity and Vodou reached its zenith, however, under the rule of François Duvalier (1957–71). The infamous "president for life" cultivated an image of father of the nation, thus earning the epithet "Papa Doc."[23] But his paternal image was complex and subtly employed the mythography of Vodou toward political ends.[24] That his dress and nasal voice bore a striking resemblance to Bawon Samdi was not lost on the majority of Haitians. While the Bawon is the head of the Gede family, he is not a vagabon. Chief arbitrator of zonbis, the Bawon can inspire dread. Duvalier, likely taking cues from the Bawon, created a paramilitary force that

 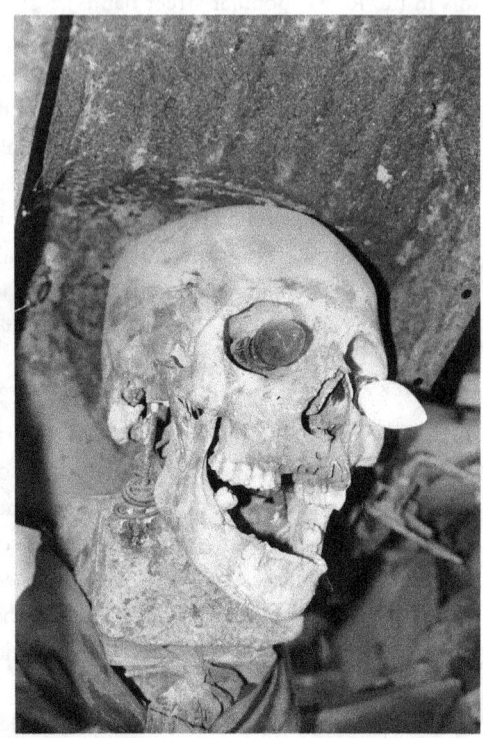

4.3A *Chef Seksyon* by André Eugene is an image of Gede that recalls, and recasts, the Duvalier era Tonton Macoutes. Photo by the author, 2005.

4.3B Detail of *Chef Seksyon* by André Eugene. Photo by the author, 2005.

appeared to raid Vodou's closet.[25] Regarding their standard-issue sunglasses, it is said that "the Tonton Macoutes took to wearing sunglasses in order to make peasants think they were zombies."[26] The implication was that Papa Doc was the controlling agent behind the Makout. But their dress had other Vodou associations as well. Their denim suits and neck scarves resembled the spirit Kouzin Zaka, who resides over agriculture. Zaka is closely related to Gede, and is the only other spirit who is said to be a vagabon. Certainly many Macoutes were engaged in vagabondaj. Yet the dress of the Tonton Makout also resembled a boogeyman of Haitian folklore, who was said to kidnap disobedient children and carry their diced remains in his knapsack (*makout*). Be they zonbis, boogeymen, or vagabons, the Makout enforced a regime of violence that was, in most respects, unprecedented in Haitian history for its intensity, duration, and penetration of civil society.

Jean-Claude Duvalier demonstrated similar totalitarian tendencies as his father, but he did not hold the same serious persona in the popular imagination. For example, it was rumored among the people that he was *masisi*, or gay, a term that is generally used pejoratively. In Vodou, masisi are associated with the lwa Ezili Freda, who is as stridently feminine as Gede is thoroughly boyish. Like Gede, Freda's hyper-gendered identity is not biologically determined. Freda is recognized by her stereotypical feminine proclivities, namely an insatiable appetite for fineries. In that sense, the younger Duvalier and his avaricious wife, Michèle Bennett, lived the Ezili lifestyle. It was not that corruption and graft were new, but that the spectacle of gratuitous consumption had reached a new level.[27] At a moment before the AIDS epidemic, when tourism was at its height, Haiti appeared to be a land of cocaine and champagne. It was an era of Ezili Freda—or at least it was for some.

For the vast majority of Haitians, little changed in the shadows of such resplendence. The graft did begin to take its toll on the economy, and in February 1986 the masses, emboldened by hunger, took to the streets and helped to topple the dynasty. Out of Duvalier's overthrow came a galvanized popular movement unlike anything seen since the early twentieth century, perhaps even the revolution. Yet this was only half the story. The old guard of Papa Doc's regime was not satisfied with the younger Duvalier's marriage or the lifestyle it entailed. As the historian and anthropologist Michel-Rolph Trouillot asserts, "What Haitians witnessed on February 7, 1986, was not the disorderly escape of an "entire leadership" pushed out by popular pressure ... but a transmission of power, orchestrated with absolute order—albeit against a backdrop of popular uprising."[28] The expulsion of Baby Doc was, in part, devised by Duvalierists, and so the era leading up to elections in 1990 came to be cynically referred to as "Duvalierism without the Duvaliers."[29]

Yet this era was not all *plus ça change*. Duvalierism was irreversibly destabilized, just not immediately. In Eugene's imaging of *Chef Seksyon*, then, the "military hat" is atop a human skull and a spine made of a camshaft, but the seriousness of bones and steel fortifiers is undermined by the Christmas tree lights in the eye sockets of the skull. One light is slightly askew and the jaw is disjointed, giving him an expression of grinning madness. The artist said of the piece, "It's a real skull. I put two lights in his eyes so he can see. He isn't dead though, he is in life, that's the reason he has the big *zozo*. He gives life always." In Creole, *zo* means "bone," and while words are often repeated for extra emphasis, in this case, *zozo* becomes slang for an erect penis. Eugene is referring to the industrial-sized exhaust pipe that juts three feet out from *Chef*'s body, a phallus that marries abundance and absurdity in its scale.

The phallus of *Chef* also has a lived presence in Eugene's home. First, there is the fact that it occupies a central, even awkward, position in what serves as the artist's living room. Every living body that enters the space must accommodate it. As an active part of the home, the phallus wears an ever-changing assortment of accessories. These appurtenances generate narratives of a certain lifestyle that may be described as vagabondaj. When I interviewed Eugene about the *Chef*, he leaned on the exhaust pipe, which was at the time bound with a rope, and explained:

> The zozo is tied with a rope because it gives too many problems.... This part is tied, but he may also use a condom. I can put a plastic sack on it for a condom. Sometimes I take it off and sometimes I tie it, and sometimes I untie it. An artist's oeuvre is never done for him. He is always improvising on things. Depends how I feel because a piece of work for an artist is never done. With the same materials [the artist] can create different things, he can create a diverse oeuvre with the same philosophy.

It should be noted that Eugene was laughing when he described the problems of the zozo and his attempts to rein it in. Yet he is also clearly making a link with the expressive and creative quality of the zozo and his role as an artist.

I asked Eugene why *Chef* was not wearing a condom, and he replied, "Now's the time for having sex *ann dezòd* (recklessly). Time to make children. When he doesn't make children he wears a condom. When the zozo stays hard though he has to tie it, to chain it." The term "ann dezòd" is significant because it is commonly used to describe the behavior of both Gede and vagabons. But Eugene pushes the humor and metaphor further when describing the singular, metal testicle of *Chef*: "You see Monsieur also has only one testicle [*grenn*],[30] a testicle that is like a grenade. . . . It's the same when you blow your load [ejaculate], there is a lot of small stuff that disperses." Eugene's analogy describes Gede's explosive sexuality in terms of a procreative bomb. The latent duality of creation and destruction in this analogy is particularly apposite, considering the population boom that stifles the city under so much vitality. Yet the image is also masculine and chaotic. There is a performative aspect to Eugene's description that demands a deeper reading. Specifically, with the image of *Chef* and his explanation of it, Eugene is making plain the linkage between Gede and the average man—or more to the point, the average vagabon.

VAGABONDAJ: HAITIAN DISCOURSES ON MISBEHAVING

Sitting outside a barbershop one afternoon, a friend explained to me, "Everyone engages in vagabondaj sometimes. Sometimes you feel good, maybe you have a little money and you get a friend and go out on the street and look for women." When he said this he was smiling broadly and leaning back with arms open wide, as if to suggest he was ready to *banbouche*, or party.[31] Often it seems that "vagabon" permeates every aspect of public discourse: from Carnival songs like "Vagabond 4 Life" to political commentary in *Le Nouvelliste*, the word has become ubiquitous. Young men are lauded as vagabons when dancing suggestively behind a Rara band, but the word is also spray painted on walls to deride a local politician or "big shot." Friends would use the word when discussing current events, especially the urban gangs that have flourished in the past decade.

It is clear that there is a deep uncertainty in the term. Its usage can be playful and sexual, but also menacing and derogatory. The vagabon is celebrated for flaunting authority in a country saddled with a long history of authoritarianism, yet the same disregard for social norms makes the vagabon an object of fear. The vagabon's transgressions may be humorous and liberating, or they may be violent and destructive. Haitians put it best with the proverb "Se ton an ki bay signifikasyon" (It's the tone that gives meaning). The word may be spat at a passing car, whispered under the breath when discussing a recent kidnapping, or used to cajole a disobedient child, but the tenor of its meaning is always contextual.

Despite the wide range of possible targets for the term, there are two defining characteristics of the vagabon. First, the vagabon does not respect the order of things. The word was repeatedly defined with the phrase "Li pa respekte prensip la" (He has no respect for etiquette, or literally, he doesn't respect the principle). The idea of the "the principle" is best summed up with the exchange performed outside the rural family compound or lakou. When an outsider approaches, he or she says, "Honor," and the host responds, "Respect."[32] This exchange exemplifies the dignified behavior that is considered normative, or at least ideal, in most of Haitian society. This is precisely what Eugene meant when he described the *Chef*'s unsafe sex practices as "reckless," or literally as "making disorder." He was indicating that Gede acts on his antisocial desires.

The second characteristic of the vagabon is his unambiguous masculinity. There is an aspect of public spectacle that marks the vagabon as male: most often one earns the moniker for doing in public what should be hidden in private. Public space may be gendered male and domestic space female, but in practice, of course, women engage in vagabondaj as well. But a woman is a *fanm vagabon*, or a woman vagabon; the term "vagabon" is therefore unmarked as male. The vagabon's aggressive sexuality is also something that would be accepted with a winking disapproval, as he would only be pushing normative gender roles to a playful extreme. I have only ever heard fanm vagabon used pejoratively, however, as synonymous with *bouzen* (whore) or *manman chyen* (bitch). The point is that the term, by being marked and unambiguously derogatory, demonstrates the inherently masculine quality of the vagabon. And this inherent characteristic is reflected in the Gede-Bawon family, in which the only female spirit, Gran Brijit, is secondary, elderly, and devoid of sexuality.

The Haitian vagabon is part of a larger identity matrix of African-Atlantic transgressive masculinities. The vagabon shares a polythetic resemblance to a host of labels applied to men who are generally poor, disenfranchised, and perform a sort of irreverence as resistance to propriety and respectability.[33] Thus in the vagabon one recognizes the style of the *malandro* (Brazil),[34] the trickiness and slackness of the rude boy (Jamaica),[35] the menace and envied coolness of the gangsta (United States),[36] the phallocentric braggadocio of the Trinidadian stickman,[37] the cunning of the Martiniquan *débrouillard*,[38] and the virility of *tíguere* street culture (Dominican Republic and Puerto Rico).[39] Even in the northern regions of the Atlantic, at the Boston Massacre of 1770, Crispus Attucks's compatriots were described as a "motley rabble of saucy boys, negroes and mulattoes, Irish Teagues, and outlandish Jack tars."[40] The point is that the vagabon is only one permutation of a broader complex of masculine identities that are intimately connected with the structures and strictures that both revile and define them. But the vagabon and his cohort are revered as antiheroes because they flaunt their exclusion.

In this sense, the identity matrix that I have described parallels the religious and spiritual complex of Afro-Atlantic tricksters. The category is broad and diverse, but it may be defined by a common marginality vis-à-vis mythical and social hierarchy. Tricksters, like the vagabon and his ilk, are defined by their position outside and against established order. Gede, for example, acts as an intermediary between life and death, but can do so only by going outside the prescribed role of respectability.[41] According to Robert Pelton, the trickster mediates the center to periphery by "means of a lie that is really a truth, a deception that is in fact a revelation and a conspiracy that should have been no secret."[42] In other words, the trickster's lies always undermine the discourse in which they are couched, in order to reveal a deeper, underlying truth. In societies where the state's "truth" and its constitutive silences have been maintained with violence and terror, the trickster can be revolutionary—hence the trickster is widely embraced as liberator and the vagabon is given more leeway than the average lout.

What, then, do the vagabon and the trickster reveal with lies and trickery? One answer could be found in unraveling the history in which they are bound. As E. Antonio de Moya has remarked on the tíguere, "The origins of this mostly transgressive culture in the Dominican Republic are probably related to a history of slavery, oppression and political instability, but few studies have been conducted in this regard."[43] Vagabondaj, in the sense of vagrancy, was, like the Trinidadian stickman, a form of "refusing to be the grist for the mill of colonial machinery."[44] The vagabon social type is common throughout the Afro-Atlantic in part because under the system of slavery, idleness was theft. Like the lie that reveals artifice, this act of theft undermined the tenets of slavery through the assertion of willfulness. The efficacy of vagrancy as a means of resistance was not lost on the colonial powers. Kate Ramsey notes that in Haiti, the legal regulation of Vodou and vagabondaj have often worked in tandem. As an example, she cites the 1931 memoir of Faustin Wirkus, *The White King of La Gonave*, who openly admitted that "whenever he needed manual labor for construction projects he would make arrests on charges of 'vagrancy' or 'spellmaking.'"[45]

The vagabon and his band of Afro-Caribbean rogues have therefore always been in opposition to officialdom, seeking power instead from acts of subversion and from the corroboration of pèp la.[46] It is my contention here, however, that the current age is characterized by a troubling of center-to-periphery modalities of power, especially when describing the relation of the state to the people. In the next section, I will begin with a sculpture by Eugene that is a departure from both *Bawon* and *Chef Seksyon* in its portrayal of Gede's phallus. The phallus here is used to comment on the state of the country in a moment of extreme political, social, and economic upheaval. In doing so, it troubles the distinction between social and semantic reproduction.

DR. ZOZO

In 2005, André Eugene created a sculpture titled *Dr. Zozo* (Dr. Boner; figures 4.4a and 4.4b).[47] It was a figurative piece that stood approximately five feet tall in the artist's courtyard. *Dr. Zozo*'s arching body was constructed of metal scrap: part of a car chassis for a spine, shock coils for ribs, with mattress springs clinging to his metal bones like veins. Eugene had dressed *Dr. Zozo* in used clothes of red and blue, the colors of the Haitian flag. Atop these scraps was a human skull covered in resin, made to resemble bones not yet cleaned by time. *Dr. Zozo*'s mouth was agape, seemingly grinning. He wore a stethoscope that extended from his skull to the head of a large wooden phallus. The phallus erected from the base of the sculpture, which was a child-sized coffin. Here

4.4A André Eugene created *Dr. Zozo*, a deeply ambivalent image of Gede, at a moment of heighted political instability. Photo by the author, 2005.

4.4B Detail of *Dr. Zozo* by André Eugene. Photo by the author, 2005.

was the namesake of the piece, an absurd, exaggerated penis that was being examined for a pulse. It appeared a sentient abnormality on the steel-boned corpse. The penis was further complicated by spikes that protruded from the underside of its head. This was Gede—vulgar, irreverent, grotesque, bawdy—but the addition of spikes negated the purpose of his regenerative font. It was an unprecedented image in Vodou, but for a brief time it became a recurrent theme in the work of the Atis Rezistans.

Speaking about nails in the penis of another piece, Eugene explained, "It is a zozo with power, with nails. The zozo has a power inside, it's the force it uses to create. If the zozo isn't hard, it can't create, it can't enter into the vagina. The nails have a force, too, that's why I put them there. It intensifies the sensation." While it is a graphic image, it is describing a concept of power that is accumulative.[48] The hardness of the penis is fortified in the strength of the nails. It is a concept of power that is essentially amoral, echoed in the proverb "Zozo a pa gen zorey" (The zozo doesn't have ears).

With the sculpture *Dr. Zozo*, however, the spikes take on another layer of meaning specific to the time when it was created. As Eugene explained to me in 2005, there were rumors that certain gangsters, mostly from Cité Soleil, were implanting spikes in their penises. This was at the peak of the kidnapping crisis, when Haitians of all socioeconomic strata were in terror of the newly established industry. The kidnappers were not common thugs, but a new breed of *djab* (devils). People perceived them to be criminal deportees returning from the United States. They were said to be implanting the spikes in order to facilitate in the transmission of HIV when they raped a woman. When I reacted to Eugene's story with some surprise, he said, "They learned it in the United States. They do that there, don't you know that?" With that very direct coda, the onus of vagabondaj, in its most malevolent and absurd form, was turned on the United States.

THE AGE OF VAGABONDAJ

The most dramatic transformation between the Duvalier era and the present one is that then the state used to have a monopoly on violence, whereas now it does not. While this democratization of violence has led a minority of Haitians to lament the days of dictatorship, it seems that the difference is not as much in the volume of violence as it is in the unpredictability of its source. When Haitians protest the conditions of insecurity afflicting the capital, they may be just as easily decrying the crimes of the police, the United Nations, gangs, or petty criminals.

Today, however, the faces behind the guns are typically younger than they were during the Duvalier era.[49] Many of these urban youth have ascended the ranks of power in their own right through ties to the drug trade or illicit alliances with state and elitist interests. For youth born in an era that is both post-factory and post-field, leaving the country presents the most viable alternative to survival by illicit means. The median age in Haiti is 18.5, meaning that most Haitians were actually born after the fall of Duvalier.[50] Haiti is a young nation, and Gede is a spirit closely associated with youth.

The phrase "age of vagabondaj" describes a shift in political significance of urban male youth of the popular class in the post-Aristide era. I realize that even the phrase "post-Aristide" is controversial, as the former president remains a divisive yet influential figure in Haitian politics. What seems less contentious is that when Aristide returned at the end of the coup in 1994, he was not the revolutionary who had been swept into office on a tide of radical democracy in 1990.[51] But it is beyond the scope of this chapter to debate whether Aristide became a demagogue or remained a radical reformer, victimized by imperial interests and duplicity.[52] Such approaches are not productive in that they focus on the personage to the exclusion of more systemic problems.

What is relevant, however, is the role of young men from urban centers in Haiti's turbulent struggle for democracy. Young, disenfranchised men have always been important to Aristide's power, as well as to the popular movement more generally.[53] Part of Aristide's initial popularity, and credibility, as the champion of the poor came from his work with the legions of street children of Port-au-Prince, most of them male.[54] These youths came to be known as "Aristide's boys," and they accompanied Aristide at nearly all of his public appearances leading up to the coup in 1991. In a move that had profound symbolic impact—appalling many of the elites and inspiring the disenfranchised majority—Aristide's boys were invited into the National Palace to sing at his first inauguration. Effectively, the most marginalized segment of society was ushered into the center of power to participate in a ceremony that would establish Haiti's first democratically elected leader. It would prove to be a moment as ephemeral as it was elated.

What Aristide accomplished in his two truncated terms was a very limited political enfranchisement of some members of this group. But this political re-centering was problematic in many ways, especially after his first term in office. While the performance at Aristide's inauguration was a profound symbolic gesture, Aristide, when confronted with the dual mechanisms of class and politics in Haiti and the interests and influences of the international community, ultimately capitalized on this power base by arming it. In the end, this strategy failed, not just for Aristide, but more devastatingly for the young men who were killed or imprisoned in the political crossfire. Under circumstances that may never be fully elucidated, Aristide left office on February 29, 2004, on a private plane contracted by American officials.[55] With the fallout of Aristide's demise begins what I term the "age of vagabondaj."

It must be stressed that this term is not pro-Aristide or anti-Aristide, as such thinking does not reflect the realities of how most people survive under conditions of extraordinary violence—not just the dramatic violence of guns and machetes, but also the more banal "structural violence" that casts a broader net.[56] All factions are guilty of what may be termed "vagabondaj" when used pejoratively. "Chimè" (chimera) became a buzzword to describe the pro-Aristide gangsters, but I have chosen to avoid the term because of its partisan associations. J. Christopher Kovats-Berat, for example, describes the vagabondaj of the two leaders of the anti-Aristide militia that took control of the north of the country in 2004: "Chamblain drank rum and danced in the streets that day with Guy Philippe."[57] In the end, the majority of people celebrated neither the demise of Aristide nor the victory of his opponents: "The people may not have embraced the opposition and rebel forces that ousted Aristide, but many of them did not believe that he was worth rescuing either—not because they no longer believed in what he once stood for, but because they could see that he had betrayed their trust and their interests to serve his own and his cronies."[58] The age of vagabondaj is characterized by such ambivalence.

While disillusionment and ambivalence characterize the attitude of pèp la toward the state, it is not necessarily a totalizing view. The notorious gangsters of Cité Soleil may be *vagabons extraordinaires*, but my visits there revealed that in addition to all the signs of chaos—such as United Nations tanks and bullet-pocked walls—small gardens had been planted in any available space.[59] These are small patches, often just a row of beans and a few stalks of corn, like the garden in the corner of Eugene's courtyard, but they highlight the fact that the young men who are blamed for so much of the current crisis are not without history. They are neither spatially nor temporally far removed from the mountains, but rather part of a larger trend of domestic diaspora, a segment of the population expelled from the ecological crisis afflicting the countryside.

The age of vagabondaj was preceded by the creation of ecological refugees and urbanization without industrialization, and it is marked by the mobilization of urban young men toward political ends and a popular disillusionment with democracy. All these tectonic social ruptures make the body vulnerable to both malnutrition and the ravages of infectious diseases. At the intersection of all these phenomena—the land, youth, masculinity, the body—one finds Gede.

GEDE AND THE AGE OF VAGABONDAJ

The role of young men in urban Haiti has always been one of contradiction: they are socially marginalized yet symbolically central.[60] Gede embodies this symbolic prominence as the spirit who is not only ubiquitous, but also perpetually young and unabashedly male. Yet, to a significant extent, the label "vagabon" has served to disenfranchise urban young men, blaming their lack of productivity on character and lifestyle rather than a class system built on their exclusion and exploitation. As Yelvington says of racial tensions in Trinidad, "The symbolization process was and is, in large part, monopolized by those who have had access to the 'symbolic capital' to perpetrate 'symbolic violence' against less-endowed groups."[61] In a perverse way, the myth of the vagabon's danger and virility exists in reverse proportion to their economic and political impotence. In the past two decades, the symbolic and economic positions of the "vagabon demographic" have only grown more extreme.

Given the current semantic and political terrain of masculinity, it becomes necessary to ask, what will become of Gede? André Eugene offers his perspective:

When technology advances, things begin to change, too. A long time ago in the Bible, it said not to come on the ground [to "waste your seed"] because there weren't many people. Now there's lots of people, so you have to wear a condom. You have to protect yourself against sickness, but also so you don't have too many children, because children can bring misery. In this neighborhood, people who have too many children have more misery. If Gede is the Chef Seksyon, he has to be able to check out these things. If technology advances, he goes that way, too.[62]

Yet the image that Eugene offers of a Gede who is au courant is profoundly dystopian. In *Chef Seksyon*, a condom may offer protection, but in *Dr. Zozo*, Gede comes to embody disease. It is a grotesque embodiment though, a contagion that is menacing and dangerous. Here technology is represented as the "spikes," but also as the stethoscope. His role as a doctor may also promise a cure.

Spirits are as subject to the vagaries of history as are their human counterparts, however, and it would be disingenuous to conclude by facilely pinning abstract hopes for the nation on Gede's regenerative potential. Gede is the embodiment of youth and masculinity, holding the promise of virility and renewal, but "young men" has proved a social and historical category that has been tenuously balanced in the crosshairs of both domestic and international powers in the Afro-Atlantic. And never more so than today, when "vagabon" has become an umbrella term for a tremendous segment of the population. The word's ubiquity is rivaled only by its ambiguity; it is in one moment embraced as freedom and in another shunned as threat.

Dr. Zozo is a shocking image of Gede, and I hasten to add that it is not a common one. The rumors about deportees and young men from Cité Soleil are not rumors about Gede, but they do represent a disturbing transformation in how the body is imagined. Where the rumors and Gede overlap is in the concept of vagabondaj, which I have argued is deeply ambivalent. We see this ambivalence in *Dr. Zozo* as the embodied disease, but also as the potential cure. In his portrayal of Gede, Eugene offers an indicator of what the grounds and means of survival will be. Undoubtedly vagabons will be agents of those means, but as *Dr. Zozo* demonstrates, vagabondaj is no longer merely a domestic affair, and likely never was.

Perhaps part of the message embodied in *Dr. Zozo* holds another kind of potential. What I have described as the festering abundance of urban Haiti has made for a fertile urban art scene. For the Atis Rezistans, trash has become the means of reflecting, critiquing, and re-imagining what I have described as the age of vagabondaj. But they are not alone in their creative endeavor. In Cité Soleil there are murals now for the first time since the late nineties. The traditional sequined flags, which had their genesis in Vodou temples, are experiencing a kind of renaissance. Their subjects, variety, and styles have expanded exponentially since the late nineties. There are also, for the first time, prominent women flag artists.[63]

While the international market consumes most of these artistic forms, other forms thrive in the domestic market. The affordability of digital media has resulted in a burgeoning of Haitian cinema. Most of the films are sold by young men who wander the streets and intersections of Port-au-Prince selling three-dollar DVDs from their backpacks. And while American hip-hop has always been popular in Haiti, it is now being produced locally in Creole by groups like Barikad Crew and Rock Fam.[64] Their lyrics can be obscene, and sometimes violent, but they are sung enthusiastically by youth all over the country and its diaspora. These lyrics become the anthem for an imperfect world.

The same can be said for the work of Atis Rezistans. The work is not pretty, but as the Creole expression has it, "Pito nou led, nou la" (Hey, we're ugly, but we're here). Haiti has survived slavery, revolutions, foreign occupations, military coups, insidious aid programs, and neoliberal structural adjustments. If its future at times appears implausible, it is no more so than its past. The courtyard of André Eugene is a small corner of a vast city, but it is a crossroads. Like the cemetery, it is a place where the dead cohabitate with the living. The image of Gede one finds there is an urban amalgamation that embodies a troubled history. It is, nonetheless, a sign of life.

NOTES

Support for fieldwork cited in this chapter came from the UCLA International Institute and the UCLA Fowler Museum Arnold Rubin Award. The chapter was written before the earthquake of January 2010. One member of the collective, Destimare Piene Isnèl (a.k.a. Louko), was killed in the earthquake and others were temporarily displaced. The collective continues to make politically charged art that draws on Vodou imagery.

1. "Dèyè mòn, gen mòn."

2. The Bawon is the head of the Gede family, though there are a number of different manifestations of him, such as Bawon Samdi (Baron Saturday), Bawon Lakwa (Baron of the Cross), and Bawon Simityè (Baron of the Cemetery). He is always ritually located in the cemetery at the tomb of the first man said to be buried there. His wife, Gran Brijit, is always situated at the first woman's tomb.

3. Guyodo left the collective in 2009, though he is still working in the neighborhood.

4. Barbara Prézeau-Stephenson, "Contemporary Art as Cultural Production in the Context of Haiti," *Small Axe* 27 (2008): 94–104.

5. *Atis Rezistans: Sculptors of the Grand Rue*, directed by Leah Gordon (London: Haiti Support Group, 2008), DVD (hereafter cited as *Atis Rezistans*).

6. Eugene stated that he was baptized in the hospital when he was born, but that it was Gede who really baptized him: "Gede came home with me from the hospital." André Eugene, interview with the author, July 5, 2007. Unless otherwise stated, quotations from André Eugene are from this interview.

7. *Atis Rezistans*.

8. For more on Charlemagne Péralte and the armed resistance to the United States occupation, see David Nicholls, *From Dessalines to Duvalier: Race, Colour and National Independence in Haiti* (New York: Cambridge University Press, 1979), 148–52.

9. *Atis Rezistans*.

10. Central Intelligence Agency, "CIA World Fact Book: Haiti," https://www.cia.gov/library/publications/the-world-factbook/geos/ha.html.

11. *Atis Rezistans*.

12. André Eugene, interview with the author, January 23, 2008.

13. Maya Deren, *Divine Horsemen: The Living Gods of Haiti* (New York: McPherson, 1953), 14. For a structural interpretation of symmetry in Vodou cosmography, see Karen McCarthy Brown, "The 'Veve' of Haitian Vodou: A Structural Analysis of Visual Imagery" (Ph.D. diss., Temple University, 1976).

14. André Eugene, interview with the author, July 5, 2007.

15. Marilyn Houlberg, "Magique Marasa: The Ritual Cosmos of Twins and Other Sacred Children," in *The Sacred Arts of Haitian Vodou*, ed. Donald J. Cosentino (Los Angeles: UCLA Fowler Museum of Cultural History, 1995), 280. Gede is described as a healer in most modern ethnographic literature on Vodou, though Maya Deren and then Karen McCarthy Brown recorded two remarkable examples. Deren described a ceremony where Gede is called on to heal a sick child. Using "seminal ejaculation" that he brings forth from the body of the woman he possessed, he cures a child, who miraculously survives. See Deren, *Divine Horsemen*, 114. Forty years later, Brown recalls that it was Gede who possessed Mama Lola when the daughter of the priestess was in the midst of a difficult childbirth. See Karen McCarthy Brown, *Mama Lola: A Vodou Priestess in Brooklyn* (Berkeley: University of California Press, 1991), 372. These examples demonstrate not only Gede's association with healing but also his special affinity for children.

16. Brown, *Mama Lola*, 362.

17. *Atis Rezistans*.

18. In *Mama Lola*, Karen McCarthy Brown describes the transformations of the family lakou in the context of an immigrant community. She likens Mama Lola's Brooklyn home and *ounfò* (Vodou temple) to a community center where recently arrived immigrants find information and resources. Yet, she notes, "participating in

ceremonies in her Brooklyn home ironically brought me close to a form of Vodou older than the form I had seen studying urban Haiti. It brought me closer to the family-style Vodou of the countryside where the patriarch of the extended family functions as priest and all those who serve the spirits under his tutelage are either blood kin or honorary members of the family" (9–10). See also Serge Larose, "The Haitian Lakou, Land, Family, and Ritual," in *Family and Kinship in Middle America and the Caribbean*, ed. Arnaud F. Marks and Rene A. Romer (Leiden: Royal Institute of Linguistics and Anthropology, 1975), 482–512.

19. The lakou is similar to the "yard" in Jamaica. Barry Chevannes describes the living space of the yard thus: "By 'yard' people refer to the space behind a fence and a gate, hidden and protected from public view where people are domiciled; where they cook, eat, sleep, relieve themselves, wash, bathe, and so on." *Learning to Be a Man* (Mona: University of the West Indies Press, 2001), 169.

20. Elizabeth McAlister, *Rara! Vodou, Power, and Performance in Haiti and Its Diaspora* (Berkeley: University of California Press, 2002). Discussing obscenity in popular discourse, McAlister perceptively observes that "when you are not permitted to say anything else, at least you can swear, drink, and sing vulgar songs" (61).

21. Frantz (Guyodo) Jacques, interview with the author, September 27, 2007.

22. Maya Deren (*Divine Horsemen*, 106) relates that during the Borno administration (1922–30), a group of Carnival revelers became possessed by Gede Nibo and marched through the gates of the National Palace to demand money. The scene caused such an embarrassment that the president is said to have paid them. Gede's triumph is remembered in the following song, which is still sung in Haiti today: "Papa Gede is a handsome guy / Gede Nibo is a guy / He is dressed all in black, / He is going up to the palace."

23. Elizabeth Abbott, *Haiti: The Duvaliers and Their Legacy* (New York: Touchstone, 1988), 59.

24. Michel Laguerre states that Francois Duvalier, like a few historical figures, became part of the Vodou pantheon. He notes a ceremony he witnessed in 1976: "I was surprised to see the priest dressed up to resemble Francois Duvalier—in a dark suit and black hat, wearing heavy reading glasses and holding a pistol in his right hand. He spoke with a nasal voice, imitating Francois Duvalier's speech." Laguerre goes on to explain that this is "*loa 22 os*," the mystical name given to the deified and deceased dictator. I have not found other examples that corroborate this, but the dress and manner of speech of "*loa 22 os*" also describes Gede's possession performance. Unfortunately, Laguerre does not identify the family of this "*loa 22 os*." Michel Laguerre, *Voodoo and Politics in Haiti* (Houndmills, United Kingdom: Macmillan, 1989), 118.

25. The Tonton Makout, as they were popularly called, were thugs who did Duvalier's bidding from the earliest phase of his regime. By 1958 they had gone from clandestine force to secret police, trading in their hoods for dark sunglasses. In 1962 Duvalier created a civil militia, the Volontaires de la Sécurité Nationale (VSN), which

he presented as an official version of the feared Macoutes. Thereafter VSN and Macoutes came to be used synonymously, at least in common parlance. See Michel-Rolph Trouillot, *Haiti: State against Nation* (New York: Monthly Review Press, 1990), 190.

26. Amy Wilentz, *The Rainy Season: Haiti since Duvalier* (New York: Simon and Schuster, 1990), 175.

27. As one example of the display made of consumption under the junior Duvalier, for his wedding Baby Doc spent a reported $7 million (much of it on the installation of televisions throughout the country so that the masses could witness the event). See ibid., 84–85.

28. Trouillot, *Haiti*, 225.

29. Ibid.

30. André Eugene is playing on words here. The Creole word for testicle is *grenn*, which sounds like *grennad*, or grenade. He pushes the jokes further by describing the moment of ejaculation as an "explosion." Interview with author, July 5, 2007.

31. Georges René, interview with the author, November 2007. The gesture he performed was reminiscent of the song and dance that was popular in Carnival in 2006, "Ouvri le Kò" (Open the body) by Raram. The song was massively popular during the protests against the stalled elections that were happening at the time. Flooding the streets with their bodies, people were calling for the interim government and the United Nations peacekeeping mission to open the way for the democratic election of René Préval.

32. Donald Cosentino references Gede's relationship to *l'honneur* when he writes, "Just as every character—political, military, or celestial—stripped of his pretenses is an avatar of Gede, so finally every motive, every action is reducible to *zozo*. Not *l'amoooour* . . . or *la vie* . . . or even *l'honneur*—only *zozo*." See "Envoi: The Gedes and Bawon Samdi," in Cosentino, *The Sacred Arts of Haitian Vodou*, 413.

33. I am borrowing from Sandra Barnes's use of the word "polythetic" to describe the inclusive principle that defines the Afro-Atlantic spirit Ogun. In the technical sense of the term, a polythetic definition is one that is not based on a single characteristic, but rather on a series of traits that may be combined differently. See *Africa's Ogun: Old World and New* (Bloomington: Indiana University Press, 1997), 13–14.

34. Bryan McCann, *Hello, Hello Brazil: Popular Music in the Making of Modern Brazil* (Durham: Duke University Press, 2004), 52–54.

35. On rude boy culture, see Obika Gray, *Radicalism and Social Change in Jamaica, 1960–1972* (Knoxville: University of Tennessee Press, 1991); Norman C. Stolzoff, *Wake the Town and Tell the People: Dancehall Culture in Jamaica* (Durham: Duke University Press, 2000); Garth White, "Rudie, Oh Rudie," *Caribbean Quarterly* 13, no. 3 (1967): 39–44. On "slackness" in Jamaican popular culture, see Carolyn Cooper, *Noises in the Blood: Orality, Gender, and the "Vulgar" Body of Jamaican Popular Culture* (London: Macmillan, 1993).

36. Tricia Rose, *Black Noise: Rap Music and Black Culture in Contemporary America* (Hanover, Conn.: Wesleyan University Press, 1994).

37. Gordon Rohlehr, "I Lawa: The Construction of Masculinity in Trinidad and Tobago Calypso," in *Interrogating Caribbean Masculinities: Theoretical and Empirical Analyses*, ed. Rhoda E. Reddock (Mona: University of the West Indies Press, 2004), 326–403.

38. Katherine E. Browne, *Creole Economics: Caribbean Cunning under the French Flag* (Austin: University of Texas Press, 2004).

39. E. Antonio de Moya, "Power Games and Masculinity in the Dominican Republic," in Reddock, *Interrogating Caribbean Masculinities*, 68–102; Lauren Derby, *The Dictator's Seduction: Politics and the Popular Imagination in the Dominican Republic in the Era of Trujillo* (Durham: Duke University Press, 2009).

40. Crispus Attucks, an African American, was the first person killed in the American Revolution. John Adams quoted in Peter Linebaugh, "All the Atlantic Mountains Shook." *Labour/Le Travail* 10 (Autumn 1982): 112.

41. For more on the relative position of the hero-trickster, see Donald J. Cosentino, "Midnight Charters: Musa Wo and Mende Myths of Chaos," in *Creativity of Power: Cosmology and Action in African Societies*, ed. W. Arens and Ivan Karp (Washington, D.C.: Smithsonian Institution Press, 1989), 30.

42. Robert Pelton, *The Trickster in West Africa: A Study in Mythic Ironies and Sacred Delights* (Berkeley: University of California Press), 79.

43. De Moya, "Power Games and Totalitarian Masculinity in the Dominican Republic," 79.

44. Kenneth Ramchand, "Calling All Dragons: The Crumbling of Caribbean Masculinity," in Reddock, *Interrogating Caribbean Masculinities*, 316.

45. Kate Ramsey, "Penalizing and Promoting 'Voodoo' in U.S.-Occupied Haiti, 1915–1934" (paper presented at the Obeah and Other Powers: The Politics of Caribbean Religion conference, Newcastle, United Kingdom, June 16–18, 2008).

46. Derby, *The Dictator's Seduction*, 292–94.

47. Dr. Zozo was created in 2005, but it did not last for long. By the time I returned the following year, André Eugene had dismantled it and used the pieces in new sculptures.

48. For comparative concepts about power and the aesthetics of assemblage among the Fon of Benin, see Susan Preston Blier, *African Vodun: Art, Psychology, and Power* (Chicago: University of Chicago Press, 1995).

49. Michel-Rolph Trouillot notes that in the weeks leading up to and immediately following his election, François Duvalier began using lumpen youth to intimidate political opposition. Many of these individuals would go onto the Tonton Makout. As Trouillot also argues, however, "the most original characteristic of Duvalierist violence, even before the taking of power, was the *extent of its social base.*" *Haiti*, 153.

50. Central Intelligence Agency, "CIA World Fact Book: Haiti," https://www.cia.gov/library/publications/the-world-factbook/geos/ha.html.

51. Aristide was still extremely popular when he returned to office in 1994; however, the "Paris Plan," the Clinton administration's agreement to return Aristide to Haiti,

compromised his radical political program and guaranteed amnesty to those behind the coup. Peter Hallward rightly contends that Aristide had little choice in these concessions, and that while the plan itself was moderate in many aspects, the international community respected none of its provisions intended to protect the Haitian economy. See *Damming the Flood: Haiti, Aristide, and the Politics of Containment* (London: Verso, 2007), 55–58.

52. I am referring here to the spate of at least seven books published between 2000 and 2007 about Aristide and his political party, Fanmi Lavalas. These vary as widely in their intellectual merit as they do in their political positions. One pole in this debate about Aristide's fate may be represented by Michael Deibert's *Notes from the Last Testament: The Struggle for Haiti* (New York: Seven Stories Press, 2005), which argues, often speciously, that Aristide held onto power through increasingly brutal and dictatorial means. Conversely, Hallward, in the more academically rigorous *Damming the Flood*, argues that Aristide remained a popular and radical leader targeted and sabotaged by elitist and imperialist interests.

53. Alex Dupuy describes the role of "professional and political organizations, workers' associations and trade unions, women's groups, religious and lay community organizations, neighborhood committees, and peasant organizations" in the movement for democracy following the fall of Duvalier in his book *The Prophet and the Power: Jean-Bertrand Aristide, the International Community, and Haiti* (Lanham, Md.: Rowman and Littlefield, 2007), 57–72.

54. Aristide's charitable works include the establishment of a large orphanage in Port-au-Prince, Lafanmi Selavi (The family is life). The orphanage was set on fire by Duvalierist militants in 1991, killing four young inhabitants, but was later reopened. See Christopher J. Kovats-Bernat, *Sleeping Rough in Port-au-Prince: An Ethnography of Street Children and Violence in Haiti* (Gainesville: University of Florida Press, 2008), chap. 5.

55. It is strongly held by Aristide and his supporters that he was kidnapped by the United States government. Officially, however, it was maintained by the interim government that he left office of his own volition on the eve of the impending fall of the capital to rebel groups, who had already taken control of the north of the country. Aristide returned to Haiti from exile in South Africa in March 2011.

56. Paul Farmer, *Pathologies of Power: Health, Human Rights, and the New War on the Poor* (Berkeley: University of California Press, 2003).

57. J. Christopher Kovats-Bernat, "Factional Terror, Paramilitarism and Civil War in Haiti: The View from Port-au-Prince, 1994–2004," *Anthropologica* 48, no. 1 (2006): 134.

58. Dupuy, *The Prophet and the Power*, 169. Hallward correctly argues that Aristide was, even in the turbulence of 2004, the most popular leader in Haitian politics (*Damming the Flood*, 200–77). What he does not fully acknowledge, however, is the larger trend of disillusionment and ambivalence toward all state politics. Hallward cites the 2006 election of the former Aristide protégé René Préval as evidence of this enduring popularity. Based on my own experience in Haiti at the time, however, I

would offer the counterargument that Préval's popularity at that time was based on opposition to the interim government and the United Nations occupying mission, and on the memory of his first administration (1996–2001) as a time of relative calm. For example, during Carnival in 2005 and 2006, I recorded no songs, performances, music videos, or visual manifestations that would indicate support for Aristide. The popular political discourse of those years was characterized instead by resistance to the interim government and the United Nations.

59. For many Haitians and foreigners, Cité Soleil is seen as the epicenter of the gang violence that has gripped the country over the past decade, despite the fact that crime exists in all levels of Haitian society.

60. Peter Stallybrass and Allon White, *The Politics and Poetics of Transgression* (Ithaca: Cornell University Press, 1986), 20.

61. Kevin Yelvington, "Introduction: Trinidad Ethnicity," *Trinidad Ethnicity*, edited by K. Yelvington (London: Macmillan, 1993), 10.

62. Interview with author, July 5, 2007.

63. Among the most prominent of these is Myrlande Constant, who pioneered the technique of solid beading. She says she learned this method in the wedding dress factory where she worked. When she was laid off in the early 1990s, she opened a workshop to create flags. She has since had several women apprentices who have gone on to become esteemed flag artists in their own right.

64. The obvious exception here is the hip-hop artist Wyclef Jean, who gained international acclaim as part of the group the Fugees. Later he started rapping in Creole on his first solo album, *The Carnival* (1997). In 2010, Jean attempted to run for president, but was disqualified by the electoral council due to his citizenship status.

PART II
Modernity and Tradition in the Making

5.

Slave Poison/Slave Medicine:

The Persistence of Obeah in Early Nineteenth-Century Martinique

JOHN SAVAGE

It is a little known fact of French literary history that perhaps the greatest author in the national canon, Victor Hugo, began his career as a writer with a story about an African sorcerer in the Caribbean. The protagonist of the novel *Bug-Jargal*, first written as a short story in 1819 when Hugo was just seventeen, specifically evoked the early events of the Haitian Revolution. A few years later, in the wake of the signing of the diplomatic accord that finally confirmed Haiti's independence, Hugo took advantage of the substantial public interest in the topic to rework his initial story as a novel that became a real commercial success. Literary critics continue to debate the political message of Hugo's story as it relates to slavery and abolition.[1]

What might be especially striking to scholars of Caribbean history, however, is the way Hugo referred to his protagonist with a term most often found in the English-speaking islands. Describing the slave Bug-Jargal, he wrote, "He inspired in [the other slaves] a sort of respectful fear which in no way resembled hostility: and when they saw him pass by their huts wearing his big pointed hat adorned with bells, on which he had traced strange shapes in red ink, they whispered low to each other: 'He's an obi!' "[2]

Of course, a short story written by a French schoolboy does not itself provide evidence of word usage in French islands like Guadeloupe and Martinique. But Hugo's reference does show that the French reading public would have been exposed to the term in the 1820s. And this is striking, since it appears to have been unknown in the francophone world during the seventeenth and eighteenth centuries. Indeed, in their consideration of the use of the word in the Caribbean, Jerome Handler and Kenneth Bilby concluded that "the term 'Obeah' was not employed—or only very minimally employed—outside the British Caribbean."[3] One might assume that Hugo himself simply lifted the word from English romantic literature of the period. After all, he had not traveled to the Caribbean, and in the years before he wrote his story England saw a wave of literary production specifically devoted to obeah.[4] But this explanation, focusing on the transmission of language from English to French metropolitan writers, is too narrowly European.

Further investigation suggests that Hugo's use of the term may well reflect a new usage in the French islands, perhaps resulting from the changing origins of African migration. Christopher Bongie has suggested that Hugo got the term, along with a number of others, from consulting an 1819 memoir of Caribbean life in the revolutionary era, which included a glossary of "terms commonly used in Saint Domingue."[5] This evidence is significant for historians of the circum-Caribbean because it demonstrates the mobility of the term "obeah" across political and cultural borders. More important, it reminds us of the term's malleability, the way it was used as a vessel to contain all sorts of different content. In the specific context of early nineteenth-century Martinique, France's largest remaining Caribbean colony, it was one term used to identify what was perceived as a new and devastating form of slave insurrection. In this chapter, I will explore the changing perception of African medical and spiritual practices in this specific place, in the extraordinary context of the period after the Haitian Revolution.

The term "obeah" does not appear systematically in Martinique, so its use should not be overstated. For the most part, it seems to have been used interchangeably with a general notion of sorcery. But it certainly does appear in documents produced in the French islands during this period. In 1819 a royal envoy, Baron Delamardelle, writing back to his superiors at the Ministry of the Navy and the Colonies, used the term when describing the shocking scourge of poisoning among the enslaved population. As in Hugo's *Bug-Jargal*, the administrator associates what he calls "obi" with an almost unfathomable blood lust. Basing his comments on conversations with various prominent planters, Delamardelle wrote that the problem was especially deep-rooted, since the "*obis* or *sorciers*" have such power over the slaves that they could bring them to kill what should be dearest to them, including their own children, close family members, and others of their own color: "This joy at the sight of their victims, this mutual congratulation and celebration before committing the crime, this unyielding refusal to reveal accomplices, this apparent calm while walking to the stake that has been prepared for them, this phrase repeated by those *nègres* who attend such executions, that 'so and so had a beautiful burial,' all of this shows how they are dominated by fanaticism."[6]

Delamardelle's understanding of the phenomenon was shaped by the island's governor, General François-Xavier Donzelot, who used the term "obi" but admitted that he himself had been unable to grasp the extent of the phenomenon upon assuming his post in 1818. "The events described were accompanied, for the most part," he explained, "with such bizarre circumstances, and supposed a perversity so extreme and often so gratuitous on the part of the accused, that for some time I had difficulty, I admit it, in believing in their reality."[7] For the most part, the "events" to which the governor was referring were tied to the rampant use of poison by enslaved people to kill or harm livestock, fellow slaves, and, on some occasions, white masters. The extreme difficulty of discovering the identity of the poisoners became an obsession for planters and Donzelot's major concern during his tenure as governor.[8] And indeed, the authorities came to see the "unyielding refusal to reveal accomplices" itself as the result of a kind of sorcery. Planters alleged that it was so hard to discover who was responsible because the poisoners were themselves controlled by a network of sorcerers, who guided their actions and then silenced their confessions by using a kind of sacred terror. It was not that planters reduced all mystical practices to the use of poison, but they saw poisoning outbreaks as controlled by an organized hierarchy of master sorcerers who were once removed from the offenders. In the words of Governor Donzelot, explaining his initial resistance to this view, "How could one easily accept that there is a society, a sect, that has leaders, recognizable symbols, sacramental oaths, a means of initiation, that is made up of individuals whose fraternal bond is the taste for crime itself?"[9]

The wave of poisonings that struck during the early years of the Restoration era (1815–30) in Martinique were therefore understood by most planters to be interrelated, the product of a concerted effort undertaken by an underground network of African sorcerers or black magicians, sometimes described as obis. They also occurred on a large scale, perhaps surpassing any comparable poisoning outbreaks identified in earlier periods around the Atlantic world. According to a report drafted in March 1827, over just the most recent five-year period poison was responsible for the death of some five thousand (presumably enslaved) "blacks," some eight thousand animals or livestock, and seventy-three whites.[10] The last statistic was the most disturbing to the planter elite, as it had commonly been believed in the eighteenth century that the poisonings commanded by African sorcerers would not target white masters.[11]

The evidence suggests, therefore, that the nature of poisoning crimes was shifting in the early nineteenth century, at precisely the moment the language of obeah was making inroads in Martinique. Indeed, beyond even the direct threat to white planters, the scale of the devastation came to be seen as a major challenge to the "survival of the colony," as several planters put it. The large number of dead livestock and murdered slaves masked an even broader economic effect of poisonings on plantations, where the loss of just a few slave laborers could hamper the complex chain of tasks that produced sugar, especially around harvest time. Poisoning deaths also created an atmosphere of extreme distrust across an entire *habitation* (plantation), and the laborious efforts to root out the guilty parties often magnified the losses to productive capacity. Beatings, torture, imprisonment in the dreaded *cachots*, or more minor restrictions on slaves had very real effects on the productivity of slave labor, as even the loss of a small number of workers for short periods of time could dramatically increase the pressure on those remaining. In a general way, the value of landed property itself was affected. "Plantations that suffer losses [from poison] are the least esteemed," wrote one planter, "since public opinion supposes that these crimes are committed by slaves that live on them and that if one wanted to sell them, no one would want to buy poisoners."[12]

In this same period, the French islands were also absorbing the effects of Louis XVIII's agreement to withdraw from the slave trade in 1818, as well as the increasingly competitive world sugar market. Given these pressures, the poisoning phenomenon exacerbated a sense of desperation among planters who saw the colony's very viability in doubt. All of this set the scene for an extraordinary wave of repressive violence, targeted at the poisoners and those sorcerers perceived to be controlling them. To this end, the early Restoration years saw the reconstitution of a system of martial courts first used in the eighteenth century that administered an intensive wave of judicial terror across the island in pursuit of those responsible for the poisonings. According to statistics of the Provostial Court, more than six hundred slaves were put to death and more than one thousand others were condemned to the galleys, forced labor, or deportation.[13]

In all, the early Restoration years witnessed nothing short of a full-blown crisis of authority in Martinique. In the historical literature, this period has most often been linked to the furor surrounding the publication of a tract demanding greater rights for free people of color. The so-called *affaire des hommes de couleur libres* led ultimately to the deportation of some fifteen hundred freedmen and women, a significant percentage of the total number on the island. Because the metropolitan backlash provoked by this case led directly to favorable legislation for free people of color by the early 1830s, historians have tended to focus on this story of rights-oriented freedmen pressing their demands. But the panicked overreaction of planters to these demands had much to do with the perception of a growing threat from African sorcerers, whose control over others was thought to extend even to the class of urban *gens de couleur libres*.[14]

MOBILITY, SOCIABILITY, AND THE MASTER'S CONTROL

Questions about the reasons for the apparent intensification of slave resistance using poisoning inevitably went to the African origins of mystical practices of the enslaved population. Officials charged with combating the poisoning phenomenon looked increasingly to any and all manner of African cultural practices that could be identified among the enslaved as potential factors in the crimes. In particular, healing practices came increasingly to be identified with malevolent witchcraft and poisoning, thereby undermining not only the survival of African spiritual practices but also the common medical practices used in plantation life.

It is true that similar concerns had appeared in earlier periods. In his research on pre-revolutionary Saint-Domingue, Yvan Debbasch found that some planters were already prepared to blame the widespread tolerance of African healing practices for outbreaks of poisoning. "Those who are guilty of the crime of poisoning and evil spells," wrote a planter in the 1750s, "started out with a few simple ones they think will cure some sickness.... Poison follows from this inevitably."[15] In fact, the medical role of the sorcerer was seen as the root of his power among the wider slave population. "Those people who call themselves poison doctors," as another planter put it, "take advantage of the knowledge they have of herbs and harmful substances ... in order to gain experience and make themselves feared and sought after by all the other blacks."[16] Planters came to see all African-born slaves as inherently dangerous. In Alexandre Moreau de Jonnès's view, "Among the Africans brought to America, there are perhaps a quarter who were sold following a judgment in which their compatriots found them to be sorcerers."[17]

Similarly, in Restoration-era Martinique, the perception was that it was this power over others that made master sorcerers especially fearsome and the crimes so difficult to prosecute. This control over the direct agents of the crimes was seen as absolute, leading not only to gruesome acts but also to extraordinarily complex subterfuges: "an evildoer, in order to avoid having suspicion fall upon him, starts by poisoning in his own *case*, either his wife, his mother, or his children; he pretends to grieve them," then goes on to poison others, after which he makes himself very sick, and so on.[18] Though the special knowledge of poisonous substances brought over from Africa made the crimes possible, the dissemination of these toxins throughout the island was a function of the slaves' extraordinary and increasing access to networks of exchange and communication, as well as their generally greater physical mobility than in previous periods. In fact, this was one of the principal differences with the pre-revolutionary period noted by contemporaries, and helps explain their increasing preoccupation with the incendiary potential of African spiritual and mystical practices in the early nineteenth century.

During the last phases of France's slave society, the enslaved population became more difficult to police because of this mobility. This was, in part, a function of the planters' increased reliance on slave provision grounds to provide food for the enslaved. For many slaves, marketing goods from the provision grounds became a minor source of income, connecting them to a commercial network that reached beyond the confines of the plantation.[19] This meant, in turn, that some slaves could purchase a few goods from itinerant peddlers. The latter sold a range of everyday items, from tobacco to candles, but generally also carried a variety of herbal cures or substances used to fill *mackandals* or *piailles*, the small pouches thought to have mystical powers. Around 1820, for example, Renouard de Sainte-Croix described large numbers of slaves wearing the piailles to protect themselves from snakebites and other misfortunes.[20]

In addition to plant-based substances, peddlers were known to distribute the small amounts of arsenic commonly used to combat rat infestations.[21] It is not surprising, therefore, that the peddlers came to be accused of playing a pivotal role in the poisoning conspiracies. One planter, for example, denounced "Maroon blacks, who peddle their poisons in all the plantations."[22] But rather than outlaw Maroons, the peddlers more often came from among the *esclaves patronnés*, the unofficially manumitted former slaves who lived and circulated relatively freely yet had no legal papers to prove their status. The growing numbers of this group made it increasingly difficult to monitor the whereabouts of the enslaved, thereby facilitating the short-term flight known as *petit marronage*.[23] According to a former magistrate, the esclaves patronnés were commonly known to "engage [either] in commerce and peddling in rural areas, or in the cultivation of little isolated plots of land. The first of these [two groups], by their ability to travel around the island, are the distributers of poison, and the others [are] its producers."[24]

Because officials saw peddlers as "for the most part, dangerous subjects, giving bad advice to the slaves and distributing poison to them," some forms of the practice were actually forbidden by decree of the Sovereign Council at the height of the poisoning scourge in 1819. Two years later, the ban was extended to the peddling of any kind of merchandise at all.[25] This legislation coincided with a broader effort to curb the free mobility of the enslaved population by imposing mandatory passes for slaves traveling on order of their owners. But like the ban on peddlers, such measures met with limited success, as the basic functioning of the plantation system had come to depend on the ability of slaves to act as messengers, to transport goods, to have their services and labor leased out to others, and to purchase and sell their own goods in local markets.[26] In fact, the paradoxical effect of banning peddlers in the short term, at least, seems to have been to increase the tendency for slaves to travel away from their home plantations, with or without the explicit permission of slave masters.[27]

There were similar unforeseen complications in the effort to ban the sale of arsenic from the small network of pharmacies found around the island. There were six pharmacies in the town of Saint-Pierre alone, seven more in Fort Royal and Lamentin, the two other larger towns, and six described as being scattered "in the countryside." In 1823, Governor Donzelot declared the need to review the entire set of regulations that applied to pharmacists, given that most were badly outdated or simply ignored. The council devoted a whole section of the regulations to the sale of arsenic. But poisoning cases in later years continued to name it as one of the likely substances used in the crimes, and the council's periodic promulgation of similar measures suggests that the regulations were largely ignored.[28] In the same period, the council banned free people of color from the profession and instituted a requirement that pharmacists had to pass an examination set by local officials, even if they had already obtained the academic degree demanded in France.[29] The requirement suggests how much planters saw the medical realities of colonial life as being fundamentally different from those in the metropole, a point made relentlessly in the correspondence relating to the epidemic of poisoning outbreaks, for example.

The relationship between a social environment in which physical mobility was possible, or even common, for slaves and the prevailing modes of health and medical care is best illustrated by the phenomenon of the so-called *associations serviles*. These associations of enslaved people, which began in the last decade of the seventeenth century as dance clubs, became identified with particular African "national" or ethnic identities. As Yvan Debbasch explains, "A flag indicated that a certain group was made up of *caplaoüs* or of *ibos*, who were also recognizable due to their costumes and musical instruments."[30] The high degree of organization and hierarchy in these groups was attested to by the naming of kings, queens, viceroys, masters of ceremonies, and ladies in waiting, as well as treasurers to collect dues from members. As many as seventeen such clubs proliferated in Fort Royal by 1830, perhaps more in Saint-

Pierre. In addition to being dance or social clubs and a kind of mutual aid society, the associations serviles were best known for their role in organizing religious services when members died. In fact, in later years the groups were less often identified in terms of their respective "nation" and referred to as *convois*, meaning the procession or assembly brought together for funeral services.

Not surprisingly, this mixture of claiming African identities and performing religious functions led many planters to suspect the groups to be a front for a society of sorcerers and poisoners. The threat here was especially the way these social networks pervaded the island, tying together slaves and freedmen in far-flung towns and isolated plantations. As we have seen, for many planters, the underground network of sorcerers was the true enemy of their authority. And planters often described this network in terms that directly recalled the associations serviles. As one planter who later presided over a martial court organized to combat the poisoning threat put it, these were true "societies, [with] leaders, secret signs and passwords, initiation rituals and ranks. . . . In a word, it is a special masonry dedicated to poison."[31] Indeed, what is perhaps most striking is how many of these associations managed to survive the most repressive crackdowns against poisoning. Later on, they even became a vehicle for the Orléanist government's plans for a kind of apprenticeship system based on the British model. In fact, with the decline of the African slave trade in the nineteenth century, the groupings by ethnicity or nation came to have little meaning.[32] Still, the example of the associations serviles illustrates how planters saw African medical and spiritual practices as inextricably tied to poisoning and witchcraft. As the same prominent planter put it in 1829, "The evil is less in the acts of the guilty that we expose than in the existence of societies that the guilty are part of. It is in vain that we punish the poisoners; as long as these societies exist, there will be poisoning. It is less important to punish the guilty, who often only turned to crime because of these deathly societies."[33]

This evidence can serve to qualify the notion that malevolent witchcraft and poisoning had their origins in particular African ethnic groupings, which has gained acceptance among some scholars. Though in comparative terms Martinique was a relatively creolized slave society, and one with an exceptionally large free population of color (which surpassed the number of whites on the island by 1815), there was indeed a shift in origins of newly enslaved Africans there starting in the late 1790s. Just as it has been argued that a uniquely Dahomean influence accounted for the development of Vodou in Saint-Domingue,[34] the increasing proportion of Igbo among the newly enslaved in Martinique could be a factor in the new concern over obeah after 1800.[35]

There is evidence that the Igbo were considered less desirable as an ethnic group for slave owners, and that Martinique's planters had to settle for them given the island's inability to attract larger shipments of slaves. On the other hand, large-scale migration from Biafran ports was by no means a new phenomenon at the end of the eighteenth century. In particular, slaves identified as Igbo were common in Barbados, Jamaica, and other English-speaking islands. While these were, indeed, places where the word "obeah" became commonplace, acts of poisoning were not nearly so common. Even in Virginia, where Douglas Chambers has argued that Igbo migration led to instances of poisoning, the scale of the crimes was small compared to what planters claimed was occurring in Martinique during the early Restoration period.[36] And the well-documented case of a shipload of Igbos, seized by Martinique's colonial council as part of the illegal trade at the height of the poisoning scare, reveals no particular concerns about the group's proclivity for such crimes.[37] To take another comparative perspective, though the proportion of creoles among the enslaved was substantially lower in Guadeloupe than in Martinique throughout this period, it was in Martinique rather than Guadeloupe that planters saw a network of subversive obis leading an effort to overthrow white authority. One source even argues strongly that there was no poison in Guadeloupe during the same period that it was decimating Martinique.[38]

In other words, while the presence of the Igbo in larger numbers may help account for the semantic shift to a new usage in French-speaking colonies, the varied phenomena associated with obi were undergoing a transformation that went beyond the original African meanings of the term or its antecedents.[39] The important work of Maarit Forde and Lara Putnam in this book further undermine the notion that "obeah practices," however defined, declined in direct proportion to creolization. Let us be clear that the notion that slave-criminals were put up to acts of betrayal by other, unseen, masters was an essential part of how *planters* understood African sorcery in the early nineteenth century. But the conflation of all aspects of obeah with its most radically malevolent forms cannot simply be explained through a demographic shift in the origins of slaves. Rather, the fact that virtually any reference to "sacred science" immediately raised an association with acts of poisoning represents a dramatic cultural shift.

What is most striking is that court records, planter diaries, and public tracts repeatedly described those accused of administering poison not as marginal African sorcerers at all, but rather as the slaves most likely to have intimate contact with white planter families—that is, their most trusted and devoted servants. In the Restoration period, white planters increasingly argued that

African-born sorcerers used their spiritual authority over the largely creole-born slave elite—"the overseers, sugar refiners, livestock herders, chambermaids, and children's nurses," as the governor described the likely poisoners.[40] Hence the intensification of concern and anxiety over African mystical practices in Martinique coincided with a pervasive anxiety over imminent acts of betrayal by the most "trustworthy" slaves. In this way, white views of obeah effectively acted to reinforce the separation of the races, precisely at a time when a growing population of free people of color was seeking greater acceptance and access to rights.

While the traceable national origins of African slaves may be overstated in some scholarship,[41] the tendency to characterize slaves according to their European "nation" was very real and consistent over time. The association between "French Negroes" and recalcitrant, criminal, or subversive behavior is well documented in both the British Caribbean and the mainland. Such slaves were often linked to mystical African medical and spiritual practices and sometimes seen to exert an ominous power over those around them. There is at least anecdotal evidence that poisoning incidents in the British islands or in colonial North America could be traced to French-speaking blacks living in those places.[42] But the perceived character traits of French-speaking residents of English-speaking Atlantic colonies likely tell us at least as much about pervasive anxieties generated by the Haitian and French Revolutions, and perhaps views of Catholicism and "Latin" cultures, as they tell us about any particular African group.

ENLIGHTENED OPINION AND THE BODIES OF SLAVES

Though planters in Martinique sometimes seemed to speak with one voice when it came to the evils of poison and the origins of the threat, a few dissenting voices could also be heard. In fact, the records of the island's governing council going back to the late seventeenth century show that several members expressed serious reservations about the idea that complex conspiracies were behind the poisoning deaths.[43] In Saint-Domingue as well, a few metropolitan visitors and some medical practitioners became convinced that fear and ignorance drove the common assumptions that planters held about poison. As far back as 1775, a Dr. Jean de Laborde penned a report titled "Effets dangereux de l'erreur et de superstition dans les colonies françaises de l'Amérique" (Dangerous effects of error and superstition in the French colonies of America), in which he argued that planters were mainly guided by prejudice and were mistaken in their diagnosis of poison. Most often, he concluded, what they assumed to be poison was nothing more than a form of cholera.[44]

Laborde was not alone in his skepticism. In 1780, a doctor in Guadeloupe expounded on the psychological dynamic behind accusations of poisoning: "He who has losses, even if it's someone of education and intelligence, is struck to the point of losing all hope. As the spirit weakens, reason is eclipsed, and the man gives himself over to vulgar prejudice, able to see nothing other than poison."[45] In this logic, the stress of perennially holding off angry metropolitan creditors and the looming threat of losing a whole plantation enterprise led planters to see conspiracies among the slaves where there were none. A few years later, a group of concerned doctors created an organization designed to combat such pervasive views of poisoning, African mysticism, and other medical disinformation. In Saint-Domingue, the Cercle des Philadelphes du Cap-François published its research on the question in 1788, openly challenging the planter elite to recognize its own superstitions by detailing the pattern of epizootic livestock disease over the previous quarter century.[46]

One member of the circle made a particular point of the lack of competent medical practitioners in the colonies. In general, he wrote in 1791, there were so many "doctors" practicing without any kind of proper credentials that the local prosecutor "preferred to let the abuse go on peacefully rather than make a splash about it."[47] This point seems particularly well supported by other sources. In 1816, Moreau de Jonnès wrote that "it is not rare in the islands to see adventurers taking on the title of doctor of medicine and providing their services to all comers."[48] As Yvan Debbasch has shown, with qualified medical men being so few and far between, surgeons (*petit chirurgiens*) were far easier, and also cheaper, to summon to rural areas than were medical doctors: "One must be able to preserve a cadaver sometimes two or three days, sometimes even longer depending on the distance, the season and the elements, in a country where extreme putrefaction is most often an affair of a few hours. One must then be able to read this cadaver after this interval of two or three or more days, when there has been time for the putrefaction to disfigure all things [so] that it's no longer possible to recognize anything."[49] In the absence of accurate medical knowledge, and given the difficulty of conducting serious autopsies posed by travel distance and climate, surgeons were under great pressure to confirm what was already often the common belief or expectation on the plantation in question. It was also a diagnosis that confirmed the importance of the surgeon's own medical role. Pierre Pluchon has written that surgeons tried to make themselves seem indispensable to great planter clans and often married into them.[50] Because of this, the social dimension of the surgeons' ties to planter families is an essential context for understanding the evolution of medical practices.

The medical examination of a dead body was important in large part because the report was a critical part of any criminal prosecution for poisoning or other forms of homicide. Assumptions about mystical African practices could therefore shape colonial medical policies in unexpected ways. The colonial council passed an ordinance in 1749 requiring the examination of the corpus delicti, and another in 1757 requiring that the examination be performed gratis. Through the last decades of the century, however, council members decried the fact that surgeons insisted on payment. As a result, planters apparently used almost anyone to fill the nominal function of *chirurgien*. Referring to the papers of an eighteenth-century planter of Saint-Domingue, Debbasch describes "a *sieur Magré* whom he refers to as his surgeon, but who cannot in any way justify this quality, and who seems for that matter to be of a profound ignorance in the surgical arts."[51] In Martinique, a leading planter lamented that "our surgeons find themselves embarrassed on the diseases of the poisoned blacks, about which they know nothing. It may be their fault and it is likely that this pretext often serves to cover up their ignorance."[52] Most striking of all is the evidence that many of the ad hoc surgeons planters employed to conduct post-mortem examinations were, in fact, slaves. Geneviève Léti argues, further, that this choice was not purely one made out of demographic necessity, but that it also came out of a widespread belief in the special power of some slaves to read afflicted bodies for signs of disease, poison, or sorcery.[53]

In fact, the untrained nature of most medical personnel is one reason the local population remained so attached to slave *guérisseurs* (healers) and resistant to more professionalized medical care. Doctors and surgeons themselves were commonly known to use some popular, plant-based remedies, despite official bans on such practices as forms of "black magic." It appears that the integration of African herbal remedies and other medical practices came especially through the female figure of the *hospitalière*, who acted as informal nurse and midwife, assisting visiting doctors and surgeons.[54] Especially common, for example, was the use of lemon rubs and immersions to heal the victims of yellow fever.[55] Every great planter household had its known remedies for certain ills that often came to be used around the island, whether they consisted of ingesting certain plants that had narcotic effects, often preserved in the ubiquitous tafia, or rubbing others directly on the body. One specific example, the so-called *purgatif Leroy*, became the island's most popular cure-all, as it was thought to purify the body of all toxic substances. In general, such purgatives were the most common means of combating attempted poisonings.[56]

The Cercle des Philadelphes of Saint Domingue was but one example of reform-minded associations that analyzed and publicized statistical information recorded by state ministries, part of a wave of Enlightenment-era intellectual sociability that began to challenge the more superstitious planter attitudes. A number of scholars have pointed to such writings as evidence of the decline of the influence of African mysticism in the Caribbean colonies and the rise of modernizing hygienist discourses at the end of the eighteenth century.[57] Others have seen this as largely a question of class, a clear indication of the gap between *grands blancs* and *petits blancs* attitudes.[58] In addition to African mysticism, enlightened reformers often saw the influence of Catholicism as contributing to the superstitious beliefs of the enslaved. The records of a 1755 trial in Martinique, for example, detailed the composition of the amulets worn by slaves, which included "incense and holy water, small crucifixes and . . . almost always holy bread from Christmas or another holy day, and wax from the great Easter candle." Some even saw Jesuit influence in the slaves' insistence on resorting to poisons.[59]

At the same time, however, it is important to emphasize that Enlightenment writings could be used to serve many ends, and diverse audiences creatively appropriated them in the pre-revolutionary period. Malick Ghachem has gone so far as to describe a "dialectic of colonial Enlightenment," in which the ideas of canonical authors were put to the service of planter ideology.[60] Further, as Sean Quinlan has shown, much of medical writing in the eighteenth century was devoted to explaining "the inherent morbid otherness" and "degenerate constitution" of the African body.[61] In this literature, physicians posited that the great vulnerability of Europeans to disease in the tropics was especially a function of the individual's inability to mediate between the exogenous and endogamous factors of illness. The "animal" ecology of the islands included, in the leading medical writings of the period, the effects of living in close physical proximity to African slaves. Planters, it was thought, would be susceptible to tropical diseases in proportion to their lack of self-discipline, in terms of both bodily hygiene and sexual restraint.

For example, in one case study, a doctor described a patient's relapse into a malignant fever, explaining that the patient had confessed to him that he had "caressed a Negress" the previous night.[62] But the need to limit and mediate contact with the enslaved went beyond admonishing planters not to pursue slave mistresses. Another doctor "noted that the patient had violated his 'curative method' by taking wine from a 'Negress' on three separate occasions." The obvious link to deadly disease was made explicit by Dr. Bertin, who warned that "blacks should be kept out of the household, lest they try to poison their masters."[63] In this perspective, purgatives were necessary not only when acute poisoning symptoms were observed, but also as an almost daily tonic to guard against the effects of contact with the enslaved. This contact was thought to accelerate the effects of extended immersion in the tropical climate, namely, the decay of the otherwise rigorous and superior European body. Creolization, in this view, was a medical and physiological process, not just a cultural one. This physiological change, from "taut fibers" to loose ones, and from balanced to bilious internal organs, both reflected and caused the individual's moral decadence.

For their part, the enslaved were marked above all else by their physiological degradation. While some medical or biological writing ascribed this condition to the institution of slavery, and most saw it as inherent to their race, all agreed on the connection between physical pathology and moral decadence. Yet where Europeans could triumph over tropical pathogens through an ordering of the self, by following the dictates of modernizing hygienist discourses, the persistence of African medical and spiritual practices demonstrated the inability of the enslaved to live as autonomous, sovereign individuals. The problem, of course, was that by the end of the eighteenth century, the creolization of the population meant that many slaves no longer had direct links to such practices. It was here that the all-controlling master sorcerer played such a crucial part. This is why the use of the African term "obi" may reflect the need for a more complex notion of sorcery than was recognized in the eighteenth century. If even the most trusted and devoted of slaves, those known to be honest, hard working, and churchgoing, were subject to the power of the obis, it simply reinforced the idea at the foundation of the slave system: that people of African descent were not capable of the kind of individual self-control that could protect them from the harmful effects of life in the tropics. The repeated waves of poisoning crimes confirmed this lack of restraint. Time after time, in situations that clearly suggested the presence of disease, or even poor nutrition or the harmful impact of extreme climactic or environmental conditions, planters chose instead to believe that fatalities were the product of willful acts of malevolent mysticism.

SORCERY AND RESISTANCE

Writing in his diary in July 1824, the prominent planter Pierre Dessalles left us a firsthand account of how a poisoning case was first recognized, and the type of response it could provoke. Learning of the death of one of his mules, Dessalles first called on his "veterinarian" to examine the corpse:

We opened the cadaver, and all the incontrovertible evidence was revealed. The part that had suffered most was the stomach.... I had it put in some tafia.... That evening I gave forty lashes to the head mule driver. I warned the workers ... that each of them would get the same punishment every time an animal died. I announced to a meeting of the whole *atelier*, that starting next Saturday, they would not get their Saturday or their Sunday off, and that all blacks, regardless of who they were, would be fed, but they would not be allowed into their huts except to sleep, [and] that things would go back to normal when, through their work, they will have paid for the poisoned animals. I counseled patience and obedience. All were submissive, sobered and attentive; it would be impossible for me to point to a guilty party, but it is necessary to show firmness.[64]

Dessalles's insistence on the need for a "firm" response extended to delivering those slaves denounced as poisoners to the martial court for summary execution, even when they were among his most faithful servants. Years later, the reformist colonial doctor Rufz de Lavison explained that the appearance of lesions on internal organs was often caused by yellow fever, and could help explain the prevalence of the poison diagnosis. Far more important than the fevers, according to Dr. Rufz, however, was a planter mentality in which misfortunes were almost invariably perceived as resulting from the malevolent actions of slaves. If immediate evidence of the crimes was not available, it was all the more reason for them to embrace the idea that sorcery, conjuring, or other mystical practices had caused the state of affairs. "A planter who has just purchased twenty or so blacks suddenly loses ten or twelve; instead of blaming the changes in their life, the inability to acclimate, he says to himself, 'I've got poison on my plantation,' and that explains it all."[65]

Dr. Rufz's investigation went on to suggest that patterns of epizootic livestock disease, along with dysentery, cholera, yellow fever, and other afflictions, could explain the vast majority of losses planters ascribed to poison. Having served as a member of one of the martial courts organized to combat the crime, the doctor had been struck by the flimsiness of the evidence presented, and the way that deaths that recalled dysentery or cholera were quickly assumed to result from slave poisoning. He also performed extensive experiments that cast serious doubt on the supposed harmful potential of many of those substances thought to be used by slaves to poison livestock or human victims. His investigations attempted to demonstrate that the extent and scale of the assumed crimes went far beyond what was possible given the limited availability of toxic substances on the island, from arsenic to *mancenillier*. Instead, Rufz de Lavison argued that poor supply lines from Europe made livestock populations susceptible to epizootic disease, and that poor nutrition was a significant factor in the high rates of slave mortality. Yet all around, belief in poison persisted and seemed to be supported by the tendency for some accused criminals to admit their guilt, complete with sordid details of the crime.[66]

There is much evidence to corroborate Rufz's assertions from medical writers of the period. Like his eighteenth-century forebears, Moreau de Jonnès contrasted the hardiness of flora and fauna originating in Africa with their European counterparts, noting the rapid muscular deterioration of European quadrupeds on the islands and their vulnerability to epizootic disease.[67] Moreau also took up the idea that climate played a central role in the spread of disease, especially associating the rainy period known as *l'hivernage* with the outbreak of a variety of epidemics.[68] In fact, Moreau would go so far as to argue that a population's death rates in any country could be derived from the effects of climate. This emphasis on environmental factors would seem to at least provide an alternative to the insistence that high death rates among livestock, for example, were principally caused by acts of poisoning committed by slaves.

It is also striking how the wave of intensive poisoning activity of the early 1820s seems to coincide with unusually lethal outbreaks of yellow fever. Nearly seven hundred deaths were attributed to the disease in 1821, nearly fifteen hundred in 1825, and more than four hundred in two other years in the period, with a far higher proportion of those afflicted succumbing to the disease than at previous times.[69] And while whites commonly believed that contagious diseases were especially prevalent during the rainy season, they also saw l'hivernage as a period of vulnerability to poisoning.[70] "It is always during the season of *l'hivernage* that plots are revealed," wrote the governor following a slave uprising in 1822.[71] A colonial doctor concurred, though he framed it a bit differently: "It is during the time of epidemics that they usually choose to exercise their crimes most freely."[72]

In both cases, the coincidence of acts of malevolent conjuring or sorcery and seasonal or climatic shifts could be used to explain heightened mortality rates. Just as the African population was assimilated to the "animal" environment of the tropics in eighteenth-century medical accounts, acts of malevolent witchcraft were described in this period as analogous to forces of nature. In a sense, poisoning was depicted as being a toxin endemic to the tropical environment, just as hurricanes characterized the climate at certain times of the year. As one planter later put it, "yellow fever is simply a poisoning caused by harmful miasmas that we breathe in" during the rainy season.[73] What is especially striking is a similar passage from the era's most prominent abolitionist figure, Victor Schoelcher, who described poison as "a sickness of slave countries, it is in the air, servitude has invested the atmosphere of the colonies, just as pestilential miasmas invest it with yellow fever."[74] As Moreau de Jonnès's writings already suggest, there was no easy distinction here between Enlightened medical writers and superstitious planters when it came to poison. Rather, the persistence of malevolent witchcraft and acts of poisoning were seen as symptoms of the deeply insalubrious tropical environment. They were also seen by most whites as the direct causes of the medical pathologies of plantation life.

Geneviève Léti remarks that "the magical dimension is *indissociable*" from the use of plants in the popular medicine of nineteenth-century Martinique.[75] What has perhaps eluded historians is the degree to which the mystical worldview of the master sorcerer pervaded the cultural world of both slaves and planters, and blurred the distinctions between "Western medicine" and what was called "la pharmacopée noire." For a number of decades, efforts to suppress an array of practices associated with herbalism and conjuring coexisted with continued borrowing from other, related African customs. The wariness planters showed toward those engaged in "sacred science," and their efforts to curtail even the most basic forms of slave medicine, such as healing snakebites, did not stop them from employing many of those very same techniques when they felt they needed to.[76]

As has been noted regarding other Atlantic slave societies, there are numerous accounts of planters using the services of diviners and sorcerers for their own ends. "I don't believe in sorcery," one planter insisted, "but I do believe in certain sciences, certain recipes they preserve mysteriously, and that surprise and disturb us, just as in the Middle Ages our ancestors were left surprised and disturbed before the most basic experiments in physics or chemistry."[77] What is most striking in this passage is the planter's association of higher knowledge with the enslaved, and his likening of Europeans to their own pre-rational medieval ancestors. But rather than serving the "progress of reason," the "modernizing" hygienist discourses first articulated in the eighteenth century actually fueled planters' anxiety about a society that seemed to be slipping out of their control. The conflation of Africans with the imbalanced natural environment, and the idea that African bodies were unable to resist the toxic natural forces surrounding them, paradoxically shaped planter views of African mystical practices.

In his study of the theme of obeah in romantic literature, Alan Richardson describes a "decade of British fascination with obi" between 1797 and 1807, which grew out of "British anxieties regarding power: the fluctuations of imperial power, the power of slaves to determine their own fate, the power of democratic movements in France, in England, and in the Caribbean."[78] Indeed, the widespread association of slave rebellions with Jacobinism is part of what led planters and colonial officials to see subversive acts virtually everywhere they looked.[79] Michael Mullin has also argued in favor of the idea of obeah men as community leaders, devoted to "serving [their] people" by employing their secret knowledge.[80] The perception of the obeah man as more of a master revolutionary than a master healer shaped white responses to both slave medicine and African cosmologies in this period. The vision of obeah as a kind of vessel for the systematic resistance to enslavement may have reached its most acute form in the anxieties surrounding the ubiquitous poisoning conspiracies of Restoration-era Martinique. But these beliefs originated with planters, and their reactions in turn shaped the social, cultural, and even physiological context of the slave system.

NOTES

1. See Kathrine Bonin, "Signs of Origin: Victor Hugo's *Bug-Jargal*," *Nineteenth-Century French Studies* 36, nos. 3/4 (2008): 193–204; Gérard Gengembre, "From Bug-Jargal to Toussaint Louverture: Romanticism and the Slave Rebel," in *The Abolitions of Slavery: From Léger Félicité Sonthonax to Victor Schoelcher, 1793, 1794, 1848*, ed. Marcel Dorigny (New York: Berghahn, 2003), 272–79; Jacques Cauna, "Les sources historiques de *Bug-Jargal*: Hugo et la Révolution Haïtienne," *Conjonction: Bulletin de l'Institut français d'Haïti* 166 (1985): 21–36; Gabriel Debien, "Un roman colonial de Victor Hugo: 'Bug-Jargal,' ses sources et ses intentions historiques," *Revue d'Histoire Littéraire de la France* 52, no. 3 (1952): 298–313; Christopher Bongie's introduction to his new translation of Victor Hugo, *Bug-Jargal* (1826; ed. and trans. Christopher Bongie, New York: Broadview, 2004), 9–48.

2. Victor Hugo, *Bug-Jargal* (Paris: Librairies Alphonse Lemerre), 28. All translations are mine unless otherwise indicated.

3. Jerome Handler and Kenneth Bilby, "The Early Use and Origin of the Term 'Obeah' in Barbados and the Anglophone Caribbean," *Slavery and Abolition* 22, no. 2 (2001): 89. Handler and Bilby emphasize the virtual absence of the term in colonial North America, though its marginal presence is attested to by Jason Young in *Rituals of Resistance: African Atlantic Religion in Kongo and the Lowcountry South in the Era of Slavery* (Baton Rouge: Louisiana State University Press, 2007), 126.

4. Alan Richardson, "Romantic Voodoo: Obeah and British Culture, 1797–1807," *Studies in Romanticism* 32, no. 1 (1992): 3–28.

5. Pamphile de Lacroix, *Mémoires pour servir à l'histoire de la Révolution de Saint-Domingue* (Paris: Pillet aîné, 1819). See also Hugo, *Bug-Jargal* (ed. Bongie), 200n.

6. Draft letter of Baron de Lamardelle, maître de requêtes, January 25, 1823, Centre d'Archives d'Outre-Mer, Aix-en-Provence (hereafter cited as CAOM), FM SG—Martinique 52/430, Documents de la Cour Prévôtale, 1822–27. Gabriel Debien explains that the burial ceremony remained a crucial "repository of African mores" throughout the eighteenth century, even as Caribbean societies became increasingly creolized. See "Les Cimetières à Saint-Domingue au XVIIIe siècle," *Conjonction: Revue de l'Institut français d'Haiti* 105 (1967): 33

7. Report of September 28, 1822, CAOM FM SG Martinique 52/430, Documents de la Cour Prévôtale, 1822–27.

8. Françoise Thésée, *Le Général Donzelot à la Martinique: Vers la fin de l'ancien régime colonial, 1818–1826* (Paris: Karthala, 1997), chap. 3; John Savage, "Between Colonial Fact and French Law: Slave Poisoners and the Provostial Court in Restoration-Era Martinique," *French Historical Studies* 29, no. 4 (2006): 565–94.

9. Donzelot letter of September 28, 1822, CAOM FM SG Martinique 123/1101, Déportation d'individus dangereux, 1819–22.

10. Rapport D'Avoust, cited in Rapport du directeur de l'interieur par interim au gouverneur, March 1827, CAOM FM SG Martinique 52/431, Correspondance du Gouverneur.

11. As one report before the Sovereign Council of Martinique put it in 1780, "They say that their poisons have no power over whites, and that they admit it themselves. What is certain is that up to now fortunately there are no examples of a white dying by these means." *Annales du Conseil Souverain de la Martinique* (1786; ed. Bernard Vonglis; Paris: L'Harmattan, 1995), I, 1:497. And as a French traveler to the region wrote, "They are persuaded that success depends on the power of their gods or their demons, which have no power over us." Jean-Baptiste Thibault de Chanvalon, *Voyage à la Martinique* (1763; Paris: Karthala, 2004), 64. See also Gabriel Debien, *Les esclaves aux Antilles francaises, XVIIe–XVIIIe siecles* (Basse-Terre: SHG/SHM, 1974), 401; Philip Morgan, *Slave Counterpoint: Black Culture in the Eighteenth-Century Chesapeake and Lowcountry* (Chapel Hill: University of North Carolina Press, 1998), 614.

12. Yvan Debbasch, "Le crime d'empoisonnement aux îles pendant la période esclavagiste," *Revue française d'histoire d'outre-mer* 51 (1963): 172n.

13. Joseph Elzéar Morénas, *Précis historique de la traite des noirs et de l'esclavage colonial* (1828; Geneva: Slatkine, 1978), 323–24.

14. John Savage, "'Black Magic' and White Terror: Slave Poisoning and Colonial Society in Early 19th Century Martinique," *Journal of Social History* 40, no. 3 (2007): 635–62. On the affaire des hommes de couleur libres, see Stella Pame, *Cyrille Bissette: Un martyr de la liberté* (Fort-de-France, Martinique: Editions Désormeaux, 1999).

15. Quoted in Debbasch, "Le crime d'empoisonnement aux îles pendant la période esclavagiste," 149n.

16. Ibid.

17. Alexandre Moreau de Jonnès, *Observations pour servir à l'histoire de la fièvre jaune des Antilles . . .* (Paris: Migneret, 1817), 1:56.

18. J.-B. Ricord-Madianna, *Recherches et expériences sur les poisons d'Amérique avec un essai sur l'empoisonnement par les miasmes des marais . . . et les maladies qui ressemblent aux empoisonnements . . .* (Bordeaux: C. Lawalle, 1826), 48.

19. Dale Tomich, *Slavery in the Circuit of Sugar: Martinique and the World Economy, 1830–1848* (Baltimore: Johns Hopkins University Press, 1990), chap. 8.

20. Renouard de Sainte-Croix, *Statistique de la Martinique, ornée d'une carte de cette île, avec les documents authentiques de sa population, de son commerce, de sa consommation annuelles et de ses revenus . . .* (Paris: Chaumerot, 1822), 2 vols.

21. Trial of November 7, 1826, FM SG Martinique 141/1271, CAOM.

22. Letter of the *Grand juge*, 10 Floréal an XII, CAOM C8a 110, Correspondance à l'arrivée.

23. John Savage, "Unwanted Slaves: The Punishment of Transportation and the Making of Legal Subjects in Early Nineteenth-Century Martinique," *Citizenship Studies* 10, no. 1 (2006): 38–39.

24. "Mémoire Rivière," 1829, CAOM FM SG Martinique 52/431, Correspondance du Gouverneur. Michael Mullin describes the itinerant peddler as "the quintessential subversive job." *Africa in America: Slave Acculturation and Resistance in the American South and the British Caribbean, 1736–1831* (Champaign-Urbana: University of Illinois Press, 1995), 153–54.

25. Report of September 28, 1822, FM SG Martinique 52/430, CAOM.

26. Savage, "Unwanted Slaves," 39.

27. Report of September 28, 1822, FM SG Martinique 52/430, CAOM.

28. Procès Verbaux des Délibérations du Conseil de Gouvernement et d'Administration de la Martinique, session of October 24, 1823, CAOM Martinique Correspondance 143.

29. Geneviève Léti, *Santé et société esclavagiste à la Martinique (1802–1848)* (Paris: Editions L'Harmattan, 1998), 340–60.

30. Yvan Debbasch, "Les associations serviles à la Martinique au XIXe siècle: Contribution à l'histoire de l'esclavage colonial," in *Études d'histoire du droit privé offertes à Pierre Petot,* ed. Pierre Petot (Paris: Librairie Générale de Droit et de Jurisprudence, 1959), 124. Michael Mullin emphasizes the major role of plays and dance in shaping the reception of Christian religious practices among slaves around the Atlantic world; see *Africa in America,* 211. On the medical and spiritual function of dance, see also Léti, *Santé et société esclavagiste à la Martinique (1802–1848),* 426.

31. "Mémoire Rivière," 1829, CAOM FM SG Martinique 52/431, Correspondance du Gouverneur.

32. Debbasch, "Les associations serviles à la Martinique au XIXe siècle," 125–27, 129n, 151n.

33. Rivière letter of October 30, 1829, CAOM FM SG Martinique 52/431, Correspondance du Gouverneur.

34. Pierre Pluchon, *Vaudou, sorciers, empoisonneurs: De Saint-Domingue à Haiti*

(Paris: Karthala, 1987). See also David Geggus, "Haitian Voodoo in the Eighteenth Century: Language, Culture, Resistance," *Jahrbuch für Geschichte von Staat, Wirtschaft, und Gesellschaft Lateinamerikas* 28 (1991): 21–51; and Geggus's summary on this issue in "The French Slave Trade: An Overview," *William and Mary Quarterly* 58, no. 1 (2001): 119–38.

35. See David Eltis and Martin Halbert, Voyages: The Transatlantic Slave Trade Database, http://slavevoyages.org/; David Eltis, *The Rise of African Slavery in the Americas* (Cambridge: Cambridge University Press, 2000); David Eltis and David Richardson, "West Africa and the Transatlantic Slave Trade: New Evidence of Long-Run Trends," *Slavery and Abolition* 18, no. 1 (1997): 21. See also Myriam Cottias, "Mortalité et créolisation sur les habitations martiniquaises du XVIIIe au XIXe siècle," *Population* 44, no. 1 (1989): 55–84; Gwendolyn Midlo Hall, Afro-Louisiana History and Genealogy, 1719–1820, http://www.ibiblio.org/laslave/; Gwendolyn Midlo Hall, ed., *Databases for the Study of Afro-Louisiana History and Genealogy, 1699–1860* (Baton Rouge: Louisiana State University Press, 2000).

36. See Douglas Chambers's *Murder at Montpelier: Igbo Africans in Virginia* (Jackson: University Press of Mississippi, 2009); and "'My own nation': Igbo Exiles in the Diaspora," *Slavery and Abolition* 18, no. 1 (1997): 75.

37. Françoise Thésée, *Les Ibos de l'Amélie: Destinée d'une cargaison de traite clandestine à la Martinique, 1822–1838* (Paris: Editions Caribéennes, 1986).

38. Thésée, *Le Général Donzelot à la Martinique*, 84 Josette Fallope's research, however, suggests that poisoning was indeed perceived as a scourge in Guadeloupe, though it was understood to be an extension of the main wave of poisoning centered in Martinique. See *Esclaves et citoyens: Les noirs à la Guadeloupe au XIXe siècle dans les processus de résistance et d'intégration (1802–1910)* (Basse-Terre: Société d'Histoire de la Guadeloupe, 1992), 204–5.

39. Recent scholarship has emphasized the need to distinguish Caribbean obeah from any single set of African practices. Kenneth Bilby and Jerome Handler have argued that the origins of the term have been difficult for researchers to pin down because of the assumption that the source words they were looking for would necessarily be expressions relating to malevolent witchcraft. See "The Early Use and Origin of the Term 'Obeah' in Barbados and the Anglophone Caribbean," 89–90. See also Juanita Barros, "'Setting Things Right': Medicine and Magic in British Guiana, 1803–1834," *Slavery and Abolition* 25, no. 1 (2004): 28–50.

40. Savage, "'Black Magic' and White Terror," 641.

41. See David Northrup, "New Evidence of the French Slave Trade in the Bight of Benin," *Slavery and Abolition* 24, no. 3 (2003): 69; Femi Kolapo, "The Igbo and Their Neighbors during the Era of the Atlantic Slave-Trade," *Slavery and Abolition* 25, no. 1 (2004): 116–17; Geggus, "The French Slave Trade," 131.

42. See Ashli White, "'A Flood of Impure Lava': Saint Dominguan Refugees in the United States, 1791–1820" (Ph.D. diss., Columbia University, 2003); Clarence Maxwell,

"'The Horrid Villainy': Sarah Bassett and the Poisoning Conspiracies in Bermuda, 1727–1730," *Slavery and Abolition* 21, no. 3 (2000): 48, 66–69; Mullin, *Africa in America*, 182; Savage, "'Black Magic' and White Terror," 647.

43. *Annales du Conseil Souverain de la Martinique* I, 1:497.

44. Laborde, "Effets dangereux de l'erreur et de superstition dans les colonies françaises de l'Amérique," cited in Pluchon, *Vaudou, sorciers, empoisonneurs*, 234–36.

45. Quoted in Debbasch, "Le crime d'empoisonnement aux îles pendant la période esclavagiste," 144n.

46. *Recherches, mémoires et observations sur les maladies épizootiques de Saint-Domingue, recueillis and publiés par le Cercle des Philadelphes du Cap-François* (Saint-Domingue: l'Imprimerie Royale, 1788).

47. Arthaud, *Observations sur les lois concernant la medicine et la chirurgie dans la colonie de Saint-Domingue* (Cap François: Impr. de Dufour de Rians, 1791), 60–61. On the background and training of a sampling of doctors in Restoration-era Martinique, see Léti, *Santé et société esclavagiste à la Martinique (1802–1848)*, 322.

48. Alexandre Moreau de Jonnès, *Essai sur l'hygiène militaire des Antilles* (Paris: Migneret, 1816), 82n.

49. Debbasch, "Les associations serviles à la Martinique au XIXe siècle," 157.

50. See Pierre Pluchon, "La santé dans les colonies de l'Ancien Régime," in *Histoire des médecins et pharmaciens de Marine et des colonies* (Toulouse: Privat, 1985), 99, 107.

51. Debbasch, "Les associations serviles à la Martinique au XIXe siècle," 147n.

52. Pierre Dessalles, *La vie d'un colon à la Martinique au XIXe siècle* (Fort-de-France, Martinique: Désormeaux, 1987), 1:497.

53. Léti, *Santé et société esclavagiste à la Martinique (1802–1848)*, 356.

54. Ibid., 390; Bernard Moitt, *Women and Slavery in the French Antilles, 1635–1848* (Bloomington: Indiana University Press, 2001).

55. Léti, *Santé et société esclavagiste à la Martinique (1802–1848)*, 378–81, 425.

56. Ibid., 374, 383, 385.

57. Christiane Bougerol, "Medical Practices in the French West Indies: Master and Slave in the 17th and 18th Centuries," *History and Anthropology* 2 (1985): 125–43; James McClellan III, *Colonialism and Science: Saint Domingue in the Old Regime* (Baltimore: Johns Hopkins University Press, 1992).

58. Debbasch, "Les associations serviles à la Martinique au XIXe siècle."

59. Lucien Peytraud, *L'esclavage aux Antilles françaises avant 1789* (Paris: Hachette, 1897), 181–82; see also 189–90.

60. Malick Ghachem, "Montesquieu in the Caribbean: The Colonial Enlightenment between Code Noir and Code Civil," *Historical Reflections/Réflexions Historiques* 25, no. 2 (1999): 183. See also Pierre Boulle, "In Defense of Slavery: Eighteenth-Century Opposition to Abolition and the Origins of a Racist Ideology in France," in *History from Below: Studies in Popular Protest and Popular Ideology in Honor of George Rudé*, ed. Frederick Krantz (Montreal: Concordia, 1985), 221–41.

61. Sean Quinlan, "Colonial Bodies, Hygiene, and Abolitionist Politics in Eighteenth-Century France," *History Workshop Journal* 42 (1996): 112–14.

62. Quoted in ibid., 113.

63. Ibid.

64. Dessalles, *La vie d'un colon à la Martinique au XIXe siècle*, 114. On the social advantages and medical role of the *chef cabrouetier*, see Debien, *Les esclaves aux Antilles françaises, XVIIe–XVIIIe siecles*, 97–98.

65. Rufz de Lavison, "Recherches sur les empoisonnements pratiqués par les nègres à la Martinique," *Annales d'hygiène publique et de médecine légale*, 1844, 31:429.

66. Savage, "'Black Magic' and White Terror," 650–52.

67. Alexandre Moreau de Jonnès's *Tableau du climat des Antilles et des phénomènes de son influence sur les plantes, les animaux et l'espèce humaine* (Paris: Migneret, 1817), 4; *Histoire physique des Antilles françaises* (Paris: Imp. de Migneret, 1822), 428; and *Des effets du climat des antilles sur le système moteur* (Paris: Imp. de Migneret, 1816), 2.

68. Moreau de Jonnès, *Tableau du climat des Antilles et des phénomènes de son influence sur les plantes, les animaux et l'espèce humaine*, 9.

69. Léti, *Santé et société esclavagiste à la Martinique (1802–1848)*, 126, 131.

70. Moreau de Jonnès, *Tableau du climat des Antilles et des phénomènes de son influence sur les plantes, les animaux et l'espèce humaine*, 9–10; Léti, *Santé et société esclavagiste à la Martinique (1802–1848)*, 70.

71. Quoted in Thésée, *Le Général Donzelot à la Martinique*, 121.

72. Quoted in Rufz de Lavison, "Recherches sur les empoisonnements pratiqués par les nègres à la Martinique," 31:393.

73. Paul Dhormoys, *Sous les tropiques, souvenirs de voyages* (Paris: Jung-Treuttel, 1864), 32. See also B. W. Higman, *Slave Populations of the British Caribbean, 1807–1834* (Baltimore: Johns Hopkins University Press, 1984), 272–73.

74. Victor Schoelcher, *Des colonies françaises: Abolition immédiate de l'esclavage* (Paris: Pagnerre, 1842), 121.

75. Léti, *Santé et société esclavagiste à la Martinique (1802–1848)*, 372.

76. See Londa Schiebinger, "Scientific Exchange in the Eighteenth-Century Atlantic World," *Soundings in Atlantic History: Latent Structures and Intellectual Currents, 1500–1830*, ed. Bernard Bailyn and Patricia Denault (Cambridge: Harvard University Press, 2009), 316–22.

77. Dhormoys, *Sous les tropiques, souvenirs de voyages*, 139.

78. Richardson, "Romantic Voodoo," 4–5.

79. James Walvin, *England, Slaves and Freedom, 1776–1838* (Jackson: University Press of Mississippi, 1986), 114–17.

80. Mullin, *Africa in America*, 210.

6.

The Trials of Inspector Thomas:
Policing and Ethnography in Jamaica

DIANA PATON

Recent studies of Afro-Atlantic culture have used the metaphor of the dialogue both to emphasize the complex processes at work in the cultural history of people of African descent in the Americas, and to move beyond a polarized debate between proponents of "African continuities" and "cultural creativity" in interpreting these processes.[1] My own previous work on the legal and cultural history of obeah has invoked this metaphor, arguing that obeah was produced "through a process of unequal dialogue," and identifying "ritual specialists, poor and struggling people, members of many churches, colonial officials, missionaries, and members of the Caribbean resident elite" as participants in this exchange.[2] In this chapter, I investigate more precisely the working of the "unequal dialogue" through which obeah was produced and reproduced as crime, as object of anthropological inquiry, and as a framework for understanding spiritual danger. Colonial knowledge of obeah, the chapter demonstrates, depended on local knowledge and strategies regarding spiritual danger and how to respond to it.

This chapter examines the day-to-day enforcement of the law against obeah, attending especially to the circumstances that led to particular individuals being arrested and prosecuted, rather than to the type of ritual practice that was subject to policing.[3] It focuses on Jamaica, because obeah law was often vigorously enforced there, and because of the relative accessibility of newspaper reports about Jamaican arrests and trials for obeah.[4] While the evidence through which we can learn about the circumstances leading to arrests is marked by important absences, it is sufficient to demonstrate that the police did not act alone in their efforts to enforce the law against obeah. Instead, they frequently relied on the cooperation of working-class and peasant Jamaicans, as well as on detective work and entrapment, to make arrests. This cooperation suggests that ordinary people made fine-grained judgments about the legitimacy of particular individuals' claims to spiritual power. By selectively reporting individuals for obeah, Jamaicans who were for the most part excluded and marginalized by the race and class hierarchies of colonial society contributed to wider understandings of what obeah was. At times, they even managed to manipulate the application of the law so that it punished those whose spiritual work was perceived—at least by some community members—as ineffective or exploitative, rather than everyone who, in the words of the Jamaican Obeah Law, "pretended to possess any supernatural power or knowledge ... for gain."[5]

The chapter argues, then, for a significant subaltern contribution to the official policing of obeah, and, as a result, to official and elite understandings of obeah. While this contribution was significant, however, it was largely limited to perceptions of obeah within Jamaica. Despite their dependence on the judgments of people outside the state, when policemen translated their experiences into an ethnographic discourse about obeah, they did so in ways that presented the African Jamaican population as subject to an unremitting and indiscriminate "superstition," rather than as making complex choices about whom to report. We see this especially clearly in the work of Herbert T. Thomas, a white Jamaican policeman who boasted about the numbers of obeah practitioners he had arrested, and who used his experience of policing obeah to contribute to the production of ethnography on the subject. Thomas produced a display that was briefly exhibited at the Jamaica International Exhibition of 1891, and he wrote about obeah in several books and pamphlets based on his policing experience. Thomas's career suggests that, although the experience of policing and prosecution fed into accounts of obeah that circulated internationally, it did so in ways that focused attention on the individual obeah practitioner and on the contest between policeman and obeah practitioner, rather than on the wider networks of people to which both sides were connected and on which both depended for information. Despite its exclusions, this way of thinking about obeah and its policing was very powerful, not least because it was attractive both to the police who made the arrests and to the spiritual workers who tried to evade them.[6]

Herbert Thomas's dual pursuit of the obeah practitioner as object of both criminal prosecution and ethnographic knowledge echoes practices of lawmaking and law enforcement around the colonial and postcolonial world. From debates about the nature of African witchcraft that took place among colonial officials in the pages of the journal *Africa*, to Fernando Ortiz's investigation of Afro-Cuban religion via newspaper reports of alleged *brujería* murders, to the reification of caste in colonial India, the work of the police and of magistrates played a significant role in producing the raw material that fed understandings of the social worlds of colonial subjects.[7] While the influence of the work of law enforcers and lawmakers on the construction of colonial knowledge has been discussed, little investigation has been undertaken of the policing on which this knowledge production drew. Studies of colonial policing, in the Caribbean and elsewhere in the British Empire, have for good reason largely focused on the quasi-military structure, training, and activity of colonial police forces, their prime focus on the maintenance of "public order," and their suppression of political opposition.[8] As a result, the involvement of members of police forces in other activities, including the policing of religion and culture, has been relatively neglected.[9] By looking more closely at the legal cases that fed into anthropological, and eventually historical, discussions of colonial cultures, we can unpack their monolithic status as impositions from above and see the hidden and subordinated contributions of colonial subjects to colonial knowledge production.

Before turning to an analysis of the practicalities of enforcing the obeah law, I explore the example of Herbert T. Thomas's contribution to the construction of knowledge about obeah. Thomas was appointed to the Jamaican Constabulary Force in 1876, at the age of twenty. As a white, though not especially wealthy, Jamaican, he was immediately appointed to the officer position of sub-inspector, eventually becoming inspector for the parish of Saint Thomas in 1887, considerably later than he thought appropriate.[10]

Thomas's most significant contribution to the translation of policing into colonial knowledge was via the Jamaica International Exhibition, held in Kingston from January to May 1891, to which he contributed a display of material confiscated from people whom he had arrested for obeah. He also published a short pamphlet, *Something about Obeah*, to accompany his contribution to the exhibition.[11] The exhibition was part of an international movement of great exhibitions and world's fairs devoted to the promotion of trade and national/imperial pride through the display of produce, culture, and people. The original Great Exhibition took place in London in 1851 and was followed by others across the empire, as well as by those in the United States (where they were known as world's fairs) and other European countries. Alongside displays of industrial and agricultural products, often paid for by their manufacturers, exhibitions usually included cultural displays of the costume, artifacts, and other "typical" material of many nations and colonies.[12]

Much recent scholarship on exhibitions emphasizes their investment in imperialism and in the production of colonized peoples for the consumption of metropolitan audiences. James Gilbert, for instance, argues that the organizing principle of the Victorian exhibition "was the idea of universal culture, a complex defined, in part, by . . . opposition between civilization and savagery."[13] Writing about the Great Exhibition of 1851, Paul Young describes its mapping of ideas of progress from savagery to civilization onto space, and argues that it ultimately queried whether all the world's peoples could attain civilization.[14]

Most of the exhibitions discussed in this scholarship took place in metropolitan centers, where the audience was easily and straightforwardly addressed as white and imperial, even while it was understood to be divided by class and gender. Metropolitan exhibitions presented exotic but domesticated others to an audience that was assumed to understand its own distance from what was represented, while presenting the home nation as a site of industry and modernity. The producers of colonial exhibitions such as the Jamaica International Exhibition found it harder to sustain the distinction between the local and the exotic. As Krista Thompson argues, Jamaican colonial officials and local elites planned the exhibition to "put Jamaica on the map as an emergent modern colony," as part of a wider campaign to produce a "New Jamaica."[15] The exhibition thus had a double audience: it was designed both to present Jamaica to the outside world, and to present the world, and Jamaica's place within it, to Jamaicans.

How, then, was Jamaica to be represented? Jamaica's history of colonialism and plantation slavery did not inspire the kind of focus on a glorious past adopted by exhibition representations of India and China.[16] Instead, in a context in which Jamaican culture was widely dismissed as primitive and excluded from the modern, much of the Jamaican displays avoided presenting culture at all, except in the narrow sense of agriculture. The exhibition regulations envisaged displays primarily relating to agricultural and industrial production, grouping potential exhibits into six groups: raw materials, implements for obtaining raw materials, machines for turning raw materials into finished products, manufactured goods, education, and fine arts, literature, and science. The large exhibit organized by the Institute of Jamaica followed these guidelines, displaying the natural resources of the island, its economic activity, and its literary and scientific culture, but neither this exhibit nor the "Industrial Village" section attempted to represent popular Jamaican music, dance, history, or religion. Most other exhibits in the Jamaican court displayed agricultural crops and other export-oriented items, as well as technological innovations for processing them.[17]

Yet the displays were not controlled by the exhibition organizers, who rented space in the courts to any "exhibitor" who would pay for them. Some private exhibitors chose to display woodcarving and carpentry, "fancy work" (for which prizes were offered by the governor), and, with some frequency, "medicinal herbs," suggesting that popular knowledge was not entirely excluded.[18] Even so, Herbert Thomas's participation in the exhibition was exceptional in its attempt to address Jamaicans' cultural connection to Africa. The catalogue described his exhibit as "Some African Fetish Charms, used by Tribes on the West Coast. A Collection of Charms, Implements and Materials used by Jamaica Obeahmen, or Practitioners and Priests of the Obeah Superstition."[19] The *Gleaner* deemed his display a "curious exhibit" made up of "a box containing many of the articles taken from Obeahmen, such as cards, chalk, medicine, . . . and other obeah curiosities—a most interesting collection."[20] Thomas's own "catalogue" of his exhibit, printed at the end of *Something about Obeah*, gives more detail. The stand displayed "charms and implements seized" from seven men arrested for obeah, all except one from the parish of Saint Thomas. These "charms and implements" included tins of natural substances such as myrrh, camphor, caraway seed, and sulfur; a pack of cards; a small mirror; a bag of rice; and a glass marble. In addition, Thomas included written material: "A book of certificates kept by a Bush-doctor, or Duppy-catcher in the parish of Clarendon, attesting his wonderful cures of 'madness, child-birth' and other extraordinary complaints," and "an agreement between one Fleming and an obeahman named Fraser."[21]

Alongside the Jamaican objects, Thomas displayed a group of contemporary "African fetish charms used by [the] Mendi [sic] tribe on [the] West Coast [of Africa]." These "charms" included an antelope horn filled with snake and alligator fat, a "switch made of leaves of the koos-koos grass stitched into a piece of African country cloth and ornamented with jeggas," and "a charm to be worn round the neck or any other part of the body, ingredients unknown." Thomas claimed that Sierra Leone, where this material originated, was "the home of the obeah superstition." His argument seems to have been driven more by expediency than by evidence: Thomas explained that he received the material "through the kindness of Inspector Alexander," who had "obtained [it] after bombardment of Robarri [sic] in 1887." Robari was a Temne (not Mende) settlement that was razed by British imperial forces in the "Yoni Expedition," a military episode in the expansion of British colonial rule outward from Sierra Leone in which the First West India Regiment participated.[22] Inspector Alexander was presumably an officer in the regiment who had acquired the items during the looting of Robari. Thomas's juxtaposition of the Jamaican with the Mende/Temne objects was intended to historicize Jamaican obeah by showing where it had come from. Yet the two groups of objects were both contemporary to their display. Thomas's display thus participated in the production of "anachronistic space" described by Anne McClintock and the "denial of coevalness" between Africa and the rest of the world described by Johannes Fabian.[23] It also participated in what was already a long-standing tradition of framing the key question regarding obeah as being one about origins: where—and, specifically, where in Africa—did it come from?

If, for Thomas, Jamaican obeah was the descendant of African "fetishism," it was an inferior and degenerate offspring. In his pamphlet, Thomas noted the "superior quality" of the African material in comparison with the "useless rubbish and filth used by the obeahmen of Jamaica." This illustrated, he claimed, "how the cult of obeah worship has deteriorated on the soil of Jamaica."[24] His designation of the Jamaican objects as inferior appears, ironically, to be a response to their incorporation of the "modern" manufactured materials acquired through the international trade that the exhibition hoped to promote, such as the mirror, playing cards, and glass marble. The Jamaican use of found and acquired objects for ritual purposes, when contrasted to the artisanal working of animal and vegetable materials attributed to the Mende, allowed the latter to be presented as superior even while the "tribe" was subject to imperial conquest.

In a sense, Thomas's presentation of the African material was a spatialized version of the approach taken by contemporary representations (including at exhibitions) of India, which presented the country as having degenerated from a better past.[25] The solution was not to return to that past but to eradicate it. Thomas presented his display as part of an effort to understand Afro-Jamaican culture in order to transform it. He noted his "great hopes that the mere fact of this exhibit; labelled with the names of the men from whom the various articles were taken will deal such a blow to obeah as shall be worthy of the 'Awakening of Jamaica,' the dawn of which is heralded by this our Exhibition."[26] The *Gleaner* took a similar view, rhetorically contrasting the "clumsy ingenuities of the obeahman" with the "thousand and one other curiosities and contrivances of art and soil" on display. When seen "in the broad light of solar and scientific day," the *Gleaner* declared optimistically, "Mr. Thomas [sic] obeah collections . . . will . . . tend, at least, forever to expel from their minds, and from their homes the baneful and baleful influences of his 'detestable enormities.'"[27]

Thomas's and the *Gleaner's* anticipation of the uplifting contribution of his display was quickly thwarted by the exhibition's management. Less than two weeks after the exhibition opened, Thomas was asked to remove his material on the grounds that "the objects will deter many country people from visiting the Exhibition."²⁸ At the same time, the owner of a sideshow illusion was required to remove the word "obeah" from his advertising sign, which originally read "The Living Obeah." W. P. Livingstone, the *Gleaner*'s editor, later explained that the decision resulted from the "awe created among the country blacks" by both Thomas's display and the sideshow.²⁹ Describing the incident in his 1927 autobiography, Thomas wrote, "It was only then that I began to realize what a real power Obeah is in the land."³⁰

The organizers were right to be concerned that the Jamaican public might not want to attend the exhibition. Claims that a very high proportion of local residents had attended the exhibition stood awkwardly alongside reports of hostile and not entirely unfounded rumors about the exhibition, including that it was a pretext for imposing taxes or even for re-instituting slavery. The event ran at an overall loss, which was subsidized by government funds—that is, by taxation.³¹ It is unlikely, however, that Thomas's exhibit in particular deterred attendance, especially since it was on display for such a short time. Rather, the concern about attendance masked wider anxieties about the image of Jamaica presented to the outside world. Although Thomas's display demonstrated one kind of Jamaican modernity, it was a decidedly poor fit in an exhibition designed to present Jamaica as an investment opportunity. Thomas's obeah material was troubling because it could not be presented as part of Jamaica's past, but neither could it represent an exotic and unthreatening aspect of its present. The small tins of substances and written contractual and testimonial documents it comprised were hard to imbue with appropriate meanings. Nor was its educational function for a Jamaican audience clear enough. Thomas assumed that the display of material taken from obeah practitioners would demonstrate the superior power of the state and would thus lead viewers to realize that practitioners' claims to spiritual power were false. The organizers, in contrast, recognized that other interpretations were possible, and they were particularly concerned that the display of these objects in an official exhibition would reinforce their prestige and strengthen the power they represented. Jamaica's culture of spiritual healing was too live to be easily understood within the folkloric slot afforded by exhibitionary culture.

Despite the very brief appearance of his display of obeah objects, Thomas's policing work had a more lasting impact in textual form. Arguments he made in *Something about Obeah* found their way into later anthropological writing.³² In his brief pamphlet, Thomas argued that there were two "classes" of obeah practitioner. The first, he claimed, was "the grossly ignorant, depraved, benighted being, generally an African by birth or parentage, who firmly believes in the art which he professes, although he lives within a stone's throw of a church or opposite to a school." This type was likely to have a facial "deformity" or a "sore foot," and was "generally miserably poor, at least in outward appearance, and his fee small, but he does a good trade."[33] These were the obeah men that Thomas had successfully prosecuted, and it was from them that his exhibited material was confiscated.

But it was members of the second "class" of obeah man that Thomas really aspired to prosecute, and against whom he pitted himself. Thomas described this type of practitioner as "often a man of strikingly good physique, respectable appearance, and always decently dressed. He does more in the 'duppy catching' line, and does not accept a small fee. . . . [He is] of too much intelligence to believe in the efficacy of his charms, his motives for adopting the calling being the ease with which it earns for him an ample competence, and the facilities it affords him for gratifying his animal passions, debauchery being the principal feature of his ceremonial, which is always conducted in the presence only of himself and his victim."[34]

This vision of the obeah man was a close relation of the obeah man as charlatan trope, which played a prominent role in late nineteenth-century legislation and enforcement.[35] This stereotype included the idea that the spiritual worker was in fact a secular non-believer motivated by a mixture of desire for financial gain and the possibility of sexual predation. Despite seeing the members of this group as a more worthy opponent than the pathetic first class, Thomas had to admit that he had not been successful in prosecuting them. Indeed, he noted that he had only "succeeded in cutting short the career of one gentleman of this class lately," although he threatened that "one or two others shall have due attention shortly."[36]

Thomas's typology of the two types of obeah practitioner was taken up two years later in an article in the British journal *Folk-Lore* by May Robinson, which patched together quotations from Thomas's article and Bryan Edwards's *History of the British West Indies*, concluding that "obeah practises of the present day seem similar to those of a hundred years ago."[37] The quotations were designed to provide context for understanding a further example of an obeah "charm," which the article included as an illustration, describing it as a "little Obeah figure [which] was brought to England in 1888 . . . and had been taken from a negro named Alexander Ellis, who was arrested in Morant Bay, Jamaica May 1887" (figure 6.1). According to Robinson, the figure had been returned to Jamaica for the international exhibition, where it formed part of Thomas's exhibit; it was, she informed readers, "regarded as a particularly powerful and evil Obeah, and no negro would willingly touch it, or be in the room with it." Robinson also listed a few items from Thomas's exhibition. Failing to note the

6.1 Image of a "little Obeah figure" taken by police from a man arrested in Jamaica in May 1887 for practicing obeah. According to May Robinson, the figure was brought to England but then returned to Jamaica to "form part of Mr. Thomas's collection of Obeah-charms at the Jamaica Exhibition." May Robinson, "Obeah Worship in East and West Indies," *Folk-Lore: A Quarterly Review of Myth, Tradition, Institution and Custom* 4 (1893): 213. Reproduced by permission of the Trustees of the National Library of Scotland.

significance that Thomas ascribed to the distinction between the African and Jamaican material, she included one of the Mende objects in a list of "obeah charms seized in possession of various obeah men."[38]

Robinson's article, and through it, Thomas's policing, influenced two individuals whose work had a more long-lasting impact on Caribbean anthropology: Martha Beckwith and Joseph Williams. Beckwith, who conducted research in Jamaica in the early 1920s, approvingly quoted Robinson quoting Thomas on the existence of the two classes of obeah man. She continued, "Today it is customary to look upon an Obeah Man as a crafty knave who practises upon the credulity of the more ignorant to enrich himself, or as a wicked one who may be bought to perform secret murder by means of his knowledge of deadly herbs."[39] Joseph Williams, whose extensive discussions of obeah greatly influenced later scholarship, quoted Robinson's claim for the continuity of obeah practice and noted her use of Thomas's pamphlet.[40]

Thomas's work is only one of many examples in which the writings of state officials became primary sources for later ethnographies and histories of obeah, although such writings were more often written by magistrates than policemen. For instance, S. Leslie Thornton, a Jamaican magistrate, drew extensively on his courtroom experience in his 1903 article on obeah for the *Journal of the Society of Comparative Legislation*.[41] Two decades after Robinson's contribution, *Folk-Lore* published another article on obeah, John Symonds Udal's study of "Obeah in the West Indies," based on the author's experience as chief justice of the Leeward Islands. Udal described at length cases that took place while he was in office, and was in turn cited by Martha Beckwith, Joseph Williams, and Elsie Clews Parsons, among other scholars.[42] Meanwhile, colonial officials drew on anthropological knowledge to make sense of the practices that they endeavored to control. Robert Earl, the commissioner of the Virgin Islands, for instance, argued that "Obeah-Voodoo or Ju-Ju is best understood if it is regarded as the whole body of primitive belief and customs of fetichistic African tribes which has undergone a certain amount of change by their fusion, by being placed in a different environment, ie. the West Indies, and by contact with a civilization having higher & different beliefs."[43] Earl, whose report goes on to refer to the social evolutionist theories of Herbert Spencer, here displays his reading of African ethnography and his knowledge of contemporary theories of social evolution. Thus a substantial stream that fed scholarly anthropological understandings of obeah derived from the accounts of policemen like Thomas and other state agents, who were in turn influenced by the work of early anthropological theory. These accounts referred to one another and frequently confirmed one another's assumptions and conclusions.

Even while the experience of policing fed into ethnographic descriptions of obeah, their representations were not full accounts of all the methods by which obeah was policed. Rather, they produced a particular narrative that stressed the dominance of obeah in Caribbean people's understandings of harm, and described the process of prosecution as one in which skilled, persistent, and intelligent detective work succeeded in bringing obeah practitioners before the courts, with little help, indeed even with hindrance, from the rest of the population. Thus Thomas, describing a prosecution of which he was particularly proud, emphasized that he had worked for nine months to be in a position to arrest David Elisha Bates.[44] Discussing another case, Thomas described the careful trap he set, sending two constables to pose as the relatives of a man accused of cattle wounding who were eager to help their kinsman escape punishment. After the suspect, J. Kellerman, undertook a ritual designed, in his words as reported by Thomas, to "blow the case away," the "bold, bad policemen" arrested him, leading to his subsequent conviction and imprisonment.⁴⁵ The *Gleaner* endorsed Thomas's sense of his own importance, referring to his work, in a report on another obeah case, as an example of positive police action.⁴⁶

Police pride in prosecuting obeah practitioners, and specialized attention to the task, was not confined to Inspector Thomas. Inspector H. McCrae of Clarendon collected articles about obeah prosecutions made by his subordinates in the wake of the passage of the 1898 Obeah Act. Several contained praise for his work from journalists and magistrates.⁴⁷ A generation later, a retired policeman boasted of having "succeeded in convicting no less than eleven obeahmen" in the days when, he claimed, "one had to risk one's life . . . to approach them."⁴⁸ Magistrates shared in a sense of pride in convicting people for obeah. One boasted in 1911 that "we've potted hundreds of them [obeah men] in the country parts."⁴⁹ Meanwhile, the press praised individual policemen or parish police forces for conducting "crusades" directed toward "ferreting out" obeah, while policemen responsible for particularly noteworthy arrests received medals.⁵⁰

This construction of obeah prosecutions as a contest between police and practitioner had some truth to it, but it significantly exaggerated the autonomous action of policemen and omitted many important factors that led to arrests. These other factors have been revealed through an examination of evidence about obeah prosecutions located by searching the digital edition of the *Gleaner* between 1890 and 1979 using the terms "obeah," "obeah man," "obeah woman," and "obeahism." The conservative writer Herbert de Lisser edited the *Gleaner* for much of this period, and its journalists wrote for an implied conservative, middle-class audience that self-consciously distanced itself from African Jamaican culture. Nevertheless, as Jamaica's longest-running and most financially successful newspaper, it had the most widespread coverage of courts, drawing on a network of correspondents across the island. Its court reports often included detailed summaries and sometimes-verbatim quotations of witnesses' testimony and lawyers' arguments, even if they frequently presented these, especially the former, in a salacious or satirical tone. Collecting case reports from the *Gleaner* generates a substantial body of material: 944 reports of trials or arrests of individuals.⁵¹ While many cases were reported very briefly, providing only bare details (e.g., the name and sentence of the accused), a considerable number were reported in some detail, enabling us to investigate the circumstances preceding arrest. Such information is available in nearly 60 percent of the cases.

There are, of course, methodological problems in attempting to use reports of court cases to understand how arrests were made. The story of any given arrest can begin at many different points and can be told in many different ways. As Sally Engle Merry argues, "court hearings are highly ritualized events" that "serve as critical sites for the creation and imposition of cultural meanings."[52] The rituals of court hearings, and in particular the conventions governing who says what in court, shape the testimony of everyone involved in a court case, whether they are a defendant, a police officer, a defense or prosecution lawyer, or a civilian witness. Police in court had a particular imperative to omit certain aspects of the process by which they made arrests—in order to maintain good relations with people who supplied them with information, or to disguise the fact that their actions had not been fully legal. At times, it is clear that they deliberately withheld information from the court in order to protect the anonymity of their informants. For instance, they frequently used formulaic phrases such as "in consequence of [or sometimes 'from'] information [sometimes 'certain information'] received" to explain their decision to arrest someone.[53]

While recognizing these difficulties, the analysis below uses what was said in court to investigate how arrests were made, attempting to read between the lines of reported testimony, and paying particular attention to which aspects of evidence were contested and which were not. It divides the cases, where possible, into three groups. The first encompasses arrests made through direct entrapment, in which a policeman or informal police agent set out actively to solicit the suspected obeah practitioner's ritual practice with the intention of arresting him or her. Second, there were arrests made through other forms of police-led activity, such as a direct raid on the premises where police suspected an obeah practitioner was working; charging someone with obeah after arresting them on suspicion of some other crime, such as vagrancy or larceny; or directly catching someone in the act of doing something that could be interpreted as obeah. Finally, some arrests resulted from reports made to the police by civilians. These categories necessarily simplify a complex set of processes. In some cases, policemen set a trap for a spiritual worker after receiving a report from a member of the public, while in many they encouraged someone who reported an encounter with a ritual practitioner to participate in a future healing ritual in order to enable them to collect evidence about the suspected obeah practice.[54] In other cases, evidence suggests that a policeman had long been hoping to prosecute a particular individual but could act only when he received a tip from a member of the public.[55] Despite these overlaps, the distinction between entrapment, other police-led arrests, and arrests following civilian reports provide a useful, broad-brush set of divisions for apprehending the overall patterns of arrests. Just over a quarter were made through direct entrapment, and thus fit reasonably well within the "police versus obeah man" paradigm through which Herbert Thomas understood his work. Somewhat fewer arrests came about through other police-led activity. Slightly more than half the arrests resulted from reports made to the police by civilians.[56]

The 1907 prosecution of John Scott of Roehampton, Saint Ann, provides a good example of how police acted in entrapment cases. Scott, who was known locally as "Doctor Scott," was a long-standing spiritual healer who had successfully appealed against a conviction for obeah in 1899. In 1904, however, his attempted treatment of a Chinese shopkeeper, who died after consulting not only Scott but also a number of medical doctors, led to his conviction for manslaughter, for which he was sentenced to eighteen months in the General Penitentiary.[57] By 1907, Scott had been released and had reestablished both his practice in Roehampton and, it seems, his reputation across a good part of Jamaica. Two constables who had been "detailed to work up the case" described in court how they had gone to Scott claiming that one of them was suffering from ill health. One testified that Scott said immediately that "he had plainly seen that ghosts were upon him [the constable]," going on to reassure him that he had cleared 170 people of ghosts that same week. Despite explaining that his charges ranged from ten shillings to five pounds, Scott reportedly agreed to accept the five shillings offered by Constable Johnson (which had been marked earlier to allow for their identification); he then used a Bible, a looking glass, and a shut pan to perform a healing ritual, which he then supplemented by providing two pints of medicine.[58] In court, Scott angrily but unsuccessfully defended himself, asking "why the policemen took such 'a liberty' with him . . . and if they knew who they were making their joke with." He also "stated that he did not see why he should be interfered with as he did not kill anyone." He was sentenced to twelve months imprisonment and eighteen lashes.[59]

Scott's case shares many features with others in which the police "worked up" to prosecuting someone. As in the contemporaneous Trinidadian cases explored in this collection by Maarit Forde, these features include the use of pairs of policemen in order to have corroborating witnesses, the deployment of marked money, the production of convincing narratives by plainclothes police (often involving ill health but also revolving around employment, the success of businesses, court cases, and other matters), and the participation of the police in ritual activity, followed by the revelation of their identity and the arrest of the practitioner. In describing cases like this, policemen such as Thomas interpreted obeah arrests and prosecutions as the achievements either of a single policeman or at most of a group of policemen. The police, according to this narrative, had to pit their wits against the clever—but ultimately not clever enough—obeah man.

At least some ritual healers shared with police officers this understanding of obeah prosecutions as resulting from a battle of wits and skill between police and practitioner. For instance, Francis Harmit, a well-known healer who worked in Allman Town, Kingston, reportedly boasted during the course of an encounter with the policeman who was posing as his client, "I do my work any time and anywhere: I will come to the Court House and do my work and no constable can catch me."[60] Harmit's claim was reported ironically in court as he stood trial, yet it had at least a grain of truth: Harmit had defeated at least one previous prosecution, in 1902, and had evaded arrest since then.[61] Moreover, the idea that spiritual power was a counterweight to the power of the state was deeply embedded in everyday ritual practice, which, after all, was (and is) frequently invoked as a means of defeating prosecutions of all kinds. An attempt to win court cases or acquittals was, after the treatment of physical or mental health problems, the second-most-common reason for consulting a ritual specialist reported in the *Gleaner* cases.[62] The witness in a case against Charles Fraser, for instance, testified that she heard a man asking him "to shut two men's mouths when they come to Court." Fraser worked on the case by turning the key in two padlocks while the names of the men were called.[63] Other evidence also suggests the significance of the intervention of spiritual workers in court proceedings. As one judge complained in a 1931 case, the courthouse was often troubled by the "smell of certain things sprinkled about the walls," the implication being that these "certain things" were designed to influence the court's decisions.[64]

Spiritual workers combined material with spiritual means in defending themselves against prosecution. When these techniques worked, of course, no prosecutions took place, and so we cannot access the techniques directly. But even the occasions when defensive tactics were ultimately unsuccessful reveal a widespread awareness of police techniques and a range of steps taken to counter them. Robert Williams came out of his house while it was being watched by police and fired into the darkness to warn off anyone watching him.[65] Joseph Reid, confronted with a putative client claiming to be in need of spiritual treatment for poor health, recognized that the man was a police constable and chased him out of the house with a cow-skin whip.[66] In another case, the suspect Joseph Donald refused to continue a ritual he had begun when his client produced the money provided to her by the police, saying that "he could not work because the money had marks on them." His comment implies awareness not merely of the possibility of arrest but also of police tactics at a precise and detailed level.[67] Charles Walker similarly told a client that "he could not do anything that night, as a trap was set up for him."[68] Nathaniel "Papie" Hall, of Saint Andrew, was likewise aware of the danger of entrapment, questioning his client closely about her family before agreeing—wrongly, it turned out, since she was a police agent—to "work" for her.[69] Such cases suggest that ritual specialists had a high level of knowledge of police tactics. It is therefore likely that on many occasions they were able to prevent police from collecting sufficient evidence to enable them to prosecute—a point confirmed by repeated statements of police frustration at their inability to prosecute the "big" obeah practitioners.

Police and spiritual workers thus told remarkably similar stories about the policing of obeah. Both portrayed the contest between state forces and spiritual workers as part of a battle between relative equals. They described this contest as one in which ordinary people were active only as bystanders evaluating the reputation of each side. As Inspector Thomas complained when, in 1894, he was investigated for suspected corruption, "My being in this trouble is regarded among the more ignorant of the people as the work of the Obeahmen in revenge for my interference with them."[70]

Yet this narrative tends to wash out intermediaries and others who were less directly involved in the struggle between police and obeah workers. In practice, both police and the people they sought to prosecute depended on contacts and communication with non-specialists in order to get the upper hand in their battles with one another. The extent of this is revealed when we examine how arrests came about: at least half resulted from the cooperation of people outside the police force.

Some of those who cooperated with the police did so for clear financial gain, acting as informal undercover police agents. In these cases, particularly prominent in the early 1930s, the operations leading to arrest were usually similar to those conducted by the police acting alone.[71] The police agents, almost always women, visited the target of the sting telling a story about their loss of a job, involvement in a court case, or ill health. They were accompanied on the first or subsequent visits by a policeman, who would hide somewhere where he could observe the ritual in order to be able to report on it in court. The arrest of Nathaniel Hall, discussed above, was obtained through the actions of one such agent. A woman named Ada Bogle was involved in the entrapment of at least seven obeah defendants between 1931 and 1934, and other women were equally prominent.[72] Acting as a regular paid police informant could be lucrative: Bogle was reported to have purchased three properties with money earned through giving evidence in obeah trials before her career as an informer came to an end.[73]

Yet individuals who cooperated with the police for direct financial gain were only a small minority. Who else chose to report people to the police for obeah, and why? In many cases, there is simply not enough evidence to say. The discourse of newspaper reporting and of the courtroom relied on two fictions: first, that any citizen would report any breach of the law to the police, and second, that the illegal act of "practicing obeah" was clearly distinguishable from other similar but legal acts. As a result, in many cases the motivations of the person who reported an alleged obeah practitioner to the police were not only omitted but also actively excluded from reports and testimony. For instance, a *Gleaner* article about the arrest of Charles Smith for practicing obeah reports that he approached the "Rector's coachman," told him that "he wanted 'looking after,'" and arranged to "do the 'job.'" Smith returned a few weeks later to "fix" the coachman, but, according to the report, "in the meantime the coachman informed the Rector who had D[etective] C[onstable] South and two others laying in wait to capture Smith."[74] In another case, the *Gleaner* reported that a man named Thomas informed a policeman that he had been approached by Thomas Mortimer Hood, who told him that he "had seen a ghost on his wife" and could remove it through spiritual means. Thomas later accompanied two policemen to Hood's house in order to trap him into contravening the obeah law.[75] The *Gleaner* reported on neither the unnamed coachman's nor Thomas's reasons for initially going along with Smith's and Hood's suggestions and then later reporting them. Nor did the magistrate who heard Hood's case raise the question. Thomas and the coachman could have simply ignored the spiritual workers or refused their offers of help. Why did they, instead, go to the trouble of reporting the situation? Such questions are in many cases unanswerable. They remind us of the limitations on the knowledge that we can achieve through written records about the encounters that led to obeah prosecutions.

As these cases show, people who offered ritual or spiritual services without solicitation risked arrest. Yet the risk, we must assume, was relatively low. Incidents in which people went to the police must have been significantly outnumbered by those in which the practitioner succeeded in recruiting a client, otherwise these approaches would not have continued.

In some cases, often those in which the defendant employed a lawyer to argue his or her case in court, testimony or contextual information allows us to see something of the reason why the person who eventually became a witness went to the police. In many of these incidents, testimony suggests a breakdown in the client's confidence in the spiritual worker. This might be because the spiritual work failed, as in a case when Anna Gordon, whose son was serving a six-month prison sentence, accepted Zachariah Thomas's offer to use spiritual means to get her son released within nine days, paying him £2 10s. When nine days passed and her son was still inside, Gordon asked for her money back. Thomas now denied having received more than six shillings, and Gordon went to the police.[76] Or it might be because the client concluded that the spiritual worker had charged too much, as in a case when a man named Moody consulted Charles Johnson in the hope of getting a job. He and his friend later reported Johnson to the police because (according to Johnson's lawyer) "they thought the amount charged was too much and they doubted the man's powers."[77] In other cases, the ritual specialist failed to return to complete the work promised, despite accepting money, and as a result the client eventually reported him. Letitia Gilbert, for instance, initially accepted William Francis's offer to remove the duppy that he said was causing her long-term sickness. Francis began a ritual, sprinkling white rum in her room, and then left, promising to return the next day. He did not come back. Gilbert took no further action until, after more than two months, she encountered Francis by chance, at which point she reported him to nearby police, who arrested him.[78] In this case, it seems that Gilbert started off trusting in Francis's powers but felt cheated by his failure to return.

The involvement of the police in cases like these seems to have been a last resort, a backup technique when informal efforts to resolve conflict between client and practitioner had failed. Anna Gordon would not have gone to the police if Zachariah Thomas had been prepared to return all her money. Letitia Gilbert would not have reported William Francis if he had returned the next day, as he had promised. In a similar case, Eliza Walker consulted Isabella Francis after two medical doctors were unable to help her sick daughter. Francis gave her "two bottles of some liquid and a little bag for the child to wear to keep off the evil spirit which was on the child." After several weeks during which her daughter's health did not improve, Walker returned to Francis, asking for the return of the bangles that, she claimed, she had given in payment. It was only when Foster refused to return the bangles that Walker went to the police.[79] In these cases, police enforcement of the obeah laws resembled not so much an effort to eradicate obeah as a kind of regulatory procedure through which unsatisfied clients could deal with unscrupulous or incompetent practitioners. Despite official rhetoric about the usefulness of prosecution in ridding Jamaica of obeah, in practice these cases often worked in response to the demand of dissatisfied clients for whom obeah was most definitely real.

On other occasions, the police were, willingly it seems, drawn into disputes in working-class communities. Individuals who could persuade the police to prosecute someone for obeah could, by doing so, damage their rivals or enemies. Thus, for instance, the prosecution of Eliza Barnett took place, her defense lawyer claimed, because she refused to lend money to a neighbor, Boaz Bryan. Angry at being turned down, Bryan worked with the local police to trap Barnett into committing ritual acts to remove hostile spiritual power. The trap led to Barnett receiving a six-month sentence for obeah.[80] In a similar case, Emanuel Faulkner and John Barnes were charged with possessing "implements of obeah." Under cross-examination, two key witnesses, who had provided information to the police leading to the raid on Faulkner and Barnes's yard, revealed that they were former tenants of Faulkner with whom he had frequently "quarrelled," and that they had left owing him rent.[81] In such cases, the person who went to the police had known the person reported for some time and could have reported him or her earlier, but chose to do so at this particular moment because of the developing conflict between them.

The picture built up through the examination of obeah trials and arrests is rather different from what we might expect from previous studies of policing, as well as from the self-image of policemen like Herbert Thomas. The few studies of Jamaican policing that exist emphasize its use of an "Irish model" of a semi-militarized police force and its focus on public order, and reveal the high levels of mistrust that have historically existed in Jamaica between the police and the people.[82] The material presented here is not incompatible with that interpretation, but it makes the picture less stark. Policing could be at some level entangled with people's everyday lives, even while they maintained a deep level of hostility and mistrust, which for many was reinforced by the experience of involvement with police and the courts in the process of arrests and prosecutions for obeah.

This discussion only skims the surface of what we can glean from newspaper accounts of obeah arrests and trials. We can, however, draw some points from comparison between the cases as reported in the press and the representation of obeah by policemen like Thomas. Thomas's distinction between the first and second classes of obeah man drew on the reality of policing strategies, which worked partly through the use of information supplied by disaffected former clients of individual practitioners, and partly through the entrapment of practitioners whose clients did not report them. But in writing about such strategies, Thomas failed to mention the reports against obeah practitioners that informed many arrests. As a result, he, like many of his peers, presented lower-class Jamaican "belief in obeah" as monolithic, despite the fact that the more detailed evidence of the day-to-day policing of obeah suggests that people operated within a flexible framework. It seems that the existence of spiritually caused harm was taken for granted but that the ability of particular healers to do their work effectively was constantly under scrutiny, rather than greeted with the universal awe and fear described in much writing about obeah.

The construction of obeah as revealed in the records of actual cases was a dialogic process, to which the actions, decisions, and thoughts of ordinary people contributed in important ways. But this was an unequal dialogue. Its inequality is revealed in the ways that, especially in translation for an international audience, the involvement of non-elite Jamaicans in describing the boundaries of obeah was simplified and thinned out. In the writings of Herbert Thomas and his peers, ordinary people might be obeah's perpetrators or its dupes, but they could not be participants in its making. Obeah was simply there, an already-constituted target for prosecution. Repeated declarations that obeah was an evil that must be eradicated, and that policing would lead to its eradication, served to enhance its significance in colonial constructs of the Caribbean. Despite the complex negotiations that underlay the enforcement of laws against it, obeah as a discursive construct remained an ever-present sign of Caribbean people's position on the margins of "civilization."

NOTES

1. J. Lorand Matory, *Black Atlantic Religion: Tradition, Transnationalism, and Matriarchy in the Afro-Brazilian Candomblé* (Princeton: Princeton University Press, 2005); Kevin A. Yelvington, ed., *Afro-Atlantic Dialogues: Anthropology in the Diaspora* (Santa Fe: School of American Research Press, 2006).

2. Diana Paton, "Obeah Acts: Producing and Policing the Boundaries of Religion in the Caribbean," *Small Axe* 13, no. 1 (2009): 4.

3. For an important study that uses newspaper reports of obeah prosecutions, alongside other sources, to elucidate Jamaica's "Afro-Creole belief system," see Brian L. Moore and Michele A. Johnson, *Neither Led nor Driven: Contesting British Cultural Imperialism in Jamaica, 1865–1920* (Mona: University of the West Indies Press, 2004), 14–95.

4. Jamaican newspaper reports have been particularly accessible since the publication of a full-text-searchable digital edition of the leading Kingston newspaper, the *Gleaner*, at http://www.newspaperarchive.com/.

5. The Obeah Law (Jamaica), Law 5 of 1898, The National Archives of the UK (hereafter TNA): Public Record Office (hereafter PRO) CO 139/108.

6. Rather than attempting to make a judgment about who was or was not a genuine obeah practitioner, I generally use the more neutral terms "spiritual worker" or "ritual specialist." The question of whether a particular individual was an obeah man or woman was often precisely what was at stake in the prosecutions discussed here. Very few people used the terms "obeah man" or "obeah woman" self-ascriptively, especially in the records of encounters with the state that are the main source for this chapter, although some of them may have embraced this identity in other contexts.

7. See *Africa: Journal of the International Institute of African Languages and Culture* 8, no. 4 (1935), especially the articles by G. St. J. Orde Brown, C. Clifton Roberts, and Frank Melland. On Ortiz and brujería, see Stephan Palmié, *Wizards and Scientists: Explorations in Afro-Cuban Modernity and Tradition* (Durham: Duke University Press, 2002); Alejandra Marina Bronfman, *Measures of Equality: Social Science, Citizenship, and Race in Cuba, 1902–1940* (Chapel Hill: University of North Carolina Press, 2004). On the role of policing in constructing caste, see Nicholas B. Dirks, *Castes of Mind: Colonialism and the Making of Modern India* (Princeton: Princeton University Press, 2001), 181–88.

8. For histories of policing in the Caribbean, see Howard Johnson, "Patterns of Policing in the Post-emancipation British Caribbean, 1835–95," in *Policing the Empire: Government, Authority and Control, 1830–1940*, ed. David M. Anderson and David Killingray (Manchester: Manchester University Press, 1991), 71–91; Howard Johnson, "Social Control and the Colonial State: The Reorganisation of the Police Force in the Bahamas, 1888–1893," *Slavery and Abolition* 7, no. 1 (1986): 46–58; David Vincent Trotman, *Crime in Trinidad: Conflict and Control in a Plantation Society, 1838–1900* (Knoxville: University of Tennessee Press, 1986); Jonathan Dalby, "A 'Cinderella Service'? The Organization and Personnel of the Jamaican Police before and after 1865" (paper presented to the Department of History and Archaeology at the University of the West Indies, Mona, November 2008). I would like to thank Jonathan Dalby for sharing this paper with me. On policing elsewhere in the British Empire, see David Arnold, *Police Power and Colonial Rule: Madras, 1859–1947* (Delhi: Oxford University Press, 1986); Georgina Sinclair, *At the End of the Line: Colonial Policing and the Imperial Endgame 1945–80* (Manchester: Manchester University Press, 2006); Anderson and Killingray, *Policing the Empire*; David M. Anderson and David Killingray, eds., *Policing and Decolonisation: Politics, Nationalism and the Police, 1917–65* (Manchester: Manchester University Press, 1992).

9. For partial exceptions, see Justin Willis, "Thieves, Drunkards, and Vagrants: Defining Crime in Colonial Mombasa, 1902–32," in Anderson and Killingray, *Policing the Empire*, 219–35; Trotman, *Crime in Trinidad*, 213–70.

10. Thomas's career is recounted in his book *The Story of a West Indian Policeman; or, Forty-Seven Years in the Jamaica Constabulary* (Kingston: Gleaner, 1927), and in numerous letters to his superiors, including his statement in response to charges of embezzlement, enclosed in Bengough to Ripon, no. 322, August 15, 1893, TNA: PRO CO 137/561; Thomas to Ripon, no. 246, June 11, 1894, enclosed in Bengough to Ripon,

no. 246, June 12, 1894, TNA: PRO CO 137/561; and Thomas to Ripon, no. 340, August 25, 1894, enclosed in Bengough to Ripon, no. 340, August 30, 1894, TNA: PRO CO 137/561. In several of these letters, Thomas complained of financial difficulties.

11. See Herbert Thomas's *Untrodden Jamaica* (Kingston: Aston W. Gardner, 1890); *The Story of a West Indian Policeman*; and *Something about Obeah* (n.p., 1891). The only copy I have located of Thomas's pamphlet is enclosed in Bengough to Ripon, no. 340, August 30, 1894, TNA: PRO CO 137/561.

12. There is an extensive literature on this topic, much of it focused on the London Great Exhibition of 1851. For international perspectives, see especially Robert A. Rydell, *All the World's a Fair: Visions of Empire at American International Expositions, 1876–1916* (Chicago: University of Chicago Press, 1984); Paul Greenhalgh, *Ephemeral Vistas: The Expositions Universelles, Great Exhibitions and World's Fairs, 1951–1939* (Manchester: Manchester University Press, 1988); Peter H. Hoffenberg, *An Empire on Display: English, Indian, and Australian Exhibitions from the Crystal Palace to the Great War* (Berkeley: University of Berkeley Press, 2001). On the Jamaican exhibition, see Frank Fonda Taylor, *To Hell with Paradise: A History of the Jamaican Tourist Industry* (Pittsburgh: University of Pittsburgh Press, 1993), 55–67; Karen Booth, "When Jamaica Welcomed the World: The Great Exhibition of 1891," *Jamaica Journal* 18, no. 3 (1985): 39–51; Krista A. Thompson, *An Eye for the Tropics: Tourism, Photography, and Framing the Caribbean Picturesque* (Durham: Duke University Press, 2006), 31, 80, 87–91; Ronald J. Mahoney, "Kingston 1891," in *Encyclopedia of World's Fairs and Expositions*, ed. John E. Findling and Kimberly D. Pelle (Jefferson, N.C.: McFarland, 2008), 110–12.

13. James Gilbert, "World's Fairs as Historical Events," in *Fair Representations: World's Fairs and the Modern World*, ed. Robert W. Rydell and Nancy E. Gwinn (Amsterdam: VU Press, 1994), 17.

14. Paul Young, "Mission Impossible: Globalization and the Great Exhibition," in *Britain, the Empire, and the World at the Great Exhibition of 1851*, ed. Jeffrey A. Auerbach and Peter H. Hoffenberg (Aldershot, United Kingdom: Ashgate, 2008), 3–25.

15. Thompson, *An Eye for the Tropics*, 206, 30–31.

16. On representations of India, see Hoffenberg, *An Empire on Display*; Aram A. Yengoyan, "Culture, Ideology and World's Fairs: Colonizer and Colonized in Comparative Perspective" in Rydell and Gwinn, *Fair Representations*, 62–83.

17. S. Lee Bapty, ed., *International Exhibition, Jamaica, 1891, Official Catalogue* (Jamaica: Government Printing, 1891), 16, 55–78; Taylor, *To Hell with Paradise*, 56–57, 62. For other descriptions of the exhibition, see *A Tourists' Guide to the Parishes of Jamaica Together with an Account Descriptive of the Jamaica Exhibition, 1891, Being a Supplement to DeSouza's Edition of the Jamaica Commercial Almanack and Pocket Journal* (Kingston: DeSouza, 1890); C. Washington Eves, "Jamaica and Its Forthcoming Exhibition," *Journal of the Society of Arts* 38, no. 1958 (1890): 661–72; Frank Cundall, "The Jamaica Exhibition," *Journal of the Society of Arts* 39, no. 2018 (1891): 734–37.

18. Bapty, *International Exhibition, Jamaica, 1891*, 55–78, Eves, "Jamaica and Its Forthcoming Exhibition," 664.

19. Bapty, *International Exhibition, Jamaica, 1891*, 73.

20. "The Exhibition," *Gleaner*, February 2, 1891, 2.

21. Thomas, *Something about Obeah*, 9–10. In addition to organizing this exhibit, Thomas undertook a trip to the Blue Mountains in order to "search for [Maroon] relics that might be of interest at the forthcoming Exhibition," although it is unclear whether he actually displayed anything from this trip. Thomas, *Untrodden Jamaica*, 35. For a discussion of Thomas's writing about his expedition, see Jenny Sharpe, *Ghosts of Slavery: A Literary Archaeology of Black Women's Lives* (Minneapolis: University of Minnesota Press, 2003), 8–17.

22. Rosalind Shaw, *Memories of the Slave Trade: Ritual and the Historical Imagination in Sierra Leone* (Chicago: University of Chicago Press, 2002), 39–40; Arthur Abraham, *An Introduction to the Pre-colonial History of the Mende of Sierra Leone* (Lewiston, N.Y.: Edwin Mellen, 2003), 155–56; Christopher Fyfe, *A History of Sierra Leone* (Oxford: Oxford University Press, 1962), 476.

23. Johannes Fabian, *Time and the Other: How Anthropology Makes Its Object* (New York: Columbia University Press, 1983); Anne McClintock, *Imperial Leather: Race, Gender, and Sexuality in the Colonial Contest* (New York: Routledge, 1995).

24. Thomas, *Something about Obeah*, 8. The idea that Caribbean religious practice represented a deterioration from an African original was and remains common. See, for instance, A. B. Ellis's nearly contemporary argument that Haitian Vodou represented the "disintegration of the [Ewe vodun] cult from its proper"—that is, African—"habit and surroundings." A. B. Ellis, "On Vōdu Worship," *Popular Science Monthly* 38 (1891): 660.

25. Hoffenberg, *An Empire on Display*, 151–65.

26. Thomas, *Something about Obeah*, 8.

27. "The Victoria Quarterly," *Gleaner*, February 9, 1891, 4. "Detestable enormities" refers to the 1544 and 1552 litanies of the Church of England's Book of Common Prayer, which included the phrase, "From the tyranny of the bishop of Rome and all his detestable enormities . . . Good Lord deliver us." See online editions at the Society of Archbishop Justus's website: http://justus.anglican.org/resources/bcp/Litany1544/Litany_1544.htm and http://justus.anglican.org/resources/bcp/1552/Litany_1552.htm. The use of anti-Catholic rhetoric was common in elite anti-obeah discourse.

28. "Exhibition Notes," *Gleaner*, February 11, 1891, 6.

29. W. P. Livingstone, *Black Jamaica: A Study in Evolution* (London: Sampson Low Marston, 1899), 197–98. The existence of this sideshow is intriguing, but I have been unable to find any further evidence about what it consisted of or how it was perceived.

30. Thomas, *The Story of a West Indian Policeman*, 314.

31. Taylor, *To Hell with Paradise*, 62, 66.

32. Similarly, Jenny Sharpe argues that Thomas's *Untrodden Jamaica* "served as an authoritative source on Nanny's legendary status among maroons for the first half of the twentieth century," and that the "terms associated with her name . . . are derived from this work." *Ghosts of Slavery*, 17.

33. Thomas, *Something about Obeah*, 5.

34. Ibid. The claim that this class of obeah man "does not accept a small fee" is meant to imply that the fees are large, not that such practitioners do not charge.

35. On the idea of the obeah man as charlatan, see Paton, "Obeah Acts."

36. Thomas, *Something about Obeah*, 5.

37. May Robinson, "Obeah Worship in East and West Indies," *Folk-Lore: A Quarterly Review of Myth, Tradition, Institution and Custom* 4 (1893): 210.

38. Ibid., 211–12. Although it seems likely that Thomas was involved in the arrest of Alexander Ellis, he does not mention the name in *Something about Obeah*. Robinson says the figure was sent back to England after the exhibition; its current location is unknown.

39. Martha Beckwith, *Black Roadways: A Study of Jamaican Folk Life* (Chapel Hill: University of North Carolina Press, 1929), 107.

40. Joseph J. Williams, *Psychic Phenomena of Jamaica* (New York: Dial, 1934), 102. On Williams and his influence, see Kenneth M. Bilby and Jerome S. Handler, "Obeah: Healing and Protection in West Indian Slave Life," *Journal of Caribbean History* 38, no. 2 (2004): 153–83; and Stephan Palmié's afterword in this book.

41. S. Leslie Thornton, "'Obeah' in Jamaica," *Journal of the Society of Comparative Legislation* 5, no. 2 (1903): 262–70. This article was used as a primary source by Francis Alexis for "Anti-obeah Laws and the Constitution," an unpublished typescript from 1973 held at the University of Guyana Library. For Thornton's background, see "Court Circular," *Times* (London), 9 October 31, 1896, which notes his transfer from the position of attorney general of Saint Vincent to resident magistrate in Jamaica.

42. John Symonds Udal, "Obeah in the West Indies," *Folk-Lore: A Quarterly Review of Myth, Tradition, Institution and Custom* 26, no. 3 (1915): 255–95. Udal was chief justice of the Leeward Islands from 1900 to 1911, according to his obituary in *Notes and Queries*, March 25, 1925, 216. For Beckwith's use of Udal, see *Black Roadways*, 107.

43. Earl to Colonial Secretary, May 9, 1905, enclosed in Knollys to Lyttleton, no. 218, May 19, 1905, TNA: PRO CO 152/287.

44. Bengough to Ripon, no. 322, August 15, 1894, TNA: PRO CO 137/561. For more detail on this case, see Moore and Johnson, *Neither Led nor Driven*, 17–18.

45. Thomas, *Something about Obeah*, 4. Kellerman's prosecution and sentence are listed in "Table Showing. . . . Cases of Obeah and Myalism Adjudicated . . . from 1 August 1887 to 31 July 1892," TNA: PRO CO 137/550.

46. "A Sensational Obeah Case," *Gleaner*, September 21, 1893, 3.

47. The articles are now contained in the McCrae Scrapbook, Jamaica Archives, Spanish Town 7/97/3, f 133. Thanks to James Robertson for alerting me to the existence of this source.

48. W. B. Fraser, "An Open Letter," *Gleaner*, July 7, 1930, 12.

49. "A Charge Fails," *Gleaner*, July 1, 1911, 6.

50. "The Past Fortnight," October 16, 1893; "The Past Fortnight," November 13, 1893; "The Past Fortnight," January 8, 1894; "In Hanover," November 1, 1898; "Obeah

Charge," October 26, 1911; "Fined £20 on Obeah Charge at Montego Bay," September 8, 1927; "Arrested on Obeah Charge at Alley," September 26, 1930; "Here and There in the News," April 30, 1934, all in the *Gleaner*. "Arrests for Obeah in Clarendon," "A Baker's Dozen and a Word of Praise for the Clarendon Police," July 28, 1899; "Crime in Clarendon"; "Obeahism Extraordinary," press cuttings from unnamed newspapers all in McCrae Scrapbook, Jamaica Archives, Spanish Town 7/97/3, ff. 63, 65 and 133 (incorrectly numbered, following 65). For discussion of representations of police work against obeah practitioners in Trinidad, see Maarit Forde, "Policing Religion in Colonial Trinidad" (paper presented at the conference of the Society for Caribbean Studies, Hull, United Kingdom, June 2009).

51. This figure counts each individual arrested or charged for an incident once. It includes reports of prosecutions and arrests for the following: practicing obeah, consulting an obeah man or woman, possession of "implements of obeah," and larceny in cases that clearly relate to obeah (such cases usually involved designation of the transfer of money from client to spiritual worker as "larceny"). Many trials involved more than one defendant: there were 766 separate incidents/prosecutions. The prosecutions were not distributed equally over time: 94 reports of trials or arrests were located for the 1890s, 96 for the 1900s, then between 121 and 236 in the 1910s, 1920s, and 1930s. The number dropped back to 96 in the 1940s, then fell again to 64 between 1950 and 1959, and to 6 in each of the decades beginning in 1960 and 1970.

52. Sally Engle Merry, "Courts as Performances: Domestic Violence Hearings in a Hawai'i Family Court," in *Contested States: Law, Hegemony, and Resistance*, ed. Mindie Lazarus-Black and Susan F. Hirsch (New York: Routledge, Chapman and Hall, 1994), 36.

53. Examples include "The Black Art: Case of Obeah Tried at Montego Bay," April 18, 1911; "Some Cases in Rural Courts," May 15, 1916; and "The Criminal Courts of the Metropolis," February 20, 1926, all in the *Gleaner*.

54. For instance, Robert Campbell was arrested after Albertha Josephs, who was "in a friendship" with him, reported him to the police after they had "disagreements." The police then set up a trap in which a policeman told Campbell a "tale of ill-luck" in order to entice him to perform a ritual that would lead to his arrest. "Arrest Made," *Gleaner*, October 14, 1913, 10. I have included this case and those like it in the group of those resulting from a civilian report, while recognizing that other cases classified as entrapment may have been preceded by similar reports to the police that were not mentioned in court.

55. For instance, a witness in the prosecution of Samuel Leslie stated that he had "boasted" that the police had been after him for four years but had not succeeded in catching him; he was eventually arrested when police got a search warrant based on "information received." "Curious Obeah Case," *Gleaner*, July 13, 1899.

56. This claim relates to the proportions of those cases where I was able to make a judgment about how the arrest was made, which was slightly more than half the total cases. The ambiguity of much of the data, along with the brevity of many reports,

explains the large number of cases that I have not categorized. I suspect that the number of cases initiated by civilians was actually larger than it appears here, because civilian witnesses had every reason to hide the fact that they had made a report to the police.

57. "The 'Doctor' Scott Case," *Gleaner*, June 25, 1904, 6.

58. A shut pan is a lidded metal pan used to carry food, and also frequently associated with spiritual matters, as its lid allows it to be used to catch duppies. F. G. Cassidy and R. B. Le Page, *Dictionary of Jamaican English* (Mona: University of the West Indies Press, 2002), 408.

59. "Obeah Trial at Montego Bay," *Gleaner*, October 1, 1907, 8.

60. "The Allman Town Obeah Case" *Gleaner*, October 14, 1907, 1. There are echoes of this attitude in contemporary Jamaica. During a 2008 interview with Alfonso Robinson, who described himself to me as a "spiritual worker," I asked whether he had heard of people in the past being harassed by police for the kind of work he does. He answered in the negative, and went on to say that anyone prosecuted was "not workman. Them are idiot, they don't do what they are doing." That is, an effective workman (ritual healer/obeah man) would by definition be able to defeat the law.

61. "The Allman Town Obeah Charge," September 24, 1902, 13; "Some News of the Day," October 9, 1902, 1, both in *Gleaner*.

62. Of the 529 cases where a reason for consulting a ritual specialist was given, 145 related to healing, while 82 related to court cases. In some cases, more than one reason was indicated.

63. "Charges Heard," *Gleaner*, January 27, 1911, 13.

64. "Obeahman Given 6 Months Term in the Penitentiary," *Gleaner*, July 10, 1931, 3. For more on the use of obeah to influence court cases, see Claudette Anderson, "Judge, Jury, or Obeahman? Power Dynamics in the Jamaican House o' Law" (paper presented at the Obeah and Other Powers: The Politics of Caribbean Religion conference, Newcastle, United Kingdom, June 16–18, 2008).

65. "Alleged Obeah in Clarendon," June 16, 1899, press cutting from unnamed newspaper in McCrae Scrapbook, Jamaica Archives, Spanish Town 7/97/3 f 62.

66. "Old Man Is Found Guilty of Practising Obeah—Fined £15," *Gleaner*, July 30, 1931, 18.

67. "Case of Alleged Obeah," *Gleaner*, July 23, 1929, 7. For a similar case, in which the alleged obeah man promised a bottle of medicine and then refused to give it because he said the police were outside, see "Charge of Practicing Obeah," *Gleaner*, April 6, 1916, 14.

68. "Cases Heard in Resident Magistrate's Court," *Gleaner*, August 5, 1915, 1.

69. "Obeahman Sentenced to 12 Months and Eighteen Lashes," *Gleaner*, June 23, 1933, 7. Hall was an experienced spiritual worker who had been prosecuted for obeah on at least three previous occasions. He described himself in court as a preacher and a Baptist.

70. Herbert T. Thomas to the Marquis of Ripon, August 25, 1894, enclosed in Bengough to Ripon, no. 340, August 30, 1894, TNA: PRO CO 137/561.

71. These have been included in the entrapment cases for the purposes of the analysis.

72. For cases in which Ada Bogle acted as a prosecution witness, see "Bog Walk Obeah Case in Spanish Town Court," March 3, 1931; "Head of Alleged Band of Faith Healers Discharged by Court," October 3, 1932; "Costs Woman £26 17/ to Take 'Ghosts' off Man," September 1, 1933; "Six Months for Obeahman," December 14, 1933; "Obeah Case Fails in the Police Court," January 13, 1934; "Convicted in May Pen Court on Charge of Practising Obeah," February 5, 1934; "Obeah Charge Fails in City R. M. Court," August 9, 1934, all in *Gleaner*. Other regular police spies were Florence Morgan (active in 1934) and Essie Brown (active in 1933 and 1934).

73. "Obeah Charge Fails in City R. M. Court," *Gleaner*, August 9, 1934, 5. Individual agents could be active only for brief periods before their reputations spread too widely among potential victims and became tainted in the eyes of the courts. Thus, in the same case that revealed Bogle's acquisition of property, the magistrate acquitted the defendant, George Scott, saying that "he did not want to see Ada Bogle to testify in obeah cases which would come up before him. He did not want her to give evidence in his court" because she "knew too much."

74. "Arrested on Obeah Charge," *Gleaner*, April 6, 1912, 4.

75. "Obeah Charges," *Gleaner*, October 20, 1913, 13.

76. "Trial of Zachariah Thomas," *Gleaner*, July 10, 1920, 4. For a similar case, in which a woman went to the police when the powder supplied to get her husband to "love her some more" had the opposite effect, see "Failing Love," *Gleaner*, October 6, 1913, 14.

77. "Full Court Continues to Hear Criminal Appeals," *Gleaner*, September 22, 1932, 18.

78. "Obeah Charge," *Gleaner*, April 14, 1909, 3.

79. "Cases Tried in the Courts of Two Parishes," *Gleaner*, April 7, 1922, 3. See "Obeah Charge," *Gleaner*, January 13, 1914, 13–14, for a case that arose after a spiritual healer who sold ritual medicine by post refused to accept an unsatisfied client taking back the horse he had given in exchange.

80. "Obeah Charge," May 23, 1907; "Obeah Charge," May 27, 1907, both *Gleaner*. Barnett denied that she had performed the ritual, and argued that Bryan and Lewis were attempting to frame her. We cannot know whether the ritual described by Lewis in court really occurred, but Barnett's claim that Bryan initiated contact with the police because of his resentment at her refusal to lend him money was the only explanation offered at the trial for his behavior.

81. "Interesting Case at Halfway Tree," *Gleaner*, May 13, 1916, 4.

82. Anthony Harriott, *Police and Crime Control in Jamaica: Problems of Reforming Ex-colonial Constabularies* (Mona: University of the West Indies Press, 2000); Dalby, "A 'Cinderella Service'?"

7.

The Moral Economy of Spiritual Work:
Money and Rituals in Trinidad and Tobago

MAARIT FORDE

Structures of capital accumulation and exchange of money have long been embedded in various Caribbean ritual practices, including those the colonial state in the English-speaking Caribbean defined as "obeah."[1] Drawing on the historical record of obeah prosecutions in early twentieth-century Trinidad and ethnography of contemporary Tobago, this chapter explores a moral economy of healing, divining, and other spiritual work and outlines the premises of a ritual sphere of exchange. Despite the prevalence of money in both ritual practice and related discourse in Trinidad and Tobago, the relationships, modality, and temporal logic of this sphere do not correspond to those of commodity exchange, or capitalism more generally. The ritual sphere of exchange is better understood in the context of generalized reciprocity: spiritual work and its compensations belong to a local transactional order marked by various types of gift exchange and ritualized sharing of food, for example in rites of passage and rites of exchange and communion.[2]

MONEY, EVIL, AND MODERNITY

Money, in the grand narrative of economic anthropology since Karl Polanyi's groundbreaking work, has been credited with the power to transform not only economic systems and transactional orders, but also values, moralities, and, ultimately, the social structure of pre-capitalist societies.[3] In this narrative, the introduction of money and commercial capitalism brings along a transition from traditional to modern society. Maurice Bloch and Jonathan Parry trace the general moral condemnation of money and trade in Western discourse, apparent in much of the transformation narrative, all the way back to Aristotle (and later, Thomas Aquinas), and locate the idea of the transformative power of money particularly in Simmel's thought.[4] For Simmel, money disintegrates preceding social ties and isolates individuals, promoting individualism at the expense of solidarity and community (particularly kinship ties), and catalyzes the transition from Gemeinschaft to Gesellschaft.[5]

Recent contributions to the anthropology of money have questioned the Simmelian view of the disintegrating and transformative power of money. Bloch and Parry point out that analyses of money as an agent of modernization have been underpinned by Western discourses and notions about money, and that culturally and historically nuanced research is needed to unveil different conceptions of money, coexisting transactional orders, and the general-purpose currencies that preceded state-issued money.[6] Whereas Bloch and Parry undermine the thesis of money as a catalyst of social change by arguing that money has no intrinsic qualities that would differentiate it from other objects of exchange, Joel Robbins and David Akin look at indigenous Melanesian currencies in the same analytical framework with state-issued currencies and delineate several qualities that, to varying degrees, these "moneys" have in common. They argue that all currencies share certain features and that Western, or "modern," money is not as radically different from other variants as has been assumed.[7]

In line with Euro-Christian ambivalence about money, much of substantivist economic anthropology portrays money as amoral or immoral: along with modernization, money brings forth a particular worldview, moral confusion or even a lack of morality.[8] A similar causality emerges in some of the numerous recent ethnographies of "witchcraft" or "the occult" in African societies. In this body of work, such practices are analyzed as reactions to or commentaries on modernity, and particularly capitalism, new forms and novel distribution of wealth, or neoliberalism.[9] Peter Geschiere suggests that witchcraft in Cameroon, and in African societies more generally, has a twofold orientation either toward accumulation of wealth and power, or toward leveling difference in wealth and power.[10] This latter, subversive type of witchcraft is more common in eastern and southern Africa, argues Isak Niehaus, who characterizes the typical witch as a marginal and subordinate person with malevolent powers.[11] In the same vein, it has been posited that witches express envy toward materially better-off people, particularly kin.[12] In many accounts, the have-nots suspected and accused of witchcraft are rural relatives and dependents of urban workers. On the other hand, wealth and power can be indicative of witchcraft: Geschiere describes new forms of witchcraft, in which the nouveau riche exploit zombie labor to accumulate wealth.[13] This accumulative function of witchcraft, then, increases rather than levels inequality. A basic tenet in this discussion is that capital accumulation and the introduction of new forms of wealth bring about inequality and antagonism, which serve as fertile ground for witchcraft accusations. While this proliferating literature includes excellent ethnography and inspiring theoretical advances, it has been criticized for an apparent lack of historicity and specificity,[14] for predictably functionalist models of witchcraft,[15] and for presenting the occult as modern (almost in the sense of contemporary), without paying attention to cultural continuities.[16] Bill Maurer's concern that the debate reproduces the emphasis on money as an agent of evil is not unfounded.[17]

Placing the Caribbean in the history of modernity complicates analyses of money and morality. Central loci of the emerging global capitalism since the earliest phases of the plantation system and populated mostly through forced migrations, Caribbean societies do not align with the evolutionary model of social and cultural transformation advanced in substantivist economic anthropology. With plantation slavery and sugar production, capitalism—and, with it, money—has been shaping Caribbean history for an exceptionally long period.[18] As little of precolonial culture has survived in most of the region, however, the long presence of capitalism cannot be analytically juxtaposed against preceding, indigenous economic systems. Inquiries into Caribbean moral economies require tools that do not replicate the modern/premodern dichotomy. The analytic categories for two distinct transactional orders as proposed by Bloch and Parry, along with the fine-tuned model of spheres of exchange in Robbins and Akin's work, seem helpful in attempts to make sense of the norms confining the use of money in Caribbean rituals. One of the transactional orders that Bloch and Parry outline is oriented toward reproducing the long-term social and cosmological order, and the other is marked by short-term exchanges involving individual gain, competition, wage labor, and commodities.[19] The ethnographic accounts in their edited collection show how money, normally indicative of the short-term order, can be symbolically transformed into a resource that can help to maintain the long-term cosmological order. In light of ethnographic and archival sources, it seems that the different logics of such orders structure religious norms on money and accumulation in Trinidad and Tobago.

Drawing on Marshall Sahlins's work, Robbins and Akin conceptualize different spheres of exchange in terms of the relationships involved, the modality of exchange, and the objects exchanged.[20] Morally appropriate exchange takes place not only within correct relationships, but also within the correct modality—be it sharing, competitive exchange, or equivalent exchange. As in transactional orders, money in many of the excellent Melanesian ethnographies of their volume has been associated with one or some, but not all, of the spheres.[21] If the modalities of exchange are transformed accordingly, then the flow of money across different spheres is acceptable in contemporary Melanesia. When boundaries between the spheres have collapsed, however, money has become morally ambiguous or evil.[22] In the Caribbean context, moral arguments about money cannot reference spheres of exchange devoid of money, but the elements of such spheres—the exchange relationship, modality, and objects—provide a suitable matrix for deciphering the moral economy within which Trinidadian ritual practitioners have operated.

PAYING FOR SPIRITUAL WORK

Money was occasionally used as payment for spiritual work in Caribbean societies in the period of slavery. Early records of cash payment for ritual practice include the case of an enslaved man, working as a butler in Jamaica in 1770, who was alleged to have "bought some obi" to revenge his sister's punishment by the master.[23] In 1831, a Jamaican slave named Polydore was alleged to have asked for two dollars, a cock, and a pint of rum for healing a man whom he had previously made "very sick" by nailing his shadow on a silk cotton tree.[24] After emancipation, as obeah legislation was rewritten throughout the British Caribbean, obeah was defined as fraud in the new laws of Trinidad and Tobago, Jamaica, British Guiana, and Barbados.[25] This meant that the exchange of money between the obeahman or woman and the client was central evidence of "assumption of supernatural powers" for financial gain. Toward the end of the nineteenth century, descriptions of payments became a standard element of court hearings and were reported in detail in local newspapers.[26]

Money changing hands is a recurring theme in the extensive reportage of the arrest and prosecution of an alleged obeahman named Percival Duval in 1920, and I want to look into his case as an example of the linkages between money and spiritual work during the period of heightened state interest in policing religion in the region.[27] Duval, of Princes Town in southern Trinidad, was a successful businessman and a popular healer. He described his healing work as "advising people about medicine," and his clientele came from all over Trinidad, seeking help for physical suffering and breaches in social relations, and paying modest fees for his consultations. In October 1920, Duval was arrested and charged with "practicing obeah[—and] thereby obtaining $5 from Alice Pamphile by the assumption of supernatural power." Like more than half of the obeah arrests in Trinidad that were reported in the *Port of Spain Gazette* between 1890 and 1930, Duval's arrest followed the deliberate entrapment of the defendant by the police. Lance Corporal Lewis Lambert, a specialist in obeah arrests, had designed the operation. He had previously sent his girlfriend, Margaret Thomas, to entrap Duval several times, but Duval became suspicious of Thomas because of her "insisting that she give him money and insisting that she wanted obeah." Finally the strategy was revised, and Constable Auguste of Port of Spain went to Duval's house with Alice Pamphile, armed with seven dollars and instructions from Lambert.[28] The two pretended to be a married couple from Port of Spain. Constable Auguste told Duval that he was a timekeeper at the Point Fortin oil fields and that the boss had started to dislike him. He wanted Duval to help him keep his job. The "wife" then complained that she was feeling ill and they asked for soda, giving twenty-three shillings to Duval for his help. Not trusting the couple, Duval suggested that they go to the pharmacy next to the police station to get their medicine; however, Lance-Corporal Lambert, who had been waiting outside, decided to go through with the arrest. A fight ensued between several civilians (including Duval and his brothers) and the police. Failing to arrest Duval, Lambert eventually charged six people, including Duval's mother, with obstructing the police, and Duval's two brothers with assault.[29]

The case got more complicated as Duval and Constable Auguste turned out to be lodge brothers. Duval was finally brought before the city magistrate in Port of Spain after he and two of his friends had offered Constable Auguste twenty-nine dollars as an alleged bribe, asking him to refrain from giving evidence against Duval. Duval was a member and trustee of several lodges, and Auguste, who belonged to the same Oddfellows lodge as Duval, had sent Duval letters in which he promised his help and guidance in the court case.[30] The prolonged process of trapping Duval depended on getting him to accept money from the agents provocateurs, but it was Duval's payment to Constable Auguste to compensate for his loyalty that finally resulted in his arrest and prosecution. Percival Duval was sentenced to serve six months of imprisonment and to receive twelve lashes with the cat-o'-nine-tails.

As this entrapment case gone awry shows, ritual healing was routinely exchanged for cash. In every obeah arrest reported in the *Port of Spain Gazette* in Trinidad in the late nineteenth and in the twentieth century, money paid for the services of the ritual specialist served as the primary incriminating evidence. Because the exchange of money was definitive of illegal practice of obeah, the agents provocateurs in entrapment cases—disguised policemen, their sweethearts, or police informers—always had to hand money, usually marked with the initials of the policeman in charge of the operation, to the ritual specialist before the arrest could be made. Ritual specialists charged relatively modest fees for their work: their clients' payments normally ranged from a few shillings to a few dollars, rarely more than ten. Witnesses often testified of having been asked to pay higher fees, but that ritual specialists had then settled for small "down payments." Some of this money was used to purchase substances and materials needed in the rituals, like candles, rum, or fowls, and according to witnesses, the ritual specialist had often carefully itemized the fee according to the necessary paraphernalia.[31]

In addition to the use of money as compensation for services, including those legally understood as obeah, Duval's story casts light on the various linkages between this "obeah" and the capitalist economy more generally. Although obeah has been mystified by locating it in distant, rural places in fiction, calypsos, and stories—as well as by colonial elites' insistence that the proper place for obeah was in "the wilds of Africa"[32] rather than in modern, civilized colonies—the majority of people charged with practicing obeah in Trinidad lived in towns and cities, like Duval. Raquel Romberg observes a similar locatedness of contemporary *brujería* in Puerto Rico—witches prosper in commercial centers, not in the bush.[33] Percival Duval was a cane and cocoa proprietor in Princes Town, who lent money on promissory notes "with good security" and owned a car, which he hired out. Denying any connections to obeah, he claimed that the dirt found in a drawer of his desk by the police and displayed as evidence against him (presumably as graveyard dirt, to be used to access the spirit world) was, in fact, a sample of soil that his brother was taking to an analyst to discover possible traces of oil in his property.[34] Henry Padmore, arrested in Trinidad in 1909, was another urban, well-established, self-employed obeah convict. Originally from Grenada, Padmore speculated in horses and provisions and had a large clientele in and beyond San Fernando, which the *Port of Spain Gazette* compared favorably with those of "many of our local medical men who have established a fairly good practice. From far and near did men and women patronise 'Doctor Padmore.'" When he was taken to the police station, a crowd of 400 people followed him, and among the evidence against him were 180 letters from clients.[35] Practices classified as obeah in Trinidadian courtrooms and newspapers took place alongside other ways of making a living embedded in the industrializing colony's cash economy.

People who consulted ritual specialists like Duval or Padmore were equally incorporated in the economy, most obviously as wage laborers. Among the problems that people sought to solve by consulting such specialists in Trinidad in this period, work-related worries and aspirations formed the largest category, followed by physical suffering, court cases, and breaches in relationships.[36] Because so many of the arrests were entrapments, we have limited knowledge of clients' genuine motives except for what can be deduced from clients' letters, witnesses' accounts, and the less numerous cases in which disguised policemen or agents provocateurs were not involved. It is noteworthy, however, that in entrapment cases, the bogus clients often quoted work-related problems as their reason for consulting the ritual specialist. Because it is likely that the police tried to make their stories as credible as possible in order to make a successful arrest, it seems that employment was a normal and common motive in encounters between clients and ritual specialists. People approached ritual specialists to get employment or to keep their jobs in shops or in the oil industry (and, less frequently, in the agricultural sector). Many, like the female client whose letter to the Trinidadian Dr. Williams is quoted below, were concerned about losing their livelihoods due to the jealousy or malice of coworkers or other perceived enemies.

In magistrates' and judges' verdicts and commentaries, "moneymaking" was singled out as a particularly deplorable aspect of the practices they classified as obeah. Magistrate S. J. P. Spicer, upon passing the verdict of Dr. Williams, declared that his was "a case of sheer robbery and ignorance,"[37] whereas Justice Deane thought that "the object of the obeah man is always so to play upon the superstitions of the ignorant or weak-minded as to induce them to part with their money in the expectation that he by his supernatural powers or knowledge may be able to obtain for them their desires."[38] Convicting the Trinidadian "Professor" Hubert Carrington to six months of hard labor and twelve strokes with the cat, Magistrate Deane pointed out that Carrington was "a young strong man, quite capable by manual labour or otherwise to support himself in an honest way.... [Deane] looked upon him as a pest and a rogue who lived entirely by this sort of thing. He was not a man who does ordinary work and when tempted, steals something, he was not like an ordinary thief."[39] A telling example of the dissemination of this image of the obeahman as a moneymaking charlatan was staged in the aftermath of the much-publicized Noitgedacht tragedy in Demerara:[40] a group of Boy Scouts played out an obeah trial and punished the "obeahman" "to make him see that it was better to engage in honest employment than to fleece unsophisticated people of their hard-earned cash."[41] The media had portrayed the main culprit in the actual Noitgedacht murder case as an itinerant "juggler and an obeahman . . . cheating people out of their money by means of tricks and obeah."[42]

As the introduction to this book suggests, obeah was an extremely inclusive and amorphous criminal category, and obeah prosecutions in Trinidad featured an eclectic array of ritual practitioners considered charlatans. In August 1920, the *Port of Spain Gazette* observed that "False magicians, 'jumbie' raisers, witch doctors and obeah 'professors' and other tricksters of that genus would appear to be getting rather numerous," going on to describe the arrest of Mahadeo, "an Indian man" of the town of San Fernando in southern Trinidad.

The report noted how the "professor" had "grown quite famous" and "did no manner of work; but he lived in style through the means of his 'clients.'" Mahadeo, like many other defendants identified as Indo-Trinidadian, was charged with practicing obeah.[43] The trope of the trickster was well established in colonial depictions of Indo-Trinidadian ritual specialists, particularly in the case of itinerant pundits, who traveled between estates and provided ritual services.[44] Aisha Khan shows that the persistent stigma of charlatanry has prevailed in both outsider and insider comments on pundits, from the colonial depictions of "the wily Babagee [sadhu]" who makes a good living by fooling uneducated laborers, to present-day dismissals of pundits as "scamps" lacking in ritual purity and knowledge.[45]

Although people like Mahadeo and Percival Duval were accused of being tricksters and charlatans, they were not charged with "obtaining money by false pretences," as the law defined fraud, but instead with "obtaining [money] by the assumption of supernatural power." When prosecuting such defendants, the state was not merely interested in protecting its subjects from fraud. The specifically targeted criminalization of ritual practices speaks of the civilizing mission of the empire; as voiced by several magistrates and local newspapers, obeah prosecutions aimed at weeding out "superstition," modes of thought and practices deemed unsuitable for a modern, civilized colony. The discourse on civilization and modernity that helped to rationalize religious persecution in British Caribbean colonies also served to produce a moral community—or in Gramscian terms, hegemony—in colonies like Trinidad, especially in the face of increasing claims for self-government and suffrage from the 1890s onward.[46] As Karen Fields argues regarding British colonial administration in Africa, it was inconceivable for the British to share the conceptual order and morality of what their African subjects identified as witchcraft; there could be no moral community of actual witchcraft beliefs integrating the rulers and the colonial populations. Therefore, witchcraft itself could not be criminalized. On the other hand, witchcraft accusations, cleansing movements, and trials were a common concern of the colonial governments in the British Africa, and this concern, albeit indirectly, helped to produce a moral community in relation to the same witchcraft that the state claimed did not exist.[47] In a similar way, the colonial legislation in the post-emancipation Caribbean did not criminalize obeah because of its assumed, negative consequences in the social lives and material realities of the people (or because of disruptive or violent "obeah" eradication movements, for that matter, since they were very rare in the British Caribbean with the exception of 1840s myalism in Jamaica). Instead, the condemnation of fraudulent moneymaking along with "superstition" tells of state concerns about the existence of alternative cosmologies and noninstitutionalized ritual practice. For the laboring people to accumulate (however modest) wealth, reputation, and power by means of ritual practice outside European-originated institutions undermined the hegemonic ways of knowing that were of vital importance to the status quo of post-slavery societies. The moderate wealth and, perhaps more important, notable social capital accumulated by successful ritual specialists went against the pyramid of power relations preferred by the colonial elites. I read the magistrates' and judges' disapproval of ritual specialists who did not make "an honest living" less in the light of the centuries-long unease in Western thought about the morality of material acquisition, but rather as stemming from a perceived threat of the uncontrolled empowerment of the underclass. What is more, the state's insistence on differentiating between "superstitious" and other charlatanry implies another perceived threat—that of the power of obeah.

THE EXCHANGE RELATIONSHIPS OF OBEAH

Whereas colonial legislation in Trinidad and Tobago framed obeah as a crime by referencing rules of commodity exchange, the social relations, modality of exchange, and temporal orientation of transactions in the realm of rituals in Trinidad did not correspond to those of mundane, commercial transactions. In line with the spheres outlined by Robbins and Akin, I suggest that ritual exchange—including payments for healing and other ritual treatments or performances, but also exchanges between human and spirits—has been qualitatively different from market exchange, although money can be, and has been for centuries, the object of exchange in both. Here my analysis departs from two outstanding ethnographic accounts of the moral economies of contemporary Caribbean religions, Karen Richman's *Migration and Vodou* (2005) and Raquel Romberg's *Witchcraft and Welfare* (2003)—largely due to the different economic development and colonial (and postcolonial) histories of Trinidad and Tobago, Haiti, and Puerto Rico. In the framework of world-system theory, Richman portrays the dual value structure of Haitian Vodou through the interdependent, although apparently opposite, moral systems of Guinea and Magik.[48] Whereas Guinea entails moral authority, tradition, and kinship ties—values of the peasant society—Magik is associated with money, wage labor, capitalist exploitation, individualism, migrants, and sorcery.[49] Accumulation, part of the Magik complex, is potentially immoral, while the morally superior peasant mode of production depends today on wage labour to survive. Contemporary Puerto Rican brujería, on the other hand, has become commodified, and values and practices inherent to consumer capitalism have been incorporated in its moral economy. Individualism and accumulation of wealth are morally acceptable, although prosperity may attract evil forces.[50] Unlike the dual morality of Vodou, brujería in Romberg's analysis inheres soundly within capitalism—with the reservation that social relations between brujos and their clients are not disembedded.

Instead of juxtaposing money and capitalism against another, morally superior system of exchange and values, or approaching ritual exchanges as inseparable from commodity exchange, I begin to investigate the proposed sphere of ritual exchange in terms of the social relations involved. In early twentieth-century Trinidad, letters written to defendants in obeah cases by their numerous clients were sometimes read as evidence in court, as they offered aggravating evidence of monetary transactions. In Percival Duval's case, the prosecution read aloud several letters in which people either "remonstrated with [Duval] for not giving a satisfactory medicine for value paid" or "eulogized him for the good his medicines had done for them."[51] When Dr. Williams, a ritual specialist of Siparia in southern Trinidad, was arrested in January 1910 and charged with obtaining two dollars by the assumption of supernatural power, several letters found at his house were read as evidence. One of the writers, a woman, thanked Dr. Williams for assisting her in a problematic domestic situation and outlined her commitment to continued remunerations: "Dear Sir, I must thank you for all the trouble you took, your work was well for the child was to be sent back—. I like advice because you see what is better for my welfare. I send you two dollars for your work, and every month I will send more to you and the same time let me know how much you charge for all your trouble. I must thank you again."[52] Another female client, asking Dr. Williams to help her husband, who she feared was about to lose his job due to a malevolent coworker, apologized as "owing to certain difficulties I cannot manage to give anything more just yet try your very best and see what you can do for him and I will keep you up fortnightly. I am sending you a bottle of fruit syrup tell when you write how you like it."[53] Such correspondence, quoted in connection to many prosecutions in this period, implies lasting exchange relationships between ritual specialists and their clients.

Transgressions of appropriate social relations, on the other hand, were reflected in a lack of solidarity between the ritual specialist and his or her clients, who often reported their transactions to the police. Spiritual discovery of treasures was a recurring example of non-normative ritual exchange. Finding lost treasures was one of the areas of ritual practice that was remunerated with money and, if discovered by the police, prosecuted under obeah legislation.[54] Fees charged for locating treasures by divination could be as high as

$300.[55] Unlike in most other types of spiritual work, the ritual specialists themselves—or, in many cases, aspiring or make-believe ritual specialists—initiated the process by telling a prospective client that there was a treasure in her or his land to be discovered. Large sums of money were also exchanged in cases, again prosecuted under obeah laws, in which an evil spirit, or jumbie, was taken off a sum of money. For example, Ms. Madeleine Hernandez, who had inherited $200 from her father, was persuaded by a man named Fitz Bishop to withdraw the money from her account, because "when people died and left money there was always a spirit on it." Mr. Bishop would then remove the spirit. When Ms. Fernandez did not get her money back from the cleanser, she informed the police.[56]

In cases like these, the practitioners usually aimed at a single contact with their client, charged or stole a notable amount of money, and made few, if any, allusions to religious symbols. Their arrests always followed reports made by the clients themselves, not agents provocateurs. On the other hand, ritual specialists like Percival Duval, Leopoldine Moise, Henry Padmore, or Dr. Williams had wide clienteles and were engaged in prolonged exchange relationships with their clients, who consulted them repeatedly. These latter types of ritual specialists, who are more numerous in the Trinidadian records, were less often turned in by their clients: in a clear majority of cases, their arrests resulted from police entrapment. The mutual loyalty between ritual specialists and the people among whom they lived and worked implies that large sections of the Trinidadian society approved of or tolerated healing and other spiritual work, as well as their moderate remuneration with money.

PASSING MONEY: THE MODALITY OF EXCHANGE

The historical record of obeah prosecutions in which defendants' or their clients' voices are heard only selectively, if at all, does not easily lend itself to an analysis of ritual practitioners' moral views about money and spiritual work. It would seem, however, that they had few reservations about charging fees for their services, neither in sense of fraudulence as postulated by the state and the media, nor in line with the Euro-Christian preoccupation with money as the root of all evil. In this section, I draw on ethnographic material to add a comparative angle to the discussion of the ritual sphere of exchange, and particularly the modality of such exchange.

In contemporary Trinidad and Tobago, people seek the help of ritual specialists for problems very similar to those revealed in newspapers and court records a hundred years ago. Physical suffering as well as problems at the workplace, unemployment, and breaches in relationships can be addressed and cured by consulting people who do spiritual work, often elders in the Orisha or Spiritual Baptist religions.[57] I lived in the household of a popular Tobagonian Spiritual Baptist ritual specialist, Mother Cleorita Robinson, for two years between 1996 and 2004 doing ethnographic fieldwork with her and various other Spiritual Baptist congregations. People from all echelons of Tobagonian society and beyond, from other Caribbean countries as well as from the United States, where Mother Cleorita regularly travels, make use of her expertise as a healer, diviner, and counselor—and these attributes do not seem sufficient to cover the range of her spiritual work. Mother Cleorita, like many of her Tobagonian colleagues, does not charge for the work she does. That is, she does not ask for money or set special prices. "You must not charge for spiritual work," stated Leader Brothers, another distinguished ritual specialist and church leader, who is well into his eighties. As the relationship between ritual specialists and their clients follows the logic of reciprocity, however, clients should offer to pay for the treatment, blessing, divination, or other service. The payment must not be too overt: leaving money discreetly on a table before leaving is an elegant way of going about the potentially awkward transaction, whereas handing over money directly to the ritual specialist would be embarrassing for both parties. In some of the obeah cases prosecuted in Trinidad in the early twentieth century, the incriminating coin or note was reported to have been found not on the person of the defendant, but rather on a table or, in the case of Leopoldine Moise, "laid on her lap."[58] Without contemporary accounts of a possible logic behind this pattern, however, it is difficult to deduce whether it matches with the present-day norm.

The voluntary nature of compensation is, of course, ostensible. Leaving without paying is embarrassing and even insulting. An intense discussion on payments for spiritual work arose one night in Mother Cleorita's yard, as she; her husband, Leader Gerald; Teacher Audrey, the second mother of their church; and I were sitting under the galvanized roof of their garage, chatting about the eventful visit of a few Trinidadian Baptists to the church. A young man walked up to us from the street and told Mother Cleorita that his "belly was giving him trouble." Laying him down on a wooden bench, Mother Cleorita inspected the man's abdomen and then treated him accordingly, including massaging his belly with olive oil. When the treatment was over, the man thanked her and went on his way. Teacher Audrey exclaimed with astonishment, and Mother Cleorita could only just disguise her humiliation with an air of indifference. The ladies started to admonish people who first go to see a doctor who cannot help them, yet pay for the consultation, and then come to Mother Cleorita who helps them and gets nothing in return. Mother Cleorita then stated that she helped "everybody," including those who did not pay, because some people left her twenty dollars or even more and, in a way, paid for the free riders as well. "The Holy Spirit did not tell me to charge for the things I do," she pointed out, and explained that she needed money only to pay for the oil, candles, Florida Water, and other ritual materials. They then went on to criticize mothers and leaders who charged too much for rituals like "mourning,"[59] and predictably, the avarice of Spiritual Baptists based in the United States. "In America," declared Leader Gerald, warming up to a favorite topic, "religion is a moneymaking machine!" From the Tobagonian vantage, Caribbean migrants' religious practice, authority, and the moral economy of American-based churches are usually distanced or negatively valued against local orthodoxy, unselfishness, and disregard of money.

Although charging excessive fees for rituals is morally condemnable, there is nothing wrong with money and material wealth received in a correct modality of exchange and through correct relationships. Money and ritual authority belong to separate conceptual categories in, for example, Mosko's analysis of the Papua New Guinea Meko society and Richman's dual model of the moral economy of Vodou, but in the early twentieth-century Caribbean, wealth did not undermine the moral and spiritual authority of ritual specialists.[60] Portrayals of a few defendants in newspaper reports of obeah-related arrests and trials make note of displays of wealth or respectability. The Trinidadian Isaac White as well as the Jamaicans Alfonso McDermott and John Henry were "well-dressed" men,[61] and Leopoldine Moise, arrested in Port of Spain in 1907, had "lots of jewelry" and "dressed very conspicuously."[62] The Jamaican Francis Harmit, a man who was blind in his right eye, lame in his left leg, and had only one arm, appeared in front of a packed Kingston courtroom wearing "a black venetian suit, a black bow, a pair of gold-rimmed glasses, and a bouquet by way of a charm, consisting of a spray of croton, a bit of aralia and a maiden blush rose being his other adornments."[63] Percival Duval reported the loss of no less than $491 from his desk during his arrest.[64] When Charles Dolly was arrested and convicted in Montserrat in 1904 for the fourth (but not the last) time, more than £100 in silver was discovered at his house;[65] in 1908, at his fifth arrest, he asked the police to keep safe the sum of £168 19s. 10d.[66]

In present-day Tobagonian discourse, ritual specialists consider mundane wealth and well-being desirable. Being well-off or at least comfortable is interpreted as a blessing from God: God provides for a person who fulfills her or his religious obligations and leads a morally acceptable life. The idea of wealth as a sign of being on good terms with the spiritual world corresponds to Romberg's description of Puerto Rican brujos' evaluation of material well-being.[67] Money is also an appropriate compensation for spiritual work. Ritual specialists receive money not only from clients but also through networks of ritually constituted kinship from the initiates of their congregation, known as their "sons" and "daughters."[68] As most ritual specialists have had to struggle (at least at some point in their lives) to make a living and provide for their families, money received from spiritual work or as gifts from spiritual children and clients is an important addition to their budgets. Unlike the discourses of witchcraft reported in the ongoing Africanist debate, Trinbagonian evaluations of the morality of money in ritual practice do not address accumulation as such. Ritual exchanges involving money between humans and spirits, or between ritual specialists and their clients, are not perceived as immoral. But the long-lived image of the charlatan, making money under the guise of religion, recurs in present-day discussions within religious groups (like Spiritual Baptists) themselves evaluating the authority and sincerity of ritual practitioners. Such conversations, as well as the indirect way in which contemporary ritual specialists are compensated, have been shaped by the colonial policies defining spiritual work as fraudulent. In this sense, current unease about payments for healing and other ritualized services may perpetuate some of the colonially imposed stigma of certain ritual practice as anti-modern superstition. Viewed more holistically, however, the moral rationale of the ritual sphere of exchange does not simply replicate the parameters that guided colonial government of religion in Trinidad and Tobago. From the viewpoint of ritual practitioners, exchanges with clients, but also exchanges with the spirits and God, follow the logic of the gift rather than the commodity, and orient toward the transcendent rather than the transient.

TEMPORAL LOGICS IN THE RITUAL SPHERE OF EXCHANGE

The seemingly contradictory attitudes toward money as payment for ritual practice help us outline the contours of the ritual sphere of exchange in Trinidad and Tobago. As shown above, money has been a legitimate object of exchange in this sphere for a long time. But unlike commodity exchange, the relationship between exchange partners is not alienated, and the temporality of an appropriate exchange relationship is transcendent rather than transient. The contemporary ritual specialists I have worked with have explained that their ability to do spiritual work like healing or divining is a gift from God. Although such gifts can sometimes be received prior to initiation into the Spiritual Baptist or Orisha religions, ritual specialists need to undergo repeated rites of passage to familiarize themselves with the often-cryptic wisdom and skills they have received. Further knowledge can be accumulated through dedication to ritual practice. This is how Mother Cleorita received her gift of healing during the prolonged rite of passage of mourning: Travelling in the spiritual world, Mother Cleorita found herself walking down a road. Soon she saw two cobra snakes dancing in front of her, beckoning her to follow. Despite her fear she forced herself to follow the cobras down a long set of stairs into a cave. There she encountered a man, St. Francis, who told her he had been trying to call her for a long, long time. He led her into a room, where she saw a skeleton lying on a table. It was disjointing itself, pulling off bones joint by joint, all the way from one hand to the other, until it was completely shattered. Then it put the bones back in their places, deliberately, one by one. Once complete again, the skeleton greeted Mother Cleorita and said that it was her turn now! She had no choice but to try and disjoint the skeleton. Horrified, she managed to pull out the first finger with shaking hands, then the next one, and so on, going all the way through. She then assembled the bones in the correct order. The man then led her to another place, where a woman was about to give birth, and Mother Cleorita had to help deliver the baby. After these lessons, she found her way to the Zion Hospital, where she met the famous Chinese doctor Dr. Lee. Dr. Lee told the exhausted Mother Cleorita that she was now qualified as a doctor herself and gave her a nametag and a chart; she also received a lilac dress. Her name on the tag was Dr. Su Ling. For forty years now she has been practicing her skills as a healer, including fixing dislocated ankles or knees just like the skeleton taught her.

Narratives like this, describing exchanges in the spiritual world, abound in Spiritual Baptist discourse. The historical record reveals some resembling interpretations of spiritual authority behind the skills and knowledge of ritual specialists. For example, Samuel Benkins, sentenced to prison for practicing obeah in Barbados in 1913, declared that he "had been taught the art by Indians in a gift from the Gods," and that "by this marvellous power he was able to divine the source from which any illness sprang."[69]

In return for spiritual gifts like these, ritual specialists commit themselves to lifelong cycles of rituals of sacrifice. Little is known of the long-term ritual practices of the obeah men and women prosecuted in the colonial Caribbean, except for lists of ritual paraphernalia and descriptions of ritual spaces or practices used as evidence in court. In contemporary Trinidad and Tobago, Spiritual Baptist elders tend to spend the money they receive through ritual practice on further rituals and their churches, rather than on private, secular expenses. Thanksgivings in the Spiritual Baptist religion and feasts in the Orisha religion are large-scale rituals of sacrifice that can last for seven days and include various offerings to God or to the orishas, as well as meals served to large numbers of participants. Failing to contribute to the ritual cycle of one's church or shrine, or dismissing the obligation to support one's spiritual parents, discloses selfishness, greed, and lack of dedication. Although short-term gains, like material wealth, well-being, or success in migration, can, and often are, perceived as return gifts for appropriately performed ritual of sacrifice, the ultimate aim in ritual practice is to maintain a permanent relationship to God or the spirits.

Although Caribbean religions have been practiced in societies forged by and contributing to global capitalism and other facets of modernity, the ritual practice classified as obeah in the colonial Caribbean, or the spiritual work done by present-day ritual specialists, do not align with the logic of commodification, short-term gain, anonymity, and impersonality of exchange typical of capitalism. Money is a standard object of exchange in the ritual sphere of exchange, and moral debates about ritually earned money do not question the legitimacy of monetary transactions themselves. They are rather aimed at cases in which the norms of this sphere are broken: when the exchange relationship becomes alienated and transitory, like in some of the early twentieth-century treasure hunts, and when the temporal orientation of exchange is toward short-term gains instead of lasting relationships between people and spirits. The bedrock of Caribbean modernity—the prolonged presence of capitalism—has not saturated local economic systems, but rather has coexisted along with other, no less modern, spheres of exchange, with different logics, norms, and temporalities. It is within such a sphere where money passes hands according to the principles of reciprocity that past and present ritual specialists have used their gifts and made their living.

NOTES

My research was funded by the Academy of Finland (2004–7) and the Leverhulme Trust (2007–9).

1. Obeah was, and in some places still is, a legal category in the British Caribbean, referencing various, locally specific practices. See Diana Paton, "Obeah Acts: Producing and Policing the Boundaries of Religion in the Caribbean," *Small Axe* 13, no. 1 (2009): 1–18. Few ritual specialists in the historical record or in contemporary Trinidad and Tobago use obeah autonymically, and as a discursive category it has no simple, essential meaning. I reserve the analytical use of the term mainly for contexts directly related to legal proceedings. By "ritual specialist" I refer here to socially recognized religious practitioners who engage in divining, healing, rites of affliction, and other ritual practice, often as part of their livelihoods.

2. I use the concept of a local transactional order with caution, as migrants' transnational connections to their families, neighbors, and friends stretch the ideals and

practices of gift giving to urban North America and Europe. See Maarit Forde, "Rituals, Journey, and Modernity," in *Constructing Vernacular Culture in the Trans-Caribbean*, ed. Holger Henke and Karl-Heinz Magister (New York: Lexington Books, 2007), 101–22; Karen Fog Olwig, *Caribbean Journeys: An Ethnography of Migration and Home in Three Family Networks* (Durham: Duke University Press, 2007); Karen Richman, *Migration and Vodou* (Gainesville: University Press of Florida, 2005).

3. Karl Polanyi, *The Great Transformation* (New York: Farrar and Rinehart, 1944); Paul Bohannan, "The Impact of Money on an African Subsistence Economy," *Journal of Economic History* 19, no. 4 (1959): 491–503; Paul Bohannan and Laura Bohannan, *Tiv Economy* (Evanston: Northwestern University Press, 1968); Paul James, "Abstracting Modes of Exchange: Gifts, Commodities, and Money," *Journal of the Finnish Anthropological Society* 26, no. 2 (2001): 4–22; June Nash, *We Eat the Mines and the Mines Eat Us: Dependency and Exploitation in Bolivian Tin Mines* (New York: Columbia University Press, 1979); Michael Taussig, *The Devil and Commodity Fetishism in South America* (Chapel Hill: University of North Carolina Press, 1980).

4. Maurice Bloch and Jonathan Parry, "Introduction: Money and the Morality of Exchange," in *Money and the Morality of Exchange*, ed. Maurice Bloch and Jonathan Parry (Cambridge: Cambridge University Press, 1989), 2–4. Bloch and Parry also identify an opposite, much more favorable stream of Western discourse on money, culminating in Adam Smith's propositions. The transformative capacity of money, they argue, is a common theme in the differently oriented debates on money and morality.

5. Georg Simmel, *The Philosophy of Money* (1907; trans. Tom Bottomore and David Frisby, London: Routledge and Kegan Paul, 1978), 297–303, 342–47.

6. Bloch and Parry, "Introduction."

7. Joel Robbins and David Akin, "An Introduction to Melanesian Currencies: Agency, Identity, and Social Reproduction," in *Money and Modernity: State and Local Currencies in Melanesia*, ed. David Akin and Joel Robbins (Pittsburgh: University of Pittsburgh Press, 1999), 1–40.

8. Bloch and Parry, "Introduction," 17–18; see also Bill Maurer, "The Anthropology of Money," *Annual Review of Anthropology* 35, no. 2 (2006): 19.

9. Jean Comaroff and John Comaroff, introduction to *Modernity and Its Malcontents: Ritual and Power in Postcolonial Africa*, ed. Jean Comaroff and John Comaroff (Chicago: University of Chicago Press, 1993), xi–xxxvii; Jean Comaroff and John Comaroff, "Millennial Capitalism: First Thoughts on a Second Coming," *Public Culture* 12, no. 2 (2000): 291–34; Cyprian F. Fisiy and Peter Geschiere, "Sorcery, Witchcraft, and Accumulation: Regional Variations in South and West Cameroon," *Critique of Anthropology* 11, no. 3 (1991): 251–79. On witchcraft rumors and accusations, see Erik Bähre, "Witchcraft and the Exchange of Sex, Blood, and Money among Africans in Cape Town, South Africa," *Journal of Religion in Africa* 32, no. 3 (2002): 300–34; Adeline Masquelier, "Of Headhunters and Cannibals: Migrancy, Labor, and Consumption in the Mawri Imagination," *Cultural Anthropology* 15, no. 1 (2000): 84–126. On persecutions of assumed witches, see Jean Comaroff and John Comaroff, "Occult

Economies and the Violence of Abstraction: Notes from the South African Postcolony," *American Ethnologist* 26, no. 2 (1999): 279–303; Isak Niehaus, *Witchcraft, Power and Politics: Exploring the Occult in the South African Lowveld* (London: Pluto, 2001). On witch-finding and -cleansing movements and rituals, see Edwin Ardener, "Witchcraft, Economics, and the Continuity of Belief," in *Witchcraft Confessions and Accusations*, ed. Mary Douglas (London: Routledge, 1970), 141–60; Mark Auslander, "Open the Wombs! The Symbolic Politics of Modern Ngoni Witchfinding," in Comaroff and Comaroff, *Modernity and Its Malcontents*, 167–92; Peter Geschiere, *The Modernity of Witchcraft, Politics, and the Occult in Postcolonial Africa* (Charlottesville: University Press of Virginia, 1997); Maia Green, *Priests, Witches, Power: Popular Christianity after Mission in Southern Tanzania* (Cambridge: Cambridge University Press, 2003); Maia Green, "A Discourse on Inequality: Poverty, Public Bads and Entrenching Witchcraft in Post Adjustment Tanzania," *Anthropological Theory* 5, no. 3 (2005): 247–66; Audrey Richards, "A Modern Movement of Witchfinders," *Africa* 8, no. 4 (1935): 448–61.

10. Geschiere, *The Modernity of Witchcraft, Politics, and the Occult in Postcolonial Africa*.

11. Niehaus, *Witchcraft, Power and Politics*.

12. Comaroff and Comaroff, "Occult Economies and the Violence of Abstraction"; James Ferguson, "The Country and the City on the Copperbelt," *Cultural Anthropology* 7, no. 1 (1992): 80–92; Fisiy and Geschiere, "Sorcery, Witchcraft, and Accumulation"; Geschiere, *The Modernity of Witchcraft, Politics, and the Occult in Postcolonial Africa*; Jane Parish, "From the Body to the Wallet: Conceptualizing Akan Witchcraft at Home and Abroad," *Journal of the Royal Anthropological Society* 6, no. 3 (2002): 487–500.

13. See also Comaroff and Comaroff, "Occult Economies."

14. Terence Ranger, "Scotland Yard in the Bush: Medicine Murders, Child Witches and the Construction of the Occult: A Literary Review," *Africa* 77, no. 2 (2007): 272–83; Rosalind Shaw, "The Production of Witchcraft/Witchcraft as Production: Memory, Modernity, and the Slave Trade in Sierra Leone," *American Ethnologist* 24, no. 4 (1997): 856–76.

15. Tuulikki Pietilä, "Noituuden ongelma Afrikan tutkimuksessa," *Journal of the Finnish Anthropological Society* 27, no. 3 (2003): 37–47.

16. Harri Englund and James Leach, "Ethnography and the Meta-narratives of Modernity," *Current Anthropology* 41, no. 2 (2000): 225–48; Richard Eves, "Sorcery's the Curse: Modernity, Envy, and the Flow of Sociality in a Melanesian Society," *Journal of the Royal Anthropological Institute* 6, no. 3 (2000): 453–68.

17. Maurer, "The Anthropology of Money."

18. Hilary McD. Beckles, "Capitalism, Slavery, and Caribbean Modernity," *Callaloo* 20, no. 4 (1998): 777–89; Richard Drayton, "The Collaboration of Labour: Slaves, Empires, and Globalizations in the Atlantic World, c. 1600–1850," in *Globalization in World History*, ed. A. G. Hopkins (London: Pimlico, 2002), 98–114; Sidney Mintz, *Sweetness and Power: The Place of Sugar in Modern History* (New York: Penguin, 1985);

Sidney Mintz, *Caribbean Transformations* (1974; New York: Columbia University Press, 1989); Michel-Rolph Trouillot, *Global Transformations: Anthropology and the Modern World* (New York: Palgrave Macmillan, 2003); Eric Williams, *Capitalism and Slavery* (1944; Chapel Hill: University of North Carolina Press, 1994).

19. Bloch and Parry, "Introduction," 24.

20. Robbins and Akin, "An Introduction to Melanesian Currencies." The writers extend Paul Bohannan's influential 1959 model of spheres of exchange; see "The Impact of Money on an African Subsistence Economy." See also Marshall Sahlins, "On the Sociology of Primitive Exchange," in *Stone Age Economics* (1972; London: Routledge, 2004), 185–276.

21. See, for example, Mark S. Mosko, "Magical Money: Commoditization and the Linkage of *Maketsi* ('Market') and *Kangakanga* ('Custom') in Contemporary North Mekeo," in Akin and Robbins, *Money and Modernity*, 41–61.

22. Edward LiPuma, "The Meaning of Money in the Age of Modernity," in Akin and Robbins, *Money and Modernity*, 192–213.

23. "Copies of Certain of the Evidence Submitted to the Committee of Council for Trade and Plantations in the Course of their Enquiry into the State of the African Slave Trade," BT 6/10, National Archives, London. In the 1770s, proto-peasant slaves controlled 20 percent of Jamaica's currency by selling the produce of their provision grounds at markets; see Jean Besson, *Martha Brae's Two Histories; European Expansion and Caribbean Culture-Building in Jamaica* (Chapel Hill: University of North Carolina Press, 2002), 87. See also Sidney Mintz's work on proto-peasantry, such as "Slavery and the Rise of Peasantries," in *Roots and Branches: Current Directions in Slave Studies*, ed. Michael Craton (Toronto: Pergamon, 1979), 213–42; and "From Plantations to Peasantries in the Caribbean," in *Caribbean Contours*, ed. Sidney Mintz and Sally Price (Baltimore: Johns Hopkins University Press, 1985), 127–53; as well as Lorna Simmonds, "Slave Higglering in Jamaica, 1780–1834," *Jamaica Journal* 20, no. 1 (1987): 31–38.

24. Governor Sligo to Glenelg, no. 315, 1831, CO 137/209, National Archives, London. "Shadow" represents one aspect of the soul in Jamaican belief systems; see for example Dianne M. Stewart, *Three Eyes for the Journey: African Dimensions of the Jamaican Religious Experience* (Oxford: Oxford University Press, 2005), 54; Joseph John Williams, *Voodoos and Obeahs: Phases of West India Witchcraft* (Whitefish, Mont.: Kessinger, 2003 [1932]), 152–54, 188. "Catching" or "thieving" shadows have been commonly used terms for harmful spiritual work in Jamaica. On Cuban slaves' involvement in the transatlantic political economy, including their buying and selling of esoteric ritual knowledge, see Stephan Palmié, "A View from Itia Ororó Kande," *Social Anthropology* 14, no. 1 (2006): 99–118.

25. Paton, "Obeah Acts," 6. The Trinidadian Ordinance 6 of 1868, sections 30–31, defines obeah as "every pretended Assumption of supernatural Power or Knowledge whatever, for fraudulent or illicit Purposes, or for Gain, or for the Injury of any Person," and renders punishable "every person who by the practice of Obeah or by any occult

means or by any assumption of supernatural power or knowledge shall—obtain or endeavour to obtain any chattel, money or valuable security from any other person."

26. Money itself—coins and notes—had ritual usages and could channel spiritual power. In Jamaica, a few shillings were often asked "for eyesight," to help the diviner see, and used together with other ritual paraphernalia for divining the nature of the problem at hand and the proper cure. The coins could be put in a glass or bowl, for example, with rum or water. *Gleaner* (Jamaica), June 16, 1917; September 5, 1929. Sometimes the prosecution's evidence included coins found amid other items allegedly used in illegal ritual practice; for example, see Udal, "Obeah in the West Indies," *Folklore* 26, no. 3 (1915): 271–73. But ritual use of money has not been as common in the Anglophone Caribbean as in many other societies; see, for example, Russell W. Belk and Melanie Wallendorf, "The Sacred Meanings of Money," *Journal of Economic Psychology* 11, no. 1 (1990): 35–67; Heonik Kwon, "The Dollarization of Vietnamese Ghost Money," *Journal of the Royal Anthropological Institute* 13, no. 1 (2007): 73–90.

27. See the introduction to this book for a review of literature on the government and policing of religion in the Caribbean during this period.

28. *Port of Spain Gazette*, October 31, 1920, 14, 16. Of the thirty-four arrests reported in *Port of Spain Gazette* between 1900 and 1930 that led to obeah charges, at least nineteen were conducted by entrapment. Twenty-four of the total of forty-five people who were charged with practicing obeah in this period were arrested by entrapment. There is too little information available in several of the remaining cases to conclude anything about police methods. Diana Paton's chapter in this collection discusses police methods, including the use of informants and entrapment, in Jamaica.

29. *Port of Spain Gazette*, October 7, 1920, 12; October 10, 1920, 16; October 31, 1920, 14, 16; November 14, 1920, 16.

30. *Port of Spain Gazette*, March 4, 1921, 9.

31. There are many cases on record showing that most cash transactions related to obeah in the early decades of the twentieth century involved small sums of money. For example, Laura de Freitas, who was sentenced in 1920, had asked her two clients for five shillings each, "to prepare a bath and a guard." *Port of Spain Gazette*, March 30, 1920, 12. Isaac White, who was arrested and tried in 1907, had initially asked his client, Jack Brown, for twelve dollars to help him in a court case, but settled for two dollars instead, as Brown stated he could not afford such a high price. White also requested a cock, a big bottle of rum, red, black, and blue candles, a bottle of essence, and an egg. *Port of Spain Gazette*, October 22, 1907, 5. Henry Padmore, arrested in 1909, had asked for five shillings and sent his client to the pharmacy for "20 cents in musk, a phial of essence, 5 cents red lavender, and half-bottle of strong rum." *Port of Spain Gazette*, November 30, 1909, 5. Sentenced for practicing obeah in 1910, Dr. Williams first called the price of twelve dollars, but his client, David Marshall, said he only had a dollar and four shillings and would owe Dr. Williams the balance. *Port of Spain Gazette*, January 16, 1910, 3.

32. *Port of Spain Gazette*, January 30, 1914, 9.

33. In brujería, the term "brujo/bruja" refers to ritual specialists and healers. See

Raquel Romberg, *Witches and Welfare: Spiritual Capital in the Business of Magic in Puerto Rico* (Austin: University of Texas Press, 2003).

34. *Port of Spain Gazette*, October 31, 1920, 14, 16.

35. *Port of Spain Gazette*, November 26, 1909, 4; January 4, 1910, 6.

36. I use the term "suffering" in the sense of a socially and culturally situated experience of pain; see, for example, Arthur Kleinman, *Writing at the Margin: Discourse between Anthropology and Medicine* (Berkeley: University of California Press, 1997).

37. *Port of Spain Gazette*, February 27, 1910, 6.

38. *Port of Spain Gazette*, March 2, 1921, 3.

39. *Port of Spain Gazette*, April 5, 1918, 5.

40. The Noitgedacht tragedy, in which four men received death penalties for kidnapping and murdering the four-year-old Molly Schultz for obeah purposes, was well covered in Demeraran and other Caribbean newspapers. See *Port of Spain Gazette*, February 17, 1918, 8; April 23, 1918, 8; May 7, 1918, 11; May 17, 1918, 2; June 11, 1918, 2; July 9, 1918, 5; July 16, 1918, 9; August 8, 1918, 3; January 15, 1919, 3; January 21, 1919, 6; February 3, 1919, 11; February 18, 1919, 7.

41. *Port of Spain Gazette*, February 23, 1919, 7.

42. *Port of Spain Gazette*, February 3, 1919, 11.

43. *Port of Spain Gazette*, August 15, 1920, 17.

44. Harriet Chalmers Adams, "The East Indians in the New World," *National Geographic* 18, no. 7 (1907): 485–92.

45. Aisha Khan, *Callaloo Nation: Metaphors of Race and Religious Identity among South Asians in Trinidad* (Durham: Duke University Press, 2004), 130, 167. Morton Klass, whose ethnography depicts the Indo-Trinidadian village of Felicity in central Trinidad in the late 1950s, writes about "Ojha Men," who could exorcise evil spirits and whose services were less costly than those of Brahmans. See *East Indians in Trinidad: A Study of Cultural Persistence* (Prospect Heights, Ill.: Waveland, 1961), 181–83. Arthur and Juanita Niehoff's study of two Indo-Trinidadian communities, Debe and Penal, in the 1950s mentions "Indian obeahmen" who charge their clients between one and twenty-five dollars, depending on their reputation. See *East Indians in the West Indies* (Milwaukee: Milwaukee Public Museum Publications in Anthropology, 1960), 174. See also Raymond Ramcharitar, "The Hidden History of Trinidad: Underground Culture in Trinidad, 1870–1970" (Ph.D. diss., University of the West Indies, St. Augustine, 2007), 74–76, on "wandering sadhus" who disseminated Hindu knowledge as well as political ideas among the Indo-Trinidadian population "under the cover of harmless charlatanry."

46. See the introduction to this book for a discussion of the colonial government of religion in the Caribbean as linked to notions of civilization and modernity.

47. Karen Fields, "Political Contingencies of Witchcraft in Colonial Central Africa: Culture and the State in Marxist Theory," *Canadian Journal of African Studies* 16, no. 3 (1982): 567–93. Diana Paton, tracing the development of obeah legislation in the British Caribbean since obeah was first made illegal in Jamaica in 1760, makes a similar

argument for the Caribbean: witchcraft itself could not be made illegal, because such an act would recognize its possibility and go against the principles of a secular, modern court and society. See "Obeah Acts."

48. Stephan Palmié describes a resembling opposition between Kongo and Lucumí moralities in Cuba. See *Wizards and Scientists: Explorations in Afro-Cuban Modernity and Tradition* (Durham: Duke University Press, 2002), 25.

49. Richman, *Migration and Vodou*, 17, 151.

50. Romberg, *Witchcraft and Welfare*, 140, 169.

51. *Port of Spain Gazette*, November 14, 1920, 16.

52. *Port of Spain Gazette*, February 27, 1910, 6.

53. Ibid.

54. In Jamaica, such treasures were often called Spanish jars. See, for example, *New York Times*, March 22, 1908; *Gleaner* (Jamaica), January 13, 1908; May 8, 1916; June 6, 1917.

55. *Gleaner* (Jamaica), September 6, 1919, 4.

56. *Port of Spain Gazette*, July 19, 1912, 7.

57. As the two religions merge in many people's and congregations' practices, numerous ritual specialists belong to both orders. See Maarit Laitinen, *Marching to Zion: Creolisation in Spiritual Baptist Rituals and Cosmology* (Helsinki: Research Series in Anthropology, 2002); Frances Henry, *Reclaiming African Religions in Trinidad: The Socio-Political Legitimation of the Orisha and Spiritual Baptist Faiths* (Mona: University of the West Indies Press, 2003).

58. *Port of Spain Gazette*, March 18, 1907, 6.

59. Mourning is a long rite of passage that involves the seclusion of initiates, fasting, and sensory deprivation. Leaving the mundane world behind, initiates journey in the spiritual world in search of "wisdom, knowledge, and understanding" (an expression often heard in Spiritual Baptist ritual speech). See Laitinen, *Marching to Zion*; Wallace W. Zane, *Journeys to Spiritual Lands: The Natural History of a West Indian Religion* (New York: Oxford University Press, 1999).

60. Mosko, "Magical Money," 45–46; Richman, *Migration and Vodou*.

61. *Port of Spain Gazette*, October 22, 1907, 5; *Gleaner* (Jamaica), February 19, 1909; July 31, 1903.

62. *Port of Spain Gazette*, January 16, 1908, 2.

63. *Gleaner* (Jamaica), October 14, 1907. On Harmit's prosecution, see Diana Paton's chapter in this volume.

64. *Port of Spain Gazette*, November 14, 1920, 16.

65. Udal, "Obeah in the West Indies," 273.

66. *Montserrat Herald*, December 5, 1908, reprinted in *Port of Spain Gazette*, December 19, 1908, 4.

67. Romberg, *Witchcraft and Welfare*, 12.

68. Forde, "Modes of Transnational Relatedness."

69. *Port of Spain Gazette*, May 21, 1913, 5.

8.

The Open Secrets of Solares
ELIZABETH COOPER

> Let us dedicate ourselves now to uncovering the uses, customs, and rites of this association whose existence has been known of for many years yet remains surrounded in the most impenetrable mystery.
> —RAFAEL ROCHE Y MONTEAGUDO, *La Policía y sus misterios en Cuba*

Cuban slave emancipation and national liberation were intertwined materially and ideologically. Put somewhat differently, the injustices of slavery and the injustices of colonialism were viewed by many *independistas*, in particular slaves, as one and the same. This was expressed in no small part by the overwhelming participation of Afro-Cubans in the war for independence—they constituted well over half of the liberation army. But there was also great slippage in nationalist discourse between the institution of slavery and the slaves themselves. Indeed, as Ada Ferrer has argued, a central claim of Cuban historical knowledge was that both "the island's demographic profile and its history of racial slavery incapacitated it for nationhood."[1] The massive participation of Afro-Cubans in the war for independence thus posed a dilemma for the white elites of Cuba, and for the United States government, which hoped to take power after independence. Afro-Cubans—the majority of whom were workers, tradespeople, and peasant farmers—could not be allowed to directly shape the new Cuban republic. Yet citizenship and political representation could not be denied to those without whom there would be no nation.

The Cuban war for independence—like all revolutions—broke down normative social boundaries. The racial boundaries of slave society were perhaps most notably dismantled as Afro-Cubans garnered high-ranking positions in the army and the independence movement administration. They also found more freedom in urban public spaces to mingle, do business, and socialize—particularly in Havana. New opportunities for Afro-Cubans coincided with a sustained state offensive against African *ñáñiguismo* in Havana that continued well after the declaration of the new Cuban republic. Both Spanish and republican authorities drew on racist fears of a "race war" and another Haitian Revolution in order to justify their campaigns.[2]

Alejandro de la Fuente has argued that although Cuba and "Cubanidad" were represented in vastly different ways, all definitions of the latter—from José Martí's vision of a raceless Cuban political brotherhood to the United States government's segregationist ideology—"shared the belief that 'race' was at the very core of the nation."[3] Repression of ñáñiguismo at the turn of the twentieth century corroborated de la Fuente's insight. Further, there can be little doubt that such racialized struggles over ñáñiguismo fueled and justified the racist ban of the Partido Independiente de Color in 1909 and the brutal massacre of Afro-Cubans in the eastern province of Oriente in 1912. But the struggles over ñáñiguismo in Havana also call into question whether race was at the core, or even at the margins, of how Cuban working people envisioned modern Cubanidad.

This chapter argues that the African-derived popular religion and culture of Havana—often referred to as ñáñiguismo—were fundamental sites in the transformation of Cubanidad at the time of slave emancipation and national independence. The cases of ñáñiguismo reveal a unique urban popular politics (in its broadest sense) rooted in the collective memory, daily experiences, and values of Havana's propertyless workers, distinct from both the politics of peasants in the eastern part of the island and middle-class Afro-Cuban organizations, such as the Partido Independiente de Color. At the same time, ñáñiguismo was a racial trope, justifying and necessitating the broad criminalization of popular culture—religion, politics, economics, and sexuality—stripping it of its challenge to white supremacist and bourgeois-liberal forms of power, as well as its historical place in the construction of modern Cuban society.

AFRICAN CONSPIRACIES OR MODERN SOLIDARITIES?

An array of groups and sodalities (associations with a devotional purpose) of first-generation Africans, known as *ñáñigos*, *cabildos de nación*, and *abakuá*, formed in Cuba over the course of the nineteenth century.[4] Many of these associations were recognized legally; others were highly secretive and operated outside the margins of state authority. But all of them, regardless of their legality, were viewed and treated with suspicion by the Spanish colonial authorities. As was typical in the post–Haitian Revolution period, they were often alleged to be the centers of uprisings against colonialism and slavery.

Two prime examples of this are the "conspiracies" of Aponte in 1812 and La Escalera in 1844.[5]

An active member of a cabildo de nación and a poet, Plácido (also known as Gabriel de la Concepción Valdés) was at the center of the Escalera conspiracy to overthrow slavery and colonialism in 1844. Many considered Plácido to be "the most inspired poet Cuba has ever seen" and the "most renowned person of color in Cuba in the 1840s." During his trial, Plácido argued that the "true seducers" were "ideas of equality" and talk of a time "when hierarchies would disappear."[6] Plácido clearly connected contemporary African and Afro-Cuban popular culture with democratic political principles, rather than depicting them as threatening sources of social chaos.

Although the Escalera conspiracy of 1844 sparked vigorous colonial repression, the popular organizations of Africans and Afro-Cubans continued to develop throughout the last half of the nineteenth century.[7] The effective suppression of the international slave trade in 1850 led to an increase in the number of multiethnic associations. Members of the same group might be African-born, Cuban-born of African descent, Cuban-born of Spanish descent, or immigrants from the growing Filipino-, Mexican-, Haitian-, Chinese-, and Spanish-born communities on the island.

The connection Plácido had drawn in 1844 between authorities' fears of Afro-Cuban organizations and the end of hierarchies was more relevant than ever during the struggle for abolition and independence. Indeed, renewed and rigorous implementation of "laws of association" took place alongside new laws of gradual abolition, such as the "Free Womb Law" of 1871.[8] By the late 1870s, the Spanish government had systematically developed local government administrations in order to register societies. The conflation of loosely organized religious and cultural groups with formal trade and civil mutual aid societies ostensibly legitimated working-class organizations. It was widely asserted by police and the press, however, that these societies—including, and at times in particular, the officially registered associations—served as mere fronts for more dangerous African-derived religious cults. Indeed, in practice the implementation of the new laws of association criminalized and politicized all such groups. Mutual aid associations were alleged to be fronts not only figuratively, but also literally. Police records repeatedly mention confidential tips regarding secret rooms beyond hidden doors and passageways within the official meeting spaces of legal mutual aid societies—implying devious activity rather than a formal place in Cuban society. It was in such rooms that members supposedly conducted their "primitive practices." Authorities relentlessly construed the popular culture and civic life of Africans and Afro-Cubans as inescapably atavistic, irrational idolatry.

On the evening of September 8, 1882—two years after the start of the *patronato* laws of gradual abolition and the second uprising in the war for independence, known as La Guerra Chiquita—the police officer Vicente Maceo and his colleagues stormed into a private room in a *solar* (typical tenement housing of late nineteenth-century Havana) on Anton Recio Street in the Jesús-María neighborhood. The police had received "confidential" information about a ñáñigo initiation ceremony that was to take place that evening in an "inner room" of the solar. According to the records, those present at the time of the police raid immediately fled the building, many taking refuge in neighbors' rooms. Meanwhile, police searched other apartments of the solar, largely in vain, for individuals guilty of ñáñiguismo.[9]

Those arrested in the Jesús-María raid were charged with participating in a *ñáñigo juramento* (i.e., an initiation ceremony for new members). In their defense, they laid claim to religious rights guaranteed by the constitution. They argued that the gathering and celebration for which they were being prosecuted was not a ñáñigo juramento, but rather a religious gathering of neighbors and friends, "something that one could not consider at all a meeting, let alone an illicit one."[10] Indeed, September 8 was Virgen de Regla day in Havana.[11] "Why are those arrested considered to adore the Virgen de Regla in a different way than the rest of the Roman Catholics?" they asked.[12] Whether their intentions were a sophisticated legal argument or sincere testimony, the men unequivocally defended popular religion and its due protection under the law. Those arrested also explicitly opposed the arrest of individuals who were not in the room at the time of the raid. They simultaneously defended the popular salience of their form of worship while rejecting the stereotyping of individuals based on their social status.[13]

The vast majority of late nineteenth-century ñáñiguismo cases, including this one, took place in solares, also known as *casas de vecindad* or *ciudadelas*. A solar was a multi-leveled building with an entrance immediately off the street and an inner courtyard. Although many had originally been private homes for wealthy Spanish and Cuban-born elites, at the turn of the twentieth century these buildings were overwhelmingly places where poor individuals and families rented rooms. María del Carmen Barcia Zequeira has suggested that the economic crisis of the 1880s caused by the war forced an increasing number of owners to rent out their properties in this way.[14] Solares were the homes of Havana's working class, and increasingly the homes of refugees from the fighting and devastation in the rural areas of the island. In other words, they housed the new urban polity. Indeed, by 1904 it is estimated that 2,839 solares existed in Havana, and that one-third of the city's population inhabited them. Within these new living and social spaces, "Cubans—white, black, and mestizo, as well as immigrants—developed collective familial and social strategies of subsistence that put into practice different forms of solidarity, as well as conflict and confrontation."[15]

In April 1894, the Havana police intruded onto a *juego de ñáñigos*[16] in the Jesús-María neighborhood, bordering with Belén, and managed to arrest a few people. While en route to the jail, however, the police were confronted by a group of local residents who demanded the release of the prisoners. The crowd attacked the police with stones. The guard Manuel Ibañez was injured with a stone while trying to hold back the crowd from the police and the neighborhood residents who had been arrested. According to one officer's testimony, some people in the crowd fired gunshots at the police.[17] At least two aspects of this case suggest a strong connection between the intensification of the anti-colonial struggle and conflicts over ñáñiguismo. First, the conflict between the police and neighborhood residents took place just two weeks after the arrival of a new battalion of Spanish troops.[18] Second, the police repeatedly expressed confusion and surprise at the size of the crowds and the fact that the majority of neighborhood and solar residents directly confronting the police were not known to be active members of ñáñigo groups. Both factors suggest that residents understood the conflict with police in collective rather than strictly individualistic terms. Moreover, many may have seen police attacks on popular culture as part of the struggle for colonial domination.

The last stages of the war for independence, between 1895 and 1898, were marked by the dramatic and heroic campaign led by Antonio Maceo—the highest-ranking Afro-Cuban leader of the independence forces—to take over the western portion of the island and Havana, the capital of colonial authority. While battles raged in the countryside and independistas took over more and more areas of rural Cuba, Spanish colonial authorities attempted to tighten their control over the cities and towns. Brigades of pro-Spanish *voluntarios* fought with the residents of the working and poor neighborhoods of Havana.

On May 17, 1896—the same year the independence forces took the western provinces, and two days after Máximo Gómez took the Spanish colonel Enrique Segura's entire battalion—Havana police clashed with residents in the San Leopoldo neighborhood. In one incident, local police surprised a group of "men and women of color" when they entered a solar on Zanja Street.[19] While crossing the courtyard of the solar, heading to the jail with those they had arrested, the police came under attack from rocks hurled by residents of the building and other neighbors the police claimed were members of the same ñáñigo. Some officers were injured, such as Don Pedro Menéndez, who was hit by a rock and injured his left leg.[20] According to the records, the vast majority of those arrested in the Zanja case lived together in the same solar. They worked in tobacco factories and as tailors, carpenters, cooks, street vendors, masons, dockworkers, and cobblers. The two women who were arrested—Polonia Junco y Arteaga and Angela Ybon y Arteaga—worked "out of their homes," most likely doing piecework as laundresses, or perhaps cooking the food sold by street vendors.[21]

Displays of solidarity among neighbors against the intrusion of the police contrasted with anonymous complaints published at the same time in the local press, such as the middle-class newspaper *El Mundo*, regarding the threat of "brujería," "pernicious rumba," and "dangerous ñáñiguismo."[22] Rather than unwelcome and pernicious outsiders, "los ñáñigos" were neighbors, coworkers, and friends, worthy of protecting and supporting.

The police involved in the 1896 San Leopoldo case were particularly perplexed by the *diablito* costume, which was described as "unusual" and "unlike" those found in other raids.[23] The police's fascination with the costume is striking given that the majority of the men and women arrested were sharply dressed, rather than wearing diablito costumes: the women were wearing white silk skirts and leather sandals, the men dark-colored linen suit pants, white shirts, leather shoes, handkerchiefs, and *jipijapa* (Panama) hats. The situation posed serious questions for the police as to whether those they arrested were indeed "true practitioners of authentic ñáñiguismo."[24] Officer Pedro Menendez voiced strong doubts: "I do not believe the figure we confiscated is that which is called 'diablito' and used in the ceremonies of ñáñigos, it appears completely different than those that are used in true ñáñiguismo." Officer Ramon de Mendoza shared Menendez's concerns: "The figure and objects confiscated from the meeting are completely different than those I have seen in other places."[25] The Havana police clearly struggled to make sense of the dynamic bricolage of popular culture and religious practices called "ñáñiguismo." Their focus on the diablito costume, and doubts regarding its authenticity, reveals, among other things, the way ñáñiguismo operated as a racial ideology sustaining the contradiction between racial essentialism and racial malleability.

POLITICS IN THE PLAZAS

The uprisings and fighting during the war for independence had wreaked devastation across the island of Cuba, and by the 1880s the country was suffering from a serious economic crisis. In the words of Ada Ferrer, "Traces of warfare were more apparent than traces of prewar daily life."[26] Property values had declined 80 percent between the 1860s and the late 1880s.[27] The destruction and disturbances of the war for independence, combined with massive United States investment and land expropriation immediately following the war, forced many farmers off their land and instigated a major migration of people from the rural areas to the cities.[28] One specific result of these processes was that by 1899 Havana was the "preferred destination of Afro-Cubans" from the countryside.[29] At the same time, the undeniable and overwhelming role of Afro-Cuban independence fighters—known as *mambises*—in Cuba's victory over Spain meant that Cubans of African descent emerged from the war with a "public presence and prestige they did not enjoy before the struggle began" at rallies, festivals, and on the streets of Havana.[30]

Travelers to Havana at the turn of the twentieth century invariably referred to the fact that "Havana lived on the street."[31] African women and Cuban-born women of African descent, called *boyeras*, sold small fried snacks on the streets.[32] Small *bohios* (named after the typical thatched roof house of the Cuban countryside) scattered throughout the city sold sugar- and honey-based alcoholic drinks called *fucanga* and *hidromiel*.[33] Musical trios moved from one bar to the next playing requests and collecting tips. Other vendors roamed selling water, fruit, bread, sweets, coal, poultry, and milk. Each had their own tune or musical instrument to let the neighbors know what they were selling, and they were sometimes followed by mules or cows wearing bells—all of which lent a musical quality to daily life.[34]

Esteban Montejo, an ex-slave and veteran of the war for independence, recalls that at the end of the war in the neighborhoods of Belén, Jesús-María, and San Leopoldo, "there was more rumba than in any other place, both the rumba of the cajón and the rumba of the kettle drum. . . . All the streets and inside the houses were filled with little leather stools. People would sit to watch, and old folks as well as young would go on dancing until they dropped. The ñáñigos' open patios were also lit up."[35] Indeed, many of those arrested by the Havana police for ñáñiguismo testified they were simply going about their daily business when music and drumming coming from within a courtyard or at the end of a cul-de-sac attracted their attention. Esteban Montejo compared the vibrant public life in Havana at the turn of the twentieth century to a "carnival," and in the same breath he noted how Havana street life had political resonances: "Some folks were dissatisfied with the way the Cubans *governed themselves*."[36]

Immediately after the end of the war, the United States government attempted to impose serious restrictions on suffrage rights, including literacy and property requirements. Ultimately the United States was unsuccessful, but debates raged in newspapers, among civic organizations, in city councils, and in constitutional conventions regarding the "appropriate" form of popular and Afro-Cuban participation in Cuban society after emancipation and independence.

The new penal code of 1900 reflected the precarious relationship of working Afro-Cubans with the new government: on the one hand, formally recognized and incorporated into legitimate political structures; on the other hand, consistently under suspicion. The new code was laden with racial euphemisms. Organizations, as well as individuals, could be charged with "illicit association" if they failed to comply with any of these requirements. It gave police authorities the right to enter private homes and continued to require all societies to register for licenses as "mutual aid associations" and provide the city authorities and police with a list of members and "directors," fiscal information, as well as predetermined days and times of group meetings. Meetings were officially required to be open to the police or any other authority.[37]

New carnival regulations also figured prominently in this repressive strategy. In addition to prohibiting traditional forms of pre-Lenten celebrations, such as throwing "eggs filled with flour or any other substance that can harm or bother someone,"[38] the carnival regulations of Havana from 1900 also barred all forms of social and political criticism during celebrations. The regulations banned "insults to people with phrases or actions" and "expressly prohibited" anything that offended "public morality, use[d] profane language, or costumes that ridicule[d] people or institutions."[39]

The same neighborhoods known for ñáñiguismo were also renowned for the *comparsa* music and dance groups that led the Three Kings' Day (Epiphany) and carnival celebrations in Havana.[40] Comparsa groups of Belén, Jesús-María, San Leopoldo, and Cayo Hueso used homemade instruments and materials, such as bells, frying pans, pots, and tire rims as costumes and musical instruments in their celebrations.[41] They also, as the carnival regulations suggested, used times of celebrations to voice political ideas and social criticism. For example, during the carnivals of Havana of 1899 and 1900, comparsa groups dressed up and mocked the Cuerpos de Voluntarios and Batallones de Orden Público, pro-Spanish brigades that had harassed the poor neighborhoods of Havana during the war.[42]

Neighborhoods of Havana were filled with both legal and illegal commerce.[43] The press frequently reported scuffles and fights in and around the central Mercado Tacón, such as when the street vendor José Pereira was beaten up and received injuries to his head and chest when discovered to be selling coal below the fixed price of the city's shops.[44] And the jipijapa hats that perplexed the Havana police looking for diablito costumes in the San Leopoldo case above were of the very sort that the street vendors like José Hurtado were caught selling under the portals of the Mercado Tacón without the necessary city license.[45] Indeed, there was a large market for jipijapas, *guayaberas*, and linen suits—many of the street vendors sold stolen or counterfeit versions of European brands, which were generally too expensive for working people to buy in a store.[46]

During the early 1900s, the middle-class Havana newspaper *El Mundo* frequently published reports of false identities, cross-dressing, and fraud. Just a few days before the 1902 celebrations of the new republic, the *El Mundo* newspaper reported two cases of individuals in disguise as police officers. In an interesting example of taking advantage of widespread state corruption, *El Mundo* reported that a pair of men dressed as "officers" stopped and bribed some people on the street.[47] In another article, the paper reported on the "early arrival of carnival." The piece related the story of a "Catalonian man" who had been found dressed as a woman. After being taken to the police station, the judge let him off, but stated that "he shouldn't hurry the carnival celebrations."[48]

Cross-dressing and disguises were just two of the many "counterfeit" practices that provoked bourgeois concerns over the control of people and things in Havana during the 1890s and early 1900s. *El Mundo* ran a regular editorial column titled "The Falsifications." One edition from February 1902 began with the following sentence: "The fact that counterfeit everything and anything exists in Havana is confirmed by the daily discovery of such products on the streets."[49] The paper also ran a separate daily column with brief descriptions of counterfeit products recently confiscated on the streets of Havana, such as watches, fake street vendor licenses, counterfeit cash and checks, and resold, used postage stamps.

The 1900 Cuban penal code specified under the category of fraud "those who pretended to be 'professors' without the appropriate degree, those who falsely wore uniforms of the military or another authority, those who pretended to be of nobility or standing when they were not, as well as those who defraud others with imaginary businesses, false documents, false signatures, illegal raffles, and those who spread false rumors, or use any other tactic to alter the natural price of things."[50] Indeed the code reflected a genuine rupture in old forms of regulation, status, and power in Cuban society.

REPRESSING THE REPUBLIC

On May 20, 1902, the United States officially ended its direct occupation of Cuba. Nonetheless the United States government maintained its right to intervene at will in Cuban affairs through the Platt Amendment, which left independent Cuba on unsteady ground. The end of formal occupation by the United States and the declaration of universal manhood suffrage on the island brought the meanings of membership in the Cuban nation into deeper and more intense scrutiny. If the occupation had initially placed the anti-colonial promise of universal manhood suffrage into serious doubt, the end of the occupation cautiously rekindled the hopes of generations of Cubans who dreamed of and fought for freedom.

Cubans, and especially residents of Havana, marked the withdrawal of U.S. forces from Havana with festivities. The preparations for and celebration of the end of the occupation took on a carnivalesque quality. According to contemporary accounts of the event, streamers, lights, ribbons, and homemade decorations of all sorts lined the streets of Havana. Neighborhoods organized dances, fairs with horse riding, food kiosks, and small *bohíos* from which vendors sold drinks.[51] The celebrations of May 20 revealed a heterogeneous polity and showed publicly, and unequivocally, how "Afro-Cubans' contribution to Cuban independence could not be hidden."[52]

Authorities did not miss a step in their attempt to constrain and define the terms of membership in the new Cuban republic.[53] There was a sharp increase in police surveillance and violence amid the 1902 festivities. An official count of criminal cases filed that day in connection to the celebrations placed the total number at ninety-three.[54] The threatening colonial gaze of the United States and new contests in the formal political realm regarding access to government resources and the role of black Cubans in the new republic had yet again brought out racist fears and police repression.[55] In one of the most dramatic cases of ñáñiguismo that took place on the day of the celebrations, nearly one hundred people were "caught" in a solar on Jesus Peregrino Street dancing, singing, and playing music. At the time of the raid, many of those present fled and hid in other rooms throughout the building; the police managed to arrest fifty-nine men.[56]

The police argued that those gathered in the solar were singing and dancing in a "manner offensive to *our* good customs." Further, they claimed that those arrested were "ñáñigos . . . who had been persecuted since time immemorial" and who, in order to protect their fellow members, would "attack other groups on the streets of Havana, and even kill persons . . . in ceremonies and practices of savage people."[57]

The socioeconomic and racial community subsumed in the phrase "our good customs" did not include the vast majority of Havana's residents who celebrated a new Cuba founded on the struggles and sacrifices of people of African descent. Further, the language of "good customs" echoed a nineteenth-century colonial sensibility. The "time immemorial" threats of ñáñigo violence and murder invoked by the police echoed fears of Haiti and slave rebellions, as well as representations of the struggle for independence as a "race war." According to the lawyer Angel Fernandez—who had an office on Calle Obispo, not far from the solar on Jesus Peregrino, and defended eleven of the fifty-nine people arrested—the entire case should have been disregarded by the courts because the police charge of ñáñiguismo rested on article 415 of the Spanish penal code, which pertained to patricide and murder and applied only to slaves.[58] The racial euphemism of ñáñiguismo legitimated new forms of state power while bridging the gap between colonial society and modern civilization.

The testimonies of those arrested in the Jesus Peregrino case were filled with descriptions of the excitement and music that permeated Havana. Men, women, and children—Havana residents as well as many people from neighboring towns, such as Regla and Marianao—wandered the neighborhoods and enjoyed the atmosphere and celebrations. Open windows and doors welcomed those passing by to join the ongoing celebrations. The scene was a far cry from police portrayals of secretive ñáñigo gatherings and induction ceremonies. Indeed, the testimonies from the Jesus Peregrino case reflect a genuine sense of confusion on the part of those arrested as to what crime they had committed.[59]

Ramon Calvo O'Farrill, a fifty-one-year-old *moreno* man, stated that men, women, and children gathered to celebrate their "incredible joy for the country." According to O'Farrill, the windows and doors of most of the houses of Havana were wide open, and one could hear drumming and singing coming through them all. Due to what he termed the "disruptions of the war," O'Farrill had been imprisoned briefly in Spain. In his defense, O'Farrill argued that he was but a working man and "a father" who "suffered many calamities, including the loss of two children to hunger." It would appear from O'Farrill's testimony that the festivities on May 20 provided a moment in which to remember suffering and sacrifices, celebrate their end, and dream collectively of different and better times to come.

Francisco Roca Ybarra, a resident of Regla, had come into Havana for a day of festivities and celebrations. While walking down Jesus Peregrino Street, he came upon the celebration in the solar. Ybarra, attracted and moved by the music and energy from within the solar, entered the building and joined the group that had already gathered there. In his defense, Ybarra explicitly challenged the police's characterization of the event as a ñáñigo meeting. In particular, he pointed out that women and children were present but not arrested, and implied that the police selectively arrested people in order to construe the gathering as ñáñiguismo and hide its thoroughly popular nature.

The police repeatedly emphasized that the group arrested on Jesus Peregrino was "in majority persons of color" as a justification for the raid, arrests, and charge of ñáñiguismo.[60] According to the testimonies of those arrested, however, the crowd gathered was predominantly, but by no means exclusively, people of color. The men arrested in the Jesus Peregrino case reflected the diverse economic structure of Havana: they worked as masons, tailors, dockworkers, painters, tobacco factory workers, day laborers, carpenters, cooks, cobblers, carriage drivers, sailors, bakers, and musicians. As Stephan Palmié has observed, the popular celebrations at the dawn of the Cuban republic made public how working people of all colors not only acquired an "African" memory, but also turned themselves into "agents of its [Africa's] social reproduction."[61]

In another case at the time of the celebrations, Pascual Garcia Almirante, age thirty-three, and Juan Llane Basallo, age twenty-three, were accused of being leaders of a juego de ñáñigos and arrested in a solar on Peñalver Street.[62] Both men had been born in Havana and worked as day laborers. In their own defense, they expressed firm and sincere reverence for the family heirlooms that police had confiscated as proof of ñáñiguismo activity. Almirante stated that the objects taken by the police were "preserved by my father as remembrances since he died and left them in my charge, and they have never been used in any *asociación ilícita* or *juego de ñáñigos*."[63] They defended their behavior and the belongings under scrutiny as legitimate and traditional ways to honor and remember family members and ancestors, as well as to honor the struggle for freedom from colonial domination and slavery. Ultimately, both men were found guilty of ñáñiguismo on the grounds that the objects confiscated from their home constituted proof of ñáñigo activity. And ironically, after the courts rejected Basallo and Almirante's claim that their possessions were valuable and historical heirlooms, the objects were handed over to the Montané Anthropological Museum at the University of Havana as "authentic" examples of African culture.

A few months after the celebrations of the republic, in September 1902, the police officer Don Emilio Menendes y Hernandez tried to slip unnoticed into a solar on San Isidro dressed in plain clothes. He hoped to surprise a "wedding" allegedly taking place between two men in an upper room of the solar. Another officer walking outside the building at the same time claimed that upon hearing "*cajones* drumming" and songs in "strange languages," he entered to investigate.[64] Police familiarity with neighborhood residents did not always work in their favor. After climbing a few flights of stairs, the residents of the solar recognized the officer and the news spread fast throughout the solar. Soon the chaos of what police and participants alike called an "immense crowd" began to spread throughout the building.

When Menendes reached the room where the alleged wedding was taking place, he found a "meeting of innumerable individuals of all the races" dancing in front of an altar. Both men and women were present, although the majority of people in the room were *afeminados* (men dressed as women). The wedding was being administered by the "ordained *brujo*" Juan Hernandez, also known as Juan el Brujo. Juan lived in another solar just one and a half blocks away on Aguilar Street, number 224. One of the men being "married" was a white man by the name of Manuel Vargas; the other groom fled and managed to escape arrest.

The captain Miguel Angel Duque Estrada claimed that the solar initially drew his attention because there were "many people hanging around in and outside the house," including two people he arrested for gambling. The police confiscated a variety of objects from the room, including a crucifix, a linen suit, and six jipijapa hats.[65] The majority of those arrested lived in the solar where the ceremony was taking place, and they worked as cooks, day laborers, masons, and painters.

In his defense testimony, Manuel Márquez y García said that the crowd had gathered in order to have a private celebration in honor of his saint, for which they requested the necessary license from the authorities, who told them they did not need a written license for such a gathering. They had borrowed candles and flower vases from the church for their altar. García claimed that the knives that had been confiscated by the police as proof of ñáñiguismo were in reality taken from the kitchen, "because the police took everything from the kitchen, even the knives!!"[66] There was both an acknowledgment here of the utter imbrication of religion and daily life, as well as a critique of the total criminalization of working people's existence.

The group partaking in the ceremony was international. José Lopez y Menendez was from Spain and Manuel Márquez y García was from Mexico, and it was in his room that the celebration was taking place. Leonardo Chacón y Gomes was from Santiago de Cuba and Pedro Velasco Isaguirre was from Haiti. The bonds among these men of different national origins interestingly contrast with divisions between native and foreign workers in the workforce more generally.[67] This case suggests that foreign and native workers of different ethnicities built connections among one another, despite economic policies intended to divide them, through religious imaginings and rituals. Moreover, the San Isidro case demonstrates, in the words of Stephan Palmié, that "'Africanity'—and indeed 'Africa' itself—is a 'project' rather than a 'primordiality' . . . a product of local social agency (whether on the African continent or elsewhere) and one that locally may or may not be aligned with racialised forms of subjectivity."[68] The majority of those arrested in the San Isidro case had been arrested twice before for public scandal and cross-dressing, in 1894 and 1896.[69] The dates of the men's prior arrests in 1896 suggest that they were charged while celebrating the victories of Maceo and the successes of the liberation army. Indeed, the records indicate that over the course of the late nineteenth and early twentieth century, these men had constructed and practiced their own vision of Cubanidad.

RACE, NATION, AND ÑÁÑIGO

Rafael Roche y Monteagudo worked as a police investigator in Havana at this time, and in 1908 he published a book titled *La Policía y sus misterios en Cuba*. Roche hoped his work would contribute to finally "exposing and extinguishing" what he, and many of his contemporaries, deemed the barbaric and dangerous practices of the poor and working-class people living in Havana at the turn of the twentieth century. "Exposure" seems a significant choice in words on Roche's part, as it invoked both the notion of bringing to light dark and hidden truths, as well as making someone vulnerable (in the sense of "dying from exposure").

According to Roche, bandits, thieves, tricksters, and scam artists of the "worst sort" were at the helm of popular associations. Indeed, those accused of and arrested for ñáñiguismo were often also charged with robbery or other petty economic crimes. Police frequently mentioned that gambling in the solares of Havana would initially catch their attention and lead them to the more secretive deviant practices at work inside. Roche states in his book that "creole" ñáñiguismo was "bastardized," that Cuban-born members who improvised and introduced new practices "lent profanity and ridicule to Catholicism," and that "these elements struck fear in the elder generation and increased the criminal element in these groups."[70] Roche's words conveyed both elite concerns regarding counterfeiting and racist portrayals of contemporary popular culture in Havana. The contrast Roche drew between early and late nineteenth-century ñáñiguismo erased many historical complexities, not the least of which was that "pure" African cabildos of the earlier part of the nineteenth century were, in part, modeled on the cabildo system of Spain.[71] Yet Roche's use of the word "bastardized" and his expressed anxiety regarding specifically creole practices, as opposed to a sealed European or African culture, points to the demographic, economic, and political changes he himself was undoubtedly experiencing in his daily life in early twentieth-century Havana. For Roche, late nineteenth and early twentieth-century ñáñiguismo was the soul of a world brimming with fraud and social degeneration.

Roche highlights, again in a severely distorted manner, the struggle of authorities and elites to reckon with and reconcile the legacy, mutations, and valence of African traditions and practices in a modern and independent Cuban society. In the first pages of his book, Roche argues that "the time has come to discover the regeneration of the lower social classes of the country." I want to focus here on Roche's use of the word "regeneration." Although he construed ñáñiguismo as primitive, degenerative, bastard, and secretive, he nevertheless—it would seem—recognized that African-derived popular culture was at the very heart of the regeneration (political, economic, social) of the country.[72]

Contrary to Roche's claims to the contrary, the practices of ñáñiguismo did not transgress otherwise real boundaries of identities and cultures. Rather, ñáñiguismo created new identities and paradigms. Specifically, attempts to make popular religion and culture fall along racial lines, disconnected from their historical and contemporary contexts, broke down repeatedly. The physical spaces where gatherings and ceremonies were held "flit among and between *cabildos*, private homes, and public spaces."[73] The objects used in ceremonies varied, as did their specific purposes. Ceremonies involved "sacred" and "familiar" things—from Catholic crucifixes and African drums to pots and pans from the kitchen. Participants could just as easily be wearing ceremonial costumes, passed down through generations, or linen suits and Panama hats. Drumming and ritualistic dancing were an integral part of political holidays in honor of emancipation and national independence. These cultural practices were utterly immediate, and at the same time strongly embedded in an imagined historical space and time that connected struggles, histories, futures, and continents. The separation imposed after emancipation and independence between "African" and the "modern" has concealed how working people of Havana fashioned their membership in modern Cuban society through the praxis and defense of cultural and spiritual practices. It has also elided the way that controlling and racializing popular culture was critical to wresting power in the post-emancipation Cuban nation.

In present-day Cuba, the term "ñáñigo" is considered by many to be derogatory—associated with ignorance, imprecision, or "impurity"—particularly when it is used to refer to secretive all-male sodalities that self-identify as *abakuá*. At the turn of the twentieth century, however, rather than a "thing" or a specific "type" of group, ñáñiguismo was something in the making—a process—both on the ground and in the official records. The broad application and uses of the term "ñáñigo," whether by police, journalists, writers, or participants themselves, was part of the historical phenomena under scrutiny in this chapter—namely, the reconstitution of the Cuban polity and the transformation of racial ideology at the time of slave emancipation and national independence. That ñáñigo becomes both derogatory and considered an inaccurate and "impure" description of Afro-Cuban religion is in part a product of struggles in the late nineteenth and early twentieth century over culture and power after slave emancipation.

DIABLITOS: WHETHER DAPPER OR IN DENIM

On October 10, 1916, the Havana police interrupted what they called "a flagrant example of ñáñiguismo."[74] The records of the October 10 case tell the standard story of the police "surprising" a "secret meeting" of a ñáñigo group holding a "juramento."[75] Ten men were arrested and charged with "ñáñiguismo" and "asociación ilícita." The majority of those arrested lived on Aguila Street, and many in the same building. They worked a range of jobs, from day laborer to street vendors, cooks, tobacco factory workers, and dockworkers. The men arrested were of all racial backgrounds: white, mestizo, and black. In their defense, they argued they did not gather for an illicit reason or to commit any crime against property or persons. Indeed, some police involved in the case themselves expressed confusion as to who precisely belonged to the ñáñigo, and moreover whether this constituted a case of true ñáñiguismo. The piece of evidence invoked as unquestionable proof of ñáñiguismo activity was the diablito costume. In the back of the police file, however, the police recorded the kind of clothes the men were wearing at the time of their arrest. All of those arrested were dressed in long pants, some in linen pants and others in denim. Most were wearing striped, long-sleeved, or solid-colored shirts. Approximately half the group were wearing the traditional Spanish farmer *alpargata* shoes, made of rope and canvas.

The date of the gathering and raid marked the anniversary of the Grito de Yará, when in 1868 Manuel de Céspedes freed his slaves, set off a revolt in the eastern part of Cuba, and instigated the war for independence.[76] Although there is no mention of this "coincidence" in the records, it seems safe to assume that rather than a flagrant example of ñáñiguismo, the police had raided a celebration of slave emancipation and Cuban independence—a joint spiritual and political event. Or, perhaps more to the point, as the cases analyzed in this chapter show, ritual was part and parcel of the production of political identity and community among working people in Havana. At the turn of the twentieth century, working men and women of Havana interwove their own visions of equality and reciprocity with memories and experiences of slavery and war, cajones drumming, music and songs, candles and crucifixes, counterfeit Panama hats, denim jeans and linen suits, and traditional Spanish farmer shoes. The open secret of the solares in a diablito disguise was the praxis of popular Cubanidad.

NOTES

1. Ada Ferrer, *Insurgent Cuba: Race, Nation, and Revolution, 1868–1898* (Chapel Hill: University of North Carolina Press, 1999), 112. All translations are my own unless otherwise specified.

2. Fannie Theresa Rushing, "Cabildos de Nación, Sociedades de la Raza de Color: Afro-Cuban Participation in Slave Emancipation and Cuban Independence, 1865–1895" (Ph.D. diss., University of Chicago, 1992), 315. See also Pedro Deschamps Chapeaux, *El negro en la economía habanera del siglo XIX* (Havana: Union de Escritores y Artistas de Cuba, 1971); Robert Paquette, *Sugar Is Made with Blood: The Conspiracy of La Escalera and the Conflict between Empires over Slavery in Cuba* (Middletown: Wesleyan University Press, 1988), 262; Stephan Palmié, *Wizards and Scientists: Explorations in Afro-Cuban Modernity and Tradition* (Durham: Duke University Press, 2002).

3. Alejandro de la Fuente, *A Nation for All: Race, Inequality, and Politics in Twentieth-Century Cuba* (Chapel Hill: University of North Carolina Press, 2001), 23.

4. Chapeaux, *El negro en la economía habanera del siglo XIX*, 43; Fernando Ortiz, "Los cabildos afrocubanos," *Revista Bimestre Cubana* 16 (1921): 9.

5. The Aponte rebellion of 1812—named after one of its leaders, José Aponte y Ubarra—resulted in a series of antislavery rebellions across the island of Cuba. In 1844 the Spanish colonial government imprisoned, tortured, and killed thousands of Afro-Cubans, both enslaved and free, for fear of a massive slave rebellion. See Matt D.

Childs, *The 1812 Aponte Rebellion in Cuba and the Struggle against Atlantic Slavery* (Chapel Hill: University of North Carolina Press, 2006); and Paquette, *Sugar Is Made with Blood*.

6. Paquette, *Sugar Is Made with Blood*, 262.

7. Stefan Palmié, "A View from Itia Ororó Kande," *Social Anthropology* 14, no. 1 (2006): 103.

8. Many of the laws of association had been formally in place since 1837. See María del Carmen Barcia Zequeira, "La sociabilidad de las capas populares en la conformación de una sociedad moderna, Cuba (1880–1930)," in *Historia y memoria: Sociedad, cultura y vida cotidiana en Cuba, 1878–1917*, ed. José Amador (Havana: Centro de Investigación y Desarrollo de la Cultura Cubana Juan Marinello, 2003), 265–80.

9. Fondo Audencia de la Habana, legajo 711, expediente 12, Archivo Nacional de Cuba, Havana (hereafter cited as ANC).

10. Ibid.

11. The Virgen de Regla is often equated with the Orisha goddess Yemayá from Yoruba-based religions, considered the main protector of sailors, fishermen, and dockworkers. This does not exclude, of course, the possibility that some people were indeed being initiated into the group on this day.

12. Fondo Audencia de la Habana, legajo 711, expediente 12, ANC.

13. Unfortunately, as is the case with many of these records, it is unclear if and how the case was resolved. The last piece of defense in the records was filed on May 8, 1883.

14. María del Carmen Barcia Zequeira, *Una sociedad en crisis: La Habana a finales del siglo XIX* (Havana: Editorial de Ciencias Sociales, 2001), 106. See also Michael Zeuske, "The Cimarron in the Archives: A Re-reading of Miguel Barnet's Biography of Esteban Montejo," *New West Indian Guide* 71, nos. 3/4 (1997): 265–79.

15. Barcia Zequeira, "La sociabilidad de las capas populares," 269.

16. A phrase used to refer to a gathering of a group that does not connote an induction ceremony.

17. Audencia de la Habana, legajo 558, expediente 21, ANC.

18. "Notice of New Soldiers Arrived in Havana," 1894, Cuba: Capitanía General Collection, Cuban Heritage Collection, University of Miami Libraries (Infantería del Distrito Militar de la Isla de Cuba, Depósito del Embarque y Desembarque de La Habana, Capitanía General Collection, "Notice of new soldiers arrived in Havana," 1894).

19. Audencia de la Habana, legajo 554, expediente 4, ANC.

20. Ibid.

21. Ibid.

22. *El Mundo*, February 13, 1902, 2.

23. "Diablito" was the name given originally by Spaniards to refer to costumes used in African-based religious ceremonies.

24. See Alejandra Bronfman, *Measures of Equality: Social Science, Citizenship and*

Race in Cuba, 1902–1940 (Chapel Hill: University of North Carolina Press, 2004) for a close and detailed analysis of how and why police took inventory of these objects.

25. Audencia de la Habana, legajo 554, expediente 4, ANC.

26. Ferrer, *Insurgent Cuba*, 100.

27. Ibid., 98.

28. Robin Dale Moore, *Nationalizing Blackness: Afrocubanismo and Artistic Revolution in Havana, 1920–1940* (Pittsburgh: University of Pittsburgh Press, 1997), 66.

29. De la Fuente, *A Nation for All*, 115.

30. Miguel Barnet, *Biography of a Runaway Slave* (Willimantic, Conn.: Curbstone, 1994), 190; de la Fuente, *A Nation for All*, 35; Ferrer, *Insurgent Cuba*, 3.

31. Barcia Zequeira, *Una sociedad en crisis*, 125.

32. "Las bolleras," Registro de Asociaciones, legajo 331, expediente 9788, ANC. By the late 1930s they had formed an official carnival *comparsa* in Havana, with a board of directors and a fixed meeting space. Their costumes include large pans and spoons.

33. Ibid.

34. María Poumier, *Apuntes sobre la vida cotidiana en Cuba en 1898* (Havana: Editorial de Ciencias Sociales, 1975), 108.

35. Barnet, *Biography of a Runaway Slave*, 191.

36. Ibid., 191; emphasis added.

37. *Código Penal de Cuba*, 1900, Archivo Histórico Municipal, Oficina del Historiador de la Ciudad de La Habana, Havana.

38. *El Mundo*, February 12, 1904, 6.

39. *El Mundo*, February 5, 1910, 3.

40. Moore, *Nationalizing Blackness*, 64.

41. Ibid.

42. Ibid., 68.

43. Ana Vera, "La fotografía y el trabajo a principios del siglo XX," in Amador, *Historia y memoria*, 183–203.

44. *El Mundo* January 11, 1903, 6.

45. *El Mundo*, January 14, 1915, 16.

46. Poumier, *Apuntes sobre la vida cotidiana en Cuba en 1898*, 110, 239. This style of dress, in particular the suits and hats the men wore, became the outfit par excellence of the stereotypical hustlers, also known as *guapos*, during the 1920s. Details on linen suits and jipijapa hats appear increasingly in the police records after 1910 as a way to connote "deviant" types.

47. *El Mundo*, May 14, 1902, front page.

48. *El Mundo*, January 23, 1904, front page.

49. *El Mundo*, February 22, 1902, 2.

50. *Código Penal de Cuba*, 1900, Archivo Histórico Municipal, Oficina del Historiador de la Ciudad de La Habana, Havana.

51. *El Mundo*, May 20, 1902, front page.

52. De la Fuente, *A Nation for All*, 37.

53. Fernando Martínez Heredia, Rebecca J. Scott, and Orlando García Martínez, eds., *Espacios, silencios y los sentidos de la libertad: Cuba entre 1878 y 1912* (Havana: Ediciones Unión, 2001); Bronfman, *Measures of Equality*, 18.

54. *El Mundo*, May 21, 1902, front page.

55. De la Fuente, *A Nation for All*, 162.

56. Audencia de la Habana, legajo 214, expediente 5, ANC.

57. Ibid.; emphasis added.

58. Ibid.

59. Ibid.

60. Police also noted other features, such as hair texture, the shape of one's nose, the color of one's eyes, and one's height.

61. Palmié, "A View from Itia Ororó Kande," 107. Aline Helg has argued similarly that in early twentieth-century Havana, "the white lower class was Africanizing its way of life." Helg's problematic use of "two races" aside, her remark points out connections among forms of popular sociability, daily life, and political identity and consciousness. Aline Helg, "Race in Argentina and Cuba, 1880–1930," in *The Idea of Race in Latin America*, ed. Richard Graham (Austin: University of Texas Press, 1990), 52.

62. Audencia de la Habana, legajo 223, expediente 4, ANC.

63. Ibid.

64. Audencia de la Habana, legajo 734, expediente 2, ANC.

65. Ibid.

66. Ibid.

67. De la Fuente, *A Nation for All*, 125–27.

68. Palmié, "A View from Itia Ororó Kande," 111.

69. Audencia de la Habana, legajo 734, expediente 2, ANC.

70. Rafael Roche y Monteagudo, *La Policía y sus misterios en Cuba* (Havana: Imprenta y Papelería de Rambla, Bouza y Cia, 1914), 38.

71. Ortiz, "Los cabildos afrocubanos," 8–9; Paquette, *Sugar Is Made with Blood*, 108–9.

72. Roche y Monteagudo, *La Policía y sus misterios en Cuba*, 38. The original Spanish reads, "Tiempo es ya de procurar la regeneración de las bajas capas sociales del país."

73. Bronfman, *Measures of Equality*, 21.

74. Audencia de la Habana, legajo 704, expediente 10, ANC.

75. Audencia de La Habana, legajo 704, expediente 5, ANC.

76. See Aline Helg, *Our Rightful Share: The Afro-Cuban Struggle for Equality, 1886–1912* (Chapel Hill: University of North Carolina Press, 1995).

PART III
Powers on the Move

9.

Rites of Power and Rumors of Race:
The Circulation of Supernatural Knowledge
in the Greater Caribbean, 1890–1940

LARA PUTNAM

In the late nineteenth and early twentieth centuries, large-scale migration created a heterogeneous cultural sphere that reached from the Caribbean coasts of Central and South America across the islands of the Caribbean and beyond. Jamaica, Panama, and Cuba formed key nodes within the migratory networks of the western Caribbean; Barbados and Trinidad did the same in the east. The western circuits also encompassed the coastal lowlands of Colombia, Costa Rica, Nicaragua, Honduras, and Guatemala; the eastern circuits tied the English- and French-speaking Leeward and Windward chains to Venezuela in the south and the Dominican Republic in the north. While the vast majority of the migrants whose travels, letters, and remittances linked these distant locales were of African ancestry, the continuous arrival of indentured East Indians to the eastern Caribbean contributed both emigrants and ideas to the circum-Caribbean migratory flows. Migrants from the Indian subcontinent, from China, and from the Spanish-speaking mestizo populations of the inland regions were present in every rimland port at the turn of the twentieth century, while indigenous populations persevered in the surrounding hinterland.[1]

This chapter examines the practice of obeah in the Greater Caribbean migratory sphere in the early twentieth century. Judicial, autobiographical, and print sources from these years reveal a complicated mixture of parallels, common origins, mutual reinforcement, and ongoing borrowing among a variety of supernatural traditions in this mobile world.[2] The search for effective knowledge brought migrants of different origins into an ongoing, decentralized conversation over human access to supernatural power. Even selecting terms to summarize that conversation is hard, and for reasons that go beyond the standard imperfections of the historian's craft. Rather, the dilemma inheres in the particularities of this system of meaning and practice, understood by those who sustained it and were sustained by it to be neither fully knowable, nor properly speakable, nor fixed in its moral valence. Although each seeker knew that she herself or he himself would recur to it only for healing, protection, or justice, he or she also knew that others might employ it toward malevolent ends. This same perspectival duality was reflected in the terms used. Individuals referenced the supernatural access they *sought* as "science," "work," or "cure"; that which they feared might have been used *against* them they labeled "humbug," "hex," or, occasionally, "obeah."[3] Meanwhile, contemporary observers from near and far used the word obeah to describe the system as a whole, a usage that on the one hand captured the unitariness and slipperiness of the powerful forces involved, in line with participants' perceptions; and on the other hand ignored the distinctions of moral intentionality on which participants insisted, and over which they argued. Scholars have largely adopted this broader usage, as I will do here.[4]

In the same years that working folks of disparate ancestry crossed the Caribbean in search of opportunity, rumors of malevolent black magic traveled between the same sites, sped by the growing circulation of Caribbean newspapers. The tales of ritual murder printed and reprinted by papers in Havana, Kingston, Panama, Colón, Limón, San José, Port-of-Spain, Bridgetown, New York, and Toronto in the first decades of the twentieth century did not describe Caribbean engagement with the supernatural as a fluid intercultural system, but rather as a definitive racial marker: obeah and "voodoo"—the terms were often used interchangeably by outside commentators—reflected "African savagery" or "Negro atavism," pure and simple. The iconic victims in the sacrifice tales that circulated in the region's press were white infants and children, drained of their blood to cure ailing black bodies. The iconic aggressors in these tales were foreign blacks: Jamaicans or Haitians in Cuba, Trinidadians or Saint Lucians in Panama or Costa Rica. The deep irony, I argue, is that rumors of obeah spread around the early twentieth-century Caribbean both due to a *reality* of cross-cultural commonality and in service of a *fiction* of racially demarcated cultural difference.

As we shall see, popular constructs of obeah drew on disparate streams of knowledge, including sensationalist print accounts, specialists' expertise, and community common sense. Each of the three streams of knowledge drew on avowedly traditional and self-consciously modern sources alike. Yet the custom within scholarly writings on obeah has been to consider that which appears traditional or African to be genuine, and to treat heterogeneous,

European, or innovative elements as distortions or accretions, extraneous to true core of belief and practice. In adopting this perspective, even sympathetic accounts have remained trapped in the paradigm established by foundational debates over "voodoos and obeahs" in the 1930s, within which the inherent Africanness of obeah was taken for granted, and the only issues up for debate were the degree of racial determinism in shaping black culture, the potential meliorability of Afro-descended populations in the Americas, and the political implications of the same.[5] In contrast, if we choose to take obeah as practiced by Caribbeans rather than obeah as fantasized by white observers as the object of our analysis, we see that heterogeneity was central to its strength and spread and that innovations and borrowing were the order of the day. Like their contemporaries in Paris, Liverpool, and Long Island, Caribbean folks sought supernatural power by means of an eclectic array of elements drawn from Victorian and Edwardian imaginings of otherness. In the cases discussed below, we see the reverberations of French romantic reengagement with the medieval *grimoire* tradition, the nineteenth-century resurgence of blood libel accusations against eastern European Jewry, and the new semiotics of the occult generated by a popularized Orientalism in which Egypt and India took center stage. Meanwhile, certain developments in Western science and commerce, in particular consumers' enthusiasm for patent medicines and the related obsession with the strength and purity of "the blood" as the underlying determinant of health, shaped the evolving practice of obeah as well. In sum, twentieth-century obeah was a multi-stranded ritual complex created by, for, and about people on the move.

POPULAR PRACTICES OF SUPERNATURAL MANIPULATION IN THE EARLY TWENTIETH-CENTURY CARIBBEAN

The attempt to understand the making and meaning of magical practice in the early twentieth-century Caribbean is beset by very specific methodological dilemmas, due both to the nature of the written sources available on the topic and to the patterns of interaction between print and popular culture within the historical process under study. Euro-American observers' writings mixed and matched anecdotes about black people's black magic in the Caribbean with cheery abandon, borrowing cases reported from one island to support claims about popular practices elsewhere. Thus print culture served as a sort of echo chamber in which a few original scenes were transformed into multiple data points. The logic at work used lines of racial demarcation to determine bounds of extrapolation. Any practice found among some black people somewhere was presumed to be common to black people everywhere. What was necessary, as W. Ralph Hall Caine wrote in 1908, was to grasp the "main essence" of "all these manifestations of belief in single, double, or black magic and serpent worship," in order to "appreciate the attitude of mind of that part of the negro family which, while accepting Christianity with a gladsome heart and every evidence of sincere conviction, still retains beliefs that link it at one step to the wild, untamed, sacrificial orgies of the West African forest." Grasping that "main essence" of Negro nature was essential for "our self-appointed task of up-lifting the negro race."[6] The political stakes of such claims could not have been higher. As Diana Paton has argued, for many white commentators, obeah became a referendum on the meliorability of Negro barbarism and, thus, on the ultimate possibilities for black people's self-government in the Americas.[7]

Euro-American observers' fetishization and reiteration of certain tales creates real dilemmas for the historian who aims to trace the chronology and spread of popular practice in the Caribbean. In essence, there are two histories here, one of popular practices and their circulation and borrowing, and one of print representations and their circulation and borrowing. Print representations claimed to be a reflection of popular practices, and to varying extents they were, albeit distorted and partial ones. But they also, and ever more stridently, reflected and refracted other print representations, and it is not always possible to distinguish which of these two is at work. In turn, popular practice itself drew on and responded to the construction of knowledge about obeah and other supernatural regimes in print culture, although we capture only suggestive glimpses of this process.[8] The old assumption that everything authentic about obeah came from Africa, and that any other aspects were adulterations to be ignored, had the advantage of epistemological parsimony, albeit at the cost of ethnographic accuracy. My not-fully-satisfactory response to this dilemma has been to search out written sources produced at the local level—most often local press coverage of police action or court cases, or court transcripts themselves. Of course, neither court testimony nor newspaper articles provide unmediated access to popular practice—in fact, quite the contrary. They reflect necessarily atypical moments of rupture; they are structured by legal codes that dictated the utility and authority of different truth claims. Nevertheless, these sources were at least generated out of local conflicts and in engagement with local practice in ways that, read cautiously, offer a more grounded picture of developments in communities across the region.

With these caveats in mind, let us begin with a baseline summary of the elements commonly mentioned by outside travelers and foreign residents as part of obeah practice in the British Caribbean in the last decades of the nineteenth century—at the moment when a surge of direct foreign investment in the circum-Caribbean rimlands was beginning to accelerate migratory flows and carry English-speaking islanders into unaccustomed lands. Outside observers in the 1880s and 1890s described obeah as a system of supernatural manipulation within which ritual specialists played a key role in diagnosing ills (which were often the result of magical attacks) and prescribing responses (which often included the preparation of specific assemblages of powerful materials). While some authors linked obeah to collective drumming, dancing, and spirit possession, most agreed that obeah narrowly understood took the form of individual, often furtive consultation with this "obeah man" or "obeah woman." Accounts describe the use of poisons and the preparation of glass bottles with specific combinations of substances that were buried at doorways or hung in trees. Materials frequently cited as part of bottles, bundles, or rituals included pieces of coffins, grave dirt, the feathers or body parts of fowl, and human body parts (e.g., hair or teeth, sometimes from the intended targets of magical action). Obeah was used to heal physical ailments, to secure or retain sexual partners, to gain favor with employers, to draw wealth and good fortune, and to influence the outcomes of court cases.[9]

Written traces generated at the local level at disparate sites confirm all these elements, suggesting that claimed commonalities of magical practice across the Caribbean were not merely an artifact of the borrowing and replication between published accounts. For example, testimonies from across the region record the preparation of bottles to be buried under a target's door. A Trinidad newspaper editorial in 1898 lamented the ability of "the Obeah-man" to "fleece Quaco out of a dollar and a Cock, under the pretence, that by means of a combination of toe-nails old rags and such like rubbish, inclosed in a bottle and buried before his neighbour's door, he will be able to do him some grievous bodily harm."[10] Similar descriptions abound, for this era and later. S. T., who migrated to Limón, Costa Rica, from Jamaica as a child in the second decade of the twentieth century, described years later the hex that had separated him from his second wife. A hex "is a thing which is planted at the doorstep, a little bottle, it's planted beneath the doorstep and you are walking over the little bottle all the time."[11]

MAGIC OF AND FOR A MOBILE MODERN WORLD

One way to explain cross-Caribbean commonalities of popular practice would be to assume a genealogy of shared West African roots, and surely some portion of the symbolism, logic, and ingredients of obeah practice did indeed draw on knowledge that had survived the Middle Passage. Yet we also need to take seriously the evidence of innovation and heterogeneity in the evolving, cohesive, yet never entirely coherent repertoire of magical practice we glimpse through the historical record. Indeed, although outside observers insisted that African "tradition" was the wellspring of supernatural practice, local sources foreground links to modern capitalism, Victorian science, and the market. Practitioners prescribed patent medicines and sent clients off to pharmacies, which gladly prepared and sold oil of this and powder of that. Commercially produced cards (playing cards, tarot cards, and other series) and colored candles appear in countless cases. These substances were utilized in combination with non-manufactured substances such as grave dirt, garlic, coffin parts, teeth, bones, and hair. Items taken from the accused obeah man King Ja Ja's house and placed on exhibit at his trial in Tobago in 1904 included garlic, powders, "a doll," bottles and vials both empty and full, cards, a "parcel of dirt," and various "indescribable exhibits."[12] An editorial published in Port-of-Spain in 1898 complained that "there are lots of things sold in Pharmacies which are used solely for superstitious practices. Quicksilver, musk, Indigo blue and lots of other things we could mention would scarcely ever be sold, if they were not bought for superstitious purposes, since the miraculous properties attached to them by the purchasers, are totally unknown to medical science."[13]

As the editorialists noted, the infusion of commercial materials with miraculous powers was not endorsed by "medical science" of the day—but it was absolutely of a piece with the debates over the boundaries of science and medicine characteristic of the Victorian moment in the West. In metropoles as in colonies, these were years in which professionals in medicine struggled to distinguish themselves from promoters of patent medicine, a time in which the line between the experimental investigation of electricity and physics and that of spiritism and metaphysics was sometimes blurry and often contested.[14] The Port-of-Spain editorial cited above explained local enthusiasm for obeah in precisely this transatlantic frame: "There is at present, a great revival of dead and gone superstitions in England, and that the 'Cult of Hocus-Pocus' as [the British papers] called it, was being vigorously prosecuted there. Omens and portents, charms and amulets are said to be having a high old time of it over there, principally among the fair sex, while the time-honoured superstition about thirteen at table, is still so vigorous, that many people would as willingly stand before a loaded cannon as to sit thirteen at a dinner table. So much for the vaunted civilization of the nineteenth century."[15] This non-racialized framing places obeah as part of transatlantic modernity rather than African perpetuity: a novelty in contrast to travel writers' standard approach, but in fact not unusual within local newspaper coverage at the time.[16]

Thus one element in the commonalities of obeah around the Caribbean was an engagement with the contemporaneous North Atlantic and the disparate and contentious technologies of healing and knowledge for sale within it. Yet what local sources also underline is the degree of communication and borrowing under way within the Caribbean, as not only products but also prints and people circulated in ever-greater numbers. The Barbados-born William Young, a client of King Ja Ja, had "first heard of obeah about six months ago in Trinidad"; with this new knowledge, when he moved to Tobago and found himself unfairly castigated by his supervisor, Young suspected someone was "humbugging him at work" and sought out the local obeah man for help. Commentators in the late nineteenth-century played up the notion of traveling obeah men. Kingsley wrote in 1871 that "the chief centre of this detestable system is St. Vincent, where—so I was told by one who knows that island well—some sort of secret College, or School of the Prophets Diabolic, exists. Its emissaries spread over the islands, fattening themselves at the expense of their dupes."[17] Perhaps drawing on Kingsley, William Drysdale reported in 1886 that witchcraft's "home in the West Indies is St. Vincent. . . . Pupils of these humbugs have spread through the other islands and a 'St Vincent Obeah Man' is considered an expert."[18]

Evidence suggests that the supposed appeal of occult expertise from afar was not merely a Euro-American fantasy. A 1913 editorial published in the Colombian island of San Andres, located off the shore of Nicaragua and peopled since the seventeenth century by English-speaking Afro-Caribbeans, lamented the "invasion of the obeahmen" from British islands. "There are several of these fellows around, West Indians most of them, who, although cognizant of the fact that said evil is punished in their country with the cat-o'nine-tails, do not seem to think it a wrong and openly threaten their fellow creatures to harm them there with."[19] A report by the administrator of the British Virgin Islands from 1903 to 1910 noted the case of "a man belonging to the Virgin Islands, who was returning home after spending several months in Santo Domingo. His belongings being extensively searched for Customs purposes a very complete outfit for an obeah man was discovered."[20] Knowledge could also circulate even when individuals did not. King Ja Ja allegedly provided consultation from Tobago via post to clients from around the eastern Caribbean: police seized in his home letters "written by different persons, some at Carriacou, some at St. Georges, some at Port of Spain, some at Manzanilla, some at Mayaro and Belmont."[21] In the same year, 1904, Theophilus Dasent was arrested in Nevis and trunks full of letters from around the region—requesting assistance in counteracting magical assaults, healing sores, vanquishing sexual rivals, and improving employment circumstances—were seized as evidence of obeah.[22]

A professional obeah practice could span the islands, it seems, and islanders of multiple origins could agree on the power of obeah. Of course, each eastern Caribbean island itself had internal fissures of language as well as ancestry, residence, and class; and at this level, too, we hear again and again of the engagement of magical specialists across linguistic and cultural divides. When Simon Joseph's four-year-old son disappeared in Tunapuna, Trinidad, in 1904, he spent days "consulting oracles and trying to obtain a warrant" for police to search the houses where he feared the child was held. He traveled to the capital to consult a "female oracle" who "lives on a hill at Laventille at about five miles from Port of Spain," he later testified, "but the [oracle] spoke English. He only understood one word." Joseph, like many others who appeared in the courts of Trinidad, Grenada, Saint Lucia, and elsewhere in these years, spoke only French creole. This did not stop him from engaging the English-speaking oracle's services. "The woman told them to buy tar and other things. His money bought the goods which only cost a shilling."[23] A court case from Limón, Costa Rica, in 1903 offers us a similar glimpse of obeah ritual as a common vocabulary among Afro-Caribbeans from far-flung origins. A fistfight began when Serafín Clutero, from Martinique, accused his neighbors, Sofía Wilson of Mosquitia, Nicaragua, and her consensual partner, Daniel Glover, from Antigua, of working witchcraft against him. Sofía Wilson told police that "Monday morning Clutero came to her house to remonstrate with her regarding a bundle with strange contents that he found in front of the door to his house."[24] Clutero testified that the problems began when "I found inside my house a packet with small pieces of plantains cut in half, this is for creating animosity in one person regarding another, for it's used as witchcraft; I assumed that an old man named Glover was the one behind this and I told him so, because that was his occupation . . . since before this he had offered [me] his services of witchcraft."[25]

Here we have English- and French-speaking migrants from Martinique, Nicaragua, and Antigua selling, using, and fearing obeah on the Caribbean coast of Costa Rica. Amid their quarrel, what they do not disagree over is most significant: none doubted that a bundle including sliced plantains placed in a doorway could create discord for the couple inside. In cases like this, we see supernatural practices functioning as a medium for communication across boundaries of language, origin, and empire. Whether in the former French islands of the eastern Caribbean or in Anglophone settlements like Mosquitia and San Andres now subsumed by the Spanish American republics of the western Caribbean, there was enough commonality in the underlying grammar and specific gestures of magical practice that newcomers could seek assistance, recognize threats, and offer services. As we saw at the outset of this chapter, such commonalities of belief and ritual confirmed European and North American observers in their conviction that the "branch of the negro family" in the New World "still retains beliefs that link it at one step to the wild, untamed, sacrificial orgies of the West African forest." Yet the functioning of obeah as a lingua franca extended beyond Afro-descended populations, further evidence that mobility, heterogeneity, and innovation, rather than simply shared African origins, were central to the regional commonalities of obeah.

Cases from the eastern and western Caribbean alike illustrate the eager participation of South Asian immigrants in the market for supernatural access subsumed under the label "obeah."[26] A Trinidad paper wrote in 1898:

> Coolies will not be persuaded that there is no such thing in existence as *charming powder*, which will, when administered to a strange dog (or for that matter an estranged wife) cause the dog (or the wife as the case may be) to follow them about very submissively. And they will go from shop to shop, until they meet up with some dishonest clerk, who sends them away quite happy, with a little magnesia scented with musk, for which they part willingly with 4 or 5 shillings of their hard earned money, fully believing in the efficacy of the potion.[27]

In Jamaica in 1905, a "coolieman" was convicted "on the charge of practicing obeah." While his clientele was apparently large and varied, in this case the client was an ailing "cooliewoman"; he "told the woman that 'duppies' were on her" and cured her using various "implements of obeah."[28] The only Jamaican *brujo* ever accused of causing a death by witchcraft in Limón was "John Gupi (culi)," identified by police as "jamaiquino," whose place of birth was "Hindustan."[29] This 1911 case was presented by the West Indian elites who published the local English-language paper as an incident of obeah, and it clearly worried them (more so than it did the local police, who dismissed the case once the forensic doctor reported that the deceased had died of malaria). In Trinidad in 1920, police caught a man who, "it is said, practices obeah" in Mayaro, "extorting 10s. from an East Indian woman named Hetea, by pretending to her that he could show her where some money which was buried by her husband could be found."[30] In each of these cases, the specific magic sought by East Indian clients and the diagnoses proffered by East Indian obeah men are identical to those of their Afro-Caribbean contemporaries. The communication of magical expertise was not a one-way street: Afro-Caribbeans also sought out and valued elements of Indian occult traditions, as did their metropolitan counterparts in this era, of course. Materials demanded by the "Obeah Woman" Laura de Freitas in order to work a protective ritual in Port of Spain in 1920 included cards, candles, and "two Indian charms," which the client was sent to purchase from Karimbocas's shop on Charlotte Street.[31]

As shifting patterns of employment and investment made international mobility ever more common in working-class lives, Caribbean people found in obeah a source of power that was likewise not limited by territorial anchors or jurisdictional boundaries. The interwar years saw Cuba replace Panama as the destination of choice for western Caribbean emigrants, while the oil fields of Trinidad and Venezuela drew ever-greater numbers of eastern Caribbean sojourners. Obeah could be used to speed migrants on their way—or to tie them more tightly to home. In Kingston in 1921, a man nicknamed "Colon," and working out of the Hotel Colon (named for the preeminent Panamanian boomtown of an earlier era), met four men about to head off for the Cuban cane fields and demanded money from them to "wash" them so they would be successful on that island.[32] In Port of Spain in 1920, Maria Ramcharan was arrested for using a pack of cards, "a lap board," "Altar Stations," and a crucifix to work obeah for Maria Thomas. Thomas testified that "someone had told her that the defendant could do many things, and she went there to hear about her husband who was at the oilfields and was not good to her. Defendant had charged her three shillings to see her business and $25 to get her husband to be as good to her as before."[33]

Supernatural recourse was well suited to the specific challenges of transnational kinship. Kin obligations in the Caribbean as elsewhere were generally managed through social pressures and informal mediation. But the extraordinary mobility of early twentieth-century Caribbean life made this far more difficult. Family ties stretched between far distant lands might well remain intact. Then again, they might not. Social pressures could be attenuated by distance; people who wished to get lost could be lost. Like the faithless Matilda who "take me money and run Venezuela," conjugal partners could break ties and put themselves beyond reach with disturbing ease. Local courts could be called on to enforce (or sever) obligations locally. But no courts had authority supranationally. There are hints that supernatural specialists, their jurisdiction unaffected by state frontiers, were particularly attractive as possible solutions to these dilemmas. In 1911, Regina Skirving sued Elizabeth Howell for slander in the Panamanian courts, saying that Howell had accused her of using *brujería* to kill the wife of the man she was living with in Panama. The wife in question had lived, and died, in Jamaica. Skirving found this accusation (which, of course, she denied) credible enough to be worth suing over. Panamanian judicial authorities, in contrast, ruled that death by witchcraft was "not plausible," and thus that Howell's words might be *injuriosos* but were not *calumniosos* (i.e., they were insulting but contained no accusation of criminality).[34]

Again, transnational love magic transcended linguistic and national divides. In 1894, the Cuban-born Rafael Lavalle Roque, a self-described brujo resident in San José, Costa Rica, claimed that the seventeen-year-old Costa Rican Ester Bestard had told him "that her husband wanted to leave for Nicaragua and that she wanted a *reliquia* [holy object] to keep him from abandoning her: [Lavalle] answered that he was going to look among the prisoners in the jail to find someone who would make it for her."[35] Lavalle found a prisoner who made a "*paquetito* [small packet or pouch] of leather," he told investigators, which he took to Ester, receiving two colones in return. "She also told him that a brother-in-law of hers named Prudencio Costiña had abandoned a shop he had in Limón, leaving his wife and daughters abandoned."[36] As the investigation into Lavalle's supernatural services continued, one man, an artisan from Costa Rica, testified that Lavalle had sold him "a composition that would serve to tie women, that is, make all the women you want fall in love with you.... Although he [the witness] doesn't believe in such foolishness he gave him a peso coin just to get rid of him, because Lavalle wouldn't leave him alone."[37] Ester's mother likewise testified that Lavalle tried to sell her "white water for tying men." Police fined Lavalle thirty colones for "abuse of credulity."

References to women "tying" men through *brujería* appear in life histories composed in Limón by men of every origin. M. G. L., a Nicaraguan from Belén de Rivas, was threatened with a whip by a Costa Rican *compañera* around 1949, and only later learned that she had attempted to tie him by means of a *bruja*, and thought she had successfully dominated him.[38] When the Costa Rican R. G. C. was working on a road-building project in Talamanca around 1950, all the men on the crew took indigenous women as temporary partners, but with some caution: "The *compañeros* would say, that *india* is going to tie you."[39] L. C. was born in the Estrella Valley in 1916, his father a Nicaraguan migrant, his maternal grandmother an indigenous Bribri, his maternal grandfather a Jamaican immigrant. While collecting rubber on an abandoned United Fruit Company plantation in the 1950s, L. C. fell ill and began suffering hallucinations. With his godfather's help, he discovered it was due to a hex. "The healer who cured me told my sister that the ones who did me this harm were the woman who had lived with me and another individual, she out of revenge because I didn't love her anymore and he because he had stolen from me and I'd had him put in jail."⁴⁰ It is impossible to pin down the cultural coordinates of the hex that injured L. C., just as (but not only because) it is impossible to pin down the ethnicity of any of the parties in the story. Such stories reveal the complicated mixture of parallels, common origins, mutual reinforcement, and ongoing borrowing between supernatural traditions in the Greater Caribbean. The crucial commonalities are that all participants understood bodily health to be inextricably tied to justice, envy, love, and revenge, and all hoped (or feared) that ritual specialists could turn human desire into tangible outcomes through intangible means.

In sum, the overall picture of popular practices of supernatural manipulation in the early twentieth-century circum-Caribbean highlights the cultural creativity of sojourners negotiating a complex modern world. Multiple traditions of supernatural manipulation—including but not limited to those of western Africa and western Europe—had coexisted and crossfertilized in this region for centuries. More recently, a common array of North Atlantic commercial products promising cures and knowledge had spread across the same terrain. The combined result was that magical practice could serve as a lingua franca in a region constantly on the move.

THE MAKING OF A BLOOD LIBEL

Thus far we have not had occasion to refer to what would become the centerpiece of European and North American writings about black people's black magic in the Caribbean: cannibalism and child sacrifice. Stories of the ritual murder of white children by brujos, voodooists, and obeah men skyrocketed to prominence in print cultural production about witchcraft in the Caribbean in the second and third decade of the twentieth century, with commentators stridently insisting that the atrocities reflected deep-rooted African traditions unleashed by the weakening of civilized controls. The modern analyst might be tempted to assume that it was instead the European fantasy of African thirst for white babes' blood that was deeply rooted in the Atlantic past. But reconstruction of the chronology and spread of ritual child murder accusations suggests a different etiology. I have found not a single mention of the possible curative use of white children's blood in any sources generated in or about the Caribbean before 1904. In that year, I will argue, multiple cultural, social, and political trends came together to create a new sacrifice tale that would then be performed—by print media and by lynch mobs—again and again, rapidly creating the belief that it had always been thus.

Significantly, the pre-1904 silence within the Caribbean on white children and their curative blood stands in sharp contrast to the deep roots of an oddly similar trope: the Old World accusation that Jews kidnapped and murdered Christian children to use their blood in religious rituals. Meanwhile, writings about Haiti from the late nineteenth century had indeed included accusations of cannibalism and child murder, but it was invariably *black* children (usually the offspring of those eating) who were the alleged victims. As scripted at the end of the nineteenth century by white writers eager to demonstrate Haiti's lamentable savagery, these tales of child sacrifice emphasized not the healing properties of innocents' blood, but rather the consumption of cooked body parts as food—in one memorable case, prepared with savory beans.[41]

Given that tales about the curative power of children's blood appear in the Caribbean for the first time at the turn of the twentieth century, we should pause to consider the array of beliefs about blood and healing that shaped commonsense perceptions in that historical moment. Europeans from medieval times onward had believed that certain people's blood had healing powers. As one 1854 history of magic explained, "To eradicate deeply-rooted diseases, a young and fresh life was necessary. Especially, pure virgins and young children were supposed to free persons from diseases by their breath, and even by their blood."[42] Victorians who discarded such traditions as superstition and embraced modern medicine found blood more important than ever. One could not pick up a newspaper in the Caribbean at the end of the nineteenth century without reading in vivid detail about the importance of blood. Blood could be strong or weak, virile or effeminate, vital or thin, purified from without or poisoned from within. The health of the body depended on the health of the blood, and a tonic to strengthen the blood was the sure route to healing almost any ailment. One might try, for instance, "Zarouba: The Extraordinary Blood Medicine. Never before was there anything like it, nor can its marvelous effects ever be equaled in all cases of poorness, impurity, or other imperfection of the blood from whatever arising."[43] Blood, of course, was also figured, as it had been for centuries, as the substance through which racial ancestry was transmitted and measured. There was white blood and black, Semitic blood and Oriental, and when individuals classed as of different race coupled, it was their "blood" rather than any other bodily fluid that "mixed." The discerning eye could spot "Negro blood," however "diluted." The articulation between the pairing of blood and disease and blood and race is clear in passages such as an 1895 meditation on Jamaica's "colored Jews" by the North American travel writer Fannie Ward. Exotic, numerous, and prosperous, these "Jewish mulattoes" were lamentably prone to disease, leprosy in particular:

"Thus the Oriental race, through all its wanderings and adulterations, has retained the primeval tendency to certain diseases: so true it is as Mephistopheles remarks, that blood is 'quite a special sap.' "[44]

The association that Ward here echoes between Jewish difference and the symbol of blood had even deeper roots. The historian David Biale argues that the notorious "blood libel" accusation that Europe's Jews used Christian children's blood in the preparation of Passover matzo was a particularly volatile development within a semiotics of blood through which Jews and Christians defined themselves in contrast to each other over millennia.[45] The first accusation that a Christian child had been murdered and mutilated for Jewish ritual purposes came in the city of Norwich in 1144.[46] Although such accusations and related mob violence tended to decline after the medieval era, the nineteenth century saw a new wave emerge, in particular in regions of the Mediterranean and eastern Europe where imperial sovereignty was shifting and contested. One 1883 case from what is today Hungary received widespread press coverage in the Caribbean. The *Kingston Gleaner* reprinted at length the *London Times*'s coverage of the trial of various Jews in Tisza-Eslar. The son of one of the accused eventually testified to having witnessed the murder of the fourteen-year-old Esther Solymosi by his father and other Jewish men; he described in detail "the manner in which they had turned her over to let the blood flow out."[47] Cuban newspapers also covered the Tisza-Eslar trial and its aftermath in repeated articles in 1883.[48] Thus, among Euro-oriented Caribbeans at least, and perhaps within their societies more broadly, by the late nineteenth century patent medicine advertisements and tales of Jewish bloodletting had joined far older medieval traditions that assigned magical healing properties to pure blood in general, and to the blood of children in particular.

Armed with a better understanding of the symbolic freighting of blood for contemporaries, we can move to reconstruct the trajectory of child murder accusations in the Caribbean. Claims of cannibalism in the Caribbean date back to the time of Columbus, but they gained new energy in the momentous half century that saw the collapse of slavery in the French and British Caribbean and the rise of debate over what forms post-emancipation social orders might safely take. Stories of Haitian cannibalism were linked to descriptions of worship, dance, drumming, and magic by people of African origin in the British West Indies, and they became key evidence for those debating ex-slaves' readiness for political rights. Spenser St. John's 1889 *Hayti: The Black Republic* and James Anthony Froude's *English in the West Indies* were particularly influential in this regard. The two formed a potent and self-referential pair: Froude cited St. John's cannibal tales in support of his claims of Negro savagery, and St. John's second edition cited Froude's approbation as evidence of the veracity of his account.[49] Two narratives reproduced by St. John would be especially influential: that of the 1863 murder of a girl named Claircine, by relatives who then consumed her body in dishes St. John described in nauseating detail; and (appearing in the second edition) the account of an anonymous North American observer, published in the *New York World* in 1886, who claimed to have worn blackface to witness a Vodou dance that culminated in the sacrifice of a "goat without horns"—that is, a young Haitian boy, and later a girl as well. While for Froude and St. John the African roots of such evil practices were self-evident (yet needed constant reiteration), some skeptical voices did sound at the time. The folklorist William Newell in an 1888 article titled "Myths of Voodoo Worship and Child Sacrifice in Haiti" argued that actual evidence of such practices was scanty and controversial, and that in any case the rites described derived not from African but from medieval European traditions and religious heresies.[50] It is also worth noting that Hesketh Bell's 1889 monograph on obeah in the British Eastern Caribbean makes no mention of either child sacrifice or human blood used for healing anywhere in its extensive catalogue of occult practice.[51]

If we move from famous authors' oft-quoted accounts down to the kinds of local coverage we depended on in reconstructing obeah practice above, we do see at least one accusation of child murder for supernatural purpose before 1904. The *New York Times* reported in 1899 that "a negro in the Island of Dominica, British West Indies, has been charged with murdering a child in order to provide a human sacrifice for obeah or voodoo worship, in connection with a search for alleged hidden treasure."[52] The race of the accused is here marked; that of the child victim is not. Testimony in the case suggested widespread popular belief that blood sacrifice (though not necessarily that of a child) was necessary to find treasure. The *Times* elaborated, "The Attorney General said that there was no doubt that the child had been made a victim of a grave and barbarous superstition which exists in the islands. This the counsel for the defense freely admitted but he argued that the prisoner was not the person who committed the murder."[53] Thus, as of spring 1904, the possibility of sacrificing a child in order to find treasure had been mentioned in the print sphere and was claimed by some to be a widespread popular concern. Yet these ideas were in no way prominent within outsiders' representations of obeah. Indeed, in April 1904 the *Times* carried a lengthy account of obeah in Jamaica, purporting to be written by one born on that island. The author mentioned poisoning, love philters, the use of obeah to influence court cases, the practice of tying duppies to trees—in sum, many of the aspects of obeah that do indeed seem to have been prominent in popular practice—but made no mention at all of either blood or children, and only mentioned any threat to white people in the form of poisoning with "seeds of tuberculosis."[54]

Six months later, the *Kingston Gleaner* carried alarming news: "Yesterday a sensational cablegram was published all over the English-speaking world, to, the effect that a ghastly and extraordinary crime had come to light in St. Lucia. We are told that the head and hand of a white child were found in the possession of an obeahman, which led to the discovery that the child had been murdered and the body mutilated in order that superstitious natives might, through possession of portions of the body, be able to work spells." The victimization of a white child was both unprecedented and appalling: "This is an awful story and we regret sincerely that it has been given such wide circulation," wrote the *Gleaner*'s editors (even as they added their own coverage to speed the circulation of the tale). "But crimes such as that said to have been committed in St. Lucia represent very abnormal outbreaks on the part of those who believe in and practice obeah. We have never heard of such a case occurring in Jamaica during the past fifty years: no deliberate child-murder for superstitious purposes, so far as we know, has been reported during all that time." Like Jamaican commentators before and since, the authors then used Haitian Negroes' savagery as a foil for British Caribbean Negroes' comparative progress. "It is in Hayti that these crimes are said to be frequently committed, and the evidence on this point is of such a nature"—one hears echoes of the mutual assurances of Froude and St. John—"that we can hardly deny the fact. In Hayti, however, human sacrifice takes place as a part of the formal rites of the prevalent snake worship, which is not by any means the same thing as obeahism. Obeah, indeed, does not necessarily demand any thing in the shape of a human sacrifice, and is usually 'worked' without it." Something new and awful seemed to have entered the repertoire of eastern Caribbean obeahism. How could it have happened? As usual, "The answer to this question cannot be given unless one has devoted some study and attention to West African superstition and religion"—and the editors went on to provide a lengthy recapitulation of colonial accounts of sensual frenzy and religious savagery on the West African coast.[55]

In light of the *Gleaner*'s framing, what is most striking about the extensive written record generated by the Saint Lucia murder case over the following months is that there is not a single indication that the child victim was white.[56] He was simply a boy from Barbados named Rupert Mapp, accustomed to run errands on the streets of Bridgetown in exchange for food, who had been taken from his informal guardian by Montoute Edmond, a Saint Lucian butcher claiming to need a boy to carry messages. Ultimately three men would stand accused of the murder of Mapp, and their mutual recriminations left little doubt that all had been physically present at the abandoned sugar estate at Monchy when Mapp was strangled, his heart cut out, and his hands severed at the wrists and placed in a pot with salt and other substances. Montoute Edmond, the apparent initiator, was in his sixties, bilingual, and literate; Ste. Luce Leon and St. Hill were younger men, the latter illiterate, and spoke only patois. According to St. Hill, Montoute claimed to have a formula to allow them to take money from the bank, for which he needed a piece of coffin shroud and the transformed hand of a strangled person. That formula appeared in a book Montoute had transcribed by hand from a text apparently encountered during his years traveling in Haiti. After a trial that reportedly drew to Castries crowds of five thousand or more shouting for the death to the defendants, all three men were condemned to hang.

What is going on here? On the one hand, the Monchy case resonates strongly with the 1899 Dominica case and other evidence of popular beliefs tying blood sacrifice to the pursuit of treasure. But it is also a clear example of the ways Caribbean practice borrowed from European print traditions of engagement with the occult. A pamphlet published locally after the trial explained that Montoute's handwritten book was in "good French" and included detailed instructions on the creation of "La Main de Gloire" (The hand of glory), a magical candle made from the hand of a hanged man, which would render the bearer invisible to all. The instructions for creating the Main de Gloire were taken, like much else in Montoute's book, from *Le Petit Albert*, a grimoire published in Nantes and, according to the pamphlet's anonymous author, in common circulation in Haiti: "In it are contained the child-murder formulae and the horrible receipts for hidden treasure, which has such an attraction for that very large class in these countries who wish to get money without working for it. The similarity of the procedure in all the cases which have come to light indicate a common origin in this pernicious volume."[57] Purporting to be the work of the medieval scholar Albertus Magnus, *Petit Albert* circulated in multiple versions in nineteenth-century France, as did similar English-language guides, such as A. E. Waite's *Book of Black Magic and of Pacts*, first published in London in 1898.[58] Thus, quite contrary to the *Gleaner*'s insistence that understanding the Monchy case required "study and attention to West African superstition and religion," what it showcased instead was a thoroughgoing engagement with the supernatural modes of fin-de-siècle Europe, from the copied grimoire to St. Hill's last-minute claim that "hypnotism" might explain his "unconscious" participation in the crime.[59]

In late December 1904, just as the trial of the three men accused in Saint Lucia was drawing to its gruesome end, an incident in Cuba seemed to confirm the spread of increasingly deadly witchcraft across the Caribbean. The *Gleaner* headline spelled out the connections: "Witches' Bad Work in Cuba: Story of the Butchery of White Babe: Like St. Lucia Horror: Result of Rampant Obeahism in Island: Story of Inhumanity." A certain Bocourt—"a vulgar, ignorant negro" and leader of a group of "witches" in Havana and Pinar del Río who "maintain over the minds of the ignorant people of their own race an ascendancy founded upon fear and superstition"—told a black woman named "Adela 'La Conga' and her husband that Adela's dementia was the result of harm done by the whites during slavery times, and could be cured only by the blood of a white child."[60] The case, of course, is the one that has entered Cuban myth and history as *el crimen de la niña Zoila*, and it touched off a quarter century in which members of black fraternal societies were accused in dozens of separate incidents of kidnapping white children to use their blood to cure the black brujos' diseased bodies. In some cases the accused were convicted and executed; in others they died at the hands of police or mobs before trials could be completed; in others, increasingly as the decades wore on, they were acquitted in the face of a total lack of evidence. The Cuban witchcraft scare has received extensive scholarly attention in recent years, with historians explaining the hysteria with reference to post-independence struggles over black political participation, the self-positioning of Cubans claiming scientific expertise, and the growing role of the island's press in racializing the boundaries of civic participation.[61] But widening the optic from Cuba to the Caribbean as a whole suggests that there were also processes at work in the brujería scare that transcended the island's borders.

It is striking, to say the least, that the first mention of the sacrifice of a white child by obeah men, voodooists, or brujos in the Caribbean preceded the niña Zoila case by only two months—and was in fact plain wrong, as far as the race of child was concerned. Why did the *Gleaner* authors mistake or misrepresent the death of Rupert Mapp as the killing of a white child? The near simultaneity of the Monchy misreading and the Zoila case would seem to suggest that the shift from stories of Haitian cannibals consuming their own young to stories of white children victimized by blacks for their healing blood was somehow overdetermined by changes under way in the Caribbean at that moment. This was an era, after all, in which accelerating migration—given a massive push by the start of labor recruiting by the United States Isthmian Canal Commission only months before—was bringing people of disparate origin together in new ways. Scores of thousands of impoverished Spaniards were arriving in Cuba each year. Barbadians and Jamaicans were heading to Panama and Costa Rica by the tens of thousands. Perhaps the idea of black threats to white children had new resonance with elites increasingly concerned about managing demographic heterogeneity; or perhaps it captured new anxieties created by communities where working folks, black and white, lived side by side.

Meanwhile on the sending islands, this was a moment when colonial authorities insisted on the need for new kinds of violence to combat alternate powers: powers they swore did not exist. A new "Obeah Act" in the Leeward Islands in summer 1904 lowered the standards of evidence and authorized corporal punishment. Under the new ordinance, Charles Dolly—nearly seventy years old and losing his sight—was flogged in Montserrat in October 1904.[62] Press accounts did not hide the brutality of the process: "The unfortunate man was pinioned from neck to toe and the full 24 strokes inflicted. His shrieks and vain appeals for mercy were heard a long distance off as the stripes which fell from a hand apparently accustomed to that kind of business fell on his nude back, the sound of which wrung pity from those outside who heard it."[63] The editors of the *Daily Mirror* (Port of Spain) stuttered, for once, in their support for colonial policy: "No one would for a moment attempt to say aught against the justice of the sentence or the necessity for stringent measures to stop the abominable practice, but flogging is, without doubt, a barbarous thing, and it is a pity that it has had to be brought into operation in this advanced and civilized age." The editors attempted to elide the dissonance between their dismissive mockery of obeah practice and the bloody severity of state punishment, quipping that obeah men's "own backs are not safe from assault in spite of their boasted supernatural skill." But could "ridiculously useless . . . charms and nostrums" really justify reducing an aged man's back to a bloody pulp? No one would have to ask. Precisely twenty-four hours later, Port of Spain papers carried the first reports of the "frightful murder" in Monchy. The *Daily Mirror*'s own account concluded on a note of vindication: "This murder is complicated with ignorance and savage superstition, and is only a startling indication of a widespread evil, making for a relapse to barbarism, to which we have been for years vainly striving to attract the serious attention of the authorities."[64] It is hard not to see in the speed with which the flogging ordinance was followed by continuous coverage of obeahistic bloodshed, Caribbean elites' need to convince themselves that the savage state power brought to bear in their name was no more than necessary.[65]

What is indisputable is that the paradigmatic story of child sacrifice shifted in 1904. Rather than Haitian peasants feasting on the flesh of their own with a macabre relish straight out of the Brothers Grimm, henceforth stories would hew with precision to the old anti-Jewish blood libel of eastern Europe: a group of men united by a menacing non-Christian religion, a child lured from home and sacrificed, the blood of the victim drained and held for ritual use. And with stunning speed, that which was newest in constructs of Caribbean witchcraft came to seem that which was oldest. A mere five years after the causes célèbres of Monchy and Zoila, Harry Johnston could write in the *New York Times* that "the last vestige of noxious witchcraft lingering among the Cuban negroes is (said to be) the belief that the heart's blood, or the heart of a white child, will cure certain terrible diseases if consumed by the sufferer."[66] As we have seen, there is on the contrary every reason to believe that ritual child murder was the most recent European addition to the lore of obeah and brujería, rather than the last lingering vestige of African belief.

CONCLUSION

In the preceding pages, I have argued that obeah and related supernatural practices gained prominence in the twentieth-century Caribbean not because Afro-Caribbean societies were traditional but because they were modern, not because people were rooted in the past but because they were moving in the present. I have suggested that obeah could be practiced across the region not because of its shared Africanness but because of its open heterogeneity and its human universality. Obeah served as a lingua franca that allowed communication across boundaries of empire, language, and continental origin, in part because so many societies in the circum-Caribbean shared the broad cultural legacies of medieval Christendom and early modern West Africa. But the integration of East Indians and indigenous Talamancans as active buyers and sellers in the market for supernatural power reminds us to avoid placing too much emphasis on even this amplified diffusionist account. People of disparate origin easily understood each other's ideas about supernatural power, and the common association of the exotic with dangerous and useful power meant that boundaries of perceived race, culture, and origin could encourage borrowing rather than impede it. Finally, historical reconstruction of obeah practice reveals not a gulf between print and popular culture, but rather a mutual exchange between the two. Evidence from across the region shows twentieth-century obeah—not only its representation from without, but also its practice from within—as very much part of the modern world. The frames and fragments of meaning from which Caribbean actors built their understanding of the plausible and the immanent, the curative and the deadly, included eastern European murder trials, late Victorian occultism, and nineteenth-century French reengagement with the medieval macabre. This, too, is a tale that deserves to be told.

NOTES

I am grateful to conference participants and the collection's editors for their input on this chapter. I thank the Vicerrectoría de Investigación of the Universidad de Costa Rica as part of Proyecto No. 806-A2-047 and the Center for Latin American Studies and the Central Research Development Fund of the University of Pittsburgh for funding in support of research reflected here.

1. On the travels and practices that created the circum-Caribbean migratory sphere, see Lara Putnam, "The Making and Unmaking of the Circum-Caribbean Migratory Sphere: Mobility, Sex across Boundaries, and Collective Destinies, 1840–1940," in *Migrants and Migration in Modern North America: Cross-Border Lives, Labor Markets, and Politics*, ed. Dirk Hoerder and Nora Faires (Durham: Duke University Press, 2011), 99–126; on the connections migrants established and the barriers they encountered, see Putnam, "'Nothing Matters but Color': Transnational Circuits, the Interwar Caribbean, and the Black International," in *From Toussaint to Tupac: The Black International and the Struggle for Liberation*, ed. Michael D. West and William G. Martin (Chapel Hill: University of North Carolina Press, 2009), 107–29; Putnam, "Eventually Alien: The Multigenerational Saga of British West Indians in Central America and Beyond, 1880–1940," in *Blacks and Blackness in Central America: Between Race and Place*, ed. Lowell Gudmundson and Justin Wolfe (Durham: Duke University Press, 2010), 278–306.

2. In using the descriptor "supernatural" rather than "religious," I make an intentional but not uncontested choice. As critical theorists have pointed out, academic traditions that label certain beliefs as religious and others as supernatural, magical, or superstitious reflect (but do not always acknowledge) a history of power-laden intercultural encounters. See articles in the *Anthropological Forum* 13, no. 2 (2003), especially Roger Ivar Lohmann, "Introduction: Naming the Ineffable," 117–24, and Erick D. White, "The Cultural Politics of the Supernatural in Theravada Buddhist Thailand," 205–7. Certainly it is true that obeah became a marker in a colonial race-making project that defined it as witchcraft, superstition, or fraud in antithesis to legitimate— that is, European—religion. See Diana Paton, "Obeah Acts: Producing and Policing the Boundaries of Religion in the Caribbean," *Small Axe* 13, no. 1 (2009): 1–18. Yet the traces of participants' understandings preserved in the documentary record suggest an emic distinction between the religious and the supernatural, with the practices described as obeah anchored in the latter realm. It is this distinction that my wording seeks to acknowledge. The individualized contracting of ritual specialists, the potential malevolence (*pace* intended benevolence) of the power sought, and the centrality of surreptitiousness, rumor, and suspicion to that power's functioning all set obeah apart

from the beliefs and practices of collective worship, whether in the established Christian churches of the day or in those faith communities dismissed by outsiders as "sects" (sometimes "diabolical sects"), such as Shouters and balm yards. See Margarite Fernández Olmos and Lizabeth Paravisini-Gebert, *Creole Religions of the Caribbean: An Introduction from Vodou and Santería to Obeah and Espiritismo* (New York: New York University Press, 2003), 131; but also the critique in Paton, "Obeah Acts." Certainly the practices labeled "obeah" drew on a spiritual landscape shared with and shaped by Afro-Caribbean religions. But if the boundary between obeah and religion was blurred and unstable, so, too, in various ways were the boundaries between obeah and science, obeah and pharmacology, obeah and fraternal lodge ritual, obeah and games of chance, obeah and self-improvement. "Supernatural" seems to me the least-wrong label for this rich complex of resonances and resources.

3. In Spanish-language sources, the common terms for supernatural support that one sought were "protección," "cura," and sometimes "sortilegio" or "hechizo," while the terms for malevolent action against one were "maleficio," "brujería," "daño," or, again, "hechizo." These are the terms employed by individuals to describe their own use of supernatural power or others' use of that power against them in oral historical accounts and in judicial testimony recorded in court documents and newspaper accounts of trials. My source base represents Trinidad, Costa Rica, and Panama most heavily. Unless otherwise indicated all translations are my own. For a similar range of terms, and a similar analysis of their perspectival divide, see Paton, "Obeah Acts."

4. On problems inhering in this scholarly usage, in addition to Paton, "Obeah Acts," see Aisha Khan, "Isms and Schisms: Interpreting Religion in the Americas," *Anthropological Quarterly* 76, no. 4 (2003): 761–74.

5. My perspective here is particularly indebted to Stephan Palmié, *Wizards and Scientists: Explorations in Afro-Cuban Modernity and Tradition* (Durham: Duke University Press, 2002); and David Brown, *Santería Enthroned: Art, Ritual, and Innovation in an Afro-Cuban Religion* (Chicago: University of Chicago Press, 2003).

6. W. Ralph Hall Caine, *The Cruise of the Port Kingston* (London: Collier, 1908), vi–vii.

7. See Diana Paton, "The Truth about Obeah: Perspectives from inside and outside the Caribbean" (paper presented at the annual conference of the Association of Caribbean Historians, Cartagena, Colombia, May 9–13, 2005).

8. But see Palmié's suggestive discussion of occult texts and Caribbean science in *Wizards and Scientists*, 207–10.

9. This paragraph synthesizes William Drysdale, "West Indian Witchcraft," *New York Times*, April 11, 1886, 12; Hesketh Bell, *Obeah: Witchcraft in the West Indies* (1889; Westport: Negro Universities Press, 1970); *Constitution* (Atlanta) "Obeahism in Jamaica: Sorcery That Does Its Work with Deadly Poison," January 17, 1894, 2. Extensive excerpts from and commentaries on the large number of writings on obeah in the eighteenth and nineteenth centuries are provided in John Joseph Williams, *Voodoos and Obeahs: Phases of West India Witchcraft* (London: George Allen and Unwin, 1933).

10. *Mascot* (Port of Spain), February 19, 1898, editorial, under the heading "Varieties."

11. "Autobiografías campesinas," vol. 26, no. 3, "Autobiografía de ST" (transcript of interview conducted in Spanish ca. 1977), central library of the Universidad Nacional, Alajuela, Costa Rica, 197–98.

12. "Tobago: The Obeah Case," *Daily Mirror* (Port of Spain), November 16, 1904, 13.

13. "Varieties," *Mascot* (Port of Spain), February 19, 1898.

14. See Reinaldo Roman, *Governing Spirits: Religion, Miracles, and Spectacles in Cuba and Puerto Rico, 1898–1956* (Chapel Hill: University of North Carolina Press, 2007).

15. "Varieties," *Mascot* (Port of Spain), February 19, 1898.

16. See, for instance, W. A. Sweany, "Spiritualism: Ancient and Modern," *Caribbean Watchman* (Port of Spain) 2, no. 9 (1904): 1.

17. Charles Kingsley, *At Last: Christmas in the West Indies* (New York: Harper and Bros., 1871), 338.

18. William Drysdale, "West Indian Witchcraft," *New York Times*, April 11, 1886, 12.

19. Francisco A. Newball, "Necromancy," *Searchlight* (San Andrés) June 1, 1913, 21. I am grateful to Sharika Crawford for sharing this source.

20. Cited in John Symonds Udal, "Obeah in the West Indies," *Folk-Lore: A Quarterly Review of Myth, Tradition, Institution and Custom* 26, no. 3 (1915): 282.

21. "Tobago: The Obeah Case," *Daily Mirror* (Port of Spain), November 16, 1904, 13.

22. Udal, "Obeah in the West Indies," 277–78.

23. "The Coroner's Court at Tunapuna: Child Lost and Found on the Eighth Day in a Ravine," *Daily Mirror* (Port of Spain), September 30, 1904, 11.

24. Archivo Nacional de Costa Rica (San José, Costa Rica), Sección Judicial, Serie Limon Juzgado del Crimen no. 309 (lesiones, 1903).

25. Ibid.

26. For an ethnographic account that makes the same point, and explores its implications concerning the creation of knowledge within and about the Caribbean, see Aisha Khan, *Callaloo Nation: Metaphors of Race and Religious Identity among South Asians in Trinidad* (Durham: Duke University Press, 2004), 102–20.

27. "Varieties," *Mascot* (Port of Spain), February 19, 1898.

28. "Another Case of Obeahism," *Gleaner* (Kingston), September 28, 1905, 6.

29. Archivo Nacional de Costa Rica (San José, Costa Rica), Sección Judicial, Serie Limón Juzgado del Crimen no. 218 (homicidio, 1911).

30. "Obeah Man Caught," *Weekly Guardian* (Port of Spain), June 12, 1920, 4.

31. "Assumption of Supernatural Powers: Obeah Woman Convicted," *Weekly Guardian* (Port of Spain), April 3, 1920, 9.

32. "The Home Circuit Court," *Gleaner* (Kingston), January 14, 1921, 3.

33. "Obeah Worker Trapped," *Weekly Guardian* (Port of Spain), February 21, 1920, 6.

34. Archivo Nacional de Panamá (Panama City, Panama), Sección Jurídica, uncatalogued boxes, Juzgado Tercero Circuito (calumnia e injurias, 1911).

35. Archivo Nacional de Costa Rica, Policia 3276 (causa, 1894).

36. Ibid.

37. Ibid.

38. "Autobiografías campesinas," vol. 26, no. 1, "Autobiografía de MGL," central library of the Universidad Nacional, Alajuela, Costa Rica.

39. "Autobiografías campesinas," vol. 26, no. 1, "Autobiografía de RGC," central library of the Universidad Nacional, Alajuela, Costa Rica, 19.

40. "Autobiografías campesinas," vol. 26, no. 3, "Autobiografía de L. Campesino," central library of the Universidad Nacional, Alajuela, Costa Rica, 126–27.

41. See Spenser St. John, *Hayti, or, The Black Republic*, 2nd ed. (1885; London: Smith, Elder, and Co., 1889), 213; and mocking commentary in James Leyburn, *The Haitian People* (1941; New Haven: Yale University Press, 1966), 131–32.

42. James Ennemoser, *The History of Magic*, trans. William Howitt (London: Henry G. Bohn, 1854), 1:117.

43. *Herald and Venezuelan News* (Port of Spain), December 21, 1894, front-page ad.

44. Fannie B. Ward, "Rambles in Jamaica," *Sunday Inter-Ocean* (Chicago), January 13, 1895, 31.

45. David Biale, *Blood and Belief: The Circulation of a Symbol between Jews and Christians* (Berkeley: University of California Press, 2007).

46. See the analysis in Jeffrey Jerome Cohen, *Hybridity, Identity, and Monstrosity in Medieval Britain* (New York: Palgrave Macmillan, 2006), 139–73.

47. "Foreign News: Extraordinary Charge of Murder," *Gleaner* (Kingston), July 28, 1883, 2.

48. "Noticias extranjeras," *La Voz de Cuba: Diario conservador* (Havana), July 25, 1883, 2–3. The acquittal of the accused was reported in "Noticias extranjeras," *La Voz de Cuba: Diario conservador*, August 10, 1883, 2. I am extremely grateful to Jorge Giovannetti for finding and sharing these citations with me.

49. St. John, *Hayti*; James Anthony Froude, *The English in the West Indies; or, The Bow of Ulysses*, 2nd ed. (1888; New York: Charles Scribner's Sons, 1900).

50. William W. Newell, "Myths of Voodoo Worship and Child Sacrifice in Haiti," *Journal of American Folk-Lore* 1, no. 1 (1888): 16–30.

51. Hesketh Bell, *Obeah: Witchcraft in the West Indies* (London: Sampson Low Marston, 1889).

52. "The News Condensed," *New York Times*, November 1, 1899, 1.

53. "Human Sacrifice to Obeah," *New York Times*, November 1, 1899, 5.

54. "Where the Obeahman Trades in Death," *New York Times*, April 3, 1904, 8.

55. "What Is Obeah?," *Gleaner* (Kingston), October 14, 1904, 8.

56. I base this statement and the summary that follows on the extensive coverage in the *Port of Spain Daily Mirror*: "Frightful Murder in St Lucia: Boy Brought from Barbadoes and Strangled and Cut Up," October 12, 1904, 2; "The St Lucia Murder Case: The Evidence," October 26, 1904, 12–15; "The St Lucia Murder Case: Capture of St Hill," November 1, 1904, 13; "Day by Day: The St Lucia Murder Case," November 23, 1904, 9; "St Lucia: The Monchy Murder Case," November 25, 1904, 9; "The St Lucia

Murders," December 6, 1904, 13. For further coverage in the *Gleaner* (Kingston) see: "The Brutal Butchery in Saint Lucia," October 29, 1904, 12; "The Horror of St. Lucia," November 12, 1904, 13; "Murderers Hanged," December 24, 1904, 13. British West Indian papers in the rimlands followed the case as well: e.g., "Obeahmen Pay Penalty with Lives," *Limón Weekly News*, December 31, 1904.

57. Udal, "Obeah in the West Indies," 286–95, quotation (transcribing pamphlet) on p. 294. The pamphlet, which I have not seen, is also quoted at length in Joseph J. Williams, *Psychic Phenomena of Jamaica* (New York: Dial, 1934), 111.

58. Waite's instructions for making the hand of glory are almost identical to those cited in French versions of the *Petit Albert*. See Arthur Edward Waite, *The Book of Ceremonial Magic: The Secret Traditions in Goëtia* . . . (New York: University Books, 1961), 310–12.

59. "The St Lucia Murders," *Daily Mirror* (Port of Spain), December 6, 1904, 13.

60. "Witches' Bad Work in Cuba: Story of the Butchery of White Babe," *Gleaner* (Kingston), December 29, 1904, 11.

61. Aline Helg, *Our Rightful Share: The Afro-Cuban Struggle for Equality, 1886–1912* (Chapel Hill: University of North Carolina Press, 1995), 109–116; Helg, "Black Men, Racial Stereotyping, and Violence in the U.S. South and Cuba at the Turn of the Century," *Comparative Studies in Society and History* 42, no. 3 (2000): 576–604; Palmié, *Wizards and Scientists*, 210–60; Alejandra Bronfman, *Measures of Equality: Social Science, Citizenship, and Race in Cuba, 1902–1940* (Chapel Hill: University of North Carolina Press, 2004), 37–65; Roman, *Governing Spirits*.

62. See Udal, "Obeah in the West Indies," 274.

63. "The Application of the Cat," *Daily Mirror* (Port of Spain), October 11, 1904, 13.

64. "Frightful Murder in St Lucia: Boy Brought from Barbadoes and Strangled and Cut Up," *Daily Mirror* (Port of Spain), October 12, 1904, 2.

65. For similar arguments regarding the construction of voodoo during the U.S. occupation of Haiti, see Mary Renda, *Taking Haiti: Military Occupation and the Culture of U.S. Imperialism, 1915–1940* (Chapel Hill: University of North Carolina Press, 2001); Kate Ramsey, *The Spirits and the Law: Vodou and Power in Haiti* (Chicago: University of Chicago Press, 2011), esp. chapter 3.

66. Quoted in Udal, "Obeah in the West Indies," 266. See also Harry Johnston, *The Negro in the New World* (1910; New York: Johnson, 1969), 66.

10.

The Vodou State and the Protestant Nation:
Haiti in the Long Twentieth Century

KAREN RICHMAN

In 1804, the leaders of the slave revolution in Saint-Domingue created a Catholic nation-state. For most of its existence, Haiti has only endorsed and protected this one religion, despite a continued struggle for autonomy with the Vatican, which continues until the present. A key event in this bitter history was the campaign of 1941–42, during which the Vatican moved to rein in ordinary Haitians' incorporation of Catholicism within a blasphemous set of African beliefs and practices. In 1983, Haiti received its first and so far only papal visit. The head of the Catholic Church came to Haiti to announce a new campaign to stem the advance of a religion "lacking the true message of the Gospel and with methods that do not respect real religious liberty." The charlatans in his sights this time, however, were not "Vodouists"—they were Protestants. Numbers of converts were increasing exponentially on the island and in the region. Immediate evidence of the futility of the pope's mission could not be ignored in 1985 with the Haitian state's official recognition of Protestantism. Within two more decades, a presidential decree made Vodou an official religion of the nation-state of Haiti as well.

This chapter explores aspects of the historical and contemporary interplay between Catholicism, Protestantism, Vodou, and the Haitian nation-state. Claims of doctrinal integrity and autonomy notwithstanding, Catholicism, Vodou, and Protestantism have defined, mediated, and reproduced one another in the fluid, plural landscape of Haitian religious history. Attention to this religious dialectic sheds new light on some of the landmark events of this history over the long twentieth century. Ethnographic research focusing on a particular community in Léogâne further reveals the hidden fluidity between these religions and brings into question the meaning and purpose of conversion. Religious conversion may not entail the radical break that separatist Protestants, and some believing scholars, claim it to be. Even the assertive, separatist stance of the Protestants cannot disguise how firmly their congregants remain within a fundamentally integrated spectrum of mystical techniques and strategies to hold illness and misfortune at bay. The tenacity of this fluid, instrumental spectrum baffles the Protestant leadership as they grapple with a proper response to their sudden "success" (about one out of every three Haitians identifies as a Protestant today).

Moreover, the dialectic of Catholicism, Protestantism, and Vodou can be understood only in relation to the actions and reactions of the nation-state. Haitians' humiliating encounters with Catholic and American imperialism at the beginning of the twentieth century inspired a nationalist search for an alternative anchor of identity to challenge that hegemonic narrative. This anchor was found and reproduced through state-sponsored folklore studies of the "African" religion of Vodou. Paradoxically, the pro-Vodou Haitian state was, at the same time, quietly welcoming intensely anti-Vodou, white Protestant missionaries into the country. The Protestant evangelists could be depended on to offer material development to the country, to refrain from interfering in political affairs, and to limit the power and colonial designs of the other Haitian state—the Catholic Church. The cultural narrative of the Haitian state is virtually silent about the nation's Protestant flirtation.[1]

CATHOLICISM AND COLONIALISM IN HAITIAN HISTORY

Saint-Domingue, as Haiti was known in the colonial period, was France's most lucrative sugar colony. In 1804, its slaves stunned the world economic order by liberating themselves and the colony. During the century following independence, the first free and feared black nation-state was isolated from the rest of the world, so the descendants of slaves established a freeholding peasantry. By entrenching themselves as small, independent farmers, they were able to resist pressures from the elite and the state to coerce them into a return to plantation labor. It took the economic and military might of a new colonial power to push the Haitian peasants into capitalist agriculture. The United States consolidated its hegemony over the region and Haiti, in particular, during the early 1900s. Over the course of the twentieth century, the Haitian peasant economy was gradually undermined and transformed into one that produces unskilled wage labor for export and increasingly consumes imported food. Intimately linked to the transformation of Haitian peasants into a contingent, mobile labor force are North American Protestant missionization in Haiti and the inevitable repatriation of Haitianized Protestant churches to Haitian migrants' settlements in the United States.

Roman Catholicism was the official religion of the colony of Saint-Domingue, which was established in 1697, and it remained the state religion of independent Haiti. As mentioned above, in 1985 the state recognized Protestantism, and it added a third official religion, Vodou, in 2003. The Catholic Church was indigenized after independence in 1804, when French colonists and their priests fled the country. Haitians controlled their own church during the six-decade-long political isolation that served as the punishment levied by the metropole for the Haitian slaves' successful challenge to colonialism and slavery. In 1860, however, as Haiti's Francophile, mulatto elite was inviting recolonization by France and Germany and ultimately the United States, authority over the church was returned to the Vatican and remained unchallenged for a century. Fabre Geffrard, Haiti's tenth president, signed the concordat with the Vatican, declaring, "Let us hasten to remove from our land these last vestiges of barbarism and slavery, superstition and its scandalous practices."[2] As a result of the accord, French priests regained control not only of the church but also of the principal schools, which were run by religious orders.

The rise of the United States as the new regional colonial power in the early twentieth century, coupled with the official occupation of Haiti by the United States between 1915 and 1934, limited the power of the French Catholic Church in Haiti. When the American administrators and soldiers finally departed, the Catholic Church interceded in the power void. In 1941, the Catholic Church launched an all-out crusade against superstition in Haiti. *La campagne anti-superstitieuse* formally began with a pastoral letter published in the Catholic daily *La Phalange*, decrying "the irreconcilable opposition" between Christianity and "the collection of religious beliefs and practices which came from Africa."[3] Many of the elements of this "collection" actually came from Europe, but identifying them as African better served the church's purpose.[4]

The "rejection" (*rejèt*) crusade moved promptly westward from the capital to the county of Léogâne. Archange Calixte recalled his father's confrontation in a hamlet in Ti Rivyè, Léogâne, with the parish priest and police during the anti-superstition campaign. His father was one of the first professional ritual leaders (*gangan ason*) in the area.[5] The iniquitous contents of the two shrines he oversaw were targets of the rejection. Archange and I were standing in the same courtyard where the encounter took place nearly seventy years before. He vividly recreated the tense scene that unfolded before his eyes as a seven-year-old:

> I remember during the rejection, a priest from Léogâne came into the compound along with two policemen. I remember it well. They had been destroying the *lwa*'s things [in the area]. They called for my father. They said to my

father, "Go into the house, get the things, bring them to us." My father said, "There is nothing I'm going to bring to you. If you want to take them, go inside and take them. I am not bringing anything to you." After that, they went across the street to the other *lakou* at Mizdor's house [of worship], and they said the same thing: "Go into the temple and bring the things to us." He said, "I'm not going to do it. If there is something you are looking for, go inside and take what you need." They didn't do anything. As they were leaving, they said to him, "Bring the things to town for us. Come to the [town] with the things." He said, "I'm not hauling anything to town. I don't have anything to sell." We fell out laughing. I remember that well. I was young. Everyone fell out laughing.[6]

Archange's father exposed the absurd incompetence of the leaders of the antisuperstition crusade. Ironically, *La Phalange* likened the campaign to a "spiritual blitzkrieg," implying that it would apply the tactical surprise, speed, and courage used in the German attack on western Europe. Fiction writers could not have invented a more ironic name for a campaign that circulated preposterous anti-Vodou catechisms and whose loud processions, led by French priests bearing crosses, sounded advance warning to potential targets. Such processions were realistically depicted in the novel *All Men Are Mad* by Philippe Thoby-Marcelin and Pierre Marcelin.[7] Literary critics in North America who dismissed the novel as incredible exaggeration[8] were no doubt unfamiliar with such firsthand descriptions of the campaign as that of the zealous French priest Roger Riou:

> I'll never forget those processions, two or three hundred people all chanting: "Down with the loas! Down with the loas!" . . . In the habitations and on the roads—wherever we found voodoo signs—we'd ask if the people were willing. If they were not, we did nothing, unless the crowd in the procession overruled us. Then the habitants were stripped of their voodoo symbols whether they liked it or not. . . . We walked behind the cross all over the *mornes*. I gave my blessings, then we gathered up voodoo signs and burned them. We were horrified to find that the three drums of voodoo—big, medium, and small—were the hiding places of snakes fattened on consecrated eucharistic offerings. Their crosses had nothing to do with the faith, so we burned them.[9]

Father Riou reminisced about leading conspicuous processions to confiscate sacred objects and burn shrines, actions that no doubt involved local citizens more zealous about settling interpersonal scores than exercising religious conviction. The French father meanwhile revealed some of his own contradictory "superstitious" beliefs in the magical powers inherent in both religious ritual objects and in the methodical collection and classification of those objects.[10] Later in *The Island of My Life*, Father Riou disclosed how rationalism prevailed when, rather than burning the commandeered magical objects, he painstakingly catalogued them, after which they were given to museums in Paris and Port-au-Prince.

Neither the real head of the Catholic Church in Léogâne, nor the actual French Father Riou, nor even the fictive Père Belloc of the Marcelins' novel could have led military-religious expeditions to stamp out superstition without the backing of the Haitian state. The Catholic Church's decision to launch a campaign against Vodou received enthusiastic endorsement from the new, pro-American president and former ambassador to the United States, Elie Lescot. President Lescot's support for the anti-superstition campaign was inseparable from his "mulatrification" project, a clumsy effort to return political and economic hegemony to the mulatto elite and their American allies.[11] Lescot took office one week after the publication of the pastoral letter decrying superstition, vowing a return to Catholic government. But when the spiritual blitzkrieg began sweeping up Protestants, too, President Lescot was compelled to demonstrate his disapproval of the attacks, which he expressed indirectly by attending worship at a Protestant church.[12]

NATIONALISM, THE VODOU STATE, AND PROTESTANT EVANGELISM

As in the late nineteenth century, the resurgence of the Catholic Church's colonialist policies provoked a nationalist response. And as in the late nineteenth century, the nationalist movement was allied with North American and European Protestantism. The writer Louis Joseph Janvier believed that Haiti should embrace the establishment of a religion that would respect the sovereignty of the state.[13] In addition, Janvier advocated the civilizing influence of Protestantism. In his 1883 treatise on Haiti's foreign affairs, he wrote, "The Protestant is thrifty and self-reliant, he does not waste his money on carnivals and other frivolities. Protestantism permits free discussion and encourages private initiative.... The Protestant is almost always a more practical worker and a better citizen than the Catholic."[14] Thus Janvier argued that conversion to Protestantism would provide the religious basis for capitalist economic development of the archaic peasant economy, echoing the bourgeois discourse of the seventeenth and eighteenth centuries that disparaged the indolence of European peasants and blamed the Catholic ritual calendar, whose many saints' days and festivals sapped the supply of labor.[15]

Yet Janvier recommended that Haiti emulate Africa rather than Europe. He went so far as to claim that Protestantism was more suited to the African temperament than was Catholicism. He offered evidence of Protestantism as a tool for introducing "primitive" populations of Africa to Western culture. Nonetheless, Janvier admitted that his vision of a Protestant Haitian society was unlikely to be realized: "Protestantism will never be a danger for Haiti and would want for it [Haiti] the affection of Protestant nations."[16] Janvier's defeatist admission was unwarranted. Over the next century, Protestant evangelization increased to the point that, precisely one hundred years after Janvier published his 1883 tract, the pope himself was compelled to intervene.

The excesses of the U.S. occupation, the Lescot presidency, and the church's anti-superstition campaign provided ample fodder for Janvier's nationalist followers to embrace an alternative narrative of authenticity and identity. The new discipline of Haitian ethnology answered the call. Studies of the peasants' religion and folklore provided the material for promotion of an authentic Haitian identity located in peasant life and rooted in African culture.[17] Jean Price-Mars, who in 1928 authored the first important text on the peasants' folklore, was Episcopalian.[18] Yet he also extolled the evangelical Protestants, even though they opposed Vodou even more strongly than did the Catholic Church. A further paradox of the nationalists' embrace of Protestantism was that Protestants made up the majority of the blatantly racist "colons en khaki," as the writer Jacques Romain, a central member of the ethnological movement, termed the occupying force.[19]

The version of Vodou studied and authorized by the Bureau of Ethnology, however, was not the authentic peasant religion—as if there ever were one— but rather a modern innovation. This religious form featured congregations whose membership was recruited based on individual choice rather than bonds of descent, professional leadership, codified styles of devotion, and spectacular performance. Each congregation was based at the temple, or "peristyle," owned by the professional ritual leader. The peristyles multiplied as the capital city of Port-au-Prince swelled with displaced rural migrants. Soon the temple organization and practices spread from Port-au-Prince to the densely settled lowlands of Cul-de-Sac and Léogâne as these areas were undergoing massive economic and social upheaval.

In a section of Léogâne called Ti Rivyè, the site of my ethnographic and historical research since 1981, the agents of diffusion of temple customs appear to have been not only redundant peasants and neophyte proletarians circulating between the capital city and the nearby plain, but also ethnologists who moved between privileged sites of the Vodou laboratory. Though their approach to Vodou was part of counter-hegemonic, nationalist discourse, it nonetheless recapitulated a modern view of tradition-bound primitives. The ethnologists portrayed Vodou as a coherent set of essentially African beliefs, ignoring and devaluing the substantial Catholic bases of much of Haitian popular religion. They also perpetuated erroneous claims of Haitians' beliefs in universalistic nature spirits and the requirement for spectacular ritual practices to worship them. In the case of Ti Rivyè, research by Odette Mennesson-Rigaud and other ethnologists seems to have encouraged the encroachment of the same invented traditions they were documenting.[20]

Vodou ascended to become a symbol for the Haitian nation and state with the election of François Duvalier to the presidency in 1957. Duvalier, who claimed Janvier as his ideological mentor, was a central member of the ethnological group and he authored or coauthored several studies of the folk religion (some of which were based on observations of performances staged in Port-au-Prince hotels). The self-declared president for life developed a reputation not only for "practicing Vodou" but also for incorporating the practices and priesthood in his ruthless politics. Duvalier appears to have fostered the myth of his promotion of Vodou, which only bolstered outsiders' stereotypes of the exotic, mysterious religion.[21]

Haiti's first pro-Vodou, pro-peasant, black nationalist president was, at the same time, the country's foremost champion of Protestantism. Harold Courlander and Rémy Bastien wryly observed that the fact that Duvalier fostered Protestantism, which opposes Vodou even more strongly than the Catholic Church ever did, demonstrates that "the relationship between Duvalier and religion should be viewed not as one of an individual to a faith, but rather it should be approached from the standpoint of the relations between church and state."[22] Fred Conway further captures the paradox of the ethnologist-president's promotion of Protestantism when he writes:

> For all his identification with Vodoun, François Duvalier might well be called the "Father of Protestantism" in Haiti. Duvalier's main potential opposition in the religious sphere was a Catholic Church dominated by foreigners. In his struggle with this adversary, he enlisted both Vodoun and Protestantism in spite of the fact that the Protestants were more inimical to Vodoun than were Catholics. At a time when Duvalier was deliberately alienating foreign governments and foreign aid organizations, he welcomed Protestant missionaries, especially from the U.S. The Protestants drew people away from an allegiance to the Catholic Church without themselves presenting a monolithic front to the government. Because the missionaries were competing with each other, fiercely at times, they were not in a position to oppose the government as a group.[23]

Duvalier finally succeeded in breaking the power of the Catholic Church. In 1966, in exchange for a promise to stop persecuting and expelling foreign Catholic priests, the Vatican capitulated to Duvalier's demand to abrogate the 1860 concordat and allow Haiti the right to name its own priests.[24]

At the same time as he was resorting to violence to oust the European Catholic leadership, Duvalier was extending a friendly welcome to evangelical Protestants from North America. The Protestants could be depended on to avoid involvement in political affairs as much as possible and meanwhile bring "development" into the country. The happy union between Duvalier and the North American Protestant missionaries was just one example, during the second half of the twentieth century, of several such alliances between a repressive Latin American state (including Chile and Guatemala) and an apparently apolitical Protestant mission. The second tenet of the Baptist faith is that "the church and the state are separate," affirms Edner Jeanty, a Haitian evangelical Baptist theologian, in his history of Protestant expansion in the country.[25] Yet in the conclusion of the same text, Rev. Jeanty rejoiced when a Protestant became the acting head of state in 1990: "The Bible has entered the National Palace through the front door."[26]

By 1965, Protestant missionaries ran more than a third of the schools in Haiti. Duvalier received the Pentecostal televangelist Oral Roberts at the palace in 1969.[27] Approximately 70 percent of the Protestant missions in Haiti in 1970 had been established in the preceding twenty years, and an estimated 20 percent of the population was Protestant.[28] The expansion of Protestant missionization in Haiti since the 1970s especially involved the growth of Pentecostal groups, which systematically covered the geography of the country and encompassed the poorest segments of the population. Echoing the findings of many observers of Pentecostal missionization in Latin America, Charles-Poisset Romain asserts that "le take-off pentecôtiste [sic]" (the Pentecostals' take-off) in Haiti was the result of their promotion of the vernacular spoken by the masses, rather than the colonial language of French, which was spoken and written only by the elite few.[29] Moreover, the Pentecostals linked their valorization of Creole vernacular to the promotion of literacy for the masses. The mainline Protestants had already presented their "religion of the book" as one of "sociability and civilization."[30] Literacy was seen throughout the colonized world as a primary means of self-improvement.

Romain claims that during the 1970s, missionization was more intense in Haiti than anywhere else in the hemisphere, and that Haiti witnessed more proliferation of sects during that period than any other country. Though this claim cannot be proved, support for it comes from the ethnographer Fred

Conway's experience in southern Haiti during that period. According to Conway, the missionary presence was so pervasive that he, like almost all foreigners in rural Haiti, was taken for a Protestant missionary.[31]

In a laudatory recounting of the history of Baptist missionization in Haiti at mid-century, Jeanty compliments North American missionaries' skillful deployment of capitalist marketing techniques. He glowingly narrates the accomplishments of one proselytizer with a special knack for selling a new religion to reluctant native consumers. In the process, Jeanty inadvertently admitted that Christian missionization amounted to creating consumer desire for a nonessential product when he praised Mme Ruben Clarke, who accompanied her husband to Pignon to spread the gospel, as "a dynamic woman who could 'sell a refrigerator to an Eskimo.'"[32]

Romain's and Conway's studies demonstrate that evangelism oriented people toward North American capitalist culture. Conway's cultural exploration of local understandings of Protestant missionization describes an unequivocal linkage between the religion and a dream of America. He argues convincingly that "missionary Protestantism in Haiti gives rise less to a Protestant ethic of self-help than to the idea that the way to worldly success is identified with direct dependence on the foreign—North American—missionary."[33] He cites villagers' discourse, no doubt mediated by their perception or hope that their North American interlocutor was a missionary, and thus a source of jobs or visas. Villagers asserted to Conway that the Protestant mission churches symbolized progress. While pointing to Protestant missions, people told him that "the country is becoming more and more civilized," in contrast to the backwardness blamed on peasant Vodou. Several converts boasted to Conway that their conversion was a contribution to development.[34]

Moreover, the Protestant churches signified modern, capitalist principles, including belief in quantitative accounting and record keeping. According to Conway, villagers understood that Americans "needed" quantities of converts and that they were willing to pay for them. No one benefited more from their "needs" to build missions and count disciples than did the pastors. The clergy was and is one of the few "jobs" for men in rural areas, and the field of candidates is vast. Romain observed that "every Protestant is a pastor and a missionary at the same time."[35] The success of the pastors reflects the convergence of the fluid, informal, lay, and entrepreneurial character of the evangelical practice with local values regarding diffuse leadership and charismatic, spontaneous power. Haitians also harbor an intense distrust of authority and bureaucracies, born of their long experience of betrayal by leaders, secular and religious alike. The religion welcomes the man who aspires to have a congregation, begins by praying with two or three people, and eventually builds a following. The speech practice of addressing any male evangelical as *pastè* (pastor) reinforces this assumption.

PROTESTANT MAGIC AND IMMUNITY

The ethnographic literature on Haitian religion took note of the strategic use of conversion during the mid-twentieth century, before the postwar expansion of Pentecostalism in the country. Alfred Métraux described the tactical use of conversion as an act of revolt against lwa. The act of conversion, he wrote, represented "a magic circle" of protection from discipline by lwa. He quoted what a Marbial person told him: "If you want the [lwa] to leave you in peace, become a Protestant." Métraux added, "No doubt it is the challenging attitude adopted by Protestants towards the [lwa] which has finally convinced the peasants that this religion confers upon its adepts a sort of supernatural immunity."[36]

Métraux's analysis of the instrumental use of conversion closely echoed the internal Protestant critique. The Haitian Protestant theologian Roger Dorsainville had previously lamented that a "true conviction and profound commitment to be saved" were "rarely" the reason people converted. "Protestantism," he asserted, "is pursued as a superior *wanga* [magical power], the pastor is like a more powerful sorcerer."[37] The magic circle also protects the convert from the very real fear of sorcery, a social weapon long used by peasants throughout the world to limit individualism and greed and enforce reciprocity.

My ethnographic work in Ti Rivyè has confirmed that many converts view their conversion as a strategic defense against sorcery.[38] Denise, who grew up in Ti Rivyè and was initiated into the temple role of *ounsi*, told me after her conversion in the mid-1990s, "As soon as you convert, nothing can harm you."[39] Her new religion has neither replaced nor diminished her belief in the reality of sorcerers' powers but rather persuaded her that it offers the most protective armor against evil forces. "Evil exists" (Le mal existe), she said (quoting the expression in French rather than Creole), during a conversation in 2002, several years after her conversion. The appeal of Protestantism as the antidote to existing forms of sorcery reverberates with analyses of many colonized and missionized African societies. In Malawi, for example, the Watchtower sect entered as a new witchcraft eradication movement, offering total inoculation to anyone who converted. As Fields explains, Protestant conversion offered an escape route for young migrant men from an increasingly onerous "traditional" system.[40]

Catholics (who serve their lwa) I interviewed refuse to accept the explanation that conversion is merely an escape from sorcery. They argue the opposite: conversion is a license to sorcery. Converts switch their religious "costume" so that they can make money illicitly, which they will not have to share or redistribute, and they do it with impunity. Converts think that their sober, separatist behavior will preempt accusations of patronizing gangan so that they can secretly pursue magic and sorcery while removing themselves from obligations to a social and ritual redistribution system that serving lwa necessarily entails.

It is widely suspected that converts secretly patronize gangan for private magic or sorcery. While conducting ethnographic research in the Ti Rivyè hamlet during the mid-1980s, I had been curious about the well-dressed strangers who occasionally walked into the compound I shared with a matrilineal extended family. They would ask for Joiecius, the husband of one of the senior residents, and a well-established gangan ason. Joie was not usually there—he oversaw two shrines in two different hamlets and had a couple of other wives whose houses he also visited. So the strangers would be offered chairs on the veranda and wait until he arrived, when he would lead them away from the compound. I finally asked the ritual leader who those strangers were. "They're Protestants," he told me, as if I were the only one who did not already know that obvious fact. "They come from the capital city."

Pepe, another gangan ason in Ti Rivyè, whom I interviewed many times over the years, also frankly admitted to me that many of his clients are Protestants. When I interviewed him at his shrine in 2003, he quickly dismissed my query about the Protestants' offer of strong protection against sorcery. "If they say they convert so nothing can harm them," he responded, "then why do they come to see gangan? And why do they have sacred things hidden in their houses?" In a curious echo of Dorsainville's 1940s lament about converts seeking stronger wanga from Protestant pastors, Pepe further asserted that "pastors get wanga and *dyab* (moneymaking powers), which they plant at the front of their yards so when foreign missionaries pass by they will notice them and give them money and send them to the States. They have to fill their churches to satisfy their sponsors. And they are good talkers, too." Pepe thus echoed Joiecius's charge that "it's a business; it's so they can make money."[41]

The Protestants' ascetic posture and their assertive attitude may not fool non-converts, but the latter are disinclined to challenge them publicly. Norms of graciousness and indirection prevail, and few are willing to give someone an incentive to retaliate against public humiliation through sorcery or political persecution. The trickster lwa, Gede, is the one agent who publicly takes on the arrogant and self-righteous, and the figure of the pretentious, sober pastor is a handy target of Gede's wicked mockery. Karen Brown describes Gede as a "transformation artist" who "redefines the most painful situation—even death itself—as one worth a good laugh."[42] Protestants' pretensions of their virtuous female inhibition and lack of sexual desire make them ideal fodder for Gede and his audience, who do not believe in childhood sexual innocence or protecting children from sexuality. When asked to draw a picture of a human being, Haitian children portray people with genitalia. As for virginity, parents care less about a young woman's protection of her purity than her strategic deployment or foolish waste of her sexual resource, sometimes referred to as "the little square of land" between her legs.[43]

At one ceremony I attended in Ti Rivyè in 1983, which coincides with the Catholic fete of All Souls' Day at the end of October, a male Gede spirit had mounted a senior woman named Clarisse. Once the Gede arrived in her body, "he" was re-costumed in denim, a triangular hat, and spectacles—a hilarious "disguise." Someone conveniently handed the nonliterate Gede/Clarisse a little Bible, and he/she took on the persona of a sober pastor. Now pastor/Gede/Clarisse stood, erect and self-righteous, encircled by an attentive crowd, the Bible, spread open, cupped in one hand, his index finger alternately stabbing at the pages and piercing the air to emphasize his points. The "pastor" taught us what the Good Book said. Out poured a deluge of rhyming sexual profanity, followed by an unbridled give and take in vulgarity between the ridiculous minister and his sanctified "congregation."

This hilarious scene was a cathartic reformulation of a tense situation. The "social drama"[44] underlying the performance turned on the conspicuous absence of two connected beings: a spirit and a kinswoman who was the spirit's favorite "horse." Josilia, the paternal niece of the gangan ason who established the shrine, had just renounced the spirits of her lineage and converted. For nearly four decades, her patron spirit and Clarisse's had danced together in the "heads" of their "horses." They had been a reliably spectacular ritual duo at the annual December rites, during which the pounding of powders in a giant mortar goes on without pause throughout the night, accompanied by nonstop ritual drumming, dancing, and singing.[45]

Now, a month before the approach of the annual rites, the timing of Gede's commentary on Protestantism was deliberate. Everyone was aware that without Josilia, the ceremony would be lacking. Indeed, as the service was about to begin, Michel, the gangan ason, Josilia's cousin, voiced what others must have been thinking when he said drearily to no one in particular, "There is no one left to dance [at the service] . . . everyone has converted."[46] Gede's imitation of the evangelist's feigned puritanical restraint was one way for her ritual community to reframe the immediate crisis of Josilia's conversion and to defuse their disappointment with vulgar humor. The use of a possession performance to satirize conversion attests to how widespread this sentiment must be. Are Protestant Evangelicals, and especially their leaders, aware of this critique?

REINING IN THE PROTESTANT WANGA

Protestant evangelization of Haitians is part and parcel of the massive global expanse of evangelical Protestantism, especially the Pentecostal and charismatic forms. Protestantism, argues Webb Keane in *Christian Moderns*, is a moral narrative of modernity.[47] Many Haitians construe conversion as a rhetoric and set of behaviors for mastering a model of individual, social, and economic success. I have argued elsewhere that some Haitians have seen conversion as a socially appropriate escape route from the fetters of obligation and interdependence that undergird their transnational domestic and ritual ties.[48] The ritual discourse of self-mastery and human emancipation fits converts with the religious armor to resist the spiritual and magical enforcement of those collective moral obligations. They model the self-assertive, individual separatist disposition that, Weber argued, was central to the religion's appeal and initial success in Europe four centuries ago.[49]

Yet far from making a clean break with local religious powers and practices associated with lwa, wanga, or dyab, Haitian Protestant discourse makes all these representations hyper-real. They are objectified and reified so that they can be ritually killed. This ritual logic explains why the evangelicals' rhetoric constantly invokes the Catholic-Vodou "other," all the while collapsing the other's internal distinctions and dismissing it all as devil worship, much as Birgit Meyer found in her study of Ghanaian Protestants' strategic incorporation and disavowal of "the devil."[50]

The need to keep the local other alive and, at the same time, at bay is widely echoed in research and scholarship on the Protestant evangelical turn across the globe. José Casanova has argued that Protestantism's swift and broad success results from two contradictory tendencies. Converts' separation from and renunciation of local culture coexists with their thoroughgoing roots in local culture.[51] Joel Robbins sums up others' research findings that "the religion localizes by accepting as real local spirit worlds and the problems they represent. This process allows Pentecostal and Charismatic Protestant converts to turn their new religion immediately to addressing local issues in locally comprehensible terms."[52]

The critique of the pragmatics of Haitian conversion goes back at least to the 1940s, when Roger Dorsainville lamented that Protestantism is pursued as a superior wanga and the pastor is like a more powerful sorcerer. To understand whether the contemporary Haitian evangelical Protestant leadership recognizes this critique, I approached the head of the Haitian Baptist Séminaire de Théologie Evangélique de Port-au-Prince, the Protestant reverend Jean Duthène Joseph.[53] At no point during my interview with this charismatic and influential theologian did he assert that Haitians' beliefs about wanga or dyab were false. He did not deny their existence. He insisted rather that such instrumentalist discourse is false insofar as it distorts the transcendental purpose of Christianity.

At the same time, the Baptist leader demonstrated extensive competence in this "distorted" rhetoric. It seems that Duthène began learning this discourse as a chronically ill child. His parents' and family's interpretations of the meanings of and treatments for his affliction tossed him among competing spiritual healing systems. Duthène was raised by his paternal aunt and his father, who alternately (or simultaneously) served his spirits, pursued magic, and sought Protestant conversion. His father tried Protestantism, first to rescue his wife (who died in childbirth) and second to heal his ailing son:

KAREN What I see among the converts is the quest for healing or for protection against sorcery. It is the magic circle Dorsainville spoke about. So many people have told me, "As long as you're converted, nothing can harm you."

REV. JOSEPH It's false. I have heard of that. It is a lie. There is nowhere in the Bible that says that. Do you know what word we use? It is that Christians are not "immunized" against suffering, against affliction. But you will find other people, pastors who say, "As long as you lift up your hands in the name of Jesus, all disease is finished, everything is finished." It is false. . . . The problem is, and that is what I'm arguing in my [doctoral] thesis, too, is that a lot of people run to convert to Protestantism so the dyab won't eat their children. You understand? Or so people won't send a wanga on them. So people won't send *zonbi* [harmful spirits] on them. It's as if they don't have to do anything else. That's false. That's what I'm saying to you. There is a lack of understanding. We're teaching people so your eyes will be open to the word so when you take up the Bible you can interpret it.

KAREN How is it false? Is it false because dyab doesn't exist? Is it false because zonbi don't exist? Really? Or is it false because people don't really have faith?

REV. JOSEPH It's false because that is not the Protestant objective. Do you understand? Christianity—that is not the purpose of Christianity. OK. And

> Jesus said, "Seek first the kingdom of justice of God and all these things will be added to you." Therefore it will come as a "byproduct." Physical protection, protection against evil spirits, material property, that can come as a byproduct but it isn't the purpose.

One interpretation of Rev. Joseph's comments, illustrated by Gede's possession by a pastor, would be that converts to Haitian evangelical sects have appropriated the utilitarian core of the Protestant ethic. After all, to Protestantism's founders, appearance and action trumped belief; quantification and accumulation were moral imperatives.[54] Today, however, the evolution of the religion exposes its inner truths and threatens to discredit its good name.[55] The Protestant leadership has basked in the glory of quantitative victory, but quantitative success has its qualitative costs.

To discipline this stubbornly immanent and instrumentalist Haitian-Protestant creation, Rev. Joseph has committed his life to religious work as a director of a seminary and a minister of a large urban congregation, and to numerous rural development projects to correct this problem. In addition, he recently completed a dissertation under the auspices of a Bible university in Indiana to analyze the etiology of this too-worldly Protestant monster. His thesis is that Haitians' "Vodou heritage affects Protestantism in the country."[56] After mentioning unexpected challenges in completing the writing of his dissertation he laughed, noting the congruence between our projects and saying, "I may need your help."

CONCLUSION: CONFRONTING THE PRESENT PROTESTANT DANGER

Reflecting on Protestant pastors' gains in Catholic Haiti over the last half century during that same interview in 2002, Rev. Joseph made much of an event that took place two decades before. Pope John Paul arrived in Port-au-Prince in March 1983, the first and only visit to date of a pope to Haiti. One hundred years after Louis Joseph Janvier's published concession that Protestantism was unlikely to ever amount to a "danger" in Haiti, the Catholic Church was compelled formally to recognize the looming sectarian threat. Rev. Joseph recounted:

> In 1983, the pope came to Haiti. He made a grand declaration: "Things must change." At that time, the bishop—Archbishop [François-Wolff] Ligondé—wrote an article that I have still. He made it understood that the Catholic Church would embark on a campaign so they could wage a campaign against what he called the "blind proselytism of the Protestants." Do you see? He was carrying out a counterattack because of the Protestants. The pope said he

would provide resources to do education on the radio across all of Latin America. It was a way for them to prevent Protestants from going further in their proselytizing.

The pope's visit took place during a conference attended by sixty-one Latin American bishops, the top agenda of which was "preparing actions to stem the rapid growth of Protestant fundamentalist sects in the region."[57] Pope John Paul said, "The advance of religious groups which at times are lacking the true message of the Gospel and with methods that do not respect real religious liberty pose serious obstacles to the mission of the Catholic Church and to other Christian confessions."[58] The Haitian archbishop, who was the host of the conference, announced the start of a national campaign to defend Catholicism in Haiti against "the blind proselytizing of Protestants."[59] Rev. Joseph recalled his rival's challenge with a sense of smug vindication, no doubt because the rate of conversions to Christianity since 1983 has only continued to increase.

The nationalist narrative of the pope's 1983 visit attributes a very different significance to the event. Rather than taking account of the pope's conspicuous counterattack on the Protestant danger in Haiti and in the Latin American region, the narrative emphasizes the political import of the papal visit. The pope's nonspecific declaration that "things must change" is interpreted as the event that set in motion the popular mobilization to uproot the government of Jean-Claude Duvalier. This history ignores processes that weakened Duvalier prior to the visit, which emboldened the pope to reverse the concessions made to Jean-Claude's father and to retake control of naming bishops and priests in Haiti, essentially reinstating the terms of the 1860 concordat. Resistance to the concordat's religious colonialism, it will be recalled, inspired the founder of Haitian black nationalism. Janvier's twentieth-century ethnological followers, chief among them François Duvalier, located the anti-colonial nation-state's authenticity in the allegedly African religion of Vodou. To this day, the Haitian state ornaments official events with Vodou symbolism and folkloric performances. (Ironically, children typically perform the mock Vodou rites and dances, even though children would hardly be appropriate agents to carry out rituals or ritual dances in actual worship. But as stand-ins for the modern ideals of innocence and authenticity, the children reinforce the authenticity of the Vodou performance itself.) At the same time, the state remains virtually silent about the nation's Protestant turn. The Catholic Church, however, could not afford to ignore the notice.

In 2007, the head of the Haitian Catholic Church took the extraordinary step of signaling that the religious pluralism of Haitians could be a route to the church's salvation from the Protestant danger. Archbishop Joseph Serge Miot took to the countryside to reach out to gangan ason. Significantly, the archbishop selected Léogâne to launch what we might call the pro-superstition campaign. "Why Léogâne?," I asked Father Thomas Streit, who is associated with the local Catholic parish and who attended the inaugural meeting.[60] "Because, as you know yourself, Karen, Léogâne is the center of Vodou in Haiti," he responded. The county's special status in the annals of Vodou history was the product of the nationalist narrative of African authenticity, in which ethnological research in Léogâne played a small but significant part.[61] Léogâne's identification with quintessential Vodou was re-inscribed in 2003 when President Jean-Bertrand Aristide, a former Catholic priest, declared Vodou an official religion.

At the meeting in Léogâne, the archbishop entreated the assembled Vodou leaders to remind their flock that they were "still Catholics." The archbishop effectively profaned the divide between Catholicism and Vodou—the very separation the church had tried to protect for the last two centuries. The campaign represented a complete reversal of the church's 1941/42 anti-Vodou crusade, whose rationale had been to uphold "the irreconcilable opposition" between Catholicism and the collection of religious beliefs and practices alleged to have come from Africa. It was a necessary and inevitable reconciliation given the present Protestant danger.

NOTES

1. This project builds on bibliographic and multilateral ethnographic research conducted in Léogâne, Haiti, and in South Florida, Virginia, and Maryland over the past two decades. The most recent phases of research on religious conversion have been supported with generous funding from the Newberry Library, the Social Science Research Council, and the University of Notre Dame.

2. Quoted in David Nicholls, *From Dessalines to Duvalier: Race, Colour and National Independence in Haiti* (New York: Cambridge University Press, 1979), 84.

3. Ibid., 182.

4. Terry Rey and Karen Richman, "The Somatics of Syncretism in Haitian Religion: Tying Body and Soul" (paper presented to the annual meeting of the American Anthropological Association, Washington, D.C., December 1, 2007).

5. Interview with Archange Calixte, Léogâne, Haiti, July 24, 2010.

6. "M sonje lè rejèt la yon prèt Léogâne vin nan lakou a ansanm ak two jandam. Yo tap detwi bagay lwa a. Yo rele papa m. Yo di papa m, 'Antre nan kay la; pran bagay; pote yo bay nou.' Papa m di, 'Nan pwen bagay m pral pote bay nou. Si ou vle pran yo, antre, pran yo. M p ap pote anyen p ou.' Apre sa a, yo travese lari, nan lòt lakou a, nan kay Mizdò a, yo di li menm bagay. 'Antre nan kay la, pote bagay ba nou.' Li di, 'M pap fè l. Si

ou gen yon bagay ou vle chache, antre al pran sa ou bezwen.' Yo pa fè anyen. Lè yo t ap pati, yo di li, 'Pote bagay yo ba nou lavil. Vin lavil avèk bagay yo.' Li di, 'M pap brote anyen. Pa gen anyen m ap vann.' Nou tonbe ri. M sonje sa a byen. M te piti. Tout moun tonbe ri."

7. Philippe Thoby-Marcelin and Pierre Marcelin, *All Men Are Mad*, trans. Eva Thoby-Marcelin (New York: Farrar, Straus and Giroux, 1970).

8. Marlene Daut and Karen Richman, "Are They Mad? Nation and Narration in *Tous les hommes sont fous*," *Small Axe* 26, no. 2 (2008): 133–48.

9. Roger Riou, *The Island of My Life: From Petty Crime to Priestly Mission* (New York: Delacorte, 1975), 154. Originally published as *Adieu la Tortue* (Paris: R. Laffont, 1974).

10. Susan Pearce, *On Collecting: An Investigation into Collecting in the European Tradition* (London: Routledge, 1995).

11. Kate Ramsey, "Without One Ritual Note: Folklore Performance and the Haitian State, 1935–1946," *Radical History Review* 84 (2002): 7–42; Nicholls, *From Dessalines to Duvalier*, 183.

12. Brenda Gayle Plummer, *Haiti and the Great Powers, 1902–1915* (Baton Rouge: Louisiana State University Press, 1992), 148.

13. Nicholls, *From Dessalines to Duvalier*, 118.

14. Quoted in ibid.

15. E. P. Thompson, "Time, Work-Discipline, and Industrial Capitalism," *Past and Present* 38, no. 1 (1967): 56–97.

16. "Le protestantisme ne serait jamais un danger pour Haïti et lui vaudrait l'affection des nations protestantes." Louis-Joseph Janvier, *La république d'Haïti et ses visiteurs (1840–1882)* (Port-au-Prince: Editions Fardin, 1883), 371.

17. Kate Ramsey, "Prohibition, Persecution, Performance," *Gradhiva* 1, no. 1 (2005): 165–79.

18. Jean Price-Mars, *Ainsi parla l'oncle: Essai d'ethnographie haïtienne* (1928; Montreal: Leméac, 1979).

19. David Nicholls, "Politics and Religion in Haiti," *Canadian Journal of Political Science* 3, no. 3 (1970): 403, 412.

20. Karen Richman, "Peasants, Migrants and the Discovery of the Authentic Africa," *Journal of Religion in Africa* 37, no. 3 (2007): 1–27.

21. Paul C. Johnson, "Secretism and the Apotheosis of Duvalier," *Journal of the American Academy of Religion* 74, no. 2 (2006): 420–45.

22. Harold Courlander and Rémy Bastien, *Religion and Politics in Haiti* (Washington, D.C.: Institute for Cross-Cultural Research, 1966), 56.

23. Fred Conway, "Pentecostalism in the Context of Haitian Religion and Health Practice" (Ph.D. diss., American University, 1978), 166–67. See also Paul Brodwin, *Medicine and Morality in Haiti: The Contest for Healing Power* (Cambridge: Cambridge University Press, 1996); and "Pentecostalism in Translation: Religion and the Production of Community in the Haitian Diaspora," *American Ethnologist* 30, no. 1 (2003): 85–102.

24. Elizabeth Abbott, *Haiti: The Duvaliers and Their Legacy* (New York: McGraw-Hill, 1988), 381.

25. Edner A. Jeanty, *Le Christianisme en Haïti* (Port-au-Prince: La Presse Evangélique, 1991), 62. Laënnec Hurbon also argues that Protestants may, on the one hand, profess rejection of participation in politics and, on the other, "express a willingness to mount the political stage to defend their churches' interests." See "Current Evolution of Relations between Religion and Politics in Haiti," in *Nation Dance: Religion, Identity, and Cultural Difference in the Caribbean*, ed. Patrick Taylor (Bloomington: Indiana University Press, 2001), 136.

26. Jeanty, *Le Christianisme en Haïti*, 106.

27. Nicholls, "Politics and Religion in Haiti," 412.

28. Conway, "Pentecostalism in the Context of Haitian Religion and Health Practice," 5.

29. Charles Poisset Romain, *Le Protestantisme dans la société haïtienne* (Port-au-Prince: Henri Deschamps, 1986), 190. Selected relevant studies of Protestant evangelization in Latin America during the period include David Lehmann, *Struggle for the Spirit: Religious Transformation and Popular Culture* (Oxford: Polity, 1996); David Martin, *Tongues of Fire: The Explosion of Pentecostalism in Latin America* (Oxford: Blackwell, 1993); and David Stoll, *Is Latin America Turning Protestant? The Politics of Evangelical Growth* (Berkeley: University of California Press, 1991).

30. Romain, *Le Protestantisme dans la société haïtienne*, 145.

31. Conway, "Pentecostalism in the Context of Haitian Religion and Health Practice," 172.

32. " . . . une dynamique femme capable de 'vendre un réfrigerateur même à un Eskimo." Jeanty, *Le Christianisme en Haïti*, 1.

33. Conway, "Pentecostalism in the Context of Haitian Religion and Health Practice," 193.

34. Ibid., 172.

35. "Tout protestant est à la fois pasteur et missionnaire." Romain, *Le Protestantisme dans la société haïtienne*, 144.

36. Alfred Métraux, *Voodoo in Haiti*, trans. Hugo Charteris (New York: Oxford University Press, 1959), 352.

37. "L'Evangile est aussi recherché comme un *ouanga* supérieur, le prédicateur est comme un bocor puissant." Quoted in Cats Pressoir, "L'état actuel des missions protestantes en Haïti," *Conférence Prononcée au Dimanche de la Bible, à L'Eglise St. Paul, Haiti*, December 13, 1942, 8 (pamphlet).

38. Karen Richman, *Migration and Vodou* (Gainesville: University Press of Florida, 2005); and "A More Powerful Sorcerer: Conversion and Capital in the Haitian Diaspora," *New West Indian Guide* 81, nos. 1/2 (2008): 1–43.

39. "Depi ou konvèti, anyen pa ka fè ou."

40. Karen Fields, *Revival and Rebellion in Colonial Africa* (Princeton: Princeton University Press, 1985).

41. "Se yon biznis; se pou yo kab fè kòb."

42. Karen McCarthy Brown, *Mama Lola: A Vodou Priestess in Brooklyn* (Berkeley: University of California Press, 1991), 330.

43. Ira Lowenthal, "'Marriage Is 20, Children Are 21': The Cultural Construction of Conjugality and the Family in Rural Haiti" (Ph.D. diss., Johns Hopkins University, 1987), 74.

44. Victor Turner, *Schism and Continuity in an African Society* (Manchester: Manchester University Press, 1957), 288.

45. Erika Bourguignon, interview with the author, June 2, 2005; Erika Bourguignon, *Possession* (San Francisco: Chandler and Sharp, 1976); Odette Mennesson-Rigaud, "Noël Vodou en Haïti," *Présence Africaine* 12 (1951): 37–59; Métraux, *Voodoo in Haiti*, 236–43.

46. "Nan pwen moun pou danse . . . denye moun konvèti."

47. Webb Keane, *Christian Moderns: Freedom and Fetish in the Mission Encounter* (Berkeley: University of California Press, 2007), 197–222.

48. Karen Richman, "The Protestant Ethic and the Dis-spirit of Vodou," in *Immigrant Faiths: Transforming Religious Life in America*, ed. Karen Leonard, Alex Stepick, Manuel A Vasquez, and Jennifer Holdaway (Lanham, Md.: AltaMira, 2005), 165–87; Richman, "A More Powerful Sorcerer."

49. Max Weber, *The Protestant Ethic and the Spirit of Capitalism* (1905; New York: Scribner, 1958).

50. Birgit Meyer, *Translating the Devil: Religion and Modernity among the Ewe in Ghana* (Trenton, N.J.: Africa World Press, 1999).

51. José Casanova, "Religion, the New Millennium, and Globalization," *Sociology of Religion* 62, no. 4 (2001): 415–41.

52. Joel Robbins, "The Globalization of Pentecostal and Charismatic Christianity," *Annual Review of Anthropology* 33 (2004): 117.

53. Rev. Jean Duthène Joseph, interview with the author, August 2, 2002.

54. Weber, *The Protestant Ethic and the Spirit of Capitalism* (London: Routledge (1992): 72, 111, 124.

55. Michael Taussig, *Mimesis and Alterity: A Particular History of the Senses* (London: Routledge, 1993), xiii.

56. Jean Duthène Joseph, "The Symbiotic Relationship between Catholicism and Haitian Vodou and the Impact of the Association on the Evangelical Community in Haiti" (Ph.D. diss., Trinity Evangelical University, 2006).

57. Marlise Simons, "Pope in Haiti, Assails Inequality, Hunger and Fear," *New York Times*, March 10, 1983.

58. Quoted in Ibid. See also Anne Greene, *The Catholic Church in Haiti: Political and Social Change* (East Lansing: Michigan State University Press, 1993), 191–210.

59. Simons, "Pope in Haiti."

60. Father Thomas Streit, interview with the author, October 27, 2008.

61. Richman, "Peasants, Migrants and the Discovery of the Authentic Africa."

11.

The Moral Economy of Brujería
under the Modern Colony:
A Pirated Modernity?

RAQUEL ROMBERG

For the last five centuries, the moral economy of Puerto Rican *brujería* (witchcraft, witch healing) has been shaped by extra- and intra-religious forms of power.[1] As with many other non-institutional vernacular religions, it has retained the symbols of hegemonic culture long after they have ceased to be relevant in the mainstream.[2] In this sense, the moral economy of brujería has been shaped by what Anna Tsing terms the "margins": those "zones of unpredictability at the edges of discursive stability, where contradictory discourses overlap, or where discrepant kinds of meaning-making converge."[3] The resulting moral economy thereby encompasses apparently incongruous manifestations, such as the presence of the Catholic cross amid African and Asian deities, the performance of Catholic and Protestant worship in the making of magic works, and the convergence of consumerist desires with the moral laws of Spiritism.

The often-amused reactions of non-practitioners to these sorts of discrepancies—when social security applications are blessed and placed under a Buddha, or when Hail Marys are prayed in litany during the making of a magic work—reveal the "attitude"[4] or "in-your-face"[5] power of vernacular, anti-institutional religious practices. On a theoretical level, they show the contention of practitioners with hegemonic social powers as they appropriate them, taming or punctuating them in order to solve their existential, practical problems. For instance, when clients bring documents produced by welfare state agents to consultations with brujos (witch healers), they seek to achieve the material benefits that might be garnered with the appropriate spiritual intervention. Also, when Catholic prayers are performed by brujos during the making of magic works, they become tangible manifestations of past challenges to the exclusivity of the Catholic Church no less than of the illicit personal takeover of its most cherished symbols and gestures. Rather than the outcome of creole "mixtures," these forms of worship are the upshot of illicit appropriations, pointing to ritual tactics that reposition the hegemonic symbols of powerful others. In this process, a dialectic of two moments—one challenging the exclusivity of hegemonic symbols, and the other recognizing their power—results in the tactical rechanneling of its purposes to something other than those intended by the dominant culture. I have characterized this process elsewhere as "ritual piracy."[6]

This characterization is inspired by, and is intended to evoke, particular frictions in Caribbean socioeconomic and cultural histories that were driven by various interstitial groups, such as pirates, buccaneers, and Maroon societies.[7] What connects these groups with creole brujos are their tactics of survival on the margins, which have depended on parasitically close, though illegal, relations to local and metropolitan centers of power. In this sense, piracy reflects a typical Caribbean pioneering, infiltrating force that depends on artful forms of partnership between centers of hegemonic power and their margins.[8] Ritual piracy, far from being a safe, mild metaphor for conceptualizing creolization processes, resonates with Stefano Harney's notion of "predatory creolization." It suggests cultural plundering in the context of scarcity and monopoly—not mixture—and recognition of powerful others and tactical imitation—not dialogue.[9] In fact, ritual piracy considers the plundering of cultures as *itself* a "culture building" tactic.[10] Such illicit tactics have shaped the moral economy of brujería and its practices—divination, healing, and magic rituals—since colonial times, providing both spiritual and material charters for solving the existential predicaments of its practitioners in the present.[11] They have also been essential to the transcendental empowerment of creole brujos—despite and because of the various religious, cultural, and state hegemonic gatekeeping practices that constantly aimed at restricting and undermining them.

From this perspective, I propose to examine power with regard to two interrelated arguments. The first focuses on issues of power as constitutive elements of this creole religion in relation to macro-ethnohistorical processes, particularly in response to hegemonic political, economic, religious, and cultural forces. The second argument complements the first by examining the micro politics of ritual performances, especially the kinds of power that constitute the goals and outcomes of actual consultations.[12] Through this combined lens I explore the current dynamism of Puerto Rican brujería, influenced by the effects of both the Americanization of the island, particularly its welfare and consumer capitalist ethos, and transnationalism.[13]

The American imposition of a capitalist economic system combined with a welfare state (commonly referred to as welfare capitalism) produced a unique hybrid form of economic, political, and cultural colonial domination, characterized half ironically by the Puerto Rican anthropologist Jorge Duany as a "postcolonial colony,"[14] and by the political scientist Ramón Grosfoguel as a "modern colony."[15] Much like the French and Dutch colonies in the postwar Caribbean, what characterizes Puerto Rico as a modern colony (in contrast to neocolonial colonies) is that it is granted (1) annual transfers of billions of dollars in the form of food stamps, health, education, and unemployment benefits; (2) participation in metropolitan standards of mass consumption; (3) metropolitan citizenship and democratic/civil rights; and (4) the possibility of migration without the risks of illegality.[16]

The economic boom of the island between World War II and the 1970s was "showcased" internationally (especially in contrast to the involvement of the Soviet Union in Cuba) as an American success story of development. For example, Operation Bootstrap ("industrialization by invitation") in the 1950s boosted labor-intensive industries and the infrastructure. In addition, the exemption from federal taxes granted to American companies on the island under the 936 Law in 1976 propelled massive foreign and federal investments for capital-intensive industries. According to the political scientist Ramón Grosfoguel and the sociologist Marietta Morrissey, the United States welfare system was extended to Puerto Rico as a social and political buffer for its various massive, postwar capitalist development programs. In addition to extending federal social insurance and public assistance, the minimum wages guaranteed in the United States were imposed on Puerto Rico. Although this improved the personal income of Puerto Ricans, it drove many companies away from the island, raising its levels of unemployment.[17] To prevent social unrest, the United States government extended its food stamp program to the island (used by approximately 60 percent of Puerto Rican families by the 1980s).[18] Most analysts conclude that these economic changes had repercussions that were not only economic and social but also political and cultural. Along with stimulating the growth of the manufacturing, financial, and service sectors and raising personal income and living standards, these measures contributed to the assimilation of and dependence on American consumerist and welfare values and practices, which eventually hindered the decolonization impetus on the island and constituted a unique *boricua* everyday practice marked by political and cultural ambiguity.[19]

In addition to transforming Puerto Rico into a modern colony, the Americanization of the island reconstituted not just the previous roles and power basis of brujos but also the material desires of their clients. New sites for economic mobility that have been opened up by U.S. federal welfare agencies and U.S.-based businesses, together with the alluring powers of the modern colony—consumerism and fame, not persecution and isolation—now inform the practices of brujería.[20]

According to the economist Jaime E. Benson-Arias, Puerto Rico's norm of consumption after the Second World War has been shaped by its participation in mainland accumulation and regulation activities, which has been maintained even during periods of economic crisis. With the recent post-Fordist neoliberal social policies that lowered considerably the buying power of many Puerto Ricans, the norm of consumption on the island has been maintained through an increase in consumer indebtedness (just as it has on the mainland).[21] Indeed, the social scientist Laura Ortiz-Negrón's investigation of consumer practices in Puerto Rico shows that shopping has become a primary social activity, confirming the adage that "going shopping is a national pastime in Puerto Rico." This is so, Ortiz-Negrón argues, not just because of the sheer amount of shopping malls and mega-stores plastered on the small island, but also because these shopping malls are always full despite relatively low salaries, an unofficial unemployment rate of 30 percent, and the fact that 60 percent of the population receives federal nutritional assistance through the program known as PAN (Programa de Asistencia Nutricional).[22] Looking at the constitutive nature of consumption on Puerto Rican subjectivities, Ortiz-Negrón's study reveals that consumer culture offers an escape from the utilitarian spaces of everyday life, that it signifies the participation in, not just the illusion of, equal access to goods and services, and that it allows for a nontraditional perception of commodities and social relations that stresses elements of desire and cultural capital.[23] Consumerism under the modern colony, she concludes in a way that pertains to my chapter here, needs not be assessed solely in terms of "the problem of consumption" or as a prevalent mode of criticism of American hegemony, cultural imperialism, and national identity.[24] Therefore, consumerism as a contemporary (some would add, postmodern) means of imagining and constructing self-images through the acquisition of commodities may be examined in relation to magic in general or the transformative potential of commodities (as in the spirit of matter, or "commodity fetishism"), and to brujería practices more specifically as one of the social arenas in which one's "blessings" could be attested or tested.

In framing the moral economy of brujería also within consumer capitalism, I also want to draw attention to the impact of consumerism on vernacular religious practices in Puerto Rico. Indeed, capitalist modes of consumption, not just production, could be considered as critical sites for the exploration of both the constitutive aspects of capitalist forms of domination and the potential agency of consumers as producers of meaning.[25] The distinction made by Daniel Miller between a priori and a posteriori differences in the kinds of rupture that the consumption of commodities might entail is useful here. By focusing on the a posteriori effects of consumer capitalism on brujería practices, I illuminate "the unprecedented diversity created by the differential consumption of what had once been thought to be global and homogenizing institutions." Rather than solve theoretical conundrums, it provides a lens to observe how brujos and their clients "commonly live out these contradictions in local practice."[26]

Since the late 1980s, the increasing transnational pool of ritual experts and commodities in Puerto Rico, together with a local multicultural identity politics, have also reshaped the moral economy of brujería with a more inclusive and positive attitude toward people and things African.[27] Taken together, these economic, political, and cultural changes have not only shaped Puerto Rico's modernity in comparison to other Caribbean nations, but also, as I will show below, distinguishes the moral economy of brujería from other vernacular religions in the Caribbean. In the concluding discussion of this chapter, these ethnographic realities will be situated within and against a growing, compelling cross-cultural literature on the modernity of magic as a first step in tracing the unique genealogy of modernity that the moral economy of brujería (under a modern colony) exposes.

BRUJERÍA IN A MODERN COLONY

Over the span of five centuries, various layered histories originating both in distant and local places have shaped the moral economy of Puerto Rican brujería. In this tortuous history, brujería has incorporated at different periods the spirituality and gestures of popular Spanish Catholicism, French Spiritism, United States Protestantism, and Cuban Santería.[28] These religious practices came together because of the political, economic, and social conditions brought by colonialism, slavery, nation building, and migration—all of which were shaped by global forces of various kinds. Similar trends were also constitutive of other Afro-Latin vernacular forms of spiritual healing and magic, such as Haitian Vodou,[29] Cuban Santería and Palo,[30] and Brazilian Candomblé and Umbanda.[31] But what sets Puerto Rican brujería apart is the added "Americanization" of its moral economy.

After three and a half centuries of being persecuted as heretic and vilified as superstitious and primitive under Spanish rule and the beginning of American rule in 1898, the practices of brujería have recently changed again because of the colonial relations that tied the United States mainland with the island under commonwealth status since 1950. These ties, which began with the invasion of 1898, are economic, religious, and cultural, as well as ideological. As noted above, they have transformed Puerto Rican modes of production and consumption under free trade and consumerism, and established a stronger dependency on the various forms of federal aid from the U.S. federal government, administered by specialized state agencies under the system of welfare capitalism.

Puerto Rico under the Estado Libre Asociado (ELA, or commonwealth) occupies an ambiguous position between total independence from, and total annexation to, the United States. Rather than the result of positive political action, the commonwealth seems to be the result of an irresolute electorate, or, as Doris Sommer suggests, an electorate very decided on not deciding.[32] After decades of deferred controversies, visible in the enactment of endless plebiscites, the future of Puerto Rico's status is still entangled in irreconcilable options between state sovereignty and annexation.[33]

In religious matters, with the separation (at least at an official level) of state and religion, American Catholic and Protestant churches mushroomed, and Cubans who arrived as political exiles following the 1959 revolution established Santería temples.[34] As a result, a general "spiritual laissez-faire" atmosphere emerged, opening up the gates to religious eclecticism and competition.[35] Trusting that the American presence would help modernize and bring prosperity to the Puerto Rican nation after centuries of declining Spanish colonial rule, many (rich and poor alike) began converting to the newly established U.S.-based churches on the island.[36] During the first decades of American rule, it was quite easy to find members of one family affiliated with different religious traditions, creating an unprecedented religious heterogeneity within each family.

It is in this eclectic religious atmosphere—with its various logics of practice—that many of the brujos I worked with were raised and later as adults developed their employment trajectories, shaping in great measure their individual ritual styles. Tonio, a famous brujo in his nineties whom I met in Loíza in 1995, for instance, followed popular Catholicism, Spiritism, and creole reworkings of African-based magic practices. In the early decades of the twentieth century, he used to work as an overseer in an American-owned sugar plantation, acquiring an insider's knowledge of the workings and effects of capitalist forms of management and employment. For sixty years (until his death in 1998), however, he dedicated himself fully to his *obra espiritual* (spiritual work). Haydée, whom I met through Tonio, followed Tonio's style with an added mode emerging from her upbringing as the daughter of a Spiritist father and a Catholic mother who converted to American Protestantism. She worked for many years as a legal secretary and then as the personnel manager of a state-run health care clinic before devoting herself fully to the obra espiritual after a series of health problems. The youngest of all the healers I met, Armando, was raised by an *espiritista* mother in New York, where he had the opportunity to expand his ritual knowledge among Cuban and Nuyorican *babalawos* as well as other healers from South and Central America, continuing his initiation in Santería under Ronny, an exiled Cuban babalawo in Puerto Rico.[37] Armando worked in an American-owned paper-goods factory in Puerto Rico and as a healer after work and on weekends, with the intention of fully dedicating himself to the obra espiritual as soon as he could leave his in-laws' house. Basi, the owner of a botanica, was in her mid sixties when I met her and lived with her during several months of my fieldwork. She was raised by a Spiritist grandmother, and since roughly the 1980s she blended New Age versions of Spiritism with an ecumenical form of Christian religiosity in her obra espiritual. Reflecting her healing style, Basi's botanica was profusely supplied with the usual potions, icons, trinkets, herbs, candles, and books, with added special sections for New Age and herbal medicine products. Ken, a forty-year-old Nuyorican healer married to Mora, a Puerto Rican *espiritista-santera*, developed a personal style that combined various Asian, Native American, and New Age modes of healing with traditional Puerto Rican Spiritism. They worked together in private consultations, and coached groups in all sorts of meditation and spiritual traditions, catering to a host of young, yuppie clients.

This short sample suggests that in addition to the eclectic religious trajectories brought forth by transnationalism and the Americanization of the island, the life and working experiences of brujos—many of whom have experienced working in American-owned factories or state agencies—shaped their ritual expertise. Having thus acquired additional cultural capital pertaining to new systems of production and redistribution under consumer and welfare capitalism, brujos are often at the center of commercial and bureaucratic circles. In this capacity, they are able, for example, to recommend their unemployed clients to companies headed by their influential clients, and to inform their needy ones of new welfare regulations that may become available. As a result, as will become evident below, the healing and magic styles of powerful brujos—those blessed by both the spirits and influential clients—encompass not only the spiritual but also the material welfare of their clients. Interceding more directly in the material conditions of their clients, and no longer persecuted as heretics or vilified as charlatans, brujos have begun to function implicitly as "spiritual entrepreneurs": as brokers among state, business, and professional networks. As such, they are sought out when mainstream medicine, psychology, or social work fail to provide solutions to a variety of health, relationship, and economic problems, but, more comprehensively, they are also consulted in order to promote one's *bendiciones* (blessings) or ultimate success in life.[38]

Within this new moral economy, material acquisitiveness and desire for success have been elevated to a higher moral and spiritual order of aspiration: brujos and their followers see material and spiritual progress as well as the attainment of high social status as not only morally legitimate quests but also visible signs of being "blessed" by the spirits. This form of "spiritualized materialism" suggests that profit and success have become infused with an ultimate moral purpose, once spiritual forces are believed to have intervened in achieving these goals.[39] Defined in terms of both material and spiritual progress, the quest for bendiciones has been molded recently by consumer and welfare capitalist values and sensibilities, adding to the hitherto exclusively Catholic and Spiritist spiritual understandings of bendiciones a concern for the material conditions of one's existence (similar to those promoted by charismatic Pentecostal churches). The connection between spiritual and material blessings is hence established: material success—measured by one's acquisitive power, social status, and overall progress—attests to having been gifted with spiritual blessings (and vice versa). This redefinition of bendiciones is embodied in rituals and orientations to reality that aim at achieving and explaining economic and social success. For instance, under the Spiritist law of love and charity, one's bendiciones (in this case, one's *cuadro*, comprising protective spirits) have to be shared in order to multiply them: the more we share, the more blessings and prosperity we are given back.

TRANSNATIONALISM

Although striking in their own ways, these local processes cannot adequately encompass the complex world in which urban vernacular religions in general[40] and unorthodox forms of *espiritismo*, *santerismo*, and *brujería* in particular operate today. This is a world in which the technologies of travel and communication have facilitated the intense movement of people (some as a result of forced dislocation, others in search of better opportunities), as well as the circulation of ideologies, commodities, and desires.[41] One of the results is that social relations in today's urban settings are no longer confined to the nuclear or extended family or dominated solely by face-to-face encounters, but rather are swayed by complex, long-distance networks of mediated relations and desires.[42] These processes have influenced brujería practices in at least three ways: by the migration of ritual experts, the circulation of ritual commodities, and the impact of Afro-American identity politics. In fact, with the recent intensification of the circulation of ritual experts and commodities, vernacular religions such as Puerto Rican brujería have entered a transnational arena of ritual experimentation and eclecticism. For example, Haydée met various santeros and babalawos—some exiled from Cuba and some Nuyoricans—during her regular visits to botanicas. It was during one of these visits that she met an exiled Cuban babalawo (who consulted with her occasionally) and his godson, Armando, with whom she initiated a collaboration that lasted a few months.

Other forms of religious change or conversion have occurred among practitioners of Santería in Puerto Rico as a consequence of their identification with the African Diaspora (as in many parts of the Caribbean and the Americas), leading to the revitalization and essentialization of their religious practices, in many cases following a highly selective regard for Yoruba origins.[43] But the re-imagining of creole religious practices with regard to an imagined Africa or an essentialized indigenousness (*indigenismo*)—pervasive within some diasporic religions[44]—was not consciously adopted by the practitioners and clients with whom I worked, and thus is outside my discussion here. I need to mention, however, the unintended effect of this revitalization on the practices of brujería. In effect, the overall public recognition of the African and Taíno heritage of Puerto Rican popular culture by state and private promoters freed practitioners of brujería from the need to hide their practices.[45] Instead of being ashamed or threatened by past stereotypes that labeled them as either heretics or charlatans, brujos are increasingly able to acknowledge their spiritual work as stemming from the magic and healing powers of African *orishas* or deities, overtly incorporating elements of Santería in their Spiritist practices. African deities are considered the most honored, potent spiritual energies of all—their ultimate value stemming, however, from their perceived ritual potency, not from their connection to Africa or any other moral geography.[46]

PROSPERITY, CONSUMERISM, AND WELFARE CAPITALISM: A PARTICULAR GENEALOGY OF MODERNITY

The choices of lifestyle offered by consumerism in conditions of "high modernity" impart a more or less integral set of practices that an individual "is forced" to choose (we have no choice but to choose) "not only because such practices fulfill utilitarian needs, but because they give material form to a particular narrative of self-identity."[47] Acquisitiveness as an endless process of materialization satisfies at the same time the possibility of enhancing and renewing oneself according to ever-changing narratives of self-identity and lifestyles. The materiality of these lifestyles acquires yet another value within brujería. As mentioned above, if achieved, material success becomes a marker of one's bendiciones; and if it is yet to be achieved, it becomes an endless motivational force that guides personal and social choices. Like the phantasmagoric nature of the fetish mentioned by Michael Taussig, bendiciones elucidate "a certain quality of ghostliness in objects in the modern world and an uncertain fluctuation between thinghood and spirit."[48] If both self and commodities become entangled in fetishist relations, one's personal power becomes materialized and desired objects become spiritualized. Having acquired and at the same time confounded their assumed qualities, the need to perceive one's personal power materialized in objects destabilizes both the self and the objects that are meant to embody it.

Since being prosperous suggests that one is blessed by the spirits, when brujos are able to invest in expanding their altars and to throw lavish spiritual fiestas for their patron saints, they are asserting their spiritual powers. And much like their clients, they display their blessings through the consumption of fancy clothes, glamorous jewels, flashy cars, and the latest technological gadgets (e.g., electronic gates, cell phones, beepers). Waiting rooms filled with clients who come to consult (often making big sacrifices and waiting for three to five hours to be seen), and clients traveling long distances, even over the Atlantic, are additional external markers of successful brujos. This sensuous moral economy fits well with the enticements and predicaments of consumer capitalism, acquiring a spiritual, cosmic meaning.[49]

An evident circularity is at work here. Similarly to the fetish and the belief in its transformative power, this moral economy implies that there is materiality in blessings and spirituality in corporeality or embodiment. In short, spirituality and materiality reflect each other: material prosperity is a sign of being blessed spiritually, and leading a spiritual life is rewarded materially.[50]

Brujería thereby operates on murky ground, articulating the desires and frustrations akin to high modernity by foregrounding the centrality of material consumption simultaneously as proof, reflection, and anticipation of one's personal power.

This moral economy is evident also in botanicas. For example, they have to have their shelves fully stocked, be well supplied, have the latest innovations, offer "new and improved" products (e.g., cleansing aerosols, which have been rapidly incorporated by successful brujos as practical, timesaving substitutes for cleansing potions made from scratch), and prodigiously expensive items in order to index that they are "blessed by the spirits." A prosperous-looking botanica attracts clients with the hope that its good fortune will also affect them. The sign of prosperity is not the size of the botanica but its displayed stock, in terms of both variety and quantity (the latter related to a sense of limitless availability and bountiful supply). Also, today you can find in these stores a gamut of mass-produced ritual objects from around the world—from South, Central, and North America, East and Southeast Asia, and the Caribbean. They are sought by brujos not because of their origin but because of their perceived potency, following the endorsement of celebrity healers or personal contact with transnational healers.

There are yet other sources and meanings of bendiciones, which come from the interventions of brujos in commercial and bureaucratic matters during consultations. Thanks to Haydée's connections, for example, a young unemployed woman found a job with a restaurant chain, since the manager of one of these restaurants is one of Haydée's clients. Through another client (a manager of a hotel chain and car-rental agency), Haydée secured a receptionist job for a young Nuyorican man who just arrived from the mainland. Interventions such as these were also public pledges to her power as a bruja, as well as a display of the bendiciones—acquired via her *trabajo espiritual* (spiritual work)—she was able to share with her clients. Through a conflation of spiritual and social responsibility to others, Puerto Rican brujería does answer to this agenda, but it does so outside an institutional setting. Stemming from its unique, non-institutional ways of operating, it offers an unorthodox, individualistic form of spiritual guidance and religiosity in achieving material success.

Clearly not the result of belief in any particular healing tradition, the choices made by business owners, professionals, homemakers, and blue-collar workers who seek brujos are mostly guided by the perceived fame and success of particular healers and the power ascribed to their particular healing style.[51] In addition to the moral economy mentioned above, and without diminishing its spiritual authenticity, the spiritual field of brujería is largely shaped by free-market consumer considerations: intense competition, self-promotion, and specialization. Asserting their fame and powers as spiritual entrepreneurs, healers often define their expertise in relation to mainstream "cloak professions": Armando, for example, defines himself as a "spiritual consultant," and Haydée sees herself as a "doctor of the soul." The marriage between market and spiritual considerations—usually viewed as problematic in modernist discourses—is actually a nonissue for practitioners and their clients. Guided by the Spiritist ethos, which foregrounds the preeminence of spiritual laws, justice, and personal civic responsibility, brujos manage to muster—for a modest fee of $10 to $20 per consultation, compared to $60 to $120 charged by physicians, lawyers, and psychologists—diverse functions commonly held by public and private institutions in addressing their clients' practical and moral problems.

Extending the area of influence and control beyond the management of spirits and saints, brujos develop their expertise by encompassing those areas of social life that fall under the control of state and commercial agents. I see this appropriation as a form of tactical opposition from within.[52] If, as Taussig suggests, "the labor of the negative" is essential to the "magical power that converts the negative into being,"[53] this power stems in the case of brujería from the transformation of exclusionary forms of knowledge into incorporated areas of intervention: knowledge and control over the transcendental world is now complemented with knowledge and control of market and state powers. Taking advantage of new economic opportunities and welfare regulations, brujos can answer the emotional, economic, and spiritual needs of their clients and at times even become adjudicators between man-made laws and policies and Spiritist ethics. In essential ways, the means of attaining material security and success are achieved by co-opting bureaucratic and commercial systems into the moral economy of brujería. An important aspect of the constitutive aspect of the labor of the negative lies in the irreverent incorporation and adaptation of key mainstream values and gestures of powerful agents in society, and the taking over of the roles traditionally assigned not only to psychologists and social workers but also to officials of the labor, justice, and public health systems. A young woman accountant came for a consultation with Haydée after she was unjustly dismissed from her job. During divination, she was advised to fight for a more just severance pay, particularly for retroactive wage adjustments (she used to work extra hours for which she was never compensated). During the divination process, she heard, "Remember that you need to demand what you deserve. You worked for three years and were in charge of that office from morning to night—you never made a case for leaving at the end of the workday—but were never paid for overtime. If you sum up all these hours in three years, imagine what you should be getting." At the end of the session, Haydée provided this woman with a personal card of one of her clients, an attorney specializing in workers' severance and wrongful termination compensation cases.

Even though brujos do not subvert dominant systems of power, they operate within and at the same time without them: they irreverently poach the liberal and religious professions, as well as state and commercial agencies, twisting the modern colony "with an attitude." For instance, when the Spiritist law of cause and effect (or cosmic causation) and notions of spiritual justice and reincarnation inspire the advice given by brujos to their clients, merely instrumental goals become spiritually endowed.

For example, new economic opportunities afforded by federal aid and tax breaks provide areas of economic mobility, following the policies of welfare capitalism, which those more savvy brujos are able to tap into when they address, say, social security issues. Adopting a bureaucratic pose and drawing on their networks with state agencies, brujos help their clients get the best of deals from governmental spheres of action. Mediating among clients, state agencies, and the spiritual world, they infuse the performance of their magic works with practical information as to where and when to apply for federal loans for housing, small businesses, or educational opportunities. In this added capacity, they also become brokers among state agencies, businesses, and individuals (similar to the roles taken over by some Protestant churches in response to neoliberal policies). When Nora, a young woman in her twenties, came for a consultation with Haydée with a health problem, aggravated by the refusal of the social security administration to recognize it and grant her work compensation, Haydée asked Nora to show her the official documents she received. Attempting to obtain social security benefits can be a complicated and frustrating process, filled with long forms and much red tape. Haydée knew that many of those who apply for disability benefits for the first time are denied until they can present the necessary evidence. Numerous impairments could qualify as disabilities, and thus it is crucial to retain a knowledgeable attorney who can gather the necessary evidence and present it to the court. After carefully examining the reasons for the rejection and identifying the agent who signed it, Haydée advised her to go see a friend of hers who works in the local social security office, and, with her help, reapply. The consultation was not over until the power of spirits of prosperity and justice were summoned, the official documents were placed under an icon of San Judas Tadeo (the saint in change of difficult legal cases), and a lit candle was offered to him.

As a final warning, Haydée said, "Remember that you can't work when you apply for disability."

The case of Tomasa, a middle-class woman in her fifties, illustrates another type of intervention of brujos with the government. She came for a consultation with Haydée because she had some legal problems with a tenant—a single mother on welfare who had failed to pay the rent for almost a year. Having won a court case in her favor, Tomasa was going to collect past-due rent money (plus interest) from her tenant, and came to give this good news to Haydée. During divination, however, Haydée stated that the judge's ruling had been "immoral." According to the tenets of Spiritism, and taking into consideration the economic straits of this poor woman, Haydée urged Tomasa to reconsider a fairer deal, one that reflected the cosmic ruling spoken by the spirits during divination: "Whatever is wrongly taken won't shine." If Tomasa were to follow this cosmic ruling instead of the judge's ruling, she could avoid breaking the cosmic law of love (i.e., all actions are to be measured against the life and teachings of Jesus) and thereby avoid risking the castigation of the spirits. This is some of what Tomasa heard during divination:

> Remember, "Whatever is wrongly taken, won't shine." How much does she owe you [for the rent]? Because for me, "What's not mine, I don't want." You need to decide what is yours . . . what you are asking for. . . . You shouldn't be taking what is not yours [interest plus legal fees]. The lawyer is demanding far more than he should—for what is not yours. But you'll pay. . . . The lawyer knows how to trick the law. . . . But remember, "The cord breaks at its weakest point" [i.e., you are going to suffer, not the lawyer]. . . . If you and your husband have social security . . . if you have that, why take the money from those that need it? But greed for money—that's terrible. "The more you have, the more you want." That woman doesn't have even a place to fall dead!

A long session of questions and answers followed, during which Haydée pressed Tomasa to break down the final calculation made by the lawyer and to explain her finances. After learning that Tomasa was not clear about ever filing taxes for the income she had received from renting rooms, Haydée made her point from a bureaucratic, legal perspective: "Remember that today everything goes into one computer. I don't ever mess with the federal government. I give them what I owe them. If that girl takes you to Hacienda [Treasury] or she takes you to DACO [Departamento de Asuntos del Consumidor; i.e., the Department of Consumer Protection] . . . and then . . . you . . . you didn't think about that, ah?"

Realizing that she might be castigated both by the federal government and by the spirits, Tomasa decided to override the judge's decision by not only allowing the poor woman to pay just the rent without interest and legal expenses, but also to forget about the debt altogether if she was not able to pay any money at all. As this and other cases illustrate, the advise given by brujos provide not only the "eyes and ears" for clients to find possible resources within bureaucratic organizations and capitalist enterprises, but also the "soul" or moral direction behind the demands and profits that one could make without transgressing the moral laws of Spiritism. In other words, the accumulation of state- and corporate-administered social goods should be pursued only in righteous ways, if one wishes to be rewarded with more blessings. Whereas some would see this and the other ethnographic vignettes as inflections of modern welfare capitalism, as "alternative" or "vernacular" forms of modernity,[54] I prefer to characterize them as "pirated"—as will become clear in my concluding discussion.

In relation to the extensive scholarship on Caribbean modernity, such an understanding of the modernity of Puerto Rican brujería stems from and is limited by the vantage point of an ethnographic insider's perspective on vernacular religious practices. It presumes answers to such questions as: To whose modernity does it refer? Who is assumed to be entitled to it? From whose perspective is it to be assessed?[55] Broadly, the modernity of dominant and subaltern groups in the Caribbean has been extensively discussed in relation to metropolitan capitalist forms of entrepreneurship, exploitation, production, accumulation, and consumption, as well as Enlightenment projects involving the scientific management, accounting, and dominance of people and nature.[56] More specifically, the modernity of subaltern groups (which was historically denied to them) has been recently recognized in postcolonial studies by circumscribing their participation in capitalist forms of domination and exploitation as either victims or resilient, inventive *bricoleurs*.

My discussion of Puerto Rican brujería under the modern colony is situated somewhere between these readings. Following Hayden White's proposed literary model for deconstructing the tropes of historical accounts, it provides an account that is neither tragic nor heroic but rather ironic, one that highlights the paradox resulting from the simultaneous submission to and rejection of hegemonic economic, social, political, and cultural forces and values.[57] In the preceding sections, I have shown how capitalist-welfare consumer desires, opportunities, and disenchantments are reworked from the inside, following the notion of "blessings" within the moral economy of brujería. One can argue that this type of participatory engagement of brujos and their clients with welfare capitalism is outside of what Bruno Latour referred to as "the Constitution of modernity" and of social theories of modernity.[58] Yet, if one takes into account the apparently twisted, irreverent ways in which the moral economy of brujería engages both consumerist and welfare practices without completely surrendering to them and without disavowing them, the idea of piracy might begin to make sense.[59]

CONCLUSION: A PIRATED MODERNITY?

Recent anthropological studies of witchcraft and magic in Europe, Latin America, and Africa have suggested their linkage to modernity. In this literature, historical anthropologists studying contemporary decolonized societies have reinserted witchcraft and magic in discourses of modernity, mainly as local practices that have arisen as forms of resistance to Western colonial and modernization processes.

In a relational account of terror and healing, Taussig challenges the view of witchcraft and magic as closed, timeless systems of belief, showing that they have emerged as the result of a joint venture tying the imaginings and fictions of the colonizers to those of the colonized.[60] Indeed, for Taussig, E. E. Evans-Pritchard's attempt to offer Western ears a clear-cut rationalization of witchcraft as a closed system is comforting but misleading. "Doubtless this 'it' we call magic, like calling into an echoing abyss, existed in third-world countries before European colonization," writes Taussig. "But surely this 'it' from that point on contained as a constitutive force the power of colonial differentiation such that magic became a gathering point of Otherness in a series of racial and class differentiations embedded in the distinctions made between Church and magic, and science and magic."[61] Stephan Palmié elaborates a similar argument with regard to the oppositional moral complementarity, historically forged in Cuba, between the Lucumí (Yoruba)–based benevolence of Santería and the Congo (Bantu)–based wickedness of Palo.[62] Also in this line of inquiry, Joan Dayan, Sidney Mintz, and Michel-Rolph Trouillot have examined the turbulence of Haitian political history as inseparable from the tribulations of Vodou, its wars, gods, and fictions.[63] Some studies suggest that the feared Haitian "zombie" and the West Indian "obeah man" are creole creations that owe more to the nightmares of slavery than to the survival of African beliefs in the Caribbean.[64]

Indigenous forms of witchcraft and magic are depicted as creole forms of empowerment that not only have emerged out of relations of inequality in colonial times,[65] but also have been mobilized in sustaining the elusive spirit power of post-independence states.[66] In other works, witchcraft appears as a cultural idiom intrinsically tied to colonial systems of inequality that has the potential to destabilize the political and economic orders of decolonized nations at the local and regional levels.[67] Peter Geschiere has noted that on the African continent, for instance, economic and political powers under modernity are inherently connected to local witchcraft practices: "Witchcraft . . . continues to be a key element in discourses of power, despite modern processes of change (or perhaps because of them), thereby creating new forms of domination and resistance."[68] Here witchcraft appears to be a form of political action—a predominantly subversive local idiom that engages in a contestation of colonial and postcolonial forces.[69] Also, Adeline Masquelier shows that witchcraft has become a local form of resistance to non-indigenous forms of trade relations in a community; and Mark Auslander in the same collection argues that witchcraft accusations reflect the lack of equitable forms of integration for members of a community into a market economy.[70]

In contrast, most historians of European witchcraft have traditionally related witchcraft and magic to the modern world in a diachronic mode, stressing the connection of witch hunts to larger and more complex political and economic realities, such as the state and the church. Equipped with economic and political models, historians have portrayed witchcraft and magic as class- and gender-motivated practices that subvert the modern state. Thus, although asserting a temporal connection between modernity and the practices of witchcraft and magic rectified the otherwise-misleading perception that the latter belonged exclusively to the world of the "primitive," it also diminished them, in my view, by foregrounding their subversive character. Witchcraft and magic were portrayed as antithetical to the social order.[71]

The modernity of witchcraft and magic in Africa, Asia, and parts of the Caribbean and South America has been conceptualized most often in one or another from of "occult economy" or "prosperity cult."[72] Promising "to yield wealth without production, value without effort," occult economies become necessary, according to Jean and John Comaroff, when an increasingly neoliberal social order fails to provide those who lack fiscal or cultural capital with the legitimate means to fulfill their capitalistic accumulation desires.[73] They are deployed in order to "conjure wealth—or to account for its accumulation—by appeal to techniques that defy explanation in the conventional terms of practical reason," pointing to an ethical aspect that emerges from "the moral discourses and (re)actions sparked by the real or imagined production of value through such 'magical' means."[74] Broadly, these economies comprise "alchemic techniques [that] defy reason in promising unnaturally large profits—to yield wealth without production, value without effort."[75]

Similarly, the anthropology of "cargo cults" (infamous in ethnographies of

New Guinea and Melanesia, recently under critique) suggests a "traditional" enchantment with Western commodities (cargo), believed to have been created by divine spirits and intended for local indigenous people but snatched unfairly by white people.[76] By means of a primitive ritual imitation of white behavior, cargo cult members were assumed to entice their ancestors to restore their control over cargo. Occult economies, like cargo cults, seem to be based on the assumption that a flawed model of causation held for modernization and capitalist processes produces unrealistic, ill-considered, and ultimately unrewarded magical rituals and ceremonies.[77] The conceptualization of occult economies and cargo cults in these cases act as "gatekeeping concepts"[78] that reinforce the temporal distance between "traditional" or "local" cultures and modernity,[79] even as they recognize their spatial coexistence and interdependence.

The moral economy of brujería stands in stark contrast to these portrayals. What occult economies seem to help muster elsewhere, the modern colony provides for brujería practices in Puerto Rico. And what cargo cults seem to summon, contemporary brujos make available through combined spiritual and practical advice. Witchcraft and magic practices in this context are not unlike the "invisible worlds" that inform the accumulation of wealth among the dynastic rich in the contemporary United States[80] and, for that matter, the "flexible" forms of capitalist accumulation under globalization. Like these unseen worlds, the moral economy of brujería works not just to adapt to the modern colony but also to reproduce it, though perhaps unwillingly and in oblique ways. Similar to the practices of Korean shamanism, which in the last twenty years increased the frequency of "prosperity rituals" against "ancestor rituals" to fit the needs of its practitioners under capitalism,[81] the spiritual world of brujería and the cosmological morality it entails are summoned for *promoting* the necessary practical means to achieve mainstream goals, not for *substituting* them. Adding the ethical tenets of Spiritism to the spectral ethos and predicaments of consumer and welfare capitalism, the moral economy of brujería can therefore hardly be seen as counter-hegemonic in the same measure as elsewhere in the world.

Unlike reports about the effects of postcolonial forms of capitalist accumulation as resulting, for instance, from "contracts with the devil,"[82] the surplus of "zombie laborers" working for "cannibalistic witches,"[83] in an "economy of the belly,"[84] prosperity is not envisioned within the moral economy of brujería as "evil" or "the labor of the negative." In addition, unlike the bureaucratic nightmares in Castro's Cuba embodied in current practices of Palo,[85] the redistributive role of the commonwealth is imagined as a blessing (except, of course, by the Puerto Rican independence movement). Rather than placing capitalistic forms of accumulation and state redistribution powers in detrimental opposition to local or traditional culture, brujería practices "tame" prosperity and the welfare state in its own terms: fame and success are believed to be rewards for leading a moral, civil life. That is, material and spiritual progress not only are not at odds but also are intimately connected. The obvious reason seems to be the historically and currently constituted conditions of brujería practice. I do not mean to suggest that the enticements of the modern colony in Puerto Rico are such that they disavow the predicaments of consumer and welfare capitalism. As with fetishism, the fetishism of the modern colony involves a powerful fascination or desire that is both *indulged* and at the same time, *denied*.[86]

Rather than destabilizing or contesting the modern colony, however, the moral economy of brujería has forged ways to twist it—with an attitude. While spatially and temporally distancing assumptions are still directing much of today's scholarly and lay perceptions of witchcraft and magic, a more participatory role should be imagined, for they are not as alien to modern economic circuits and political developments as assumed. Both the relational and subversive models mentioned above fail to address what I see as the "positive power" (in Foucault's terms) or the "making power" of Puerto Rican brujería. Following the discussions in *Magic and Modernity* about the intrinsic imbrication of (and affinity between) magic and modernity,[87] I want to argue that the participation of brujería in the modern colony is apparent and active, albeit invisible and mostly irreverent, speaking in it and with it. This is perhaps the reason why I think plural, relativized, or alternative views of modernity[88] fall short of addressing the disciplinary effects of Latour's Constitution of modernity—of what it allows and forbids—on the creation of multiple versions of modernity or its "hybrids."[89] Further, what plural views of modernity tenaciously forget is that "we have never been modern," at least in the totalizing ways we think about, in the sense that the modern world "has never functioned according to the rules of its official Constitution alone."[90] In response to dominant (not alternative) capitalist and welfare desires and opportunities, the moral economy of brujería strategically articulates, in unorthodox ways, capitalist and welfare values with the ethical values of Spiritism in order to promote their clients' prosperity or blessings. Brujos and their clients, far from offering a counterculture to modernity[91] or being endangered species or subversive, are thus active participants in the modern colony, perhaps suggesting a form of participation that is not so much *entitled* or *alternative* but rather *pirated*.

NOTES

1. "Brujería" is an emic or native term imported to the Spanish colonies at the time of conquest and in use ever since. Similarly to its closest translation in English, "witchcraft," brujería carries negative stereotypes stemming from a long history of persecution (paralleling that of European witchcraft). For this reason, some Puerto Rican healers when talking to outsiders refer to what they do by using the more neutral term "espiritismo." Yet, espiritismo is also entangled in a local politics of labeling and spiritual authenticity. Scientific spiritists, for instance, differentiate and disparagingly refer to *popular espiritistas* as *espiriteros* (fake *espiritistas*). See Raquel Romberg, "Whose Spirits Are They? The Political Economy of Syncretism and Authenticity," *Journal of Folklore Research* 35, no. 1 (1998): 69–82; Romberg, "From Charlatans to Saviors: Espiritistas, Curanderos, and Brujos Inscribed in Discourses of Progress and Heritage," *Centro Journal* 15, no. 2 (2003): 146–73. I thus initially offer "witch healing" as a working translation; yet, in the following pages, I use "brujería" in keeping with what it means for practitioners. Among insiders, *brujos* today deliberately call themselves "brujos" and what they do "brujería" to index not only their ability to heal and solve spiritual problems, but also their pride—even arrogance—in their trade, a far cry from the dread and shame of the past. See Romberg, *Witchcraft and Welfare: Spiritual Capital and the Business of Magic in Modern Puerto Rico* (Austin: University of Texas Press, 2003).

2. Raymond Williams, "Base and Superstructure in Marxist Theory," in *Problems in Materialism and Culture: Selected Readings* (London: Verso, 1980), 31–49.

3. Anna Lowenhaupt Tsing, "From the Margins," *Cultural Anthropology* 9, no. 3 (1994): 279.

4. Johannes Fabian, "Culture with an Attitude," in *Anthropology with an Attitude: Critical Essays* (Stanford: Stanford University Press, 2001), 87–100.

5. Roger D. Abrahams, discussant of the panel "Creolization: Mapping New Territories in Creolization" (annual meeting of the American Folklore Society, Rochester, N.Y., October 16–20, 2002).

6. Raquel Romberg, "Symbolic Piracy: Creolization with an Attitude?," *New West Indian Guide* 79, nos. 3/4 (2005): 175–218. This particular view on creolization, though applicable to certain processes of cultural change and other vernacular religions on the Americas, is limited to those that arose in late nineteenth-century urban slave and highland-peasant-Maroon societies under Spanish colonial rule—societies that were intensely linked to European settlers and their mores.

7. See Peter T. Leeson, *The Invisible Hook: The Hidden Economics of Pirates* (Princeton: Princeton University Press, 2009); Peter Linebaugh and Marcus Rediker, *The Many-Headed Hydra: Sailors, Slaves, Commoners, and the Hidden History of the Revolutionary Atlantic* (Boston: Beacon, 2001); Marcus Buford Rediker, *Between the Devil and the Deep Blue Sea: Merchant Seamen, Pirates, and the Anglo-American Maritime World, 1700–1750* (Cambridge: Cambridge University Press, 1989); Rediker, *Villains of all Nations: Atlantic Pirates in the Golden Age* (Boston: Beacon, 2004).

8. Indeed, mutual dependency and ambiguity have inspired various kinds of parasitic relationships in the Caribbean since colonization until today, such as those between piracy and imperial commerce, privateering and anti-colonial revolutions, Maroon and plantation economies, and informal and global markets. Such native trickster modes of economic and cultural survival have been characterized by Ramón Grosfoguel, Frances Negrón-Muntaner, and Chloe Georas as *jaibería* (astuteness)—a folk term that denotes a wide range of popular practices of resistance to, and negotiation with, colonialism, "of taking dominant discourse literally in order to subvert it for one's purpose, of doing whatever one sees fit not as a head-on collision . . . but a bit under the table." See "Beyond Nationalist and Colonialist Discourses: The *Jaiba* Politics of the Puerto Rican Ethno-Nation," in *Puerto Rican Jam: Essays on Culture and Politics*, ed. Negrón-Muntaner and Grosfoguel (Minneapolis: University of Minnesota Press, 1997), 30–31.

9. Stefano Harney, *Nationalism and Identity: Culture and the Imagination in a Caribbean Diaspora* (Mona: University of the West Indies, 1996), 114–15. For a parallel interpretation of creole economics as oppositional and subversive, see Katherine E. Browne, *Creole Economics: Caribbean Cunning under the French Flag* (Austin: University of Texas Press, 2004).

10. Jean Besson, discussant of panel "Moral and Political Economies" (Obeah and Other Powers: The Politics of Caribbean Religion conference, Newcastle, United Kingdom, June 16–18, 2008).

11. I conducted fieldwork and archival research in Puerto Rico between the summer of 1995 and the winter of 1996. The names of some places and people have been changed to protect their privacy. All the dialogues were spoken in Spanish, and some of the textual sources were in Spanish as well. All translations are mine.

12. This joint agenda is also reflected methodologically: the first argument is based primarily on a combined archival and media research, and the second on my ethnographic work at various Spiritist centers, home altars, botanicas, and, most essentially, my work with healers and their clients during consultations—in particular, during my close apprenticeship with Haydée for over a year.

13. I refer to "welfare and consumer capitalism" strategically in order to contextualize my discussion of the moral economy of Puerto Rican brujería. The theoretical-historical discussion about the emergence of these concepts and the differences and connections between them is beyond the scope of my argument.

14. Jorge Duany, "Nation, Migration, Identity: Rethinking Colonialism and Transnationalism Apropos the Case of Puerto Rico" (paper presented at Swarthmore College, Department of Sociology and Anthropology, November 30, 2001), 6.

15. Ramón Grosfoguel, "The Divorce of Nationalist Discourses from the Puerto Rican People: A Sociohistorical Perspective," in Negrón-Muntaner and Grosfoguel, *Puerto Rican Jam*, 57–76.

16. Ibid., 66–67.

17. In addition to raising the income of Puerto Ricans 1,000 percent—annual per-

sonal income rocketed from $118 to $1,200—these measures also propelled the exodus of unemployed Puerto Ricans to the mainland. See Karl Wagenheim and Olga Jiménez de Wagenheim, eds., *The Puerto Ricans: A Documentary History*, updated ed. (Princeton: Markus Wiener, 1994), 183–84.

18. Marietta Morrissey, "The Making of a Colonial Welfare State: U.S. Social Insurance and Public Assistance in Puerto Rico," *Latin American Perspectives* 33, no. 1 (2006): 23–41; Ramón Grosfoguel, *Colonial Subjects: Puerto Ricans in a Global Perspective* (Berkeley: University of California Press, 2003), 57–66.

19. Frances Negrón-Muntaner, ed., *None of the Above: Puerto Ricans in the Global Era* (New York: Palgrave Macmillan, 2007).

20. This is no coincidence. As Jean Besson noted in her comments at the conference, these practices are the result of a long legacy of colonial capitalism in the Caribbean.

21. Jaime E. Benson-Arias, "Puerto Rico: The Myth of the National Economy," in Negrón-Muntaner and Grosfoguel, *Puerto Rican Jam*, 86.

22. Laura L. Ortiz-Negrón, "Space out of Place: Consumer Culture in Puerto Rico," Negrón-Muntaner, *None of the Above*, 40.

23. Ibid., 41–42.

24. For example, Arlene Dávila connects the production of national identity to consumerism in Puerto Rico, showing that big companies that sponsor popular national and local festivals have become sponsors of Puerto Ricanness along with (and often substituting for) more traditional state-sponsored agents, such as the Instituto de Cultura Puertorriqueña. See *Sponsored Identities: Cultural Politics in Puerto Rico* (Philadelphia: Temple University Press, 1997).

25. Mimi Sheller, *Consuming the Caribbean: From Arawaks to Zombies* (London: Routledge, 2003).

26. Daniel Miller, "Anthropology, Modernity and Consumption," in *Worlds Apart: Modernity Through the Prism of the Local*, ed. Daniel Miller (London: Routledge, 1995), 3, 18.

27. Raquel Romberg, "'Today, Changó Is Changó': How Africanness Becomes a Ritual Commodity in Puerto Rico," *Western Folklore* 66, nos. 1/2 (2007): 75–106.

28. Santería, also called *la religión de los orishas* or *la regla de ocha*, is an Afro-Cuban religion. "Ocha" in Spanish and "orisha" in English derive from the Yoruba word for deity, "òrìṣà." Espiritismo refers to the belief in spirits as encoded by the French scientist and man of letters Allan Kardec (1804–69). Its orthodox practice is referred to as *espiritismo científico* (Scientific Spiritism). Yet any follower of espiritismo, whether in its orthodox or popular form, is generally called an *espiritista*. See Romberg, "Whose Spirits Are They?"

29. See Karen McCarthy Brown, *Mama Lola: A Vodou Priestess in Brooklyn* (Berkeley: University of California Press, 1991); K. Brown, "Staying Grounded in a High-Rise Building: Ecological Dissonance and Ritual Accommodation in Haitian Vodou," in *Gods of the City: Religion and the American Urban Landscape*, ed. Robert A. Orsi

(Bloomington: Indiana University Press, 1999), 79–102; Elizabeth McAlister, *Rara! Vodou, Power, and Performance in Haiti and Its Diaspora* (Berkeley: University of California Press, 2002); Karen Richman, *Migration and Vodou* (Gainesville: University Press of Florida, 2005).

30. See David H. Brown, "Altared Spaces: Afro-Cuban Religions and the Urban Landscape in Cuba and the United States," in Orsi, *Gods of the City*, 155–230; D. Brown, *Santeria Enthroned: Art, Ritual, and Innovation in an Afro-Cuban Religion* (Chicago: University of Chicago Press, 2003); Katherine J. Hagedorn, *Divine Utterances: The Performance of Afro-Cuban Santería* (Washington, D.C.: Smithsonian Institution Press, 2001); Stephan Palmié, *Wizards and Scientists: Explorations in Afro-Cuban Modernity and Tradition* (Durham: Duke University Press, 2002); Johan Wedel, *Santería Healing: A Journey into the Afro-Cuban World of Divinities, Spirits, and Sorcery* (Gainesville: University Press of Florida, 2004).

31. See Roger Bastide, *The African Religions of Brazil: Toward a Sociology of the Interpenetration of Civilizations*, trans. Helen Sebba (Baltimore: Johns Hopkins University Press, 1978); Rachel E. Harding, *A Refuge in Thunder: Candomblé and Alternative Spaces of Blackness* (Bloomington: Indiana University Press, 2000); David J. Hess, *Spirits and Scientists: Ideology, Spiritism, and Brazilian Culture* (University Park: Penn State University Press, 1991); Hess, *Samba in the Night: Spiritism in Brazil* (New York: Columbia University Press, 1994); J. Lorand Matory, *Black Atlantic Religion: Tradition, Transnationalism, and Matriarchy in the Afro-Brazilian Candomblé* (Princeton: Princeton University Press, 2005).

32. Doris Sommer, "Puerto Rico a flote: Desde Hostos hasta hoy," *Op. cit* 9 (1997): 253–62.

33. The indeterminate political status of the island under the commonwealth forged a particular variety of cultural nationalism, which strongly draws on primordial ethnic and historical ties and minimizes the jural aspects of national sovereignty. For excellent debates on the ways in which Puerto Rico defies classic definitions of "nation," see Jorge Duany, "Nation on the Move," *American Ethnologist* 27, no. 1 (2000): 5–30; Duany, *The Puerto Rican Nation on the Move: Identities on the Island and in the United States* (Chapel Hill: University of North Carolina Press, 2002); Grosfoguel, *Colonial Subjects*.

34. See Nélida Agosto Cintrón, *Religión y cambio social en Puerto Rico, 1898–1940* (Río Piedras, Puerto Rico: Ediciones Huracán, 1996); Jorge Duany, "La religiosidad popular en Puerto Rico: Resena de la literatura desde la perspectiva antropologica," in *Vírgenes, magos y escapularios: Imaginería, etnicidad y religiosidad popular en Puerto Rico*, ed. Ángel Quintero Rivera (San Juan: Centro de Investigaciones Sociales de la Universidad de Puerto Rico, 1998), 163–85; Samiri Hernández Hiraldo, *Black Puerto Rican Identity and Religious Experience* (Gainesville: University Press of Florida, 2006); Jaime R. Vidal, "Citizens Yet Strangers: The Puerto Rican Experience," in *Puerto Rican and Cuban Catholics in the U.S., 1900–1965*, ed. Jay P. Dolan, and Jaime R. Vidal (Notre Dame: University of Notre Dame Press, 1994).

35. Romberg, *Witchcraft and Welfare*.

36. See Hernández Hiraldo, *Black Puerto Rican Identity and Religious Experience*; Samuel Silva Gotay, "Social History of the Churches in Puerto Rico, Preliminary Notes (Presented at the Ecumenical Association of Third World Theologians, Geneva, July 17–21, 1983)," in *Towards a History of the Church in the Third World*, ed. Lucas Vischer (Bern: Evangelische Arbeitsstelle Oekumene Schweiz, 1985), 53–80; Gotay, *Protestantismo y política en Puerto Rico, 1898–1930: Hacia una historia del protestantismo evangélico en Puerto Rico* (Río Piedras: Editorial de la Universidad de Puerto Rico, 1997).

37. A babalawo is the highest priest in Santería.

38. See Romberg's "From Charlatans to Saviors"; and *Witchcraft and Welfare*.

39. Romberg, *Witchcraft and Welfare*.

40. Orsi, *Gods of the City*.

41. See, for example, Brown, "Altared Spaces"; Brown, "Staying Grounded in a High-Rise Building"; and Brown, *Mama Lola*, for excellent insiders' portrayals of the creative tactics that Santería and Vodou practitioners need to devise in order to turn public and private spaces into new places of worship when they migrate to new urban frontiers. See also McAlister, *Rara!*; Richman, *Migration and Vodou*; Paul Christopher Johnson, *Diaspora Conversions: Black Carib Religion and the Recovery of Africa* (Berkeley: University of California Press, 2007).

42. Arjun Appadurai, *Modernity at Large: Cultural Dimensions of Globalization* (Minneapolis: University of Minnesota Press, 1996).

43. Some Santería houses in Cuba sought not just to "purge" any vestiges of their Catholic colonial past, but also to recover their "authentic" West African Yoruba components. Lázara Menéndez Vázquez characterizes this particular type of "re-Africanization" as "Yorubanization," because it is the Yoruba influence that is being stressed, not just any African influence, in constructing an Afro-creole heritage that allocates a higher cultural currency to Yoruba influences in the African Diaspora. See Menéndez Vázquez, "¿Un cake para Obatalá?!" *Temas* 4 (1995): 38–51. For similar cases in Cuba and the United States, see George Brandon, *Santeria from Africa to the New World: The Dead Sell Memories* (Bloomington: University of Indiana Press, 1993); and Brown, *Santeria Enthroned*. Lorand Matory explores similar processes in Candomblé houses in his *Black Atlantic Religion*.

44. Johnson, *Diaspora Conversions*.

45. Raquel Romberg, "Glocal Spirituality: Consumerism, and Heritage in an Afro-Caribbean Folk Religion," in *Caribbean Societies and Globalization*, ed. Franklin W. Knight and Teresita Martínez-Vergne (Chapel Hill: University of North Carolina Press, 2005), 131–56.

46. Romberg, "Today, Changó Is Changó."

47. Anthony Giddens, *Modernity and Self-Identity: Self and Society in the Late Modern Age* (Stanford: Stanford University Press, 1991), 81.

48. Michael Taussig, "Maleficium: State Fetishism," in *Fetishism as Cultural Discourse*, ed. Emily Apter and William Pietz (Ithaca: Cornell University Press, 1993), 217.

On the phantasmagoria of the fetish, see also Taussig's *The Nervous System* (New York: Routledge, 1992); *Mimesis and Alterity: A Particular History of the Senses* (New York: Routledge, 1993); and *Magic of the State* (New York: Routledge, 1997).

49. In this line, Stephan Palmié, in comments at the Obeah and Other Powers: The Politics of Caribbean Religion and Healing conference, Newcastle, United Kingdom, June 16–18, 2008, noted that in most Caribbean religions there are hidden regimes of accumulation behind healing, rituals of sacrifice, and so forth, and that these add to the reputation, prestige, and ritual authority of religious practitioners. At the same conference, Claudette Anderson argued that this moral economy contrasts with some other religious economies in Jamaica, in which ritual specialists are believed to lose their power if they charge money for their work. This belief also guides the practices of Scientific Spiritists in Puerto Rico; it is used to distinguish "authentic" Spiritism from popular, "inauthentic" forms, such as those practiced by espiritistas-brujos or espiriteros, as they are condescendingly called.

50. This circularity also ties the technologies of magic and their expected effects. For instance, by manipulating certain objects, desired effects are summoned, tying the object of magic through chains of resemblance and contact with its desired effect. I develop this idea in *Healing Dramas: Divination and Magic in Modern Puerto Rico* (Austin: University of Texas Press, 2009).

51. See Claude Lévi-Strauss, "The Sorcerer and His Magic," in *Structural Anthropology*, trans. Claire Jacobson and Brooke Grundfest Schoepf (New York: Basic Books, 1963), 167–85.

52. Michel de Certeau, *The Practice of Everyday Life*, trans. Steven Rendall (Berkeley: University of California Press, 1984).

53. Michael Taussig, *Defacement: Public Secrecy and the Labor of the Negative* (Stanford: Stanford University Press, 1999), 107.

54. Bruce M. Knauft, ed., *Critically Modern: Alternatives, Alterities, Anthropologies* (Bloomington: Indiana University Press, 2002).

55. Although in some cases it might be useful to examine social modernization (the actual organization and management of society) and cultural modernity (the ideological premises that sustain and legitimate social modernization) separately, these processes are purposefully considered here in tandem. See Michel-Rolph Trouillot, "The Otherwise Modern: Caribbean Lessons from the Savage Slot," in Bruce M. Knauft, ed., *Critically Modern: Alternatives, Alterities, Anthropologies* (Bloomington: Indiana University Press), 220–37.

56. See, for example, Richard Drayton, *Nature's Government: Science, Imperial Britain, and the "Improvement" of the World* (New Haven: Yale University Press, 2000); Paul Gilroy, *The Black Atlantic: Modernity and Double Consciousness* (Cambridge: Harvard University Press, 1993); Sidney W. Mintz, *Caribbean Transformations* (New York: Columbia University Press, 1974); David Scott, *Conscripts of Modernity: The Tragedy of Colonial Enlightenment* (Durham: Duke University Press, 2004); Sheller, *Consuming the Caribbean*; Michel-Rolph Trouillot, "The Otherwise Modern."

57. Hayden White, *Metahistory: The Historical Imagination in Nineteenth-Century Europe* (Baltimore: Johns Hopkins University Press, 1973).

58. Bruno Latour, *We Have Never Been Modern*, trans. Catherine Porter (1991; Cambridge: Harvard University Press, 1993).

59. A reviewer of *Witchcraft and Welfare* noted her disappointment that brujería is not depicted as an oppositional practice. See Eileen Moyer, review in *American Ethnologist* 31, no. 1 (2004): 1024–25. I wonder why scholars should have this expectation. Must vernacular religions, by definition, always be expected to openly and intentionally oppose the social order and whatever oppressive, exclusionary systems it entails? Could participation "with an attitude" be entertained as a viable if non-tragic or non-heroic way of accommodation and empowerment? Similar questions have been posed in other ways and contexts by scholars such as J. Lorand Matory (in *Black Atlantic Religion*) and David Scott (in *Conscripts of Modernity*), in their revision of the symbolic inclusions and exclusions of subaltern groups in conceptualizations of the "African Diaspora" versus the "black Atlantic."

60. Michael Taussig, *Shamanism, Colonialism, and the Wild Man: A Study of Terror and Healing* (Chicago: University of Chicago Press, 1987).

61. Ibid., 465.

62. Palmié, *Wizards and Scientists*.

63. Joan Dayan, *Haiti, History, and the Gods* (Berkeley: University of California Press, 1995); Sidney W. Mintz and Michel-Rolph Trouillot, "The Social History of Haitian Vodou," in *Sacred Arts of Haitian Vodou*, ed. Donald J. Cosentino (Los Angeles: Fowler Museum at UCLA, 1995), 123–47.

64. See, for example, Margarite Fernández Olmos and Lizabeth Paravisini-Gebert, *Sacred Possessions: Vodou, Santeria, Obeah, and the Caribbean* (New Brunswick: Rutgers University Press, 1996).

65. Sidney W. Mintz and Richard Price, *An Anthropological Approach to the Afro-American Past: A Caribbean Perspective* (Philadelphia: Institute for the Study of Human Issues, 1976), reprinted as *The Birth of African-American Culture: An Anthropological Perspective* (Boston: Beacon, 1992).

66. See Palmié, *Wizards and Scientists*; and Taussig, *Magic of the State*.

67. See, for example, Jean Comaroff and John L. Comaroff, eds., *Modernity and Its Malcontents* (Chicago: University of Chicago Press, 1993).

68. Peter Geschiere, *The Modernity of Witchcraft: Politics and the Occult in Postcolonial Africa* (1995; trans. Peter Geschiere and Janet L. Roitman, Charlottesville: University of Virginia Press, 1997), 7–8.

69. For a comparative historical treatment of the moral economy of witchcraft in Africa and Europe, see Ralph A. Austen, "The Moral Economy of Witchcraft: An Essay in Comparative History," in Comaroff and Comaroff, *Modernity and Its Malcontents*, 89–110.

70. Adeline Masquelier, "Narratives of Power, Images of Wealth: The Ritual Economy of Bori in the Market," and Mark Auslander, "'Open the Wombs!': The Symbolic

Politics of Modern Ngoni Witchfinding," both in Comaroff and Comaroff, *Modernity and Its Malcontents*, 3–33, 167–92.

71. See Christina Larner, *Witchcraft and Religion: The Politics of Popular Belief* (Oxford: Basil Blackwell, 1984); Alan Macfarlane, *Witchcraft in Tudor and Stuart England* (London: Routledge and Kegan Paul, 1970); H. C. Erik Midelfort, *Witch Hunting in Southwestern Germany, 1562–1684* (Stanford: Stanford University Press, 1972); E. William Monter, *Witchcraft in France and Switzerland: The Borderlands during the Reformation* (Ithaca: Cornell University Press, 1976); Monter, *Ritual, Myth and Magic in Early Modern Europe* (Brighton, United Kingdom: Harvester Press, 1983); Keith Thomas, *Religion and the Decline of Magic: Studies in Popular Beliefs in Sixteenth- and Seventeenth-Century England* (London: Weidenfeld and Nicolson, 1971). Following these lines of inquiry, recent scholarship on early modern witch hunts points to alleged witches (often but not always older women) as scapegoats for the ills of society at a time of rapid and fundamental changes, whether demographic, economic, political, or religious. See, for example, Bengt Ankarloo and Stuart Clark, eds., *Witchcraft and Magic in Europe: The Period of the Witch Trials* (Philadelphia: University of Pennsylvania Press, 2002); Lyndal Roper, *Witch Craze: Terror and Fantasy in Baroque Germany* (New Haven: Yale University Press, 2004).

72. Jean Comaroff and John L. Comaroff, eds., *Millennial Capitalism and the Culture of Neoliberalism* (Durham: Duke University Press, 2001). See also Palmié, *Wizards and Scientists*; Taussig, *Shamanism, Colonialism, and the Wild Man*; Taussig, *Magic of the State*.

73. Jean Comaroff and John L. Comaroff, "Millennial Capitalism: First Thoughts on a Second Coming," in J. Comaroff and J. L. Comaroff, eds., *Millennial Capitalism and the Culture of Neoliberalism* (Durham: Duke University Press, 2001), 23.

74. Ibid., 19.

75. Ibid., 23. In this line, James Howard Smith, in *Bewitching Development: Witchcraft and the Reinvention of Development in Neoliberal Kenya* (Chicago: University of Chicago Press, 2008), presents a close ethnographic account showing how some groups in Kenya have appropriated and made sense of development thought and practice by focusing on the complex ways that development connects with changing understandings of witchcraft and magic.

76. See Martha Kaplan, *Neither Cargo nor Cult: Ritual Politics and the Colonial Imagination in Fiji* (Durham: Duke University Press, 1995); Holger Jebens, ed., *Cargo, Cult, and Culture Critique* (Honolulu: University of Hawai'i Press, 2004).

77. Richard Drayton, in his comments at the Obeah and Other Powers: The Politics of Caribbean Religion and Healing conference, Newcastle, United Kingdom, June 16–18, 2008, also noted the similarity of cargo cults to the quasi-magical ways in which wealth, politics, and modernity are incorporated in some postcolonial religious moral economies in the Caribbean.

78. Michel-Rolph Trouillot, "The Caribbean Region: An Open Frontier in Anthropological Theory," *Annual Review of Anthropology* 21, no. 1 (1992): 19–42.

79. Johannes Fabian, *Time and the Other: How Anthropology Makes Its Object* (New York: Columbia University Press, 1983).

80. George E. Marcus, "The Problem of the Unseen World of Wealth for the Rich," in *Ethnography through Thick and Thin* (Princeton: Princeton University Press, 1998), 152–60.

81. Laurel Kendall, "Korean Shamans and the Spirits of Capitalism," *American Anthropologist* 98, no. 3 (1996): 512–27.

82. Taussig, *Shamanism, Colonialism, and the Wild Man*.

83. Rosalind Shaw, *Memories of the Slave Trade: Ritual and the Historical Imagination in Sierra Leone* (Chicago: University of Chicago Press, 2002).

84. Jean-François Bayart's notion, mentioned in Geschiere, *The Modernity of Witchcraft*, 7.

85. See Palmié, *Wizards and Scientists*; Wedel, *Santería Healing*.

86. Stuart Hall, ed., *Representation: Cultural Representations and Signifying Practices* (London: Sage, 1997), 267.

87. Birgit Meyer and Peter Pels, eds., *Magic and Modernity: Interfaces of Revelation and Concealment* (Stanford: Stanford University Press, 2003).

88. Dilip Parameshwar Gaonkar, ed., *Alternative Modernities* (Durham: Duke University Press, 2001).

89. Bruce M. Knauft. "Critically Modern: An Inroduction," in B. M. Knauft, ed., *Critically Modern: Alternatives, Alterities, Anthropologies* (Bloomington: Indiana University Press, 2002), 3; Latour, *We Have Never Been Modern*, 10, 34.

90. Ibid., 39, 46–48.

91. Gilroy, *The Black Atlantic*.

Afterword

Other Powers:

Tylor's Principle, Father Williams's Temptations,

and the Power of Banality

STEPHAN PALMIÉ

Let me begin with a reflection on the title of this book, *Obeah and Other Powers*, for it strikes me that whatever it is we are talking about here, and whatever the term "obeah" may have meant at any one time, and in any one context, the fundamental epistemological problem we face remains uncannily akin to the way in which the Barbados Council, in 1789, summed up the state of their knowledge about the practice of obeah on the island: "Of their arts," the council members wrote then, "we know nothing."[1] Or do we? Clearly, as Elizabeth Cooper in this collection aptly puts it, apropos the semantic volatility of the term "ñáñiguismo" in late nineteenth- and early twentieth-century Cuba, what we are looking at is neither a "thing" nor a "group," and least of all perhaps a "system" (of beliefs, ritual, or what have you). It is "something in the making—a process—both on the ground and in the official records." Sign and referent, in other words, lead independent lives. What Edwin Ardener called the "language shadows," cast on the pages of our archives by certain "on-the-ground" facts, were already hopelessly compromised by a historiographical version of Heisenberg's dilemma (where every attempt to pin down the object of inquiry obscures the path of its historical morphing and vice versa).[2] What is more, as Lara Putnam points out in this book, the source of our troubles also lies in the fact that the referents of the signifying practices we encounter in our documentation were never simply "natural kinds," but rather "interactive ones," in Ian Hacking's sense.[3] In other words, unlike plants or chemical compounds that remain indifferent to their naming and description, the phenomena in question reacted to their uptake into discourse—at least to some degree, though usually in anything but foreseeable ways. As a result, we are dealing with a tangle of several complexly articulated histories. These consist not only in changing popular practices developing locally and circulating throughout the Caribbean region in the course of post-emancipation migrations, nor merely in the proliferation of representations of such practices that, as Alasdair Pettinger's and Diana Paton's contributions show, by the late nineteenth century had begun to mesh into a densely intertextual discursive formation. Instead, as Putnam argues, "popular practice itself drew on and responded to the construction of knowledge about obeah and other supernatural regimes in print culture." Empirically, we are dealing with a singularly dense mesh of social praxis with its representation.

This is due, to a considerable extent, to the fact that the language deployed to capture such practices was saturated with violently antagonistic intent right from the start, and underwrote no less violent projects of domination. Paradoxical though it may seem, such projects—and the archives they generated—have now become our prime source of evidence on the practices we aim to characterize here. With very few exceptions (such as the highly unusual case of the writings of Henri Dumont discussed by Alejandra Bronfman in this collection), what we are facing is a record of negativity through which we, at times (and whether rightly or wrongly), imagine to discern that which "changed on the ground": those "other powers" whose work within a fundamentally "colonial" and aspirationally "modern" economy of representations not only secured contemporary Western senses of "civilization," "rationality," and so forth, but also bequeathed to us a hopelessly contaminated vocabulary. In fact, this language, as Erna Brodber, Kenneth Bilby, and Karen Richman note (albeit in different ways), nowadays also structures the ambivalence with which the descendants of those to whom colonizers or postcolonial elites attributed such powers (or the belief in them) confront the contemporary transformations of the Afro-Caribbean occult traditions their forbears are said to have originated. The work of historical iniquity thus transforms into the image of the "worker of iniquity"—a figure that (as Bilby points out) present-day Jamaican Rastafarians have come to identify with the moral corruption and spiritual decay of "Babylon" itself.

The result, for the contemporary ethnographer and historian, is a truly transcontinental palimpsest of inter-articulated occult modernities. For the descendants of Caribbean slaves who have begun to opt into rapidly globalizing neo-African religious forms to reclaim the spirituality of their ancestors, Brodber sees a "knowledge vacuum that [makes] positioning themselves in the stream of spiritual history impossible, and that [forces] them to wonder if their newfound spiritual rituals would really lessen the sense of wearing the wrong robes that had driven them out of the Euro-American churches and in search of the African spiritual forms." Living "with burning candles, wearing full white, keeping their heads covered, and leaving plates of food in their yards for the ancestors," young Afro-Caribbean intellectuals in search of a spiritual past still don't "know if they [are] connected with the feared obeah man down the road, formerly the butt of jokes in their friendship networks." Of their ancestors' arts, we might say, they, too, know but little.

How has this situation come about? At least as far as anthropology is concerned, it might be apt here to turn to one of the more tender-minded architects of the vision shaping a good deal of the evidence at our disposal, and briefly revisit Edward Burnett Tylor's conceptions of the "other powers" that underwrote the Victorian rationalism of which we continue to be unwitting heirs. As is well known, Tylor's famous theory of "survivals" hinged on a long-standing syllogism that translated cultural difference not only into degrees of spatial or social distance, but temporal/evolutionary antecedence as well. "The modern educated world," he writes, "rejecting occult science as a contemptible superstition, has practically committed itself to the opinion that magic belongs to a lower level of civilization. It is very instructive to find this judgment undesignedly confirmed by nations whose education has not advanced enough to destroy their beliefs in magic itself. In any country an isolated or outlying race, the lingering survivor of an older nationality, is liable to the reputation of sorcery." What is more, "The usual and suggestive state of things is that nations who believe with the sincerest terror in the reality of the magic art, at the same time cannot shut their eyes to the fact that it more essentially belongs to, and is more thoroughly at home among, races less civilized than themselves."[4] "All this is of one piece," he continues a few pages on, "with the survival of such ideas among the ignorant elsewhere in the civilized world. Many a white man in the West Indies and Africa dreads the incantations of the Obi-man, and Europe ascribes powers of sorcery to despised outcast 'races maudites,' Gypsies and Cagots."[5] In sum, "By a vast mass of evidence from savage, barbaric, and civilized life, magic arts . . . may be traced from the lower culture which they are of, to the higher culture which they are in."[6] Or, as none other than Malinowski put it in one of his lesser-known canards, it is a "well-known truth, that a higher race in contact with a lower one has a tendency to credit the members of the latter with mysterious demoniacal powers."[7]

Of course, Tylor's concept of survivals was, among other things, an effort to make sense of the perplexing wave of occultism washing over Victorian Britain in his day and age.[8] Yet while his contemporary Frederick Engels—who, like Tylor, attended several spiritist séances—was content to write the "fourth dimension" off as a homegrown form of vulgar materialism, there were other issues involved than merely a protracted boundary dispute between "religion" and "science" that had barely been decided in favor of the latter, or the ironies of a dialectic that spiritualized the materialism of what Marx called the religion of everyday life in capitalist society, just as ectoplasmic emanations or table rappings materialized the spirits of the dead.[9] Rather, and given Tylor's reference to the dread inspired by the incantations of the "Obi-man" among otherwise perfectly "advanced" white colonizers, we might pause to note not just the trope of the magical prowess of the subaltern (common in European discourse since Roman antiquity),[10] but also of the ways in which notions of higher civilization, racial superiority, rationality, science, modernity, or even religion have always hinged (and continue to hinge) on the play of what Reinhart Koselleck called "asymmetrical counterconcepts": in our case, that of "other powers," the occult knowledge and sorcerous prowess accorded the other not despite, but precisely because, of his or her mundanely transparent subjugation.[11]

It may thus not be overly far-fetched to argue that just like "voodoo" or "ñáñiguismo,"[12] and indeed the concept of the "fetish," "obeah" is perhaps best approached, at least initially, not as an element of any one particular Afro-Caribbean culture, but as belonging to a rapidly universalizing culture of European colonialism.[13] Not only did Diderot's *Encyclopedie* feature an article (penned by Baron d'Holbach) on "mumbo jumbo,"[14] but at least since the aftermath of the 1760 Jamaican slave rebellion (on which I will have to say a bit more), terms such as "obi," "obia," and later "voodoo" came to energize whole genres of literature cast in what Michael Taussig has aptly called a "colonial hall of mirrors."[15] That Matthew "Monk" Lewis is generally better known for his gothic novels than his posthumously published *Journal of a West Indian Proprietor* should not surprise us here; nor that gothic fiction itself thrived on what Karen Halttunen calls the "pornography of pain" characterizing much popular antislavery literature.[16] By the same token, however, what lent attractiveness to such literary productions (of which Conrad's *Heart of Darkness* was only a particularly crass, though belated specimen) is that their multiple displacements (of agency, power, sadistic intent, and so forth) speak to a frighteningly concrete historical reality: the sheer terror unleashed in the "preservation of civilized order" against what Laënnec Hurbon has called "le barbare imaginaire," a being whose uncanny powers, as Taussig or Margaret Wiener have argued, were not only the creation of, but visceral to, the project of colonial domination.[17] Indeed, as Randall Styers notes with appropriate sarcasm, our own scholarly efforts at separating out and analytically circumscribing objects of knowledge such as "obeah," "voodoo," or "brujería" continue to be haunted by this "logic of disavowal," manifesting itself as it does in "a widespread, explicit consensus among scholars that magic incites antisocial appetites and subversive passions among the dispossessed and thus places good order at risk."[18]

Since I have dealt with this theme to a considerable extent in my book *Wizards and Scientists*, suffice it to say that much of what historians today find themselves working with are the records of what Vincent Brown has aptly called "spiritual terror": the calculated anticipation and imaginary preemption—call it counter-transference, if you will—of African by civilized savagery.[19] What is particularly striking here is that while the violence English planters unleashed in attempting to "seize and manipulate" what they thought were "African visions of the afterlife in an effort to govern the worldly actions of the living," their ghastly actions in dismembering dead slaves corresponded not so much to any clear conceptions of what such "African visions" might be, than to what might "represent a compelling metaphysical threat to English Protestants."[20] Nor is this merely an instance of premodern histrionics of power. If waterboarding finds its earliest documented record in the American campaigns in the Philippines after the conclusion of the Spanish-American War,[21] it might not surprise us that torture by electricity has its precedent in the trial of some Jamaican obeah men in 1760 who, as Bryan Edwards tells us, were submitted to "various experiments . . . with electrical machines and magic lanterns." "After receiving some very severe shocks," Edwards gloats, one of them "acknowledged that his masters' Obi exceeded his own."[22] And there you have it. We do not, of course, know when the term "science" entered Anglophone Caribbean usage as a synonym for assault sorcery.[23] But this instance of eighteenth-century high-tech savagery may well provide an apposite starting point for any inquiry into such matters.[24] Abu Ghraib and Guantanamo, we might say, are older than we think.

Indeed, fast-forwarding to the present may be instructive here. If the "moral artifact" of terrorism has become routinized in Western cultures to the degree where the United States Department of Homeland Security's orange warning signs at U.S. airports are no longer noticed by all but the most infrequent flyers; where the Bush administration's dismantling of habeas corpus would cause little public outcry; or where "harsh" interrogation methods would seem justified in light of that administration's fabulously illogical claim that these have averted several hundred terrorist strikes on American soil, then we might perhaps be facing an analogy worth exploring.[25] Regardless of whether we believe in the reality of evil Muslim conspiracies, we might still welcome that our fellow passengers are made to take their shoes off and have their luggage searched in a rather poorly modernized version of anti-witchcraft screenings. Which is to say that invoking doubt (or reductionism)—principled or otherwise—ill serves us to unravel the luxuriously tangled skein of language games that we find roped up with one another in the historical record at our disposal. To say the very least, as Wittgenstein reminds us, "the game of doubting itself presupposes certainty."[26]

Wiener, who has explored this theme in the context of colonial Java, may have put her finger on a decisive issue when she speaks of the titillations of ineffable certainties on the part of the "civilized" regarding the colonial occult as constituting a "twilight zone."[27] In this zone, inscrutable "other powers" became the frightful equivalent of what metropolitan skeptics like Engels or Tylor could write off into a fantasy world of elemental category mistakes, but which was not so easily put aside for the metropolitan expatriate awash in a sea of nonwhite others. That disincarnate Indian swamis, Negro spirits, or dead Native Americans were turning tables in London, Paris, or Boston was one thing. But that otherwise reliable, rationalist metropolitan witnesses would be swayed toward expressing disbelief in the *nonexistence* of occult power in the colonies was another. Thus, only four years before E. Edward Evans-Pritchard famously told his (lastingly astonished) European audience that he himself had seen witches flying across the night sky in 1927 Zandeland, and then proceeded to rationalize not only the episode but also the entire ontological system within which it could have assumed concrete significance, the American Jesuit Father Joseph J. Williams, in a lecture delivered at the 1934 International Congress of Anthropological and Ethnological Sciences in London—in fact, the same occasion where Evans-Pritchard presented some of the first results of his work among the Azande—took the opposite course.[28] Father Williams is best known for his fanciful, but surprisingly influential, speculations about the origins and etymology of obeah.[29] But on that occasion he decided to confront the demons hovering over the entire debate in a manner reminiscent of the hermeneutics deployed by the Department of Homeland Security under President George W. Bush when it comes to the ontological status of a global terrorist threat. Presenting seven detailed cases of unaccountable phenomena derived from observations of his own and of reliable fellow missionary witnesses in Jamaica, Williams concluded that "the collective evidence, I feel, compels us to acknowledge that we are dealing with preternatural agencies or forces, call them what you will."[30]

In his aptly titled book *Psychic Phenomena of Jamaica*, Williams thus, for example, takes issue with a successful appeal mounted by none other than

Afterword

Norman W. Manley in defense of one Viola Phillips, who had been convicted of practicing obeah. Given that Jamaica's obeah laws at the time penalized the pretense to supernatural power, Manley had apparently argued that "it was necessary, in order to constitute obeah, not merely that a person should do something utterly foolish and futile on a pretence that it would accomplish something, but that they should definitely use occult means or pretend to supernatural power." Yet, since the "framers of the statute did not believe there was any such thing" as supernatural powers involved in "obeah," the statute either forbid something that did not exist, or wrongly criminalized what "might be considered a mere obtaining of money by false pretences."[31] For Williams, this would not do. Like other "educated Jamaicans," Manley, he felt, lacked "appreciation regarding the real attitude of the 'bush' towards witchcraft. The law may assume the impossibility of the fact and stress the pretense at supernatural power," but this did not mean that such powers did not exist. On the contrary, "It is the conviction of the practitioners of obeah that the obeah-man can and does control a super-human influence that can destroy life itself without any physical contacts, and further that this projection of power does not arise from the obeah-man himself."[32]

Well and good. Similar considerations led the panelists at the London congress, such as Evans-Pritchard himself, G. St. J. Orde Brown, or Frank Melland, to the conclusion that "to reason against African belief in witchcraft is useless because intellectually it is perfectly coherent,"[33] or to acknowledge the absurdity of an anti-witchcraft legislation that targeted those who perceived themselves as victims of sorcery,[34] and instead to propose to enlist "the better class witch-doctor" in the project of indirect rule.[35] Of course, as Karen Fields has shown, proposals such as the latter directly implicated the metropolitan skeptic in the reproduction of the very "irrealities" whose proliferation colonial African anti-witchcraft legislation had originally aimed to curtail.[36] Needless to say, British Caribbean anti-obeah laws never produced such legal and political embarrassments—if only because their logic reversed that of colonial African anti-witchcraft legislation in penalizing not the accusers, but rather the alleged perpetrators of mystical assaults.[37] Still, as Manley seems to have perceived, the persecution of imaginary crimes arising from simple category mistakes ("doing something utterly foolish and futile on a pretense that it would accomplish something") would implicate the British colonial juridical system in unwarranted metaphysical arbitrations (did the accused "use occult means or pretend to supernatural powers"?). These, in turn, were likely to produce their own forms of embarrassment—as, for example, when it came to the production of suitably incriminatory evidence. And Manley was right: as the case of Percival Duval recounted by Forde in this collection shows, the assumption that the soil found in a desk drawer of this successful Trinidadian cocoa and cane proprietor and money lender was "graveyard dirt, to be used to access the spirit world," rather than "a sample of soil that his brother was taking to an analyst in order to discover possible traces of oil in his property," was not Duval's, but rather that of the persecutory authorities. Whatever Duval himself may have thought about such matters, and for whatever reasons he had stashed such dirt in his drawer, *they* were the ones who *believed* that he believed in its supernatural potency and so was practicing obeah.

It is precisely this conundrum—highlighted by Slavoj Žižek in his discussion of the "subject supposed to believe"—that the good Father Williams's anguished objections throw into relief.[38] This is so because for Williams, the entire question of belief was a nonissue. Unlike the inspector Herbert T. Thomas, who suspected that his exhibit of confiscated obeah paraphernalia was removed from the 1891 Jamaica International Exhibition because the organizers feared that it encouraged, rather than dissuaded, the audience's belief in occult powers (and so ran counter to the exhibit's secular, modernizing, pedagogical mission; see Paton's contribution to this book), Williams felt "driven to the conclusion that just as in the days of slavery, obeah was too long regarded with amused toleration merely as a foolish superstition devoid of real efficient power to do harm, so to-day there is a tendency in Jamaica to shut the eyes to the nefarious influence of the cult on the entire Negro population of the island, and to regard this practice of the black art as an exuberance of superstition and nothing more."[39] This, however, would be a grave mistake, because "the real menace comes not from the quixotic external practices, professing by a sort of sympathetic magic to control ghosts, to prosper some love affair, or assist in legal disputes and commercial transactions, but from the underlying conviction of the potency of a spiritual force which is nothing more nor less than an assumption that if properly invoked, his Satanic Majesty will exert an efficient directive force in the affairs of man's daily life."[40] Nor is this—and here is the rub—only "an assumption" on the part of deluded would-be sorcerers or their credulous clientele. For Williams, "the Obeah-man is merely an agent of the Evil One who really produces the effects desired in virtue of the incantation of the devotee and the acceptance of the client, both of whom are placing themselves in communication with him in full reliance on his co-operation. The obeah-man only directs the necessary power or force which ultimately comes from the Author of Evil."[41] No wonder then that, according to Williams, even Jamaica's Fabian Socialist governor, Lord Sydney Olivier, had seen fit to mount an inquiry into the nature of Jamaican "poltergeist" phenomena:

When the atmosphere has been properly surcharged electrically, we may anticipate a thunderstorm with all its usual disturbances of wind and rain. So, too, once the obeah-man has created what I might call a diabolic atmosphere in a district, when his communications with the Devil has given His Satanic Majesty some standing in the spiritual life of the community, and the co-operation of the clients of the obeah-man has firmly established a practice which is nothing less than demonolatry, we need not be surprised if the Power of Evil begins to manifest material phenomena, perhaps of the poltergeist type, seeking to weaken church control and so to gradually augment the tendency to evil throughout the district.[42]

Unlike his seventeenth-century predecessor, Père Jean-Baptiste Labat, Williams no longer believed in torturing African demonolatry out of black sorcerers as a method of choice. But he also seems to have felt deeply skeptical of the rationalistic "proofs" of the superiority of the white man's "Obi" obtainable, for example, through the use of "electrical machines and magic lanterns" that Edwards had favored in the eighteenth century. Rather, and much like many a missionary before him, Father Williams was busily translating the devil into something of which he, by his own admission, had neither direct knowledge nor clear understanding, but was deeply convinced existed—ominously lurking in the Jamaican "bush," and manifesting in preternatural occurrences attested to by reliable, civilized witnesses.[43] Note here the difference between the anguish of a metropolitan rationalist like Tylor, or Sir James Frazer's much-quoted warnings that civilized disenchantment merely constituted a "thin crust which may at any moment be rent by the subterranean forces slumbering below."[44] But notice also the contrast to the sheer "ordinariness" of occult dangers that, as Evans-Pritchard or Melland took pains to point out, characterized the life-worlds and moral economies of early twentieth-century Africans, and that—I should add—characterize those of present-day denizens of the Caribbean whose lives and livelihoods remain precarious (see Putnam's chapter in this collection).[45] If obeah and the other powers unleashed by the "Author of Evil" were a reality for Williams—even as he spoke to his (undoubtedly queasy) colleagues at the International Congress in London—was this because he (perhaps mistakenly, but not entirely inappropriately) read the workings of the "Evil One" into the interpretations of social iniquities on the part of those whose everyday experience rendered the presumption that obeah and other powers were at work in and on their lives a rather reasonable proposition?[46] Much as he might have detested a Durkheimian conclusion that the collective representations circumscribing the realm of the occult in late colonial Jamaica would *eo ipso* reflect the moral state of Jamaica's society under British rule, it is nonetheless tempting to read Father Williams's anguished testimony in precisely that way. Could he have foreseen that Forbes Burnham would legalize the practice of obeah in Guyana? That the government of Basdeo Panday was to institute Spiritual/Shouter Baptist Liberation Day and Orisha Family Day as national holidays in Trinidad? Or that Abel Prieto, Cuba's minister of culture, would declare the practice of Afro-Cuban religious traditions as a contribution to the global fight against capitalist cultural imperialism?[47] Could he have even dreamed that, as Richman in this book tells us, Haiti's archbishop would decide to reach out to the once-demonized *gangan ason* in the Haitian countryside, reminding them that they are "still Catholics," and recruiting their powers to the common cause of stemming the tide of evangelical Protestantism? He might. But not on terms that we—as social scientists—might be ready to call our own.

Obviously, the twilight zone opened up by the good Father Williams's temptations are the civilized rationalist's (legal or metaphysical) nightmare come true, and we can only speculate what conclusions Evans-Pritchard might have drawn from Williams's enchanted presentation at the 1934 congress. This is not the place to explore the question of whether belief in occult powers may constitute what we could call, with a nod to Monica Wilson's definition of witchcraft, social science's "standardized nightmare."[48] "Is not everything good fi eat, good fi talk," we might say with Brodber. Yet since the topos of "participation" has played such a tremendous role in the constitution of ethnography as a modernist literary genre, a few remarks are in order.[49] After all, part of the "ethnographer's magic," in Malinowski's terms, has always been to skillfully evoke, but remain outside, what Raquel Romberg (in this book), quoting Anna Tsing, calls "'the margins': those zones of unpredictability at the edges of discursive stability, where contradictory discourses overlap, or where discrepant kinds of meaning-making converge."[50] Of course, Father Williams's case is rather more than a minor nuisance disturbing the discursive stability of social scientific authority, in a manner akin to the fleeting scandal occasioned by the publication of Malinowski's rather ominously Kurtzian *Diary in the Strict Sense of the Term*. Still, it once more points us to the epistemological quandary at the core of this book: unless rationalized as simple fraud and trickery, or written into a reductionist narrative about the social or psychological "function" of occult practices and beliefs, the "other powers" wielded by the subaltern other do not easily yield to "objective knowledge," unless the observer herself adopts the policy of Father Williams (or the U.S. Department of Homeland Security) and agrees to come under its influence.[51]

I hasten to add here that this is by no means to say that Caribbean slaves, peasants, or workers *did not* believe in something called "obeah," "voodoo," or "ñáñiguismo," and on occasion acted on such belief (if "belief" really is the right word here, as Romberg astutely points out). They did—and do, although in ways that largely escape the documentary record,[52] and have yet to be put into proper historiographical and ethnographic perspective.[53] It is to say that much of what our evidence actually tells us is that their masters or social superordinates (including anthropologists) *strongly believed* that slaves, peasants, and workers might believe in such things. This, as Karen Fields has pointed out, does not at all invalidate the reality of the objects of such belief.[54] On the contrary: as "moral artifacts" that *no one* could ignore, beliefs in obeah and other powers (and imputations thereof) structured the texture of everyday life, and so perversely integrated otherwise morally divided social formations in which the obeah man or *bruja* next door were just as "real" for *both* colonizer *and* colonized (although in somewhat different ways) as the astrologer who, to Tylor's dismay, set up shop near his metropolitan home. As semiotic practices aiming to produce their own signifieds, campaigns to suppress barbaric occult practices invariably produced new evidence for the existence of such practices (not just through fraud and entrapment, but also through patterns of deliberate subaltern cooperation with persecutory authorities; see Paton's contribution to this collection). Unsurprisingly, the late nineteenth- and early twentieth-century searches for the "real" *ñáñigos* in Cuba (see Cooper's chapter in this book) sent a police force casting about to pin criminal intent on working-class people supposed to violate "our good customs." They did so by sweeping up just as motley a crowd of suspects as they did in their efforts to construe wildly disparate objects into evidence of a crime the nature of which remained as unknown as it was, in truth, unknowable. But the forensics involved here were merely late permutations of a more general and usually far more violent pattern. As John Savage's account in this collection of the stunning brutality with which planters reacted to an apparent epidemic of poisonings in early nineteenth-century Martinique shows, the violence unleashed by such campaigns was not just a means to an end, but also an end in itself. Given that, in the aftermath, yellow fever and dysentery seem at least as convincing candidates to explain the heightened slave mortality as mystically inspired vengeance, one might well conclude that the wave of slave executions unleashed to contain poison-wielding enslaved sorcerers fueled rather than allayed planters' fears of mystical attack on their lives, enslaved capital assets, and other business interests.

Indeed, given the horrific ironies that Savage's chapter implies, one might venture to say that if one thinks of oneself as in danger of falling prey to campaigns *against* "occult practices" (whether of "primitive" nature or not), it might be a reasonable course of action to acquire ritual protections against such misfortune. We should not forget here that just as the idea of Caribbean subalterns' proclivities toward "obeah" and "voodoo" acquired their ominous salience within European colonial cultures, so must collective representations of European proclivities to unleash repressive violence against presumed practitioners of the "black arts" (or legal fraud, if you will) have entered the cultures of the colonized as well. That contemporary *lucumí*, the ritual language of Cuban *regla de ocha*, features a term such as *el achelú* (meaning "the police" as a source of misfortune to be warded off by apotropaic rituals) would seem to point in no other direction. As does the (rather less dramatic) practice of placing a social security form under an icon of San Judas Tadeo (see Romberg's chapter in this collection), in a fine illustration of Max Weber's notion that the mystifications arising out of bureaucratic rationalization and control call forth their own forms of reactive re-enchantment—if, at times, only as a last ditch effort to render the workings of the "dialectics of modernity" morally comprehensible through forms of symbolic recoding of that which is otherwise too meaningless to bear.[55]

Nor is this only a matter of projections across the interface between metropole and colony (or neo-colony), or the social distance separating elites and subalterns in one and the same society. To briefly elaborate on a particularly striking example, we see the same circular logic at the core of such processes clearly at work in the contemporary Dominican Republic.[56] Here national geography provides an exemplary case in point, materializing the boundaries between civilized self and barbaric other along the line of a notoriously porous (and in many ways imaginary) international demarcation. Perhaps not surprisingly, the vigorous anti-Haitianism in the Dominican Republic combines with no less vigorous traffic in magical powers across the Haitian-Dominican border. To be sure, we might well say that a good part of Dominican nationalism—especially in its most violent aspects—is a symptom of the price Haiti has continued to pay for becoming the world's first nonwhite nation-state, militarily "liberating" the Spanish colony of Santo Domingo, and eventually releasing it into (unwanted and unplanned) nationhood when Spain failed to recolonize the eastern part of Hispaniola. Rafael Trujillo and Joaquín Balaguer certainly did not need Tylor (or Malinowski, for that matter) to tell them why control over the labor power exported by their westerly neighbor could be profitably phrased in terms of a struggle between civilization and barbarism. But it is certainly striking that even such drastic measures as the 1937 massacre of perhaps as many as fifteen thousand Haitian migrant workers in the Dominican Republic did nothing to undermine the perceived utility of Haitian magical imports in the eyes of the Dominican citizenry. On the contrary, and as with obeah in the British Victorian case, Haitian magical prowess is part and parcel of Dominican culture—only that (different from the case of colonial British planters resorting to mutilating their slaves to discourage their belief in ancestral presences, or metropolitan consumers of lurid gothic fiction) residents on the Dominican side of the border can always hitch a ride and buy *pwen* or *wanga* across the international frontier—from people, one should add, whom the majority of them might treat like dogs were they to show up on the wrong side of the border. Again, we might say that the point is really *not* whether Haitians do or don't have access to occult powers superior to those homegrown in the Dominican Republic. Nor is it whether they do or don't sell their Dominican customers "the real deal." It is that what Jean and John Comaroff have called the "violence of abstraction" characterizing the political economic relations between the two nations has generated a cross-border zone of transcultural mercantile semiosis that continues to endow Haitian occult export goods with unrivaled utility.[57]

A similar point could be made concerning the endless fascination the ostensible cultivation of mystical reputations among the politically powerful in the postcolonial Caribbean has exerted on the scholarly imagination. There is, of course, no question that the former country doctor and amateur ethnographer François "Papa Doc" Duvalier purposely crafted for himself an image of occult prowess, replete with zombified political opponents in the National Palace's basement. Nor is there reason to dispute that it "was not lost on the majority of Haitians" that "his dress and nasal voice bore a striking resemblance to Bawon Samdi," or that "Duvalier, likely taking cues from the Bawon, created a paramilitary force that appeared to raid Vodou's closet" by sporting standard-issue sunglasses that made "peasants think they were zombies" (from Katherine Smith's chapter this collection). Yet as Richman's chapter shows, such interpretations thrive on a shortsighted historical logic that fully disregards Duvalier's avid courting of evangelical Protestantism from the United States as a "more powerful sorcerer." What is more, such interpretations potentially also contribute—as in the case of Andrew Apter's Africanizing reading of the occult histrionics of Duvalier's rule[58]—to what Rosalind Shaw might call the "jujuization" of the political issues involved in blatantly Cold War–driven, U.S.-sponsored Third World dictatorships, or the spread of neoliberal silences about the international constellations of business interest fuelling the "deep weirdness" of neo-traditional warlordism in sub-Saharan

Africa and beyond.⁵⁹ That Mobutu liked to sport leopard-skin caps and (like Duvalier) styled himself as a mystically empowered patriarch who killed by law during the day and by witchcraft during the night, explains neither his rise to power nor the endless prolongation of his infamous rule.⁶⁰ Scholarly reveling in such emulations of "other powers" on the part of violent peripheral stooges of core capital interests may do little else than give Tylor's principle a new lease on life by inappropriately harnessing it to spuriously "internalist" explanations of the politics of postcolonial domination.⁶¹ As Robert A. Hill pointed out in his presentation at the conference on which this book is based, Marcus Garvey, ever the shrewd enigmatic operator, seems to have understood the logic underlying this moment better than many of us: while openly castigating the proclivities of his Jamaican constituency toward occult explanations and ecstatic practices, Garvey's famous Atlanta speech leaves little doubt about the complex nature of his intentions. Not only did he cast his failed claim to the "provisional presidency" over Africa in a prophetic idiom of mystical redemption, but he also sought to monopolize secular rationalist interpretations of his transhistorical stature in a manner not altogether dissimilar to Fidel Castro's 1956 evocation of "history" as a redemptive force in his "la história me obsolverá" speech. To be sure, the line is thin. Once properly invoked, history, as Taussig reminds us, can enact its sorcery, too, "disappearing" (in the classic Latin American sense) the past in the very act of its representation.⁶²

We see the latest products of such civilized belief in the savage beliefs of the non-Western other in the discursive contortions the British police and press underwent when, in 2001, the torso of a young black boy washed up on the banks of the Thames in the former core of the British Empire. As Todd Sanders tells the story, not only was the supposition that "ritual murder" by "African witchdoctors" was involved virtually a forgone conclusion in the investigations that ensued; rather, and perhaps even more ominous, the London Metropolitan Police, Scotland Yard, the BBC, and Britain's major dailies immediately embarked on the construction of a vast metonymic chain, linking a mutilated black body to a Yoruba name scribbled on candles wrapped in a white sheet to South African markets in "muti medicines" and on to "followers of *obeh* [*sic*]."⁶³ Guided, one presumes, by a logic stipulating that one place in Africa was as good (or "as witchcraft ridden," for that matter) as any other, Scotland Yard detectives flown to Johannesburg to liaise with South Africa's Occult Crimes Unit, in a bizarre attempt to uncover the facts of "African witchcraft" at the source, were told by a "traditional healer" to look for the perpetrators "in West Africa, from Nigeria onwards."⁶⁴ Worse yet, an (eventually aborted) investigation of a Nigerian asylum seeker in Glasgow, undertaken to prove that the boy was a "child slave" taken to Britain for the express purpose of ritual slaughter, produced "strange voodoo-like items" in the suspect's home, including "several objects associated with curses, including whisky jars containing chicken feathers"—in other words, the same kind of "evidence" that allowed persecutory agents, in virtually all the cases discussed in this book, to objectify their own belief in other people's occult beliefs.

Alas, a DNA test of the suspected woman cleared her of any forensically relevant connections to the case (at least in the eyes of the investigators looking for the boy's West African blood relatives who, or so they presumed on South African advice, would have sacrificed their own child). But her asylum application failed, and she was eventually deported to Nigeria. Sanders, who steers clear of putting the case in its historical context,[65] nevertheless identifies three moments that we might also do well to ponder: (1) the sheer reduction of African witchcraft to a unitary phenomenon affecting the entire continent in an undifferentiated manner; (2) the reduction of people of African descent to equally undifferentiated vectors of "savage" and "sinister" belief, capable and willing to act on these even in civilized Britain; and (3) the role of globalization in bringing about this deplorable state of affairs. As the vice chairman of the London Metropolitan Police Independent Advisory Group noted, "We are talking about either witchcraft, ju-ju, or voodoo. . . . In promoting cultural diversity we import the good and the bad. If this is a ritual killing then unfortunately—as bad as it may sound—we have imported those aspects of culture into mainland Britain."[66] I do not think I need to waste many words on the resonances of this case, multiple and truly disgusting as they are, with the matters of concern to this book. If anything needed to be added here, it is that what the press and British police subsumed under "globalization" had been a long time in the making. All that the London Met, Scotland Yard, BBC, and the press achieved was to once more succumb to, and write forward, the syndrome Tylor had diagnosed more than a century ago. That they wrecked the lives of several people in the process (such as that of the Nigerian woman in Glasgow) may have been a small price to pay for the defense of European civilization against the "other powers" now emanating from the council estates of urban mainland Britain's burgeoning immigrant neighborhoods.

We finally move on then from the "banality of power" to the "power of banality." At the conference on which this collection is based, the analytical necessity for such a switch in emphasis was, perhaps, most clearly articulated in a presentation by Kate Ramsey. This was so because Ramsey purposively circumvented the sterile and misleading practice—so common in this line of research—to set "voodoo" apart from what ostensibly is not "voodoo": Haitian law, American military directives, persecutory campaigns, the prurient exoticism of popular travelogues and United States Marine memoirs, indignant reactions from the Haitian elite, or early zombie films (which, one needs to add, hit the American silver screen just as the circulation of "wish you were here" photo postcards of lynchings in the U.S. South reached its zenith).[67] Instead, Ramsey folded them all into a total scenario—a strategy that allowed her to monitor the emergence of a thoroughly hybrid, and multiply overdetermined, moral artifact that, regardless of whether we want to call it "voodoo" was the product of what Bruno Latour might call the conjunction of several uneasily articulated strategies of "purification."[68] Clearly, whichever way you want too look at it, "bad magic" was proliferating in U.S.-occupied Haiti—and not just because Haitian peasants driven off their land by local comprador elites and into chain gang road work, or abusive labor contracts in American-owned sugar mills, were beginning to compare their lot with that of *zonbis*, or arming themselves with new forms of commodified counter-magic.[69] Rather, we see Tylor's principle go into effect once more in the agency of U.S. Marines slashing confiscated drums. They did so, Ramsey argued, not only because they fetishized them as instruments of "both ritual and revolution," but because their "maddening effect" on white people had been "known" since the time of Moreau de St. Mèry's admission, on the eve of the Haitian Revolution, that whites lurking in the bushes on the periphery of the orgiastic "vaudoux" rites, which he described in lurid detail, were prone to being plunged into trance themselves![70] But, of course, defaced ritual implements were among the less gruesome artifacts by means of which the occupation forces conjured "voodoo" into being. For every officer's casino or hotel bar story—such as John Houston Craige's bizarre account of the cannibalization of Sergeant Lawrence Muth at the hands of Benoît Batraville's Caco troops—there is, it seems, a documented version of U.S. Marines creating an archive of terror in the name of order and progress, such as the photographs they took of Batraville's commander Charlemagne Péralt after they had nailed his corpse on the door of a Haitian police station.[71] Again, the misadventures of Private Lynndie England in Abu Ghraib seem merely a technologically enhanced, fast-forwarded version of a much older syndrome.

What is fascinating about this archive is that it is frighteningly coextensive with what we nowadays are inclined to see as the first (more or less) disciplined ethnographic endeavors in the region. To be sure, Melville Herskovits ultimately seems to have rejected the services as a professional expert informant that Craige tried to offer him after they first met in 1928. Yet however much this may have stung Craige—who appears to have wished to add a scientific imprimatur to his lucrative publishing and lecturing career as an expert on Haitian savagery, it is striking that apart from two passing references concerning massive military engagements in the Mirebalais Valley during the Caco uprising, and the mass destruction of ritual objects shortly before Herskovits's arrival, his monograph *Life in a Haitian Valley* completely disregards what Ramsey aptly called the "affirmative logic and productive effects" of legal and extralegal strategies aiming to produce "voodoo" as an object of recognition and annihilation.[72] Indeed, the closest Herskovits ever came to describing the historical sorcery that had gone into the making of twentieth-century Haitian culture was when he noted, in the introduction of this book, that the "liberty tree" in Mirebalais's central square bore not only an inscription to the memory of the nineteenth-century Haitian military hero Pierre Cazimir de Vincent, duc de Mirebalais, but also a crude graffiti that an American Marine had cut deep into the tree shortly after the end of the fighting in the region. It reads:

> L. MARLOW
> AUG. 1ε, 1920
> U.S.M.C
> DRUNK
> AS
> HELL
> J. F. BROWN

We might take this as an apt testimony to the banality of power. But in the context of Herskovits's—by all means well-intended—book, it also testifies to the power of banality in the ethnographic inscriptions produced by him and many other practitioners of my craft. Clearly, by authorizing reified, ahistorical, and sheer endlessly iterable ethnographic counter-images to the malign swirl of imperial tropes that came to envelop the more exotic aspects of social life in the Caribbean ever since the time of Moreau de St. Mèry, Bryan Edwards, and Matthew "Monk" Lewis, they "purified" them once over (in Latour's sense), and so made sure that Tylor's principle would not come to haunt (or unduly titillate, for that matter) their readership. In that sense, they did more to obscure than to illuminate the other powers at work within the representational economies in which they participated, along with rural Haitians or Jamaicans, residents of the Dominican border zone, urban working-class Cubans, American occupational troops, international hack writers, movie producers, Jesuit priests, and local elites bent on salvaging the "civilized modernity" of their nations while often drawing tangible benefits from the denigration of racialized lower-class practices as primitive savagery.

It is pleasing to think, though perhaps not overly realistic to assume, that our contemporary reflexive sensitivities might inoculate us against perpetuating their mistakes. Obviously, there is a real danger that the anthropology of Afro-Caribbean cultures might degenerate into an omphaloscopical historical anthropology of Afro-Caribbean ethnography.[73] Yet it seems to me that if there is a single remedy to our further complicity in a naively ill-conceived, if not, at times, outright hypocritical, anthropological or historical empiricism, then it lies in our initial, principled concurrence with the disarmingly frank admission of the members of the 1789 Barbados Commission. When it comes to those who partake of obeah and other powers, it would behoove us, too, to concede that "of their arts we know [next to] nothing." That way, we might stand a chance of actually learning something.

To come to such a conclusion may seem overly pessimistic. But it need not be read in such a way. On the contrary, the virtue of the chapters gathered in this collection is that they do not, as Terence Ranger has charged in a related context, proceed from the assumption, so characteristic of colonial and postcolonial witch hunters, that "we know it when we see it," and then conveniently proceed to explanations that might fit slave poisonings in the nineteenth-century French Caribbean (real or imagined) just as much as early twentieth-century searches for the "real ñáñigos," "obeah men," and alleged child sacrificers—or, for that matter, late twentieth-century healers in Tobago or neo-brujas in Puerto Rico.[74] The numinous worlds of the Caribbean past or present are neither monolithic, nor unchanging, nor even necessarily "supernatural" (in the contemporary secular rationalist sense of the term). And it is only upon confusing names such as "obeah," "voodoo," and "ñáñiguismo" with the multifarious and historically changing practices to which they seem to refer that we could come to render them visible to us as such. Unless accompanied by stringent efforts at establishing historical specificity and local distinctiveness, such visibilization of the Caribbean "occult," I would argue, will remain little else than a spurious and misguided updating of Tylor's (let alone Father Williams's) views on the matter. If, in this sense, this book contributes to advancing our knowledge of obeah and other powers, it does so perhaps as effectively in pointing out what we, in fact, do not (and possibly cannot) know, as in outlining and contextualizing the shady contours of what the data at our disposal more often tend to hide than reveal to us.

NOTES

1. Cited in Jerome S. Handler, "Slave Medicine and Obeah in Barbados, circa 1650 to 1834," *New West Indian Guide* 74, nos. 1/2 (2000): 69.

2. Edwin Ardener, *The Voice of Prophecy* (Oxford: Blackwell, 1989).

3. Ian Hacking, *The Social Construction of What?* (Cambridge: Harvard University Press, 1999).

4. Edward B. Tylor, *The Origins of Culture*, vol. 1 of *Primitive Culture* (New York: Harper, 1958), 113.

5. Ibid., 115.

6. Ibid., 116.

7. Bronisław Malinowski, *The Sexual Life of Savages in Northwestern Melanesia* (New York: Halcyon, 1929), 199.

8. George Stocking, "Animism in Theory and in Practice: E. B. Tylor's Unpublished 'Notes on Spiritualism,'" *Man* 6, no. 1 (1971): 88–104; Peter Pels, "Spirits of Modernity: Alfred Wallace, Edward Tylor, and the Visual Politics of Fact," in *Magic and Modernity: Interfaces of Revelation and Concealment*, ed. Birgit Meyer and Peter Pels (Stanford: Stanford University Press, 2003), 241–71.

9. Frederick Engels, *Dialectics of Nature* (New York: International Publishers, 1971); Peter Harrison, "'Science' and 'Religion': Constructing the Boundaries," *Journal of Religion* 86, no. 1 (2006): 81–106; Jacques Derrida, *Specters of Marx* (New York: Routledge, 1994); Willy Maley, "Spectres of Engels," in *Ghosts: Deconstruction, Psychoanalysis, History*, ed. Peter Buse and Andrew Stott (New York: Macmillan, 1999), 23–49; Tomoko Masuzawa, "Troubles with Materiality: The Ghost of Fetishism in the Nineteenth Century," *Comparative Studies in Society and History* 42, no. 2 (2000): 242–67.

10. Including, as Peter Brown points out, the early Christians. See "Sorcery, Demons, and the Rise of Christianity from Late Antiquity to the Middle Ages," in *Witchcraft: Confessions and Accusations*, ed. Mary Douglas (London: Tavistock, 1970), 17–45.

11. Reinhart Koselleck, *Futures Past* (Cambridge: MIT Press, 1985).

12. A note of clarification may be in order: here, and in the following, I am using terms such as "voodoo" and "ñáñiguísmo" not in reference to practices nowadays more correctly designated as Vodou and Abakuá, but to colonial and other Western representations of such practices.

13. On "the fetish," see William Pietz, "The Problem of the Fetish, I," *Res* 9 (Spring 1985): 5–17.

14. John Lough, *Essays on the Encyclopédie of Diderot and D'Alembert* (London: Oxford University Press, 1968), 165.

15. See Michael Taussig, *Shamanism, Colonialism, and the Wild Man* (Chicago: University of Chicago Press, 1987); Alan Richardson, "Romantic Voodoo: Obeah and British Culture, 1797–1807," *Studies in Romanticism* 32 (1993): 3–28. See also John Savage's chapter in this collection.

16. Matthew Lewis, *Journal of a West India Proprietor, 1815–1817* (London: Rout-

ledge, 1929); Karen Halttunen, "Humanitarianism and the Pornography of Pain in Anglo-American Culture," *American Historical Review* 100, no. 2 (1995): 303–34; Joan Dayan, *Haiti, History, and the Gods* (Berkeley: University of California Press, 1995).

17. Laënnec Hurbon, *Le barbare imaginaire* (Paris: Editions du Cerf, 1988); Taussig, *Shamanism, Colonialism, and the Wild Man*; Margaret J. Wiener, "Hidden Forces: Colonialism and the Politics of Magic in the Netherlands Indies," in: Meyer and Pels, *Magic and Modernity*, 129–58; Margaret J. Wiener, "Dangerous Liaisons and Other Tales from the Twilight Zone: Sex, Race, and Sorcery in Colonial Java," *Comparative Studies in Society and History* 49, no. 3 (2007): 495–526.

18. Randall Styers, *Making Magic: Religion, Magic, and Science in the Modern World* (New York: Oxford University Press, 2004), 16. Or, as he states elsewhere in more analytical language, "Scholarly debates over magic regularly turn on questions of social order. Issues of class, authority, and social control have been central components of theoretical formulations of magic commonly configured as the province of women, children, foreigners, primitives, and other deviants. The rhetoric of magic's self-seeking, irrationality, and futility reverberates with broader gender and racial ideologies, both lending its weight to those ideologies and taking on greater resonance through them. Magic is invoked as a marker of social difference, and by highlighting magic's preoccupation with power, the efforts of socially marginal actors to obtain or exert power is overtly stigmatized. At the same time, with the theme of power deflected onto magic, the forms of control exercised by the dominant classes are eclipsed and naturalized. . . . Modern theories of magic have regularly conformed with the interests of dominant groups, both in configuring an unruly and benighted colonial periphery and in stigmatizing marginal groups within the domestic population" (223).

19. Stephan Palmié, *Wizards and Scientists: Explorations in Afro-Cuban Modernity and Tradition* (Durham: Duke University Press, 2002); Vincent Brown, "Spiritual Terror and Sacred Authority in Jamaican Slave Society," *Slavery and Abolition* 24, no. 1 (2003): 24–53.

20. Brown, "Spiritual Terror and Sacred Authority," 27.

21. Paul A. Kramer, *The Blood of Government: Race, Empire, the United States, and the Philippines* (Chapel Hill: University of North Carolina Press, 2006), 140–43.

22. Bryan Edwards, *The History, Civil and Commercial, of the British Colonies in the West Indies* (London: G. and W. B. Whittaker, 1819), 2:119.

23. Donald Hogg, "Magic and 'Science' in Jamaica," *Caribbean Studies* 1, no. 2 (1961): 1–5.

24. After all, none other than Benjamin Franklin (who had plenty of experience with electrocuting turkeys and other animals) participated in the French Royal Commission charged with "the examination of animal magnetism as now practiced at Paris." See *Report of Dr. Benjamin Franklin and Other Commissioners Charged by the King of France with the Examination of the Animal Magnetism as Now Practiced at Paris: Translated from the French with an Historical Introduction* (London: J. Johnson, 1785). Although the report discredited Franz Mesmer's theories of magnetic fluid, by then

mesmerism had arrived in Saint-Domingue with the French cartographic mission of 1784. And as early as 1785, Jean Trembley reported that a "plantation owner on [the Artibonite] plain made a big profit in magnetizing a consignment of cast-off slaves he bought at a low price. Restoring them to good health by means of the [mesmeric] tub, he was able to lease them at prices paid for the best slaves." Cited in James E. McClellan, III, *Colonialism and Science: Saint Domingue in the Old Regime* (Baltimore: Johns Hopkins University Press, 1992), 178; see also Brown, "Spiritual Terror and Sacred Authority in Jamaican Slave Society," 38n86. For the further career of electrocution in the service of humanitarianism, see Iwan Rhys Morus, "A Grand and Universal Panacea: Death, Resurrection, and the Electric Chair," in *Bodies/Machines*, ed. Iwan Rhys Morus (Oxford: Berg, 2002), 93–123; Michael B. Schiffer, *Draw the Lightning Down: Benjamin Franklin and Electrical Technology in the Age of Enlightenment* (Berkeley: University of California Press, 2003).

25. Karen E. Fields, "Political Contingencies of Witchcraft in Colonial Central Africa: Culture and the State in Marxist Theory," *Canadian Journal of African Studies* 16, no. 3 (1982): 567–93; Colin Dayan, "Legal Terrors," *Representations* 92 (2005): 42–80.

26. Ludwig Wittgenstein, *On Certainty* (New York: Harper and Row, 1972), 115. Risking serious anachronism by further extending this riff on eighteenth-century analogies, we might say that the Obama administration's vexations about how to deal with prisoners who cannot be tried on U.S. soil because their confessions were extracted under torture, will turn those inmates of Guantanamo into true twenty-first-century global obeah men: liminal figures whose dangerousness consists not in any proved illegal acts but in the extralegal nature of the technologies of violent proof production applied to them. See Elaine Scarry, *The Body in Pain: The Making and Unmaking of the World* (New York: Oxford University Press, 1985).

27. Wiener, "Dangerous Liaisons and Other Tales from the Twilight Zone."

28. Edward E. Evans-Pritchard, *Witchcraft, Oracle and Magic among the Azande* (Oxford: Oxford University Press, 1937).

29. Namely, as a degenerate New World "survival" of aspects of Asante religion: given that slavery inhibited the continuation the public cult of higher deities and destroyed their priesthood, so Williams argued, what emerged was the proliferation of hypertrophied versions of the secretive magical practices of witch doctors who, in Africa, had been held in check by the legitimate priesthood. See Joseph J. Williams, *Voodoos and Obeahs: Phases of West India Witchcraft* (New York: Dial, 1932).

30. Joseph J. Williams *Psychic Phenomena of Jamaica* (New York: Dial, 1934), 21.

31. Ibid., 135–36.

32. Ibid., 139–40.

33. Edward E. Evans-Pritchard, "Witchcraft," *Africa* 8 (1935): 421.

34. G. St. J. Orde Brown, "Witchcraft and British Colonial Law," *Africa* 8 (1935): 486.

35. Frank Melland, "Ethical and Political Aspects of African Witchcraft," *Africa* 8 (1935): 503.

36. Fields, "Political Contingencies of Witchcraft in Colonial Central Africa."

37. Diana Paton, "Obeah Acts: Producing and Policing the Boundaries of Religion in the Caribbean," *Small Axe* 13, no. 1 (2009): 1–18.

38. Slavoj Žižek, *The Plague of Fantasies* (London: Verso, 1997).

39. Williams, *Psychic Phenomena of Jamaica*, 106.

40. Ibid.

41. Ibid., 140.

42. Ibid., 258.

43. Birgit Meyer, *Translating the Devil: Religion and Modernity among the Ewe in Ghana* (Trenton, N.J.: Africa World Press, 1999). In a passage uncannily reminiscent of Evans-Pritchard's attempts to acquire firsthand knowledge of Azande magic, Williams candidly admits, "time and again I sought to draw out in conversation the professional obeah-men, but I invariably found them evasive and non-committal. As occasion offered, I closely questioned youngsters who, according to common report, were apprenticed to obeah-men as disciples to acquire the art, but they had already learned their lesson of secrecy and I could make no impression on them. I repeatedly watched a black boy whom I knew well, the son of a notorious obeah-woman, as he stood motionless for long periods staring straight into the sun,—a sure indication that he was in preparation for the practice of obeah, yet despite the fact that I remunerated him generously for trifling errands and otherwise strove to win his confidence, I never succeeded in gaining from him any information of value. It was only from disillusioned clients of obeah-men who shame-facedly made admissions connected with their own experiences, that I was really able to gather directly any reliable facts." Williams, *Psychic Phenomena of Jamaica*, 4–5. See also Evans-Pritchard, *Witchcraft, Oracle and Magic among the Azande*, 202–57.

44. James G. Frazer, *Man, God, and Immortality: Thoughts on Human Progress* (London: Macmillan, 1927), 219.

45. Evans-Pritchard, *Witchcraft, Oracle and Magic among the Azande*; Melland, "Ethical and Political Aspects of African Witchcraft."

46. If so, he would have turned the logic animating Taussig's thesis about the devil and commodity fetishism effectively on its head. See Taussig, *The Devil and Commodity Fetishism in South America* (Chapel Hill: University of North Carolina Press, 1980).

47. Stephan Palmié, "The Cuban Republic and Its Wizards," in *Permutations of Order: Religion and Law as Contested Sovereignties*, ed. Thomas Kirsch and Bertram Turner (Aldershot, United Kingdom: Ashgate 2008), 67–84.

48. Monica Wilson, "Witch Beliefs and Social Structure," *American Journal of Sociology* 56 (1951): 307–13; Jeanne Favret-Saada, *Deadly Words: Witchcraft in the Bocage*, trans. Catherine Cullen (Cambridge: Cambridge University Press 1980); Katherine Ewing, "Dreams from a Saint: Anthropological Atheism and the Temptation to Believe," *American Anthropologist* 96, no. 3 (1994): 571–83.

49. Marilyn Strathern, "Out of Context: The Persuasive Fictions of Anthropology," *Current Anthropology* 28, no. 3 (1987): 251–81.

50. See Anna Lowenhaupt Tsing, "From the Margins," *Cultural Anthropology* 9, no. 3 (1994): 279.

51. One of the more intelligent and subtly argued refusals comes from the folklorist Jane C. Beck, who recorded the life history of a self-declared St. Lucian obeah man who claimed not only to be dealing with the devil (whatever he meant by that) on a regular basis, but also to have killed a neighbor through defensive sorcery. See *To Windward of the Land: The Occult World of Alexander Charles* (Bloomington: Indiana University Press, 1979), 271–74. See also Jean-Pierre Olivier de Sardan, "Occultism and the Ethnographic I: The Exoticizing of Magic from Durkheim to 'Postmodern' Anthropology," *Critique of Anthropology* 12 (1992): 5–25; Peter Pels, "The Magic of Africa: Reflections on a Western Commonplace," *African Studies Review* 41, no. 3 (1998): 193–209; and Harry West, *Ethnographic Sorcery* (Chicago: University of Chicago Press, 2007) on the epistemological conundrums presented by "suspensions of disbelief" in ethnographies of the occult.

52. See particularly Putnam's remarks in her chapter in this collection about the moral credibility of early twentieth-century child sacrifice rumors. No doubt—and just like Latin American organ stealing rumors, Andean pishtako tales, or East African vampire firemen—the moral universes in which such rumors congealed into believable "facts" have to be calibrated in light of *very real* dangers suffusing everyday life for members of Caribbean lower classes that print-mediated elite visions helped congeal into what Evans-Pritchard might have called "secondary elaborations of belief." More obviously, perhaps, regardless of how much some of us may keep repeating the mantra that "race is a social construction," for the victims of racism the belief that race is a category mistake will have little to commend for itself. See Nancy Scheper-Hughes, "Theft of Life: The Globalization of Organ-Stealing Rumors," *Anthropology Today* 12, no. 3 (1996): 3–11; Nathan Wachtel, *Gods and Vampires: Return to Chipaya* (Chicago: University of Chicago Press, 1994); Mary Weismantel, *Cholas and Pishtacos: Stories of Race and Sex in the Andes* (Chicago: University of Chicago Press, 2001); Luise White, *Speaking with Vampires: Rumor and History in Colonial Africa* (Berkeley: University of California Press, 2000).

53. See Hildred Geertz, "An Anthropology of Religion and Magic, I," *Journal of Interdisciplinary History* 6, no. 1 (1975): 71–89; Stuart Clark, "French Historians and Early Modern Popular Culture," *Past and Present* 100, no. 1 (1983): 62–99; Adam Ashforth, *Madumo: A Man Bewitched* (Chicago: University of Chicago Press, 2000); West, *Ethnographic Sorcery*.

54. Fields, "Political Contingencies of Witchcraft in Colonial Central Africa"; Fields, "Witchcraft and Racecraft: Invisible Ontology and Its Sensible Manifestations," in *Witchcraft Dialogues*, ed. George C. Bond and Diane M. Ciekawy (Athens: Ohio Center for International Studies, 2001), 283–315.

55. Max Weber, *Economy and Society*, ed. Guenther Roth and Claus Wittich (Berkeley: University of California Press, 1978), 506.

56. See, for example, Lauren Derby, "Haitians, Magic, and Money: *Raza* and Society in the Haitian-Dominican Borderlands, 1900 to 1937," *Comparative Studies in Society and History* 36, no. 3 (1994): 488–526; Samuel Martínez, *Peripheral Migrants: Haitians and Dominican Republic Sugar Plantations* (Knoxville: University of Tennessee Press, 1995); Richard Turits, "A World Destroyed, a Nation Imposed: The 1937 Haitian Massacre in the Dominican Republic," *Hispanic American Historical Review* 82, no. 3 (2002): 589–635.

57. Jean Comaroff and John Comaroff, "Occult Economies and the Violence of Abstraction: Notes from the South African Postcolony," *American Ethnologist* 26, no. 2 (1999): 279–303.

58. Andrew Apter, "On African Origins: Creolization and *Connaissance* in Haitian Vodou," *American Ethnologist* 29 (2002): 233–60.

59. Rosalind Shaw, "Robert Kaplan and 'Juju Journalism' in Sierra Leone's Rebel War: The Primitivizing of an African Conflict," in Meyer and Pels, *Magic and Modernity*, 81–102.

60. Michael G. Schatzberg, *The Dialectics of Oppression in Zaire* (Bloomington: Indiana University Press, 1988).

61. To be sure, I have come across many intelligent people—both in Miami and Cuba—who deeply believe that Fidel Castro's charisma has mystical sources. But while I would not discount such beliefs as irrational at all, I simply do not think they are adequate for explaining the history of the past fifty years of Cuban socialism. For my own take on such matters, see Stephan Palmié, "*Fascinans* or *Tremendum*? Permutations of the State, the Body, and the Divine in Late-Twentieth Century Havana," *New West Indian Guide* 78, nos. 3/4 (2004): 229–68.

62. Michael Taussig, "History as Sorcery," *Representations* 7 (1984): 87–109; Steven Feierman, "Colonizers, Scholars, and the Creation of Invisible Histories," in *Beyond the Cultural Turn*, ed. Victoria E. Bonnell and Lynn Hunt (Berkeley: University of California Press, 1999), 182–216; Stephan Palmié, "Slavery, Historicism, and the Poverty of Memorialization," in *Memory: Histories, Theories, Debates*, ed. Susannah Radstone and Bill Schwartz (New York: Fordham University Press, 2010), 363–75.

63. Todd Sanders, "The Torso in the Thames: Imagining Darkest Africa in the United Kingdom," in *Auto-Ethnographies: The Anthropology of Academic Practices*, ed. Anne Meneley and Donna J. Young (Peterborough, Ontario: Broadview, 2005), 126–42; see also Terence Ranger, "Scotland Yard in the Bush: Medicine Murders, Child Witches, and the Construction of the Occult: A Literature Review," *Africa* 77, no. 2 (2007): 272–83.

64. Sanders, "The Torso in the Thames," 128.

65. The reflections of both Putnam (in this book) and myself (in *Wizards and Scientists*) about African child sacrifice in the New World would have been pertinent to his argument.

66. Quoted in Sanders, "The Torso in the Thames," 135.

67. The fact that George Romero's reinvention of the 1930s zombie genre in *Night of the Living Dead* and its sequels has occasionally been read as a commentary on the civil rights and black power movements of the 1960s seems highly relevant here.

68. Bruno Latour, *We Have Never Been Modern* (Cambridge: Harvard University Press, 1993).

69. Karen Richman, *Migration and Vodou* (Gainesville: University Press of Florida, 2005).

70. Médéric Louis Elie Moreau de Saint Mèry, *Description topographique, physique, civile, politique et historique de la partie francaise de l'isle Saint-Domingue* (Paris: Librairie Dupont, 1797).

71. John Houston Craige, *Cannibal Cousins* (New York: Minton, Balch, 1934); John D. Kuser, *Haiti: Its Dawn of Progress after Years in a Night of Revolution* (Boston: R. G. Badger, 1921), 28–29; Bernard Diederich and Al Burt, *Papa Doc: The Truth about Haiti Today* (New York: Avon and Burt, 1969), 40.

72. Melville J. Herskovits, *Life in a Haitian Valley* (Garden City, N.Y.: Doubleday, 1937).

73. See Brian Brazeal, "Dona Preta's Trek to Cachoeira," in *Africas of the Americas*, ed. Stephan Palmié (Leiden: Brill, 2008), 223–53.

74. Ranger, "Scotland Yard in the Bush."

Contributors

KENNETH BILBY is the director of research at the Center for Black Music Research, Columbia College Chicago, and research associate in the Department of Anthropology at the Smithsonian Institution. He is the author of *True-Born Maroons* (University Press of Florida, 2005) and coauthor (with Peter Manuel and Michael Largey) of *Caribbean Currents: Caribbean Music from Rumba to Reggae* (Temple University Press, 1995, 2006). His current projects include a comparative reexamination of practices and beliefs coming under the rubric of obeah, and a comparative study of the Jankunu festival. The two parallel projects draw on a wide range of ethnographic and other underused kinds of data to provide new perspectives on both the historical and contemporary significance of these highly charged cultural manifestations in various parts of the Caribbean.

ERNA BRODBER was born in 1940 in rural Jamaica. She studied at the University College of the West Indies, later University of the West Indies, and worked there as a researcher and lecturer. She has taught at universities in the Caribbean, the United States, and Europe. She is the author of several books and papers in fiction and nonfiction, including *Myal*, the winner of the Commonwealth Writers' Prize in 1989. She is currently working on a set of essays called *African American/African Caribbean Relations, 1782–1944*, as well as a novel called *Nothings Mat*.

ALEJANDRA BRONFMAN is an associate professor in the Department of History at the University of British Columbia in Vancouver. She is the author of *Measures of Equality: Social Science, Citizenship, and Race in Cuba, 1902–1940* (University of North Carolina Press, 2004) and *On the Move: The Caribbean since 1989* (Zed Books, 2007). Her current research revolves around a book project, *Talking Machines: Histories of Sound, Violence, and Technology in the*

Caribbean, that records the unwritten histories of radio and related sonic technologies in the Caribbean.

ELIZABETH COOPER is based in the Americas Department at the British Library. Her research and teaching address the interrelated histories of European colonialism; slavery and slave emancipation; race and racism; expressive culture and popular politics in the nineteenth- and twentieth-century Atlantic world, with a focus on the Caribbean and Brazil. She is currently at work on a book, *Of Things and Souls*, that tells the history of why new constructions of Africa emerged in Brazil in the period immediately following the abolition of chattel slavery and the declaration of the republic. The project engages one of the most enduring and perplexing historical problems of the twentieth century—the interconnected development of racial ideology and the nation-state—through an investigation into the uses, meanings, and struggles over African culture and identity.

MAARIT FORDE is a lecturer in the Department of Liberal Arts at the University of the West Indies, St. Augustine. Her research interests in Caribbean anthropology have centered on religion and migration, and she has published journal articles and book chapters on the Spiritual Baptist religion, transnational ritual practice, and the government of religion. She is currently engaged in a research project on death and mortuary rituals in the Caribbean.

STEPHAN PALMIÉ is a professor of anthropology at the University of Chicago. His research centers on Afro-Cuban religious formations and their relations to a wider Atlantic world, conceptions of embodiment and moral personhood, practices of historical representation and knowledge production, biotechnology, and constructions of race. He is the author of *Das Exil der Götter: Geschichte und Vorstellungswelt einer afrokubanischen Religion* (P. Lang, 1991) and *Wizards and Scientists: Explorations in Afro-Cuban Modernity and Tradition* (Duke University Press, 2002), and editor of *Slave Cultures and the Cultures of Slavery* (University of Tennessee Press, 1995) and *Africas of the Americas: Beyond the Search for Origins in the Study of Afro-Atlantic Religions* (Brill, 2008). He is coeditor of *Empirical Futures: Anthropologists and Historians Engage the Work of Sidney W. Mintz* (University of North Carolina Press, 2009) and a five-volume critical edition of C. G. A. Oldendorp's late eighteenth-century manuscript on the history of the mission of the Moravian Brethren in the Danish Virgin Islands (2000–10).

DIANA PATON is a reader in Caribbean history at Newcastle University. She is the author of *No Bond but the Law: Punishment, Race, and Gender in Jamaican*

State Formation, 1780–1870 (Duke University Press, 2004), coeditor of *Gender and Slave Emancipation in the Atlantic World* (Duke University Press, 2005), and editor of *A Narrative of Events, since the First of August 1834, by James Williams, an Apprenticed Labourer in Jamaica* (Duke University Press, 2001), as well as the author of articles in journals including *Small Axe, Gender and History,* the *Journal of Social History,* and *Slavery and Abolition.*

ALASDAIR PETTINGER is an independent scholar based in Glasgow. He is the editor of *Always Elsewhere: Travels of the Black Atlantic* (Cassell, 1998) and has published a number of essays reflecting his (overlapping) interests in travel literature, the cultures of slavery and abolitionism, and representations of Haiti. His current projects include a study of Frederick Douglass's visit to Scotland in the 1840s and a history of the word "voodoo" in English.

LARA PUTNAM is an associate professor of history at the University of Pittsburgh. She is the author of *The Company They Kept: Migrants and the Politics of Gender in Caribbean Costa Rica, 1870–1960* (University of North Carolina Press, 2002) and multiple essays on migratory restriction and black internationalism in the interwar Greater Caribbean. She is concluding a book titled *Radical Moves: Caribbean Migrants and the Politics of Race in the Jazz Age* (University of North Carolina Press, forthcoming).

KAREN RICHMAN is the author of *Migration and Vodou* (2005), a multi-sited ethnography of a transnational Haitian community, and of numerous articles and book chapters on Haitian and Mexican migration, family, religion, and expressive culture. She won the 2009 Heizer Award for her article "Innocent Imitations? Mimesis and Alterity in Haitian Vodou Art." She is the director of Academic Affairs and the Center for Migration and Border Studies at the Institute for Latino Studies at the University of Notre Dame.

RAQUEL ROMBERG teaches anthropology at Temple University and is the author of *Witchcraft and Welfare: Spiritual Capital and the Business of Magic in Modern Puerto Rico* (2003) and *Healing Dramas: Divination and Magic in Puerto Rico* (2009), both published by the University of Texas Press, as well as several articles and chapters on Afro-Latin religions, spiritism, possession, and creolization. She is currently engaged in bridging her previous ethnohistoric and ethnographic work on Latin American spiritism with the broader issue of Western mysticism and magic, particularly the fusing of science and spirituality in constituting modern, progressive subjectivities.

JOHN SAVAGE is an associate professor of history at Lehigh University, where he teaches modern European and Atlantic world history. He has published research on France's Caribbean slave society in *Citizenship Studies*, *French Historical Studies*, and the *Journal of Social History*, and has recently coedited the volume *Napoleon's Atlantic: The Impact of Napoleonic Empire in the Atlantic World* (2010). He is currently working on a manuscript that examines the implementation of the Napoleonic Code in the French colonies of the Caribbean during the final phase of slavery.

KATHERINE SMITH is currently a Mellon-Cogut Postdoctoral Fellow in Africana studies and history of art and architecture at Brown University. Her research focuses on religious frameworks for understanding displacement, death, and regeneration in Port-au-Prince. She has studied urban Vodou and contemporary Haitian art for more than ten years. Through extensive ethnographic research, Katherine's dissertation, "Gede Rising: Haiti in the Age of Vagabondaj," examined historical transformations of the trickster spirit Gede in the visual and embodied cultures of Vodou. Katherine's recent publications include contributions to *e-misférica*, the *Southern Quarterly*, and *Kanaval: The Photography of Leah Gordon*. In 2012, Katherine will cocurate an exhibition of post-earthquake art titled "Haiti in extremis: Vodou Arts at the Crossroads" at the UCLA Fowler Museum.

Index

abakuá, 221, 235. *See also* Lucumí
abolition, 13, 82, 105, 149, 222
accumulation, 29, 199–200, 206–7, 282, 302, 304–6
Admiral Bailey, 50
Africa: inventions of, xi, 11, 13–14, 18, 284
Africa (journal), 173
AfricAmerica, 123
African continuities, 17–18, 172, 200, 247
African mysticism, 159, 161–62
Afro-Cubans, 17, 90, 173, 220, 224–26, 229
Afro-Jamaican religion, 47, 177
agents provocateurs, 202–3, 208
Age of Revolution, 87–88
Ainsi parla l'oncle (Price-Mars), 16
Akan, x
d'Alaux, Gustave, 81–82
All Men Are Mad (Thoby-Marcelin and Marcelin), 271
Ally, Sheik, 51
Anacaona, 84, 89
ancestors, x–xi, 47, 56, 58–59, 66–67, 231, 305, 317–18; Gede and, 121, 126
ancestral anger, x, xii
ancestral power, 49
An Anthropological Approach to the Afro-American Past (Mintz and Price), 18
anthropology, 3, 14, 35 n. 37, 105; America and, 23, 114–15; Brazil and, 23;
Cuba and, 23, 103–5, 114; economic, 198–99; France and, 105, 115; Karl Polanyi and, 198; religion and, 106. *See also* Dumont, Henri
Antigua, 1–2, 24, 250
anti-Semitism, 245, 255–56, 262
archive, 103, 316–17, 331
Aristide, Jean-Bertrand, 135–36, 143 n. 51
Artists of Resistance (Atis Rezistans), 121, 123, 126, 134; Mario Benjamin and, 123; Nasson (Camille Jean) and, 123, 138–39. *See also* Eugene, André
authenticity, search for, 21–22, 30, 67, 92, 96, 225, 232, 246, 273, 283–84, 312 n. 49
Aya Bombé, 84–85, 87

Bahamas, 63, 76
Barbados, 18, 52, 157, 201, 212, 243
Barbados Council, 316, 333
barbaric, Caribbean religion defined as, 6, 14, 16, 233, 318, 326–27
Bastide, Roger, 20
Bawon, 121–22, 125, 127, 132, 139 n. 2, 142 n. 32. *See also* Gede
Beckwith, Martha, 13, 180–81, 194 n. 42. *See also* anthropology
Belgian Congo, 89–91. *See also* Bourgeois, René
Black Jacobins, The (James), 86–88

black magic, 160, 244–46, 254
blood, 112–13, 244, 255–57, 260, 262
body, African, 160–62, 255; Gede and, 125, 129, 133, 137–38
Bongo, 47
Bourgeois, René, 91–94
Brathwaite, Kamau, 20–21
Brazil, 22, 68, 105; Penal Code (1890), 16
British Guiana. *See* Guyana
brujería, in Cuba, 8, 16–17, 114–15, 173, 225, 252–53; in Puerto Rico, 5, 25, 203, 206–7

cabildos, 221, 234
Cable, George Washington, 82. *See also* chants
calypso, 49, 52, 64–65, 72 n. 21, 73 n. 25, 203
Candomblé, 16, 293
cannibalism, 12, 27, 34 n. 33, 254–56
capitalism, 5, 20, 96, 198, 200, 213, 248, 305; consumer, 28–29, 206–7, 292, 297. *See also* welfare capitalism
cargo cults, 304–5, 314 n. 77
carnival: in Cuba, 227–29; in Haiti, 126–27, 272; in Trinidad and Tobago, 79 n. 66
Castellanos, Israel, 103, 106–7, 114–16
Catholicism: Cuba and, 223; Haiti and, 16, 94, 158, 268–70, 272–75, 279–82, 284; Jean Cuvelier and, 89; Puerto Rico and, 292–93; symbolism of, 20–21, 25, 234, 289
Céleur, Jean-Hérard, 121–24. *See also* Artists of Resistance (Atis Rezistans)
chants, 82, 85–90, 94–95, 97
charlatan, obeahman as, 53, 179, 194 n. 35, 204–6, 211, 218 n. 45, 268, 295–96
Chéf Seksyon (sculpture), 127–31, 133, 138. *See also* Eugene, André
Chevannes, Barry, xi, 141 n. 19

children, 91, 95, 105, 211, 244, 250, 330; Children's Resistance, 123; in Cuba, 230–31; in Haiti, 123, 125–26, 128, 131, 136, 138, 140 n. 15, 279, 283; tales of ritual murder of, 254–62, 333, 338 n. 52
China, 5, 175, 243
Christianity, 7, 14, 21, 62, 115, 246, 281, 283
citizenship, 96, 106–7, 116, 205, 220, 227, 229, 290
class: hierarchy of, 115, 136–37, 172–73, 178–80, 189–90, 194 n. 34, 221–23; power relations and, 7, 25, 153, 175, 233–34, 252, 303–4, 322, 326, 333
climate, theories of disease and, 162–64
Cold War, 328
Colonialism: British, xi, 3, 13, 111–12, 176, 322; Dutch, 59–60, 67, 95, 290; French, 66, 81, 158, 270; Spanish, 221, 224, 236 n. 5, 292–93
Columbus, Christopher, 11, 256
commodity exchange, 198, 206–7, 211
conspiracies: Aponte (1812), 222; La Escalera (1844), 222
consumerism, 291–93, 297, 309 n. 24
conversion, 11–12, 20, 26, 58, 67, 268, 276–81, 293–94
Convince (Bongo), 47–48
Costa Rica, 247, 253. *See also* ritual specialists
Craige, John Houston, 331–32
Creole: as ethnic term, 19, 59, 66, 82, 157–58; languages, 60, 139, 145 n. 64, 162, 250, 275, 277; religions, 30, 289, 293–94, 296
creolization, 19–21, 25, 156–57, 162, 234, 289, 303, 307 n. 6
cross-dressing, 228, 233
Cuba: Antionio Maceo and, 224; Cubanidad, 221, 236; Free Womb Law of 1871, 222 in; Grito de Yara and, 235; Havana, 220–26; Manuel de Cés-

pedes and, 236; *ñáñiguismo* and, 221, 223–26, 231, 233–35, 316; palo and, 5, 9; penal code (1900) in, 227–28; plantations in, 103, 109; race and, 221, 227, 230, 235; Rafael Roche y Monteagudo and, 233; *regla ocha* and, 5, 7; slave emancipation and, 220; slavery and, 105; social science and, 104; war for independence in, 220–26, 236. *See also* carnival; ritual specialists

Cuba primitiva (Bachiller y Morales), 84

cultural reclamation, 49, 61, 64–65

cultural reproduction, 19, 21–22, 26, 30

Cuvelier, Jean, 89–92, 94

Dagara, x

d'Alaux, Gustave, 81–82

dance, 13, 27, 81–82, 136, 155, 168 n. 30, 175, 227, 229, 256, 283

dancehall, 49, 54–58, 74 n. 40, 77, 79

Delamardelle, Baron, 150

de Laurence, Lauron William, x, 23, 68

De l'égalité des races humaines (Firmin), 15

Description topographique, physique, civile, politique et historique de la partie Française de l'isle Saint-Domingue (Moreau), 13

Dessalines, Jean-Jacques, 84, 87

Dessalles, Pierre, 162–63. *See also* poisoning

diablito costume, 225, 228, 235–36, 237 n. 23

Dillon, Leonard, 54, 73 n. 31

disease: in Americas, 105–6; Gede and, 138; livestock and, 159, 163–64; slaves and, 160–64, 255; swelling and, 109, 111, 113; tropical, 108–9, 161. *See also* yellow fever

divination, 30, 207, 209, 289, 299, 301

Dolly, Charles (obeah defendant), 210, 261

Dominica, 3, 20

Dominican Republic, 24, 84, 132, 243, 326–28

Donzelot, General François-Xavier, 150–51, 167 n. 9

Draytons Two, 52

Drouin de Bercy, Louis Marie Cesar Auguste, 83–85, 87, 89

drumming, 35 n. 43, 226, 230, 232, 234, 236, 247, 256, 279

drums, 83, 234, 331

Dr. Zozo (sculpture), 133–34, 138, 143 n. 47. *See also* Eugene, André

Dumont, Henri, 103, 107–12, 114–15. *See also* anthropology

Dunham, Katherine, 17

duppies, 17, 46, 60–62, 71 n. 6, 176, 179, 188, 251, 257

Duval, Percival (obeah defendant), 201–3, 207–8, 210

Duvalier, François, 10, 127, 141 n. 24, 143 n. 49, 274–75, 328–29

Duvalier, Jean-Claude, 127–29, 135, 283

Edwards, Adolph, x

Edwards, Bryan, 13–14, 34 n. 32, 320, 324, 332

Eh! eh! Bomba hen! hen! (chant), 13, 80–82, 86, 88, 90, 95–97

El Mundo (newspaper), 225, 228

emancipation, 86, 105, 220, 234–36, 280, 317

Enlightenment: view of religion in, 6; writings of, 161

entrapment, 10, 172, 183–84, 186, 189, 197 n. 71, 201–4, 217 n. 28, 326

Estado Libre Asociado (ELA), 293

ethnicity, 21–22, 25, 67, 113–14, 116, 155–57, 233, 254

Eugene, André, 121, 124, 129, 136–37; Children's Resistance, 123. *See also* Artists of Resistance (Atis Rezistans); Gede

evil, 46, 54–55, 61, 67, 75 n. 45, 179, 190, 200, 208, 257, 277, 323–24
exhibitions. *See* Great Exhibition (1851); Jamaica International Exhibition (1891)
exoticism, 15, 24–28, 97, 255, 262, 332

family, 150, 231, 252, 293, 296; Gede and, 121, 126–27, 132, 139 n. 2, 140 n. 18
Fantasías indígenas (Pérez), 84
fetishism, 14, 27, 90, 246, 306; as African, 176–77; commodity and, 291, 297
Firmin, Anténor, 15
flogging, 261
folklore, 17, 128, 269, 273
Folk-Lore (journal), 179, 181
folk religion, 21, 273–74, 283
fraud, spiritual work perceived as, 53, 201, 208, 211
Frazer, James G., 7, 14
Freda, Ezili, 129. *See also* Gede
French Guiana, 47, 58, 65–66
Froudacity (Thomas), 15
Froude, James Anthony, 14, 16, 256–57

Garvey, Marcus, 26, 329
Gede: *Bawon* and, 121, 125; *Chéf Seksyon*, 127, 129; *Dr. Zozo*, 133–35, 138; Fet Gede, 126, 136; Gran Brijit, 131; Kouzin Zaka and, 127; *lakou* and, 126; lwa Ezili Freda and, 129; masculinity and, 135–36; Papa Doc, 127; as spirit of the people, 122, 125; as *vagabon*, 123, 126
gender, 7, 25, 52, 113, 115, 127, 129, 131, 175, 304, 335 n. 18. *See also* masculinity
ghosts, 184, 187, 297, 323. *See also* duppies
gift exchange, 198, 211–13
globalization 33 n. 19, 305, 330
Graham, Leo, 51, 72 n. 19. *See also* Jamaica

Great Exhibition (1851), 175, 192 n. 12
Grenada, 20, 24, 32 n. 16, 203, 250
Grito de Yara, 235
Guadeloupe, 12, 21, 150, 157, 159, 169 n. 38
Guérin, Théophile, 81
Guianese Maroons, 67–68. *See also* Maroons
Guinea, 206, 210, 305
Guyana, 21–22, 24, 32 n. 16, 51, 73 n. 23, 108, 201, 325
Guyane. *See* French Guiana

Haiti: Catholicism in, 269–275; chants from, 80, 84; earthquake of 2010 in, 29, 99 n. 32; Faustin Solouque and, 81; human rights and, 87; Léogâne and, 268; Port-au-Prince and, 121, 124; Protestantism in, 269–275; religious conversion and, 268; Revolution of 1804 and, 81, 269–70; slave rebellion of 1791 and, 90; Vodou and, 269–72, 274. *See also* Saint-Domingue; violence
Harmit, Francis (obeah defendant), 185. *See also* Jamaica
Haydée, 294, 296, 298–300
healing: African, 153; Afro-Caribbean, 112; blood and, 255–56, 260; payment for, 206, 211; ritual and spiritual, 21, 47, 69, 178, 183–84, 201–2, 208, 212, 244, 281, 290, 292, 294–95; slavery and, 106, 113–14; witchcraft and, 153
hegemony: cultural 50, 205; of the United States, 269, 272, 291
Herskovits, Melville, 17–18, 20, 114, 331–32
heterogeneity, 11, 17, 20, 22–23, 27, 229, 243, 248, 261
Hinduism, 8, 10, 15, 21
History, Civil and Commercial, of the British Colonies in the West Indies (Edwards), 13
History of Jamaica (Long), 13

Hosay massacre (Trinidad), 15, 22, 35 n. 41
Howe, Thomas (obeah defendant), 3–4, 31 n. 2
Hugo, Victor, 149–50
Hurston, Zora Neale, 17

Igbo, 156–58
I Maroon, 46
imprisonment, 1–3, 12, 24, 136, 152, 184, 188, 202, 212, 224, 230, 236 n. 5, 253, 336 n. 26
independence: in Cuba, 106, 227, 229; Cuban war for, 220–26; in Haiti, 149; in Jamaica, 49; in Puerto Rico, 293, 306, 315 n. 86
India, 5, 14–15, 21, 111, 173, 177
Indians in the Caribbean, 5, 14–15, 18, 21–22, 23, 35 n. 40, 38 n. 81, 243–44, 251, 262
industrialization, 18, 137, 290
iniquity, 46, 50–51, 54, 317
initiation, 13, 89, 92, 151, 156, 211, 223, 294
International Slavery Museum, 123
Islam, 23, 115
Island of My Life, The (Riou), 272

Jacques, Frantz (Guyodo), 121. *See also* Artists of Resistance (Atis Rezistans)
Jamaica: "Black Candle" (Graham) and, 51; John Scott and, 184; musical representations of obeah in, 50, 53–54, 56–58, 60, 62, 71 n. 4, 72 n. 21, 74 n. 34, 75 n. 48, 77 n. 55, 78 n. 65; obeah arrests in, 175, 182–84, 251; "Science Again" (Bailey) and, 50; spiritual practitioners in, 47–48, 178–79, 185; views on obeah in, 46–48, 62 69. *See also* entrapment; ritual specialists; Thomas, Herbert J.
Jamaican International Exhibition (1891), 173–78, 323

Janvier, Louis Joseph, 272
Jarvis, Cornelius (obeah prisoner), 3
Journal of a West Indian Proprietor (Lewis), 319
Journal of the Society of Comparative Legislation, 181

kanga, 91–93
King Ja-Ja (obeah defendant), 248–49
Kingsley, Charles, 14, 249
kinship, 199, 206; ritual, 211; transnational, 252
Kouzin Zaka, 128
Kumanti (Kromanti) tradition, 58

Labat, Jean-Baptiste, 12–13, 324
Laborde, Jean de, 158–59. *See also* superstition
labor rebellions (1930s), 18
Lachatañere, Rómulo, 8
lakou, 121–22, 126, 131, 141 n. 19
La Phalange (newspaper), 270–71
Las Casas, Bartolomé de, 12
de Laurence, Lauron William, x, 23, 68
Lavison, Rufz de, 163–64. *See also* poisoning
law, x, 16, 88, 124, 172–73, 187–88, 190, 196 n. 60, 201, 208, 222–23, 237 n. 8, 322, 331; Brazilian Penal Code (1890), 16; Free Womb Law (Cuba, 1871), 222; Jamaican Obeah Law (1898), 173; Leeward Islands Obeah Law (1904), 1, 261; Moret Law of 1870 (Cuba), 105; Puerto Rico and Section 936 of U.S. Internal Revenue Code, 290; Shouters Prohibition Ordinance (Trinidad and Tobago), 9, 16; Spiritist, 295, 299–302
Leeward Islands, 1, 181, 194 n. 42, 261
Léogâne, 268–70, 272–73, 284. *See also* Haiti
Lescot, Elie, 272
Lévy-Brühl, Lucien, 14

Index 349

Lewis, Matthew "Monk," 319
Liebig, Justus, 112
Lima Valdes, Alejandro, 110
literacy, 227, 275
Liverpool, Hollis, 65, 77 n. 60
Long, Edward, 13
Louis XVIII, 152
Love, Robert, 15
Lovindeer, Lloyd, 58
Lucumí, 8, 110, 303, 327
lwa, 5, 7–8, 25–26, 94, 125, 277–78, 280
lynching, 254, 331

McKay, Tony, 62–64, 75, 76 n. 15
Mad Professor, 63–64, 77 n. 57
Magik, 206
Malinowski, Bronislaw, 318, 325, 327
Manichean theology, 50
Manley, Norman W., 322–23
Marcelin, Frédéric, 82, 97
Marcelin, Pierre, 271
Marley, Robert Nesta, 46, 62
Maroons: Guianese, 67–68; Ndyuka, 45, 65–67, 78 n. 65; Saramaka, 60, 65; Surinamese, 45, 58, 65, 68
Martinique, 12–13, 21, 149–51, 156–58, 165; deportation to, 21, 152; Igbo in, 156–57; peddlers and, 154–55; white planters' views of obeah in, 151–53, 156–58, 161, 166
Marx, Karl, 124
Marxism, 25, 318
masculinity, 123, 127, 130–32, 137–38
Mbumba, 91–93
medicine: Cuban, 23; French 104, 106, 109; herbal, 47, 62, 154, 160, 165, 294; slave, 62, 76, 104, 108–16, 149, 165–66; tropical, 108–9, 111
Melanesia, 200–201, 305
memory, 221, 231
mesmerism, 24, 28, 335–6 n. 24
mestizo, 12, 33 n. 26, 224, 235, 243

methodology, 6, 106, 182, 245–46, 308 n. 12, 316, 325
Métraux, Alfred, 277
Mighty Chalkdust, 64
Mighty Sparrow, 52, 74 n. 41
migration, 24, 243, 247, 250, 252
Mintz, Sidney, 18–19, 40, 107–8, 118, 215–16, 303, 312–13
missionaries, 12, 15, 21, 47, 50, 81, 89, 275–76, 278, 321, 324
modernism, 86
modernity, 26–27, 107–8, 175, 205, 248, 280, 319; capitalism and, 28, 199, 213; as pirated, 298–302; of witchcraft, 304–5
Moise, Leopoldine (obeah defendant), 208
Monchy murder, 259–62
money, 198–99, 201, 211, 213. *See also* Trinidad and Tobago
Monsieur Toussaint (Glissant), 97
Montané, Luis, 103
Montané Anthropological Museum, 232
Moreau de Jonnès, Alexandre, 165
Moreau de Saint-Méry, Médéric Louis-Elie, 13, 80, 89, 94
Moret Law of 1870 (Cuba), 105
Morton, John, 15
Music: ancestral power and, 48–49; as antisocial sorcery, 50, 61; as challenging hegemonic views, 70; "The Coming of the Obeah Man" (Mad Professor), 63–64; dancehall, 54–58; "Exuma, the Obeah Man" (McKay), 62–64; evil representations of obeah in, 58; Hollis Liverpool, 65; "Madjo So We Madja" (Sangrafu), 59; "Neighbour Working Obeah" (Sheik Ally), 51; "Obeah Book" (Dillon), 54; "Obeah, Obeah" (McKay), 63; "Obeah Wedding" (Mighty Sparrow), 52; "The Oil" (Lovindeer), 58; politics

and, 65; positive representations of obeah in, 56, 59, 61–62, 65; representations of obeah men in, 53, 63; Romeo Murphy and, 75 n. 46; "Samfie Man" (Pioneer), 53; "Sang Versé" (Obia), 65; "Scratch" (Perry), 62; Surinamese, 59–60; "Try Obeah" (Mighty Chalkdust), 64; tying a lover and, 52; use of humor in, 51, 58, 60, 64; Wyclef Jean and, 145 n. 64
mutual aid societies, 156, 222, 227. See also *cabildos*
myalism, 13, 27, 76, 195, 205

ñáñiguismo, 10, 25, 221, 223–27, 229–36, 316, 319, 326, 333. See also Cuba
Nasson (Camille Jean). See Artists of Resistance (Atis Rezistans)
nationalism, 20–21, 122, 272, 283
Ndyuka Maroons, 45, 65–67, 78 n. 65. See also Maroons
neoliberalism, 139, 199, 291, 300, 328
New Orleans, 82, 109
New Orleans as It Was (Castellanos), 82
newspapers, 243, 245–46, 258; *Daily Mirror*, 261; *El Mundo*, 225, 228; *Gleaner*, 176–78, 182, 184, 187, 257; *Guardian*, 29; *New York Times*, 257, 262; *Port of Spain Gazette*, 201, 203–4
Nine-Day William (ritual specialist), 61
Nouveau Voyage aux Isles de l'Amerique (Labat), 12–13

oaths, 87–88, 151
obeah: as African, 245; capitalist economy and, 203–6; cultural confusion and, 46–47; cultural expressions of, 45; of exchange relationships, 206; Maroons and, 47, 68; policing of, 10, 15, 30, 172–74, 180–81, 186–90, 201; as sorcery 11, 24, 47–48, 50–51, 61, 69, 73, 93, 150, 153; as spiritual force, 45–46;

as supernatural, 6, 173, 201, 243, 245, 247–48. See also obeah defendants
Obeah Act, 1904 (Leeward Islands), 1, 261
obeah defendants, 24, 184, 186–89, 201–5, 207, 210, 275
"Obeah in the West Indies" (Udal), 181
Obeah Law, 1898 (Jamaica), 182, 190 n. 5
obeah practitioners. See ritual specialists
obeah trials, 23, 161; in Jamaica, 172, 182, 185, 187, 189, 195 n. 51, 197 n. 76, 197 n. 80, 320; in Tobago, 248; in Trinidad, 201–5, 210
obi, 150–51, 162
obia, 47–48, 58–60, 67, 69, 70 nn. 1–2, 75 n. 44, 78 n. 65, 319
Obia (rap group), 65–66, 71 n. 11, 78 n. 62
obiya. See obeah
occult economy, 304–5
oil industry, 18, 24, 202–4, 252, 323
Orisha religion, 7, 20, 22, 29–30, 77 n. 55, 209, 211–12, 325
Ortiz, Fernando, 16, 89, 94, 103, 106, 173

Padmore, Henry (obeah defendant), 203, 208
Palmié, Stephan, 231, 233, 303, 312 n. 49
Pané, Ramón, 12
Partido Independiente de Color, 221
Patterson, Orlando, 13
peasant: economy, 220, 269, 272; society, 206, 273, 276–77, 326, 328, 331
Pentecostalism, 275, 277, 280, 295
Pérez, José Joaquín, 84
Perry, Lee "Scratch," 62
phallocentrism, 122–25, 129, 132–33
Phalange, La (newspaper), 270–71
photography, 1–3, 124, 126, 331
physicians, 106, 110–12, 161, 299
pioneers, 53, 73 n. 28
Plácido (Gabriel de la Concepción Valdés), 222

plantations: as industry, 24, 26, 28, 159, 200, 269, 294, 308 n. 8; medicine and, 13, 104, 109–14, 153–54, 165; as a society, 20, 81, 104, 155. *See also* poisoning

Platt Amendment, 229

poetry, 84, 86, 222

poisoning, 12, 150–66, 167 n. 11, 169 n. 38, 247, 255–58; Pierre Desalles and, 162–63; in Restoration era, 151–52

Polanyi, Karl, 198. *See also* anthropology

policing, 10, 15, 30, 172–74, 178, 180–81, 186–90, 191 n. 7, 191 n. 8, 201, 217 n. 27; Irish model of, 189. *See also* Thomas, Herbert J.

politics, 29, 246, 256; in Cuba, 17, 25, 227, 229, 234, 236, 260; cultural, 30, 221–22; in Haiti, 91, 127, 133–37, 143, 144 n. 52, 144 n. 58, 269–70, 278, 283; identity, 21, 30, 296; in Martinique, 149; in Puerto Rico, 290–93, 304–6; in Trinidad and Tobago, 64–65. *See also* citizenship

Présence Africaine (magazine), 91. *See also* Bourgeois, René

Prézeau-Stephenson, Barbara, 123. *See also* AfricAmerica

Price, Richard, 18–19

Price-Mars, Jean, 16–17, 273

print culture, 243–46, 249, 254, 259, 262, 317

Psychic Phenomena of Jamaica (Williams), 321. *See also* Williams, Joseph

Puerto Rico, 3, 5, 25, 84, 108, 132, 206, 290–93, 296, 302, 305–6. *See also* ritual specialists

Pullen-Burry, Bessie, 13

race, 7, 24–25, 86, 96, 103, 158, 173, 244–46, 318; anthropology and, 104, 106–7; medicine and, 109, 111, 162, 255–56, 260. *See also* ñáñiguismo

racism, 14–15, 86, 95, 221, 229, 234, 273, 338 n. 52

Ramsey, Kate, 133, 330–32

Rastafarianism, 46, 48, 61–62, 68, 70

rationalism, 272, 318–19, 321, 324–25, 329

rationality, 41 n. 101, 317

reciprocity, 198, 209, 213, 236, 277

religious plurality, 19, 21, 24, 115

resistance: colonialism and, 283, 303, 308 n. 8; creolization and, 9; cultural, 63, 66, 91; slavery and, 85, 110, 153, 166; vagrancy and, 133

Restoration era (France), 151–53, 157, 166

Revista Bimestre Cubana, 103. *See also* Castellanos, Israel

Richardson, Alan, 165

Riou, Roger, 271–72

ritual exchanges: between human and spirits, 206–7, 212; of money, 198–205, 208, 211; social relations and, 207–9

ritual murder, 254–61

ritual piracy, 25, 289

rituals: of healing, 21; of sacrifice 21

ritual specialists, 3, 7, 10, 22–24, 26, 47, 58–59, 247, 254, 263 n. 2; in Costa Rica, 250; in Cuba, 225–27, 229, 231–36; in Haiti, 8, 16, 29, 32 n. 12, 80; in Jamaica, 47–48, 53, 58, 65, 75 n. 48, 172–73, 178, 182–88, 191 n. 6, 196 n. 60, 196 n. 69; in Puerto Rico, 8, 16–17, 22, 25, 114–15, 173, 203, 206–7, 225, 252–53, 260; in Trinidad, 201–13, 213 n. 1, 217 n. 33

Robinson, May, 179–80

Robinson, Mother Cleorita, 209–10, 212

Roche y Monteagudo, Rafael, 220, 233–34. *See also* Cuba

romantic literature, 149, 165

Saint-Domingue, 80, 82, 87, 159, 268

Saint Lucia, 258–60

Samfai, 53, 73 n. 27, 74 n. 38. *See also* tricksters
Sangrafu, 59
Santería, 3, 8–10, 40 n. 94, 46, 292–96, 303, 309 n. 28, 311 n. 37, 331 n. 41
Schoelcher, Victor, 165
Schoolcraft, Henry Rowe, 83
science, 6, 175, 245, 248; boundary of, with magic, 303, 318–19; as sacred, 157, 165; as term for spiritual power, 50, 57–58, 61, 244, 320
Scott, John (obeah defendant), 184
sculpture, 121, 123–25, 127, 133–34
Seabrook, William, 85
sexuality, 56, 78, 85, 125, 130–32, 221, 279
Shakti, 21–22
Shouters. *See* Spiritual Baptists
Shouters Prohibition Ordinance (Trinidad and Tobago), 9, 16
Sierra Leone, 176
Simmel, George, 198, 214 n. 4
Simpson, George Eaton, 17
slave rebellion. *See* conspiracies; Haiti; Tacky's Rebellion (Jamaica)
slave trade, 5, 106, 114–15, 156–57; abolition of, 109, 152, 222
solares (Cuba), 223–25, 227, 229, 231, 233, 236
sorcery. *See* witchcraft
Souloque, Faustin, 81
Souls of Black Folk, The (Du Bois), 95
South Africa, 144 n. 55, 199, 329–30
Spanish Inquisition, 12, 33 n. 26
Spencer, Herbert, 181
Spiritism, 23, 248, 291–95, 301–2, 305–6, 312 n. 49
spirits, 10, 60, 206; *brujería* and, 5, 297, 299–301; exchange of, with humans, 206, 211, 213; of iniquity, 46; Vodou and, 25, 121–28, 274, 281; witchcraft and, 49. *See also lwa*
spirit possession, 17, 247

Spiritual Baptists, 7–10, 15–16, 27, 209–11, 236 n. 2, 325
state power, 1, 5, 7, 10, 230, 261
St. John, Spenser, 14
sugar, 26, 28, 111, 152, 200, 294, 331
superstition, 6, 205, 248, 261, 273, 318, 323; anti-superstition campaign (Haiti), 16, 36 n. 52, 270–73; in French colonies, 158–61; racialized, 29, 81, 173; in Sierra Leone, 176; Victorians and, 255; West African, 258–59
Suriname, 17, 21, 60, 67; Maroons in, 45–47, 58–59, 65–66, 68
syncretism, 19–20

Tacky's rebellion (Jamaica), x, 319
Taíno, 11–12, 196
Tambiah, Stanley Jeyaraja, 7
Taussig, Michael, 297, 299, 303, 319, 329
Ten Years' War (Cuba), 105
Thoby-Marcelin, Philippe, 271
Thomas, Herbert J., 173, 178, 181, 187–89; *Something about Obeah* (pamphlet), 174, 176. *See also* policing
Thomas, John Jacob, 15
Thomas, Zachariah, 188
Thornton, S. Leslie, 181
Tobago, 3, 24, 199, 209–10, 248–49
Tonton Makout, 128. *See also* Gede
Torture, 152, 236 n. 5, 320, 336 n. 26
Toussaint Louverture (Césaire), 90–91, 94–96
Tradition: African, x, 11, 67–68, 234, 248, 254–55; Caribbean religion as, 11, 26, 274; as counterpoint to modernity, 114, 198, 244, 248, 262, 274, 305–6; European, 245, 256–57, 259; Indian, 252; invented, 274; multiple, 254
translation, 14, 81, 83–85, 89–91, 96, 104, 324; of *brujería*, 307 n. 1, of policing into colonial knowledge, 173–74
transnationalism, 30, 40 n. 88, 253, 280, 290, 292, 294–96, 298

Index 353

treasure, hunting for, 155, 207–8, 213, 257, 259
tricksters, 132, 205
Trinidad and Tobago, x, 17; calypsos and, 52, 72 n. 21; entrapment and, 201–2; Orisha and, 8, 212; paying for spiritual work and, 201, 203, 210; Spiritual Baptists and, 8, 212; trials and, 201–8, 248. *See also* ritual specialists
Trouillot, Michel-Rolph, 27, 41 n. 101, 129, 143 n. 49, 303
Tylor, Edward B., 7, 14, 318–21, 324, 326–27, 329–33

Underhill, Edward Bean, 81
United States: Cuba and, 227–28; Department of Homeland Security, 320–21; Haiti and, 85, 124, 270; Marine Corps, 86; Native Americans and, 83; Puerto Rico and, 290–91; *vagabondaj* and, 135

vagabon, 123, 126–28, 130–33, 135–37. *See also* Gede
vagabondaj, 133–36
vaudoux, 80, 91, 94. *See also* Vodou
Veracruz, 108. *See also* Dumont, Henri
Verteuil, Louis de, 15
violence: in Cuba, 229; in Haiti, 128, 132, 135–36; justification of, 29, 261, 320, 326; racism and, 86, 137, 152
Vodou, 3, 7–8, 16, 68, 81, 244; Americanized, 85; Enlightenment and, 96. *See also* Gede
Voodoo. *See* Vodou
Voodoo Fire in Haiti (Loederer), 84

wanga, 277–78, 280–81, 328
welfare capitalism, 290–91, 293
Williams, Joseph, 13, 180–81, 321–25, 333, 337 n. 43. *See also* anthropology
Winterbottom, Thomas, 13
Winti, 22, 60
Wisi, 60, 66–67, 75 n. 45, 78 n. 62, 78 n. 65
witchcraft, 11–12, 16, 47–50, 60, 69, 92–93, 150–53, 156, 160–65
World Congresses of Orisha Tradition and Culture, 9
writings, 14; Francophone, 12, 80; Haitian, 82; North American, 254; Spanish, 12, 84; travel, 14–15, 18, 84

yellow fever, 103, 109, 111, 163–64
Yoruba, x, 9, 46

Zoila case, 260–62
zombies, 62, 127

DIANA PATON is a reader in Caribbean history at Newcastle University.

MAARIT FORDE is a lecturer in the Department of Liberal Arts at the University of the West Indies, St. Augustine.

LIBRARY OF CONGRESS CATALOGING-IN-PUBLICATION DATA

Obeah and other powers : the politics of Caribbean religion

and healing / Diana Paton and Maarit Forde, editors.

p. cm.   Includes bibliographical references and index.

ISBN 978-0-8223-5124-5 (cloth : alk. paper)

ISBN 978-0-8223-5133-7 (pbk. : alk. paper)

1. Obeah (Cult)—Caribbean Area. 2. Voodooism—Caribbean Area.

3. Religion and politics—Caribbean Area. 4. Caribbean Area—Religion.

I. Paton, Diana II. Forde, Maarit

BL2565.O24 2012

299.609729—dc23

2011036577

www.ingramcontent.com/pod-product-compliance
Lightning Source LLC
Chambersburg PA
CBHW061343300426
44116CB00011B/1967